Also by Margaretta Barton Colt

Defend the Valley: A Shenandoah Family in the Civil War

Martial Bliss

Harris and Margaretta Colt, 1985.

Martial Bliss

The Story of The Military Bookman

Margaretta Barton Colt

NEW YORK

Library of Congress Cataloging-in-Publication Data
Colt, Margaretta Barton.
Martial Bliss: The Story of The Military Bookman / Margaretta Barton Colt
Originally published: New York, 2015
ISBN 9781508849445
ISBN 1508849447

Perhaps the greatest pleasure of my career

has been to place books with their friends.

Harris S. Colt
September 16, 2000

Contents

Prologue

Once upon a time there was a little boy who loved to play with toy soldiers. He was a solitary little boy, an only child, and his parents were busy with grown-up concerns. His nanny certainly wouldn't play soldiers with him, but sometimes his friend Tony came over and together they conjured up battlefields and victories. After a while the first little soldiers were wounded or had succumbed to battle fatigue or were missing in action, and he moved on to Mignots, French lead soldiers painted in colorful and elaborate Napoleonic uniforms. Napoleon's battles became his favorites, and he revived his first language, French, by reading their stories.

It was wartime in New York, and his parents were especially alive to the war news. His mother was from the small island of Malta, and she was worried about

her family and all the people there. Malta was of great importance because of its position, in the middle of the Mediterranean Sea, and it was one of the most heavily bombed places during the war. His mother worked for Malta war relief, which gathered clothes and food to send to the devastated island, and the little boy helped her collect the clothes and preserve the food.

His parents and grandpa explained the war news to him, and later he read about it in school. When he was twelve, his history teacher Mr. Mullin wrote in his report card that he was "the Clausewitz of his class." Clausewitz was a Napoleonic general who later wrote an important book about war. His mother was not pleased because the teacher added that the little boy did not pay the same attention to peacetime affairs.

His father and his grandpa appreciated and collected old and rare books on their favorite subjects, especially New York history and pictures, so it seemed natural to the boy to do the same with what he liked. Sometimes he visited special rare book dealers with his father, who taught him what to look for and even helped him buy some beautiful and rare books of Napoleonic soldiers in their great variety and magnificence.

In later years, he decided to repaint his Mignot soldiers to conform to his more critical and knowledgeable eye for the splendid uniforms' many details, and they marched across the fireplace mantel in his home.

And he decided that the only way to have enough books about war was to start his own bookstore.

CHAPTER ONE

"What bookstore?"

1975 – 1976

Under the portentous skies of an approaching hurricane, Harris came home early from Wall Street with a couple of colleagues. It was September 1975, and many small brokerage firms were suffering. Their firm had just decided to close, and over drinks, they lamented its passing and its pleasant associations. Talk of course turned to "what next," and Harris, leaning back in his rocker, said, "It's time for the bookstore."

"What bookstore?" I innocently asked. We had been married for a year and a half but had known each other much longer, and it was the first I had heard of a bookstore. It was soon revealed to me that Harris, long an avid reader of military history, believed that there should be a store devoted to the history of warfare. He had never been able to find the older books he wanted to read. Many ideas were bandied about in the next months as alternately he interviewed for financial analyst jobs and we explored the viability of his vision. He said, "It would be nice to find something we could do together." I said, breezily, "You try this and I'll help you out between my publishing freelance jobs." Famous last words: before long I found that none of the work I was offered intrigued me as much as the bookstore-to-be.

It surprised me then and in retrospect how sure and confident Harris was in this interim period and afterward. In fact neither of us was ever nervous—I kept mentally taking our pulses—he unemployed and I underemployed. His confidence seemed to have permeated mine. While we were in this career limbo, he calmly repainted his Mignot soldiers, and started to collect Malta stamps. He knew exactly what he wanted. Little did he know he had married a woman whose mother had told her, a young bookworm, "You should work in a bookstore some day." It was almost as if we were waiting for events to take a certain course. And they did: we had remarkable good luck together.

We talked to several out-of-print book dealers; they all agreed that there were many potential customers, but none of them knew if we could find enough inventory. We talked to a representative of the Military Book Club; he was guarded and somewhat suspicious, but Harris, as financial analyst and professional interrogator, elicited worthwhile information. We looked at Sky Books on East 50th Street, an emporium of new military books, with the stress on hardware rather than history. We talked to the Soldier Shop, a memorable store dealing in antique militaria, soldier models, and new military and uniform plate books, with perhaps a shelf of old books taken in trade. Harris was a good customer of theirs and viewed our projected enterprise as complementary; but the proprietor, Peter Blum, seemed to feel threatened.

We discussed it with friends; Amy Cummings, in England, was the first to send us a favorite bookstore book, Helene Hanff's *84, Charing Cross Road,* and a television adaptation of it aired that winter. Through her quirky letters and a British book dealer's staid responses, the New York author captured her long and affectionate relationship with him and British books—and added a new dimension to our imaginings.

Harris thought we should try a "pilot inventory program," vacuuming up the titles of interest from the then-numerous out-of-print bookstores in Manhattan, to see how much we could accumulate. The most familiar to us was the nearby Movable Type Bookshop, whose gregarious proprietor, Herb Weitz, frequently waylaid one or the other of us on our way up Lexington Avenue from the subway. Herb's wild curls were an expression of his manic energy; he freely gave his guidance and opinions (many of them funny, outrageous or crazy), and generously offered us his basement for our accumulations. Herb's father had been a rare book dealer, from whom he had inherited the shop and some knowledge, but he was usually more interested in playing chess, smoking pot, and shooting the breeze with his customers.

Across the street from Herb, and up one flight, was Academy Books and Jack Feldman, an old bookman who was not a businessman. Our first buy from him was by flashlight; when we went back for another try, he had been able to pay the electric bill and we found more.

I wonder how many old bookstores there were in Manhattan then. We canvassed the shops on the East Side, among them Appelfeld Rare Books, a fine bindings boutique, which turned out to have military books in their storeroom around the corner, and Lou Nathanson on 85th Street near the post office. Lou also had some books right for us in his storeroom on 96th; I told Harris that he should never have a storeroom; I thought it would be an albatross.

We mined the old shops on Fourth Avenue, visited Mendoza on Ann Street, where Harris had occasionally shopped on Wall Street lunch hours, combed the West Side and the Village, and each time took the accumulated cartons back to Herb's in a taxi. In between, Harris began to catalogue our purchases and his own extensive collection of World War II literature, which he had put into the inventory. He seemed to know about cataloguing and just how it should be. I was continuing a couple of freelance picture-editing projects.

Harris came back from the West Side one day with leads in Westchester, which we pursued in a borrowed station wagon on a cold March Monday. Our final and most productive visit was in Tuckahoe, where we met Carl Pugliese, a semi-whole-saler with a strong military specialty. A reticent man, Carl did not seem to respond to our ideas. We happily bought ten cartons of good material, and as we were leaving, Carl unbent and said, "Have you seen this week's *AB*?" The *Antiquarian Bookman's Weekly*, bible of the out-of-print book trade, made for bizarre and some-times hilarious reading for the uninitiated, as we already knew. Sample box ads: "Wanted: anything on witchcraft" or "locks" or "fore-edge paintings" or "Adam Smith"; curiosa was a regular listing.

"There's a guy in Boston, never heard of him, who's selling 3000 books on the World Wars." It was a half-page ad for the Military History Bookshop in Boston. If Carl had not had a first-class subscription to the *AB* (which meant he received it and read it on Monday), and we had not visited that day. . .

We drove back to Herbie's excited with our purchases and possibilities, and talking so hard that we missed the Manhattan turnoff on the Triborough Bridge and went to Queens. The next morning, our second anniversary, Harris called the Military History Bookshop in Boston, and had a lengthy conversation with the proprietor, Ray McGuire. He got off the phone and I said, "Well?"

"I dunno, he says he has a lot more than he advertised, he doesn't know how many, and he figures on selling the lot to a library."

"How," I said with some disdain, "can he not know how many books he has?" How soon I would eat those words.

"Anyway, I'm going up there on Friday." "I'm going too."

Friday morning, crisp and clear, we boarded the Eastern Airlines shuttle to Boston, arriving at Ray's by ten-thirty. His establishment, on the unfashionable back of Beacon Hill, was the ground floor of an old building, a space very much as ours was to be, except that Ray and his cat Charlie lived in the midst of his books. We spent the day talking books, browsing the shelves, marveling at how Charlie could walk along their edges, leaving a hairy reminder on some of the spines. The books were shelved helter skelter, by size, so that Napoleon stood shoulder to shoulder with the Roman legions and Roosevelt's Rough Riders. A title's where-abouts was noted on its catalogue card. We did not know exactly what we were looking at except that it looked good. Ray, a tall, taciturn Yankee in his forties, had been in the business for years, first working with Charles Dornbusch, the Civil War bibliographer and dealer, later on his own with Aerophilia Books and then the Military History Bookshop. A fine bookman, he preferred reading the books to selling them. His business was not an open store but by mail order, and most of his clients were libraries. When he was feeling poor, he would issue a catalogue.

The orders would come in but he could be woefully slow in shipping. By the mid-seventies, the library funds were drying up and Ray wasn't doing well. He wanted to sell out if he could, and go to the Caribbean and paint. He had never advertised; the ad in the AB was his first.

Ray was unprepared for a serious buyer to appear four days after the ad did. He certainly was unprepared for the likes of us: a short, dark, intense, intellectual businessman and a tall, blonde, serious researcher.

Harris, the career investment analyst, tried to engage in dollars-and-cents talk, profit and loss, cost of goods, value of inventory, number of mailing list customers. Ray didn't have much of a mailing list: mostly libraries, then of little use, and some zealous collectors who had tracked him down. His card catalogue files, which embodied so much of his knowledge and experience, were more precious. Ray was pretty hazy about his business details. He had several large lots of military books but no numbers on anything. When pressed, he said he might have $70,000 at retail all together. Harris elicited information in bits and pieces, and then someone would go out to get coffee and Ray would discourse on how Patton's book would always be only $5.00, and we would prowl the shelves some more and Ray would dispense pithy comments on the book business and nuggets of advice. By early afternoon, I was thinking, "We have to do this" (note the "we"). But we took no opportunity to confer privately.

Somewhat later, jettisoning all his financial training, Harris told Ray he wanted to buy the whole inventory, including card catalogue files and mailing list, for $41,000. The seasoned analyst was winging it, going on no representations other than what was before our eyes. Ray's expression did not change, and we continued to ramble on. The offer hung in the stuffy air. About ten of five, a customer called and Ray said, "No, Jim, I can't sell you that book, I'm selling the business to Harris Colt." We looked at each other, stunned, then jubilant. Lightning had struck for all of us.

The deal was made with a handshake, as with most in the years to follow. Hastily making plans for Harris's return in ten days, we bolted for Logan Airport, had a quick drink, boarded the Eastern shuttle, and straight from the plane, without even discussing it, went to Christ Cella, our favorite steakhouse.

We were never to know how many books we bought that day (although when weighed for the trucking to New York, they added up to six tons), or what was their "value." Their value was that they put us in business.

The next day, Harris's sons came for spring vacation, so only gradually did it come home to us that now we would need a store. After the boys left, Harris went off to Boston for the week, to learn from Ray, shop the Boston stores, and pack the books, tossing over his shoulder, "See if you can find a store while I'm gone."

Reader, I did.

Even in 1976, a New York rent was the scariest part of starting the eccentric and uncertain enterprise that became The Military Bookman. We had no idea what this little off-the-wall bookstore might support.

I did not have much time that week, being tied up with plumbing problems at home, attended to by the aptly named José Flo. I read the real estate ads, worried and obsessed, looked at one or two places (ruling out those with steps, Ray's valuable advice). Friday afternoon, I saw a place that had been vacant for seven years following a fire. It was a wreck, but our apartment, in an East 93rd Street brownstone, had looked much worse when we first saw it. Somehow I thought it could be fixed up for about $2000. The space was adequate, about the size of Ray's place, and it was a storefront at 170 East 92nd Street, not far from our apartment, a virtue in itself. We had agreed that our convenience was more important than the customers'—the devotees would come to us. The building, an old-law tenement, was in receivership. Even as Harris was flying home, I met the lawyer administering the bankrupt building and told him our plans. He was kindly but bemused, to say the least, by the idea of our business, and had so little faith in our prospects that he later wrote into the lease the stricture that the bookstore was on no account to include pornography. The pornography of war is perhaps a subject for another time.

He offered us a "five and five" lease—five years and the option to renew for another five—for a rent to start at a $175.00 a month, to escalate by 1986 to $225.00. This was a pittance, even then, almost a free ticket to try Harris's idea, and we could proceed without that anxiety.

An old-law tenement typically was a five-story walkup building, about thirty-five feet wide, with the street entrance in the center and two small stores flanking that. The apartments above were the legendary "dumbbell" layout. The stores at 170 East 92nd were about ten feet wide and forty feet deep, with very high ceilings. The space was good, with a large front window, and a bit of old-fashioned charm. The east wall, our wall, had a couple of windows onto a courtyard, making the store a little less like a tunnel. The other store was occupied by Burgess Movers, who were to become friendly allies.

A *New Yorker* cover that April showed a young couple fixing up just such a store. We didn't do the fixing; Dev, the brother of a friend of an old friend, Deborah Harkins, was a contractor, and soon a long bright room came out of the ashes. I was out visiting the steel-shelving market in the West 20s, learning that used shelving was really beat up, and getting estimates for new, chasing down used filing cabinets and finding at Marimekko a length of boldly striped oilcloth for the curtain that would separate the duplicate shelving and packing table from the main store. Harris was in Herb's basement cataloguing the books to conform to Ray's format, and planning the big move from Boston. And we kept buying, a return to Fourth Avenue Bookstore (where a weedy, bleached-blond young clerk named Peter took us up to the fourth floor storeroom), Dauber and Pine, Biblo and Tannen, et al. Memorably, we visited Walter Schatzki, an eminent dealer on East 57th Street, and bought two books, one a 1612 artillery treatise by Diego Ufano, one of the oldest books we ever had. We took a day for a flying trip to Baltimore with Herb, to Harris Auction Galleries, with a few bookstores thrown in; we spent twice as much at John Gach Books as we did at the auction. When visiting my family in Wilmington, Delaware, we went out in the country to the nearby Baldwin Book Barn. And I bought a few World War I posters at a remarkable sale at the New Jersey Historical Society; I have always wished I had bought more, some so rare and striking, and never seen again. That winter, partly for fun and partly because we hoped to have a store to decorate, we had pieced together, down on the living room floor and sometimes with tweezers, a huge World War I Fourth Liberty Loan poster which had come to us in fragments in a shipment of Colt family odds and ends; the fierce goddess of war hung near the store desk for a long time.

Jeffrey Kleinbardt, a young guy who had been the nicest and most knowledgeable person at the Soldier Shop, heard what we were doing and came to talk to us. He had left the Soldier Shop and was planning to open the Grenadier Guard, in competition. He proposed that we advertise together in *Campaigns Magazine*, then the best magazine in our specialties, announcing these new ventures, and shared his many contacts. One was Peter Hlinka, a militaria dealer with a small shop on East 89th Street and a large mail order business. Peter gave Harris some old military book catalogues, and Harris began to mine them for bibliographic and pricing information.

The steel shelving arrived in waves, and went up, a clangorous process, to an unbrowsable nine shelves; on the high ones we would stash long runs of periodicals. On the east wall, we planned only four tall shelves for oversize books, allowing wall space for pictures. As a picture editor, I thought that "war art" such as relevant posters and prints would be an attractive and entertaining sideline.

The painting and the rough but handsome floors were done. Dev's friend Harold the electrician, accompanied by his lovely dog, took care of the wiring. The lights went on after I had to struggle to open a Con Edison account, the representative not believing the premises existed because it was not in the computer. Who would open an account for nonexistent premises? A painter from Circle Signs applied THE MILITARY BOOKMAN in red on the big store window.

The store looked nice. It was on an interesting block with one of the few old frame houses in Manhattan and with the 92nd Street Y up the hill at the corner of Lexington Avenue; there were also a number of small shops, including a furniture restorer, an architect's office, and a studio with a very large architectural model of Palladian buildings. The model-maker was a bearded man whom we saw coming and going; we nodded, but did not speak. The eccentric furniture restorer seemed to spend most of his time sitting around, out on the sidewalk in good weather. It wasn't hard to imagine a little row of book specialists in the other small stores, like Cecil Court in London, which we did not then know. On the north corner of Third Avenue was an Irish bar—what Herb termed a "jernt"—remaining from the days of the Third Avenue El and the immigrant neighborhood, with a low-rise extension across from us. The area was a bit down at the heel, but Ruppert Towers, a large development, was rising across Third Avenue on the site of the huge old Ruppert brewery, and that seemed likely to bring in more life and retail; before long the old bar was transformed into an upscale restaurant, perhaps ahead of its time. Some people asked before coming, "Is it safe?" Well, we were there, after all ... but at that time what Harris called the DMZ was 96th Street.

Jeffrey Kleinbardt told me about a guy who had a lot of old desks. That lead took me to the Lower East Side and the lair of Richard Strich, a man of many parts: collector, dealer, electrician, self-styled "Number One in air conditioning in New York," and imp. Richard lived and worked way east on 9th Street, then such a rough neighborhood that I took the subway to 14th Street and then a cab. A large, rotund, fair, bearded man with an earring and a merry eye, Richard had wide-ranging interests, a generous nature, and a large imagination in his work. Richard had just what I wanted in his workshop, an old oak teacher's desk, and drove me and the desk uptown to the store, and engaged to air condition it, the beginning of a long friendship.

To their everlasting credit, our family and friends kept their reservations to themselves and helped out in material ways. Michael Wray, Wall Street colleague and station wagon lender, heard that I wanted to sell related posters and prints, and pulled out from under his bed his boyhood collection of World War II posters, giving them to us on consignment. Some World War I Liberty Loan posters arrived from Harris's stepmother. My old boss from Time-Life brought in some Civil War books for which I am sure we underpaid him, and later gave us a beautiful, big, French 1895 lithograph, *Sur les Ailes,* embodying the élan of the French Army. A family connection with a printing facility offered to print our first lot of stationery gratis. My parents drove up from Delaware one weekend in May with Granddad's old wicker chairs and brass umbrella stand from their basement.

Harris had picked a questionable moment to tell my parents about his book-store idea. We were driving north from Virginia on I-95 the previous October, and Daddy asked about his plans. Harris mentioned his Wall Street interviews, but said, "We are thinking about a bookstore, just military history." It's a wonder my father didn't drive off the road. The backs of their necks seemed, to me, to take on a different aspect. They were admirably noncommittal.

Eight months later, after the Boston windfall, and our getting set up in the 92nd Street store, but before we opened, we were with my parents in Wilmington and I planned to see George Theofiles, dean of printed ephemera, in nearby New Freedom, Pennsylvania. They wanted to drive there with me, Harris having gone back to New York for an auction. On the way back, I was very wound up about the posters I had bought and about the new enterprise. They were both listening hard, and I will never forget my mother's beautiful, bright face as she turned around to me over the front seat and said, "I think you're going to be famous!"

Bill Waters, a colleague from my last big book project, on transatlantic steam-ships, was closing down the office where we had worked together, and brought us leftover supplies including carbon paper and an adding machine. Bill was available part-time and started helping us on a regular basis; he got first crack at the posters I had acquired and snapped up the rare and irresistible "Loose Lips Might Sink Ships," published by Seagram's during World War II. We recycled Harris's Wall Street pendaflex files. We did everything we could cheaply, with one exception.

That spring, when I was finishing off that book project, with its most talented designer Jim Ward, I naturally told him about our plans. Jim offered to design our letterhead, for a friendly price. We had not given a thought to that; we had barely decided on a name. Harris thought this was a frill, and it was. Jim developed the basic idea: a horseman riding full tilt but (unrealistically) sitting erect, the image to be in profile and preferably in line, an engraving or drawing. He sent me off to look for such a picture, as commissioning the art would have been much too expensive. It was the most difficult picture research I ever had to do, because there was no avenue to pursue a type of image rather than a subject. After floundering for a while it occurred to me to look at a collection of scrapbooks in the New-York Historical Society, put together by Bella Landauer, an early twentieth-century lady with time on her hands and a passion for ephemera. Big, unwieldy albums, a bit of a struggle. Finally, there he was: a bugler on an 1830s New York militia order. Harris edited him for military details, and the bugle was changed to a book, and the Bookman turned to ride in the opposite direction. We now had a logo that we used always, in ads, on catalogues, calling cards, the store sign, shopping bags, even T-shirts. He conveyed the idea of antiquarian books but also was fresh, crisp and sprightly, and was recognizable, memorable.

The Burgess guys moved the books over from Herb's. By late May we were ready to bring in the Boston books; it would take two trips. Harris had engaged the services of a Jack Feldman hanger-on and would-be bookman named Jim, who said he could drive a truck. Jim looked into truck rentals in Boston and lined up a cheap one. He didn't want to fly, so he took the train while Harris and Herb flew. Herb was up for the excursion and wanted to buy Ray's art books. That didn't work out, but Herb pitched in as if ours were his books coming to New York. Jim's train was very late and the truck was feeble and barely made it up the long hill at New Haven, and altogether they had a terrible trip back, arriving as dawn was breaking. On the next run ten days later, Harris practically shackled Jim to his wrist, flew to Boston, got a better truck and they were back by five in the afternoon. We had already figured out where to shelve which subjects, and Bill was there to help unload, then unpack, by sections, checking everything in with Ray's cards and creating a new file, then shelving the books by subject, for browsing.

The card files, which we kept on the windowsill, were in five boxes of about a thousand cards each; there were more than that in the "dead files" in the steel supply cabinet behind the curtain. By July, Harris had "bookseller's bursitis" from putting the books on the high shelves.

The Bicentennial was coming and it seemed an auspicious time. We were eager to open for business, but had a particular deadline. Thanks to Deborah Harkins, my friend who was an editor at *New York Magazine*, the "Best Bets" feature writer Ellen Stern visited us and wrote us up. We would be listed in the July 6th issue, as "Martial Bliss." We had to open!

Margaretta and Harris in the store at 170 East 92nd Street.

CHAPTER TWO

"From rocks to rockets."

In those days, New York had a multitude of bookstores, for old and new books. On Fifth Avenue, Doubleday's (in several spots) and Brentano's and especially the handsome landmark Scribner's harked back to the days when publishers sold through their own stores. Brentano's and Scribner's had rare-book departments, as did Altman's department store. There was a host of out-of-print and rare book specialists in Asian, Russian, French, Irish and Celtic, German, Spanish and Portuguese, Italian, Central European; science fiction; mystery; political and radical publications; children's books; several on architecture and art; two on New Yorkiana; fine bindings; music, theater, and ballet; and travel. The rare-book stratosphere included H. P. Kraus, Lucien Goldschmidt, Walter Schatzki and others. There were also the long-established out-of-print stores concentrated on Fourth Avenue and vicinity, sometimes a whole four-story building taken over by the business. Argosy and the Strand are the survivors of this type in Manhattan.

Harris Colt thought it needed one more. Since his youth a collector and student of military history, he could never find enough books to satisfy him. Even when he traveled on business and had a little free time to look in other cities, the out-of-print bookshops all seemed to have more or less the same four shelves of common titles. Harris envisioned carrying the whole range of the subject, encompassing all that could be found, from antiquarian titles to the recently out-of-print. In this I believe the Military Bookman was unique: dealing in a range from rare and expensive titles all the way down to the recent books, and appealing to sophisticated collectors but also offering entry-level readers a lead-in to more scholarly interests.

Military history, always a more seriously regarded subject especially in England, as well as in Europe, was under a large post-Vietnam cloud here in the mid-seventies. Not much was being published. There were a few out-of-print dealers with a military specialty, none of whom dealt exclusively in the subject or had such an ambitious scope, and none with a walk-in store. There were several long-established dealers in the Civil War, that undying subject, with whom we could not really compete.

Later I said we covered "rocks to rockets," and liked to find books on even the most obscure wars. Curiously, we found that interest in a given war seemed to be directly proportional to the number of books available. In that measure, the Second World War was the most popular and numerous subject; conflicts like the Opium Wars, the Maori War, the Chaco War, the Seminole War, the Boxer

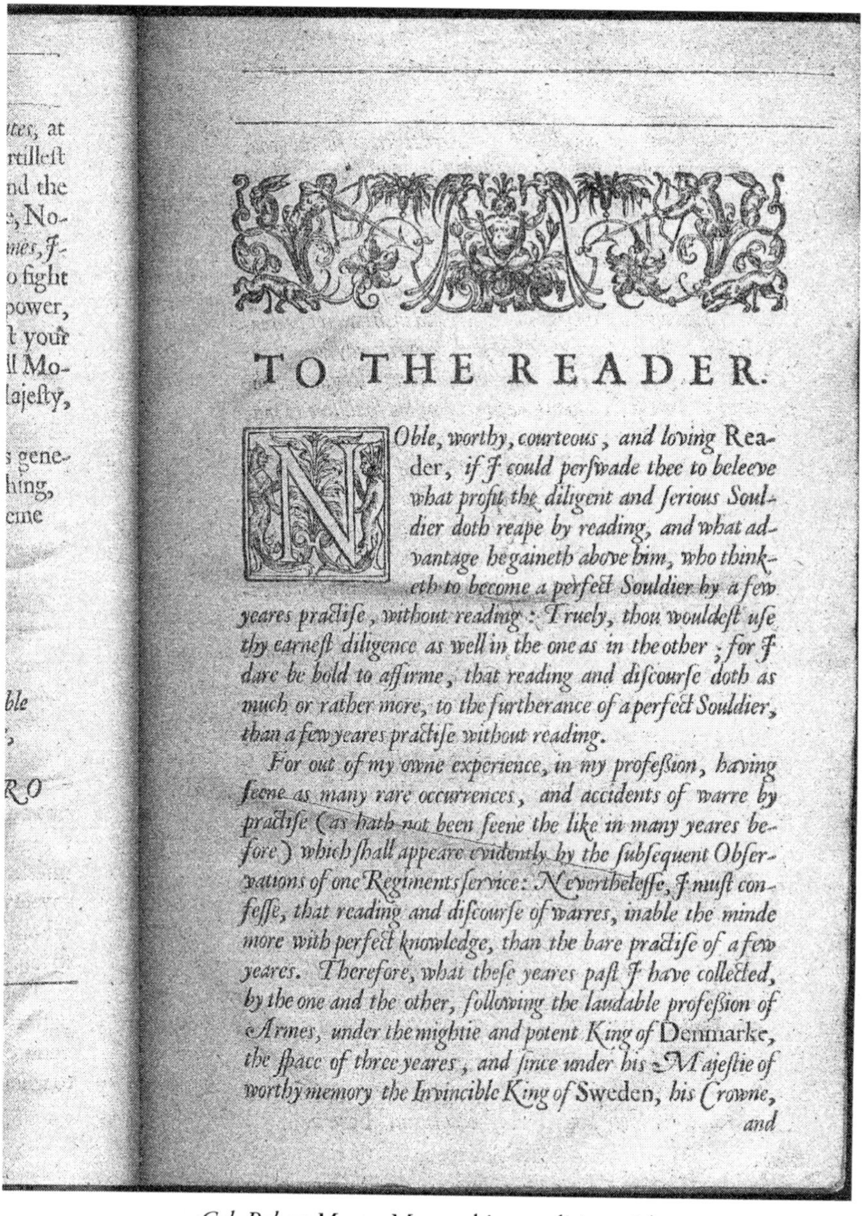

TO THE READER.

Noble, worthy, courteous, and loving Reader, *if I could perswade thee to beleeve what profit the diligent and serious Souldier doth reape by reading, and what advantage he gaineth above him, who thinketh to become a perfect Souldier by a few yeares practise, without reading: Truely, thou wouldest use thy earnest diligence as well in the one as in the other; for I dare be bold to affirme, that reading and discourse doth as much or rather more, to the furtherance of a perfect Souldier, than a few yeares practise without reading.*

For out of my owne experience, in my profession, having seene as many rare occurrences, and accidents of warre by practise (as hath not been seene the like in many yeares before) which shall appeare evidently by the subsequent Observations of one Regiments service: Nevertheless, I must confesse, that reading and discourse of warres, inable the minde more with perfect knowledge, than the bare practise of a few yeares. Therefore, what these yeares past I have collected, by the one and the other, following the laudable profession of Armes, under the mightie and potent King of Denmarke, *the space of three yeares, and since under his Majestie of worthy memory the Invincible King of* Sweden, *his Crowne,*

and

Col. Robert Monro, Monro, his expedition with the Worthy Scots' Regiment, *London, 1637.*

Rebellion, the Second Anglo-Sikh War, the Guano War, the Ashanti War, or the Philippine Insurrection had not so many books, but also not so many readers.

A Scottish mercenary with a Scots regiment in the religious wars of the seventeenth century could have been one of our customers.

> *Noble, worthy, courteous, and loving Reader, if I could persuade thee to beleeve what profit the diligent and serious Souldier doth reape by reading, and what advantage he gaineth above him, who thinketh to become a perfect Souldier by a few years practise, without reading; Truely, thou wouldest use thy earnest diligence as well in the one as in the other; for I dare be bold to affirme that reading and discourse doth as much or rather more, to the furtherance of a perfect Souldier, than a few yeares practise without reading.*
> Col. Robert Monro, 1637

Our subject ranged over the whole history of human conflict—that is, human history. A scarce book by H. S. Cowper, *The Art of Attack,* actually depicted rocks and clubs. (The first copy we had bore an ingratiating signed inscription from a young George Patton to his commanding officer. I wish we had sequestered that book for a while, until we knew more.)

The antiquarian books were theses on The Art of Warre: tactics of ancient warriors by Aelian, Edmonds's mid-seventeenth century editions of Caesar's *Commentaries*, Xenophon on Cyrus the Great, Roman warfare by Vegetius, Polybius on the Punic Wars, Polyaenus's *Strategems,* Machiavelli, and Marshal Maurice de Saxe. Contemporaneous accounts of warfare: the Turks; "the troubles of Hungary;" Babur and the Mughal conquerors of India; civil-cum-religious wars in France; the religious wars that ravaged Flanders in the sixteenth century and the German states in the seventeenth; Italian Renaissance warfare and the *condottieri*; the Saracens; Prince Eugene of Savoy; Gustavus Adolphus of Sweden, "Lion of the North," vs. Marshal Tilly; Don John of Austria, victor at Lepanto. Orme on the British Transactions in Indostan. Battles observed or by participants who called themselves "Eye-Witness" or "Officer who Served." The Marlborough Wars, so-called by the self-referential British; Louis XIV must have thought they were his wars.

They were often epic accounts, ravishing as physical objects: the gently aging rag paper, the so-black ink bitten into the page; leather bindings showing their age (perhaps repaired crudely or cleverly); vellum, occasionally gently nibbled by mice; the aroma of books marinating for centuries in an unheated library in northern Europe. Many were enhanced with handsome engraved plates of heroic marshals and kings brandishing swords, on rearing war horses; or battlefield maps with all the trees in place and the hillocks and river courses carefully delineated, with furry woods and feathery marshlands, and tiny castles in hierarchical sizes, and with hand-colored troop positions. Naval books with plates that showed fat-sailed ships propelled by the chubby-cheeked personifications of winds, and adorned with compass roses. Manuals of infantry movements and drill, with toylike engraved soldiers. Cannon and castles, the elaborate geometry of seventeenth- and eighteenth-century fortifications following the template set forth in the treatises of Maréchal de Vauban, Louis XIV's military engineer.

Manuals that had seen use in the field, rain-darkened, worn, stained from the dirt of a bivouac. We rarely saw a good copy of General von Steuben's manual, so important to and so hard-used by the Americans in the Revolution; most were battered, weathered, and often missing at least one plate. (After a while, we kept a xeroxed set of the plates on file, to provide the missing information.) An early nineteenth-century naval tract crudely rebound by a sail maker, in canvas with big stitches—how evocative. (Richard Strich, a former merchant seaman, snapped that up.) A leather-bound treatise on strategy in fine condition, with a few flowers and leaves delicately pressed between the pages, as if the reader had been wandering over an ancient battlefield.

The seduction of bindings: fine leather, on which finely cut pictorial or decorative tools had gilt-stamped the heraldic emblems of the marshals and princes or the bees of Napoleon; marbled covers or endpapers. The mid-nineteenth century stamped cloth, often silk, that gleamed softly with a little polishing. The latter nineteenth century's attractive and stylized pictorial embossed cloth that decorated many Spanish-American War or Boer War titles. Or even the blue "sugar paper" covers of early nineteenth-century titles waiting in vain for a proper, custom binding.

Nineteenth-century histories and memoirs were richly written in prose shaped by Latin in the curriculum—full of gerundives, as Harris said—and by the King James Bible. General Grant's memoir is noted for its prose as well as its history. Early on, we took turns reading the memoirs of Lord Roberts, *Forty-One Years in India,* to each other. The British biographies and memoirs represent the sprawl and complexity of Britain's empire; a single life might encompass service in Africa, Australia, and India. Napoleon dictated his memoirs at St. Helena, and many of his generals and opponents recorded their service.

Nineteenth-century books introduced more color, at first with hand-coloring of engravings and lithographs, in stunning plate books of generals and conquering armies; small, plebian, plain Bonaparte was made handsome and heroic. Accounts embellished with plates of magnificently uniformed figures, or leaders popularized in children's books illustrated by the inimitable J. O. B. (Jean Onfroy de Breville). Battle glorified, by Vernet, Detaille, Meissonier, Caton Woodville, Lady Butler: sweeping scenes of cavalry charges. One of my favorites was an anomaly, the rare depiction of Napoleonic battles by a Chinese artist, with a godlike view above the fray, almost aerial perspectives of tiny, ignorant armies on a not-too-darkling plain.

War reporting first took place in the Crimea, for the London papers. The pioneer was William Howard Russell, for *The Times* of London; coincidentally war photography began there with Roger Fenton's work. The ubiquitous Richard Harding Davis covered the war in Cuba, the Boer conflict, the Greco-Turkish War, and Salonika in World War I; Frederick Palmer was in Manchuria for *Collier's*.

Popular and accessible American periodicals, such as *Leslie's* and *Harper's Weekly*, covered the Civil and the Spanish-American wars and were heavily illustrated with wood engravings, many made from photographs by Mathew Brady, or with art by the likes of Winslow Homer, Frederick Remington, and Rufus Zogbaum. P. F. Collier's took over with photographic histories of the Russo-Japanese and the Great War. These periodicals and others, such as the *Illustrated London News* and *L'Illustration* (each founded in the 1840s), and the specialized *Navy and Army Illustrated*, were precursors of *Life* and *Look* magazines, as well as of *Yank* and other wartime publications like the German *Signal* and *Der Adler*.

The study of uniforms is a large subject in itself. As long as there have been uniforms there have been uniform studies. Technically, any army needs to be able to recognize the units and rank designations of friend or foe, even if by pieces of holly uniformly stuck in the caps of a baron's men-at-arms in medieval times. Most uniforms were designed to impress and intimidate; headgear such as shakos, bearskins, and czapskas, all made the wearer taller and more threatening. (This changed, not quickly enough, with the development of more accurate guns of greater range.) The uniforms could be glorious, that is, imbued with the glory of tradition and history and also just aesthetically beautiful in color, materials and craftsmanship. As color printing flourished in the late nineteenth century, the pre-1914 panoply was aptly and amply portrayed by new printing techniques: finely detailed color lithographs spelled out every variant of every rank, insignia, and decoration. Uniform books became more than just a celebration or record but a subject of special study, and various groups were dedicated to this research.

Galerie Militaire, an extensive series of uniform plates of the armies of Europe, compiled in the mid-nineteenth century by Dero-Becker and Martinet, is a collection of small gems. Studies such as this and the equally splendid series by Alfred de Marbot were often published, unbound, over a period of ten or fifteen years and so were rarely found as complete sets. Later, there were French uniform plate books by Detaille, *Types et Uniformes . . .,* and several studies by Susanne. Charlet and Fallou took an almost academic approach. The stricter and less attractive documentation, with synoptic plates almost like paper dolls, of Lienhart's five-volume opus on the nineteenth-century French army went to a new level. As the German Empire came to the fore, their multi-army uniform studies over decades were published by the firm of Moritz Ruhl in Leipzig. Ruhl produced small, usually folding-plate books from the 1890s on, the most dazzling uniform periods before World War I, of the armies of Europe and China, Japan, even the United States, and continued in a limited way into the 1920s. The color and detail were scrupulous; and the slim volumes probably fit handily into a uniform pocket or a sabretache, a uniform accessory serving the purpose of pockets when pockets did not conform with the de rigueur tight pants.

Rudolf von Ottenfeld splendidly portrayed the greatly varied, multi-ethnic Austro-Hungarian uniform history. William Walton, H. A. Ogden, and Fritz Kredel documented the U.S. forces; Ogden's work was semi-official, and the lithographs were a bit heavy-handed. Walton's, less well known, was reproduced from watercolors, the detail more delicate, and to me much more appealing. Charles Lefferts did a fine historical work on the uniforms of the Revolution.

The British were recorded by Harry Payne, Walter Richards, Richard Simkins, and others. Every nation had its chronicler, for instance, five handsome, recent volumes on Polish uniform history as well as many smaller works (one of which, on czapkas exclusively, contained a twenty-nine-page text and plates and was issued with a lengthy errata sheet). There was a multi-volume work on the Swedish Navy. There were hundreds of works on orders, medals, decorations, ribbons, sometimes even an exhaustive history of a single medal and its recipients.

We later designated as "war art," illustrated and plate books and those showing the war work of great artists, official or otherwise, as well as war posters and great combat photography.

There were biographies, official histories, memoirs (at first only of the literate command but slowly of all ranks), campaign studies, battle accounts; many technical studies on logistics, terrain, armaments, ships and naval equipment. Manuals, the "how-tos", were published as early as the seventeenth century, and the informative military and naval atlases and "dictionaries," starting in the eighteenth century, taught and aided the art and trade of warfare.

Naval history was first addressed by the British; after all, it was their strength and their heritage, and the Royal Navy their "Senior Service." William James was the first, followed by Julian Corbett and William Clowes. But the first great writer on naval strategy was the American Alfred T. Mahan.

Americans did not immediately write about their long revolutionary struggle. There were fine eighteenth-century British works on our War of Independence by Charles Stedman and David Ramsay, and lots of finger-pointing documentation by Generals Clinton, Cornwallis, and Howe to fix blame for the loss of the Colonies. Generals George Washington and Andrew Jackson did not write memoirs, although a few lesser lights did. A number of interesting works apparently surfaced around the time of our Centennial, when people's awareness was heightened— memoirs, diaries, letters, rosters, and order books turned up in dusty repositories and were often collected in small editions published privately or by local historical societies. There was a momentum to this; original documents kept turning up and still do. Civil War material and its publication seem to have no limit.

Strategy and tactics, at their core, appeal to the most intellectual interest, and those were Harris's specialty, both in the store and in his reading. When we opened, the most-requested strategic writers were B. H. Liddell Hart, J. F. C. Fuller, both British, and S. L. A. Marshall, an American. John Keegan's first important book, *The Face of Battle,* was published and reviewed in the *New York Times* in 1976, and we each devoured it. It seemed to herald a renaissance in military history publishing and interest.

The earliest known treatise on strategy was by Sun Tzu, a sixth-century B.C. Chinese general and philosopher who wrote the influential *Art of War.* It was translated into French in the late eighteenth century and was said to have been known to Napoleon, but, curiously, not available in English until a hundred years ago. It has come to general attention here only in the last generation, although our military produced various editions fifty years ago.

Frederick the Great's *Instructions to His Generals* appeared in several editions, and Napoleon's precepts were collected. A couple of Napoleon's generals, the Prussian Carl von Clausewitz and Swiss Baron Antoine-Henri Jomini differed in their interpretations, both famous, of the science of the Little Corporal's warfare.

Official histories first appeared in the mid-nineteenth century, and were at first semi-official, such as A. W. Kinglake's opus on the Crimean War. They were compiled by an army's historians (not just the victors) in the wake of a war: the American Civil War (both sides, in one hundred and twenty-eight volumes), Franco-Prussian, Russo-Japanese. There were eight volumes on the Russo-Japanese War, rarely seen as a set, and the same for the Franco-Prussian, which we saw only once complete. The individual volumes of these two sets were valuable in themselves. The busy Prussian Great General Staff was at the same time producing eighteen volumes on the wars of Frederick the Great, and innumerable other studies. Since they had more than a casual interest in the Boer War, they issued two volumes on it, while the British wrote three. Sir John Fortescue spent the early decades of the twentieth century compiling *A History of the British Army*, in twenty books, a monumental endeavor covering imperial warfare in the eighteenth and nineteenth centuries.

On a smaller scale, there were analyses by military attachés assigned to observe other people's wars. U.S. Col. Richard Delafield and others were sent to the

Crimea. The prolific Francis V. Greene, then American military attaché in St. Petersburg, viewed the Russo-Turkish struggle in the Balkans; twenty years later, Gen. Nelson Miles was present at maneuvers in Europe in 1897, and was on hand for the brief Greco-Turkish fracas. There were European observers at our Civil War, most notably Lt. Col. James Fremantle of the Coldstream Guards, who wrote an entertaining memoir. Our army fielded observers simultaneously in China, Russia and South Africa at the turn of that century.

The "small wars" of the nineteenth century were the subjects of many army staff studies. I particularly liked two British series of, as it happens, small books: the *Special Campaigns Series,* twenty-one wide-ranging titles in ocher cloth, and the *Pall Mall Military Series,* twelve in red. Published as texts for students at Army Staff Colleges, they were physically unprepossessing and in my opinion undervalued when we were first shopping in England. I was grabbing them here and there, never paying more that two or three pounds, if that. The authors were fine military historians, and they sold very well here. At some point I was fool enough to mention them to Peter de Lotz, dean of British military book specialists, and after that we found few in our wanderings in England, and a very large stack of them at Peter's. He had vacuumed them up and we paid a pretty penny for them.

World War I literature ranges from the individual exploits of the air war (soon to add a new dimension of carnage) to the massive killing grounds of the Western Front and Russia. The British Empire, exhausted by conflict in France, the Near East, Africa, and Turkey produced exhaustive official histories: nine multi-volume sets on the Army, four on the Navy, nine volumes on air operations. The Germans produced a massive official history, with fourteen volumes on the war at sea alone, and the thirty-six-volume *Schlachten des Weltkrieg,* studies on individual battles.

Our Army recorded the briefer American involvement in seventeen volumes. We bought the fifteen-volume Austro-Hungarian official history in strange circumstances, at an auction, and then again, years later. France published its large history in the 1930s, on the brink of another war. We found Italian battle studies of their campaigns in the north. And a rare piece on a rare hero: an aviator, Francesco Baracca, who was awarded what his general proclaimed to be the rarest medal, the Italian gold medal for bravery. I couldn't believe it; at the time, there were running jokes called "The Thinnest Books in the World," and one was "Italian War Heroes."

The writings are numerous and diverse. For instance, there was a remarkably detailed series of guidebooks to the French battlefields put out by the Michelin tire company. Our original inventory included the first, German edition of *The Sexual History of the World War* by Dr. Magnus Hirschfeld: two volumes, heavily illustrated, including color art. Large numbers of unit histories of all forces were compiled, sometimes labors of love published many years later.

World War I exerts a continuing fascination. Larry McMurtry, apparently come late to military history, recently wrote, "The Great War itself was so astonishing, so personality-rich, so ambiguous still, that one could spend a lifetime reading about it and its aftermath."

Between the big wars the Spanish Civil War inspired the most literature. The Russian Civil War was a follow-on to World War I, and the conflicts in Ethiopia, China and then Spain, precursors of what was to come.

The sheer number of U.S. government publications during and just after World War II in itself reflected the scale of the conflict: the Army chronicled its war in sixty-seven thick green volumes; the Marine Corps produced a five-volume official history and an excellent fifteen-part series called *Marine Corps Monographs,* an island-by-island study of the Pacific campaigns. The Navy's history by Samuel Eliot Morison was in fifteen volumes; the Air Force in seven, edited by W. F. Craven and J. L. Cate. The *Strategic Bombing Survey* included well over three hundred analyses of the Air Force's devastating effect on German and Japanese installations and industry.

The Army published its *American Forces in Action* series in the late forties: fourteen after-action studies of pivotal battles, including several on D-Day and other landings. A D-Day veteran who came in did not know of the Army study on Omaha Beachhead; it was prepared shortly after the invasion and was based on interviews with the soldiers, with good maps and many photos. Harris placed it in his hands at the rare book cabinet, and he found photos of men pinned down in the waters approaching the beach: it may have been his unit. He was in tears.

Innumerable field and technical manuals were being produced and updated during the conflict, as the participants were learning and applying the lessons, on subjects as various as command, maneuvers, *Don't Get Killed by Mines and Booby-Traps,* how to service a truck or a gun or deploy a hand grenade, pigeon communications, army cookbooks, *How to Abandon Ship,* a military ski manual. Harris impishly deposited a technical manual, *Mess Management,* on my perennially cluttered desk. There were pocket guides to the countries or cities where a G.I. might find himself, cute little touristic pamphlets with practical pointers about what to see and how to behave in another culture.

The Pamphlet-20 series analyzed the immense Russo-German war, with titles like *Combat in Russian Forests and Swamps* or, even more grimly suggestive, *Effects of Climate on Combat in European Russia.* There were twenty-one of the small but cogent studies, compiled from the debriefings of captured German generals.

The individual armies and army groups produced their own histories, and the self-aggrandizing Gen. Mark Clark saw to it that his Fifth Army in the difficult Italian campaign was well publicized by his busy historians, who cranked out half-a-dozen small studies on their way up the boot—to say nothing of a nine-volume after-action report. Unquestionably the army history that weighed in with the "mostest" was Patton's Third Army *After Action Report* at thirty pounds. They were justly proud of their peerless logistics, and volume two gave the details, even recording how many loaves of bread were baked. The most egomaniacal general of the war's four-volume record of the Pacific battles was titled *MacArthur Reports*. Other generals fought their battles and wrote their memoirs when they were done.

The British official histories of both wars were multitudinous and comprehensive and fine, and there were very many Commonwealth official histories. Their output during the war and afterward was comparable to ours, ranging from the numerous and varied Ministry of Information pamphlets down to Canned Food Manuals.

We bought the rare, five-volume Polish official history of World War II wondering if we would ever sell it. France documented the Free French contribution. The Soviet Union published a number of wartime propaganda pieces in English on the Great Patriotic War.

British regimental histories were in a class by themselves. Their chronicles, covering the British Empire's enormous history, geographically and chronologically, made for rich traditions and detailed historiography, and were typically beautifully produced, often with color uniform plates, in editions limited to members of the regiments. The regimental structure in the last sixty years has virtually collapsed upon itself as the British Army has shrunk to a fraction of even its mid-twentieth-century size, and regiments have been amalgamated or even obliterated. There was nothing comparable in American military history, where the army was never of the size or prestige to foster such distinct identities and traditions.

American unit histories were the stories, compiled by their members, of divisions, regiments, battalions, groups, companies, the myriad subdivisions of all branches of service, of any unit's service in a given war, as tiny and obscure as, for instance, the 118th Signal Radio Intelligence Company or the 718th Railway Operating Battalion.

Civil War regimental histories were a special category, already scarce and expensive when we went into business. Our Indian Wars in the West were cavalry affairs—the John Wayne stuff. In sheer numbers of published titles the Seventh Cavalry dominated; Custer's larger-than-life personality and mistakes sold a lot of books. In the second place, numerically, of twelve cavalry regiments was the Tenth Cavalry, the "Buffalo Soldiers," the famous black Indian fighters. The Spanish-American War was brief, but nevertheless its units were commemorated in regimental histories. Here also, personality played a part, and there was much on Roosevelt and the Rough Riders. The World War I unit histories form an extensive body of literature.

Many of the World War II unit histories greatly resembled high-school yearbooks, about same size and format, usually in embossed leatherette covers, heavily illustrated with photos of the members—and often about the same level of historiography, although they sometimes contained information not found elsewhere. They were published soon after the war, just for members of the unit, so the number of copies was limited. The Navy vets compiled "cruise books" of their ship's service and its roster. The Marine Corps's individual divisions all wrote their histories, as did the multitude of Air Force units: Fighter Groups, Bomber Groups, supply units. For Ray McGuire, and for us at first, the big demand was for the World War II units.

The customers for unit histories fell into two categories. Many G.I.s had not received their books or had lost, misplaced, or lent them along the way. The requests of those veterans or their families were touching; we often had the satisfaction of being able to provide them with their histories.

There was also a sizable group of collectors in the next generation, whose interest was probably founded on the war stories they grew up with. But these guys wanted everything; as with baseball cards, an avid collector strove to find every number. This category of books had not been known to Harris before, but characteristically he gave himself a crash course and became an authority quickly. He developed close relationships with several of these collectors, his "trading buddies," with whom he did complicated deals, inscrutable to the rest of us. Later on, Harris began classifying any book relating to a specific unit—memoirs and diaries, roster books, songs or poetry, humorous accounts, slang, lists of commendations, the little pamphlets called *G. I. Stories,* veterans' reunion programs, ephemera such as the 73rd Infantry Division menu card—by unit, and this was very successful.

There was a substantial body of reading matter on prisoners-of-war and escape-and-survival, mostly from World War II. Colditz Castle in Germany, where captured Allied officers were imprisoned, inspired at least a shelf of its own.

The Holocaust, as a term for Hitler's genocide of the Jews, was just coming into general use when our store opened. Ray had not included it, but we believed the subject to be an essential part of Second World War coverage, and found many serious and devoted readers. In time, when Holocaust books became more widely available, and many more memoirs especially were published, it seemed less important to carry an extensive selection so we concentrated on the rarer titles.

There were official histories and unit histories of the Korean War, but not so many overall histories or memoirs, sometimes a source of frustration to its veterans.

The stories of the many conflicts of the later twentieth century were being produced during the time we were in business. Vietnam books came along only gradually; it was still a fresh wound in the American experience. On the other hand, a seemingly inexhaustible demand for books on irregular warfare and Special Forces information produced publications of widely varying merit.

One might think that espionage by nature would not display its history and technique, but there are five volumes on *British Intelligence in the Second World War* alone. There were intriguing memoirs, starting with Fouché, spymaster to both Napoleon and his successor Louis XVIII, down to Allen Dulles and William Colby. Somerset Maugham was a spook, and fictionalized his experience in *Ashenden*, at one time required reading for MI5 agents. Sidney Reilly, "Ace of Spies," a mysterious Russian active from the 1890s until the mid-1920s, was the subject of several books and even a BBC TV series, and incidentally was himself a major book collector especially of Napoleonic pictorials. One of Harris's favorite volumes, which he acquired as a teen-ager, bore Reilly's bookplate. Erskine Childers, a Boer War memoirist and sometime intelligence officer and author on strategy, wrote *The Riddle of the Sands,* a prescient 1903 espionage novel of emerging German naval might: a best seller in many editions and then adapted as a movie. There were innumerable spy accounts; we usually had about eight long shelves, always very popular, and ripe fodder for Hollywood.

Thematically treated subjects later made for variety in the catalogue. For instance, Bill Waters brought us a catalogue and T-shirt from a show at the Imperial War Museum, *Animals in War* (how British). That inspired us to list it as a special subject—everything from carrier pigeons to Hannibal's elephants—and there was enthusiastic response. We never listed sex or religion as categories although there was a body of "I found God in the trenches" memoirs, and Harris remarked, from time to time, that without religion we wouldn't have a bookstore.

There were unusual collectibles like cigarette-card albums, mostly German but also by Players in England, especially popular in the 1930s. Published by different cigarette companies in an effort to entertain and addict and build brand loyalty, there was a numbered card in each pack; albums were available, with numbered spaces for the cards, and with some text to enhance it. The German albums typically had space for about two hundred and fifty cards. There were historical uniform series by the likes of Herbert Knötel; albums of flags, aircraft, decorations, or ships, and two wonderful ones of zeppelin photos. Others were creatures of the Third Reich, several replete with Heinrich Hoffmann photos of Der Führer, and were political and cultural as well as military. Many of these albums, and other stray Nazi items, came to us from G.I.s who had found them, intact or otherwise, in the ruins of the Reich.

There were changing tastes in collecting. The intensity of unit history collecting diminished somewhat during the years we were in business. Initially we saw little interest in the First World War and almost none in the Spanish-American War, and Harris even thought, not seriously, of dropping them. But World War I interest soon came on strong and continued unabated and, as I had facetiously predicted, when imperialism came back into fashion in the Reagan era, so did the Spanish-American War.

Our readers were primarily concerned with content. The first edition was the only edition of the very great majority of our titles; most never saw a second edition or even printing. Consequently we did not pay much attention to editions except with the antiquarian books—or book-club editions, which we tried to avoid. When we acquired a library containing a large chunk of Winston Churchill's work, and a handy bibliography, it was time to detail and differentiate those editions.

Ours was not a dust-jacket business either, although we noted their presence in our records, and I liked to reproduce some of them in the catalogues; but we did not price them differently or cater to collectors fixated on dust covers. A well-designed and visually arresting wrapper in good condition is a plus, but that is not what the book's about. I never understood the cult of the dust jacket. To me, an untouched, unread book is analogous to the untouched collectable antique toys in the original boxes, flying in the face of their purpose, to be handled, played with, or read.

CHAPTER THREE

"Ooh, you have a Holocaust section!"

1976 – 1977

Harris, opening day, July 5, 1976.

Harris said he wanted to "make the market." I didn't even know what that meant. Harris knew how he wanted to do things, how to describe the books, how to track the inventory. Sometimes, at the beginning, I just sat and watched him work, not knowing what I could do to help. Unknowingly, I was learning by watching, getting the feel, and also beginning to learn my own subjects, like illustrated books, and develop my own province, which might be called customer relations: systems for building a mailing list, tracking customers, and filing their "wants," their long-term requests.

I watched him sell, too. Harris was a natural, because he knew and believed in what he was selling, knew its merits, and was completely forthcoming and friendly, comfortable with anyone, wanting to engage in a dialogue with the customer and share his own knowledge of the books. He would take people to the right section and work to find things for their interest. Deborah Harkins said the store was "electrically charged by Harris's intensity." He was a great salesman and could often significantly add to an order with his suggestions, sometimes titles the customer didn't know he wanted or didn't know existed. He only got better over the years, constantly learning from the books and the customers, and having a wonderful time, never stale. One customer was so pleased with Harris's "service" he tried to tip him.

I was shy about selling at first, even what I liked. Two brothers who came in from New Jersey on Saturday mornings were interested in French illustrated books. I pulled several by J. O. B. from the rare-book cabinet in the back for Harris to show them, but he gently forced me to do it and sell them myself.

Together and early we had agreed to go beyond Ray's coverage and include, when found, more ancient, medieval, and early modern history; uniform studies; and fine illustrated and antiquarian books. Those were my subjects, too.

Our first customer was a young boy with a book allowance. That seemed to bode well. That summer a fair number of odd characters turned up among the many people who would become regulars for years.

Big Joe Ward, a knowledgeable collector, had stumbled across our accumulations in Herb's basement in March when trolling his Upper East Side bookshop rounds, and sat silently staring at the shelves figuring out how to allocate his resources once we opened. He probably passed the word to Henry Sirotin and Dan David, who became regulars and sold us some of their books to finance their new desires. At first they wanted to do it on a trading basis, but that quickly became too entangled, and perhaps led to our first policy decision: no trading.

We had done a mailing to Ray's list, and Nate Kaufman was among the first to answer the summons. His interest was World War I aviation, always a strong suit of Ray's. Nate drove in from Long Island on Saturday mornings, often with his little boy, and they would also go around the corner to Third Avenue, where there was a man who dealt in, among other old toys, Lionel trains. Nate was a wonderful customer for many years, a mild, soft-spoken man who often brought us a box of cookies or some other treat. He liked to sit and chat, along with buying some very unusual books. When we got busier on Saturday mornings, he was a little disappointed that we didn't have time for a real visit. Nate bought what he didn't have, and we enjoyed helping him add to what must have been a very fine collection.

Charles Juroe was an American living in England, and his work then was developing the introductory story that preceded every James Bond movie; his career was James Bond but his pleasure was early aviation. We soon heard from two more of Ray's customers for that subject who lived in Florida and were rivals, the ever-gracious George Banister and the cheap and churlish Fred Andrews; and from another one in Tenerife, in the Canary Islands. One of George Banister's first purchases was the Second Army Air Service history, published in France in 1919, which we perceived to be a rare book; we were really nonplussed when another copy arrived within months. It seemed to have been drawn in by some unseen force. After that we didn't see another until 2002; we had been right, it was rare.

We inherited Léon Croulebois, in Paris, from Ray. Léon collected American air unit histories, and wrote eloquent letters in green ink on blue air-letter forms:

This book is very precious . . . is sacred books, but, after the last hero is dead only this book speak before the world the courage and heroism of the wonderful US boys. I possess a great respect and gratitude for the United States for the terrific payment of my liberty the blood price during 2 wars . . . Special kisses from Paris to Margaretta.

Stanley Katz burst into the store like Kramer plunging into Seinfeld's apartment. *"Some Still Live?"* he said without preamble. That rare, Spanish Civil War aviation memoir by Lon Tinker passed through our hands only two or three times, and the first copy we saw went to Stanley. A wry Brooklynite, he also wanted World War I aviation and contented himself with that until we sent him a postcard saying simply, *"Some Still Live."* He was over to 92nd Street like a shot.

Two letters responding to the *New York Magazine* mention threw me for a loop: a neatly typed, very literate business letter from upstate: *I am currently an inmate at the Auburn Correctional Facility, and as such it would hardly be feasible for me to visit at this time.* He wanted to make arrangements to shop by mail and was interested in the notorious Waffen SS, Hitler's elite corps. What, I thought, have we gotten ourselves into?

The other, from Chicago, was on the letterhead of "The Polish Military Historical Society." So esoteric—we had to laugh. He wanted anything on Polish Winged Hussars. I was floored. But soon I learned that the Polish Winged Hussars' getup was perhaps the most extreme manifestation of "uniforms designed to intimidate." This heavy-cavalry unit rode into battle with huge wings affixed to their backs and arching several feet above their heads. This request was a challenge, and we were pleased eventually to be able to offer something unusual, but then he was too cheap to take it.

But there were interesting and even charming letters. Some correspondents were living their own fantasies to which we became privy. A young Canadian, Brian Pieper, was engrossed in the wars of Frederick the Great, and wrote playful letters signing himself "part-time Marshal of France." One was datelined "Winter quarters on the Rhine."

Nov. 27 1757 near the village of Leuthen

Hard campaigning in Silesia against Old Fritz's Prussians has left everyone pretty worn out. We look forward to winter quarters at Konigratz with its warm fires, delightful wine and good books. I've enclosed a money order in Imperial Florins of course.

The backs of his envelopes were inscribed with neat little exhortations such as *"En avant!"* or *"A la baionette!"* Nice drawings of eighteenth-century soldiers decorated some orders. It was a shock for him when we responded in kind; and it shocked us, years later, when he went on to the nineteenth century.

Jim Controvich, to whom Ray had declined to sell a book the day he decided to sell us the business, became a regular in more ways than one. A couple of times a year he came down from Springfield, Massachusetts, to go through our shelves of unit histories. While shopping for himself in Springfield and environs, he started scouting for us to support his habit.

Carmen Perrotti, another Massachusetts customer of Ray's, also collected unit histories and cruise books. "Ca'men" was a car salesman, and his letters, densely typed with a very black ribbon, all single-spaced and in capitals, captured his drive and intensity.

On the phone, Tom sounded like a woman, and Harris kept calling him "ma'am." Young Tom, with thick glasses, buckteeth, and straggly blond hair, was a sweet, funny guy and not meant for this world. Tom was a Luftwaffe devotee, a soldier -figure painter for hire, and later something of an authority on German uniforms, co-authoring several uniform books on the Wehrmacht. He had collected many original German World War II books, most notably their wartime periodicals, and sold us a number of them, and he spoke German pretty well. One of Tom's books was the scarce Von Wedel, *Der Kampf im Westen*, with a minimal text but with a hundred loose stereopticon photos and viewing glasses in an album tailored for it: Wehrmacht troops leaping over trenches and seemingly into your lap.

Walter Terzano, another of Ray's Massachusetts customers, was probably an ex-Marine: that is what he collected. But he stood out because of his pronounced accent—"Ma'garetta, this is the piano movah in Bahston"—and his astonishing letterhead. He ran Deathwish Piano Movers, and his logo was variations on the theme of a skeleton playing the piano, sometimes a skull with piano-key ivory teeth. Macabre, memorable, and very funny.

A rather dashing fellow stopped in to see if we had any unusual Flying Tiger material, and it became clear that he had been one. The Flying Tigers, the stuff of "Terry and the Pirates" comic strip, were American volunteers flying in China and "over the Hump" from Burma against the Japanese, right after Pearl Harbor. Our Tiger regaled us with a report that the bar from a dive in Kunming on which many Flying Tigers had carved their names, had recently been spirited out of then-closed China and installed somewhere in Arizona.

Several French readers came along, among them a courtly and charming Italian banker long resident in New York, Renato Guadagnini, who was interested in Napoleonic narratives, and Henry Denis, a slight, reserved Canadian who spoke and read French but was primarily interested in the beautiful nineteenth-century Napoleonic pictorials by fine war artists such as J. O. B. and Detaille, Vernet and Bucquoy, Bellangé and Charlet.

The next generation of readers started finding us, too. The reticent, good-looking David Feinberg was not a frequent shopper but his taste was impeccable. Miles Navaretta, an enthusiastic Napoleonic reader, was eventually lost to law school. Serious young Will Shrenk did chores for us after school for book credit.

I thought perhaps I should be watchful when a young guy in work clothes (when denim was not ubiquitous) came in for a look. But I watched, and changed my preconceptions when he bought an expensive book for cash. Shoplifting was never much of a problem for us, with a couple of significant exceptions, two of whom wore suits.

The "poor soul" discovered us, who knows how. He was a messenger, unlikely as it seemed: he looked and acted as if he wouldn't know uptown from downtown. But he was an idiot savant. His taste in books was excellent, and he really couldn't afford the ones he wanted. He would approach one or the other of us saying, "If I buy this book, will I have enough money until the end of the week?" showing us the contents of his wallet. It was excruciating. On one occasion, Harris refused to sell him a book too expensive for him by far, and he left angry and stood ranting on the sidewalk. Funny and sad. He buttonholed an old lady coming down the hill and complained; she listened closely and then said crisply, "I think he was quite right." That stopped the tirade and he went on his way.

Peter Stulting, brilliant, fast-talking, and hyperactive, and always nattily dressed, went through one inheritance and went broke a few more times due to his addictions to books and blondes. He finally joined the Army in desperation, later turning his knowledge and facility with the spoken word into a radio show. There were periods of silence, but it was usually because he was "regrouping" or relo-cating. He was an erratic but frequent customer, who would turn up and charm us into taking him to dinner.

A Virginia gentleman, John Richardson, called and came in bearing a large roll of World War I posters, which had been aging in his family house of generations, near Berryville. At the outset, we took them on consignment to give him a better price and because it was an uncertain commodity for us, but eventually he offered us the unsold balance at a very reasonable cost.

Harris was alone in the store when the hussar first visited. Although they spoke seven or eight languages between them, they had not one in common. Never-theless, Harris figured out that the World War I cavalryman, a Galician who had fought with the Austro-Hungarian forces, had lived in New York for perhaps fifty years. In the microcosm of Central Europe then existing on the Upper East Side he had never learned English; he did not need to. Somehow, he had made his interest known, and Harris found him a most unusual German book that dealt with his campaigns on the Eastern Front, with fine maps. Since it was expensive (maybe $40.00), Harris had agreed to xerox "his" chapter—not our usual practice. Who, after all, could say no?

I was in the store when he returned for the copies. Slight, wiry, fine-featured and faintly Asian looking, with a shrewd sharp eye, he had a military zip to his bearing; he sported a stiff beret with a tassel behind, and carried a walking stick that one would never mistake as being necessary. Tom, who spoke German well, was in the store and engaged him in conversation about his service; it was easy to hear the hussar's slushy accent, except for military terms that were delivered in precise, clipped *haupt deutsch*. He received the copies and paid for them with the greatest satisfaction, and departed. Never to be seen again, like an apparition or a time traveler.

The voluble guy in the silver bomber jacket made an instant impression. His jacket was pretty outré for 1976, and all he wanted was Holocaust material. Stuart Elenko was building, with his own efforts and often his own funds, a pioneering collection at the Bronx High School of Science. We gave him a ten percent discount always because, Harris said, he bought like a dealer, in quantity, and because it was for the school. Stuart, a regular, was pushy for his "cause" and he was funny. And he knew himself. When he was browbeating me for more of a discount, he said, "C'mon, I bet you do better for other libraries, what do they get?" Nothing, I replied, and it was true. It stopped him in his tracks.

Joe Garabrant was a different creature altogether. He appeared in the store in his habitual contractor's overalls and sized up the shelves like a pro. He was the sort, like Joe Ward, whom Harris later called the professional collector: one who really knew his subject and the books in it, someone from whom we could always learn. In between his construction jobs, Joe was always on the prowl for World War II books. Lean and mean, with a crew cut, he was a real right-winger, collecting Holocaust memorabilia while being a Holocaust denier: a misanthrope with a sour sense of humor and guns in a secret closet. Joe had been a jazz drummer in the palmy days of the great clubs in the forties and fifties, and it fit right in with his favorite construction job, demolition.

He became a frequent visitor, usually looking and not buying. It was startling to find him back in the stacks, where the aisles were narrow and high, about four shelves up straddling the aisle and perusing the books on the top shelves. Our introduction to the barter system came when Joe undertook to put a new handle on an old ax Harris had found in our apartment. Bill Waters and I suspended work on the catalogue and watched, hypnotized by his skill. When he finished, he plucked a book from the shelf and said, "That's for the ax!"

Aaron Popok discovered us that first summer, as did Rita Wolfson, each by walking the dog. Aaron, tall and saturnine, made me think of the Knight of the Woeful Countenance. He would arrive, cigarette in one hand and Corgi on leash in the other. The little dog, so excited to see us, would promptly pee and someone would go for the paper towels. Aaron, unperturbed, would sit down for a chat. I don't remember his ever buying anything,

Bill Waters and his poster.

but under the name Aaron Norman he had written a fine book, *The Great Air War,* on World War I aviation. He and his wife had enjoyed searching for the primary source books together: scarce memoirs by the veterans, or almost more often, it seemed, memorials or collections of letters privately published by grieving families. So many of the Americans were New England prep school and college boys who had quixotically volunteered before the United States entered the war. One unit, the Lafayette Escadrille, became part of the French Air Force, and a legend. These books and their collectors were in a class by themselves: both the fliers and the readers were romantics attracted to the new, in 1914, idea of flying and the old ideas of chivalry and heroic single combat. Knights, falcons, eagles, sky kings, abound in the titles, and one title presents air combat as *The Great Adventure.*

Not long after Aaron found us, he offered to sell us his fine books. That was, I believe, the first private collection we bought.

But others followed quickly. Collections are distinctive for a variety of reasons and often recognizable as the books are sold and pass through your hands on their way out the door. Some collectors had signed their names, heavily, in even the lowliest books: Malcolm Thomson, Stanley Grimm, Craig Cassen reminded us of their ownership for years. Another lot had been in boxes in an attic for a while, and someone prudent had thoroughly sprinkled them with mothballs. We always knew when they sold.

Richard Strich heard about a collection in Queens and I drove out with him while Harris and a helper took a rented station wagon, both of which we filled up. A curiosity of this lot was that there were three copies each of the owner's chosen titles: one for his reading, one to keep in pristine condition in dust jacket, one custom bound in red cloth. Harris kept the three red *Horatio Hornblower* volumes for himself, and I, the red-bound *Black Lamb and Gray Falcon*, Rebecca West's classic on the Balkans' complex history.

An early wild-goose chase was in response to a call from a Baltimore cousin, Eleanor Thomas, who dangled "Sam Morison always said my husband had nice books." Sam was Samuel Eliot Morison, the well-known historian of the U.S. Navy in World War II and Eleanor's brother-in-law, and we couldn't get on the road fast enough. Our hostess was out beagling as we went through the shelves, and we carried off only about a wheelbarrow full of books, when we had figured on at least a station wagon. We did make up for it to a degree, by buying her Derrydale Press books (predictable, I guess, in the horsey Green Spring Valley), and immediately reselling them to Herb.

We had a good number of customers, more than we knew, who were writers—scriptwriters, historians, novelists—reading for business and pleasure. Ernie Volkman was a local writer, and a regular in those years, who later authored several espionage books. We acquired John Toland as a customer on an early call at the Fourth Avenue Bookstore, because, I confess, I read his name and address upside down on their desk. On his first visit to us, John spotted and bought a copy of his own book, *Ships in the Sky*. Many authors need more copies of their own books and he was the first we were able to supply. Aaron's was only the first collection we bought from an author finished with a project, and later we bought from John.

Seymour Reit was our first writer, that is, the first we helped find material in the course of his writing. Best known as the creator of Casper the Friendly Ghost and myriad children's books, he had served in World War II in a camouflage unit, which drew on his cartoon experience, mobilized as were the talents of Disney to create illusion and deception. Later he was with the Army Air Forces in Europe, analyzing reconnaissance photos. When Sy came to us, he was working on his first adult book, *Masquerade: The Amazing Camouflage Deceptions of World War II*. We had a good time with him and his book was the first to mention us in the acknowledgments.

Rita Wolfson, with baby daughter in carriage and big white Samoyed in tow, wandered down 92nd Street one day.

I was trying to think of a good birthday gift for Mike. I knew he loved Charles Oman, as he had bought two of his books when we were vacationing in England, so I decided to just walk in one day. Harris was there talking to a customer. He looked up and said. "Can I help you?" I said I wondered if he had any books by Charles Oman.

The customer, whose back was to me, swung around and in the most condescending voice possible said, "Don't tell me YOU read Charles Oman," as if women should stick to Barbara Cartland and household-hints books.

I was so ticked off I put on my most vacant stare, looked him in the eye, and said, "Oh, he's my favorite author."

Harris, bless him, caught on in less than two seconds, said, "Why shouldn't she love him, he's a great writer," took my arm and said, "Let me show you where I keep the Oman books." He had three books Mike didn't yet own—we picked one out, and after Mike opened his present, he asked where I had gotten it and became a regular.

Rita had immediately put in a request to be kept secret: Mike deeply desired a scarce and important history by Charles W. C. Oman, *A History of the Art of Warfare in the Middle Ages,* which he called the most astounding history he had ever read. Sooner than might be expected, the Oman title came in, probably in a trade from Joe or Dan or Henry, and I called Rita. Alas, Mike was home and I left an inept message. The secret was blown: Mike said calmly, "It must be the Oman." Within the hour and not acting so cool, along came the whole family, baby and big white dog too, to collect the treasure.

Mike Wolfson, short, slight, dark, soft-spoken and rather exotic looking, was a regular for the duration of the Military Bookman. He seemed to have been led by Oman's writings to concentrate on medieval warfare; the technological advances and the lag time in understanding them intrigued him. But Oman also wrote about the Peninsular Wars, and Mike read that, which led him to the Sharp's Rifles novels on the side. Eventually he concentrated on the Mongols and their empire and Central Asia, especially Genghis Khan. He regarded himself as a reader, more than a collector, and kept just the books he knew he would go back to. But there were hundreds of those.

Scott Palter was so excited to find us that he soon brought in his new girlfriend Holly, who shared his interest in World War II. As they rounded the turn into that section, she exclaimed as if she had been turned loose in Tiffany's, "Ooh, you have a Holocaust section!" They were both chubby, and as they cavorted ecstatically up and down the store they reminded me of Picasso's balloon-like Bathers.

Whenever we saw Philip Kamil walking down the hill, the pockets of his polyester suit full of cash, we knew it would be a good day. He found us three weeks after we opened. Tall, dark, impassive but far from humorless, he was knowledgeable in many subjects. He ran a dye works factory, processing fabric for Seventh Avenue manufacturers, across the Hudson in Union City, but his interests were in stamps and many other collectables. Philip was led to the books because he collected British "Army of India" medals, and to us by Jeffrey Kleinbardt or maybe Peter Hlinka. Army of India medals were awarded to survivors of British battles in India before 1826. British medals were unusual because the recipient's name was engraved on the rim; serious collectors pursued all the medals won by an individual and put together the story of his Army service as demonstrated by the medals and associated documentation, for instance the description of the action or campaign and the award's citation. Usually a medal collector's focus was narrow; he wanted only books on battles or campaigns in which his soldier had served. But Philip's interest was broader and went much deeper and eventually he left the medals behind, devoting himself to the British Army in India before the Sepoy Mutiny of 1857. At first all the books were new to him. In later years his library grew to such proportions and contained such rarities, between the attentions of the Military Bookman and British dealers, that it became a triumph to find something to tempt him.

The store was already a social place. A number of customers liked to hang out as well as shop, and some of our former associates and friends came out of curiosity to see what was happening and how we were doing. Occasionally on weekdays, Peter Miletic, proprietor of our local favorite, Piro's Restaurant, would stop in on his way back from marketing on Second Avenue. Richard Strich and Aaron Popok first encountered each other on the front step, waiting for Harris to unlock. They sized each other up, and Aaron, ever inscrutable, said, "What's with the earring?" Richard, equally deadpan, but with a droop of the eyelids that indicated mischief, replied, "I'm gay." An earring was an anomaly then, but it suited Richard's buccaneering personality.

On my way uptown one winter night in 1975, Herb Weitz had spotted me, yelled, and reeled me in. He had something special for Harris, he said. An unprepossessing but thick stack of legal-size, paper-bound, mimeographed pamphlets, replete with great maps: it was a run of "Weekly Intelligence Summaries" issued by G-2, the intelligence arm of SHAEF, Supreme Headquarters Allied Expeditionary Force, Eisenhower's command. Stamped in red, "Secret," the run started in June 1944, the week after D-Day, and continued until May 1945. It had been compiled under the supervision of Gen. Kenneth Strong, Ike's British head of intelligence. It was even well written (the British component), and contained all the reports gleaned from a legion of sources. A vet living near the Movable Type Bookshop had served with G-2; he had kept the pamphlets all those years and then took them to Herb.

"Don't give them to Harris all at once," said Herb, "you won't see him for a long time. Give him one each week, even Ike had to wait a week!"

The movie, *A Bridge Too Far*, came out in 1977. It was the story of the Battle of Arnhem, when British Field Marshal Montgomery's elaborately planned campaign in the Netherlands overreached and was foiled by the surprise presence of a German tank division. We made a date to see the film with Michael Wray who came up for a drink before the movie; Michael, good-looking, urbane, literate and witty, was an occasional summer movie companion. Harris pulled out the SHAEF issue for the week before the battle, and found and read us the report of a Dutch observer's sighting of the German tanks refitting in that vicinity. Monty and staff had chosen to disregard the intelligence, leading to a debacle. Fully briefed, we went off to the movie.

An older dealer from the West Coast, who styled himself in the *AB Weekly* as "Mr. Arnold Jacobs," was a bit of a thorn in our collective side. He appeared a couple of times a year and depleted our shelves of unit histories, then one of our prime specialties. What he must have charged for them, after only a ten percent dealer's discount, I cannot imagine. We would have loved to have his customer list.

I was in touch with an older generation of fine bookmen in my correspondence with Louis Epstein, founder of the distinguished Pickwick Books in Los Angeles. By then retired, he was still keeping his hand in, amusing himself with a little scouting. He was complimentary about our catalogue and found us some good books from time to time, generously cutting me some slack as I learned. "I was quite confident that on examination of the two books you would find them worth more than the tentative offer."

On his first visit, Jamie Delson worked his way to the back of the store, and we found him on tiptoe, futilely trying to reach a boxed set of books on a high shelf in the Strategy and Tactics section. He was a little guy, and he had recognized the distinctive and scarce Laffont publication by Jacques Boudet, *The Ancient Art of Warfare*. Of course he had to have it.

Customers sometimes had trouble articulating what they wanted, or were shy about asking because to them it seemed so unlikely that there might be such a thing. Jamie, on a later occasion, beat around the bush, but Harris questioned him closely, and Jamie finally said he needed pictures of a World War I trench, for a film project. Harris was able to put in his hands a rare British World War I manual on how to construct a trench. Jamie was incredulous. He became a regular, and eventually translated his love of the subject into The Toy Soldier Company. Most little boys like to play with soldiers, and many of our customers and his were the ones who never outgrew it.

An open-faced, salt-of-the-earth Jersey boy, Mike Mullins, was a industrial chemist, but his passion was the Civil War, and he went to all the shows, where he sold books that he had found in the course of collecting and upgrading his own library. Mike proposed to Harris that he take a selection of our books along too, to flesh out his lot, for a commission on what he sold. Since we were not yet doing much business in the Civil War it seemed like a good idea—and became something of a tradition.

A tall, genial, John Wayne-type, but better looking, was interested only in World War II pilots' accounts. I played with the idea of asking John Hartnett to impersonate John Wayne in a commercial for us. Irwin Holtz, a Saturday regular from north Jersey, wanted World War II aviation too, but just the planes, and always hung out to schmooze with Harris about the Yankees.

We started developing a network of related specialists, such as Bob Brooks, a New York dealer in antique arms, and Stan Blake, an insignia dealer in Delaware (and you thought we were specialized). Neil Reynolds, a poster dealer from Virginia, and George Dembo, a military poster authority in New Jersey, both sold to me. Bleecker Williams, from Connecticut, was a dealer in antique guns, as the "Ordnance Chest." Big, bluff, and hearty, he bought early American military manuals. We knew a dealer in Ohio whose business was called "War Horse" —was it just cavalry books?

Sidney Lynn could always be counted on to buy several cartons of medium-priced books. An eclectic collector-accumulator, a single man in his forties, he told us he had bought a new house, in a subdivision on Long Island, which he was having built to his very particular specifications: almost no windows so that he could shelve all the walls, a drainage trench outside the walls—it sounded like a moat—to avert flooding, and as a further precaution, a plan to let all the grasses in his yard grow up to absorb water. What must the neighbors have thought, or speculated? It must have looked like a bunker. Before long, alas, his interest turned to records and he started buying them with the same aggressive zeal he had previously put into books, and we saw him no more.

He looked as if he had just walked out of a Salvation Army thrift shop, but Lewis Gordon was an old-line WASP snob. Maybe he had checked us in the Social Register before he came. He was interested in Colonial Wars and the Revolution, for his forebears presumably, and bought a little. When the new, enlarged Social Register was published, he carried on in his affected drawl, decrying their inclusion of not only the whole East Coast but also points west which he considered beyond the pale, "It's as big as the Gutenberg Bible."

Customers never failed to amaze. My first eye-opener was a man who had been searching for an airplane book he had loved as a child, long since misplaced. Such attractive period pieces came in sometimes in a lot, and had some valid information though they were juvenile books. Consider the odds. We had it; he was thrilled; the original price of $2.50 was on the dust jacket. We had marked it at $7.50 or $10.00. Why, he wanted to know, wasn't it the original price? Well, it was about thirty-five years old, and there it was for goodness sake, in front of his eyes. Unbelievably, he did not buy it. I hope he was kicking himself for a long time thereafter.

That first summer, Time-Life Books was beginning work on its massive World War II series, and placed several sizable orders. Only a couple of their writers found us. Rafael Steinberg was one, and later sold back to us his accumulated books on the island campaigns in the Pacific.

At my behest, Harris had sent in a small notice about our new venture to his prep school's alumni magazine, and Frank Crocker must have seen it. He walked in one winter evening in his Chesterfield overcoat, and maybe it was that, or his demeanor, that made me feel there was some connection. In fact they were school-mates, Frank a few years ahead of Harris. Frank was, and remained, a little irritated that Harris did not remember him, because after all Frank was one of the big boys. Tall, balding, elegant, with a wonderful laugh, Frank had been with the Marines in Korea, but that was far from his only interest. He really zeroed in on British India, the Northwest Frontier, Gurkha regiments and Afghanistan, and fretted about his supposed competition with Philip Kamil for the books. But their periods of interest did not really overlap; they never jostled each other at the shelves.

The East 90s had been "little White Russia" in Harris's youth, and indeed two Russian churches remained. An old crone who looked like Baba Yaga, the scary witch of Russian folktales, sat in the sun and fed the pigeons on 93rd Street, and the Russian priests and handsome town houses gave the block between Madison and Park a flavor of *émigré* Paris in the twenties. We were told that there had been a caviar shop in the other store at 170 East 92nd Street. So it was almost in context when, on a snowy day in that snowy winter, a Russian came to call. So complete was his image that he could have been from Central Casting: beard, fur hat, fur-collared coat. He halted just inside the door and asked, in thickly accented English, if we had the plans for a nuclear submarine for sale. It was so far-fetched it was hard not to laugh, but Harris briskly replied that if we did it would be highly illegal. Without another word, the spy? military attaché? turned and beat a retreat. Joe Ward humorously maintained that the F.B.I. had a watcher stationed on the low roof across the street from the store. This would have been his moment.

The next summer, we received a summons from Lou Appelfeld to see a most unusual, probably unique, set of books. It was a big collection of World War I posters handsomely bound by Brentano's shortly after the war into very large, elephant folios, probably six or eight volumes in all. The posters had been folded and then hinged into the books, which made them less precious as posters but a rich assortment, with many rare foreign examples—altogether remarkable. Lou had a very large price on them (maybe $20,000), and although it was certainly not viable for us, it was fun and educational to see and good to know about them. And who knew, maybe a poster addict with deep pockets would show up at the store.

Not much later, Lou called to say that his shop had been burgled and the poster set had been taken. There had probably been talk in his neighborhood about such a valuable item or maybe it was an inside job. And not long after that, a purported book dealer from Brooklyn showed up at our store and described the set to Harris, inviting him to see it. There could not be two sets like that floating around New York. Harris played along, showed interest, then later called Lou who reported it to the police.

The police asked Harris if he would wear a wire and go to Brooklyn to see the books. Don't throw me in that briar patch! Harris was thrilled, I was a bit apprehensive, and the customers who came in the afternoon he was absent laughed to think of his adventure and how he must be enjoying it. I did too, but worried a little. It turned out that the dealer was an innocent. The books were recovered, a little scuffed; and Lou Appelfeld, to thank us, took us out for a hamburger at Dorrian's on Second Avenue.

A landmark event in July 1977 was the Blackout, the second one I experienced. We were with a friend in a Chinese restaurant where they could no longer see to cook, and made our way home for scrambled eggs by candlelight, taking Fred, who lived on the fifteenth floor and gladly spent the night on our fourth floor. The next day we still had no power. Harris went to the store to protect it, guarding it with a stout Afghan goat tether from my brass collection, rather than one of his swords. There were break-ins and looting uptown, but no trouble on 92nd Street, and that night Fred had us for dinner because he had regained electricity and air conditioning and we had not.

The blackout was in the midst of orders from our first catalogue, and action resumed immediately. Our first big library order was from the S. L. A. Marshall Collection at the University of Texas at El Paso—very exciting. General Marshall had been a prolific Army historian and was well known for his after-action interviews in World War II. His own library was the nucleus of UTEP's fine collection, and this order was the start of a long relationship with the library. The curator later wrote a polite letter expressing consternation about a book in that first order, which was listed at $75.00, but then in the second catalogue for $7.50. We reassured him that UTEP had been charged the latter price, not that with the slipped decimal point in the typo.

CHAPTER FOUR

"Please do nothing that will increase the already cutthroat competition."

1977 – 1978

Recently, I was called as a last-minute-substitute judge for a New York University rare-books class's assignment to present business plans for a book business. I went, I judged, but confessed to realizing as I listened to the presentations that we went into business without a plan at all. We needed to know if the books were out there first. We did not have a budget, a space, an advertising plan, a mailing list, suppliers for either books or printing or shipping or mailing—and no out-of-print book experience or even retail experience. One intelligent and deeply knowledgeable reader with business training, and one history researcher with publishing experience and organizational skills, going into the unknown.

We learned by doing. Harris knew we needed an accountant and a lawyer, and lined them up. There were certainly mistakes, in buying especially—entry fees, Harris called them. (The *Source Records of the Great War* springs to mind: an attractive and authoritative-sounding six-volume set that no one wanted.) Customer policies were developed in reaction to our experiences, usually the negative ones. We didn't need employee policies for a few years because we didn't have any employees.

We never debated whether or not to have an open, walk-in store, with regular hours, it was a given. And we needed to be open Saturdays, so had a Sunday—Monday weekend. We were organized by subject, for browsing, the hands-on book experience, which is increasingly rare today. We made up our own methods for dealing with customers; for building and tending and trimming the mailing list; and for compiling catalogues with a mix of subjects as we worked our way through the inventory, eventually evolving ideas for catalogue subscriptions and elaborate methods of filing customers' want lists.

We used the talent at hand. We needed a lawyer, and Howard Friedman, whom we had met at a stamp show, vetted the lease and later incorporated us. He soon played a big part in events we could not anticipate. During our brief tenure at Herb's, we met two very different people who became prime assets for the duration of our business life.

Melvin Kushel became our accountant and, in our first sessions in Herb's basement under a bare, ceiling light bulb, it struck me how much he resembled a Gothic Old Testament prophet. He dispensed wisdom and know-how for small-

Harris at the unit history shelves.

business owners, and occasionally sample garments for me from one of his clients on Seventh Avenue. Melvin said if there should be a problem with the taxman he would "go downtown." Herb cracked, "One of these days, Mel's goin' downtown and he ain't comin' back."

Lloyd Gayle, a bookbinder from Jamaica via London, was a sweet, gentle man who did more than decent work, from serviceable cloth to leather and marbled boards. His prices were low, and over the years he made it worthwhile for us to buy books in disrepair or worse. Lloyd made them whole and they went on to a new life.

He also did special binding to our customers' orders, and mine at Christmas, the year's catalogues for Harris.

Harris had learned a lot from Herb about book repair that we could do ourselves. (Herb's slogan was "Glue it together so it lasts long enough for them to get it home.") We used Lloyd for the more complicated things: rebacking, rebinding, and major repairs. Lloyd carried only a limited range of binding cloths and marbled papers.

When we found our second set of the rare, Lienhart French-uniforms opus at the Soldier Shop, it was in its original mud-brown bindings. It soon attracted a buyer, and it was perhaps understandable that the client wanted it rebound; but we were too green in the business to try to dissuade him from the bright and inappropriate kelly-green cloth he chose for it. Maybe it was his Irish background kicking in. We soon became more sophisticated and assertive about choosing and suggesting bindings more compatible with the contents.

Harris and I took an excursion to Talas, the bookbinders' supplier, in the grungy West 40s near the Port Authority bus terminal. It was another little world, a fascinating specialized place. The large, open loft space was full of the arcane tools of the trade: fabrics, leathers of unimagined variety, papers, glues, presses, hundreds of patterns of tools for gilt-stamping leather and on and on. What Harris wanted were the "bones," implements made of bone, used to manipulate the binding and spine and facilitate mending. I got into the flat files of marbled papers and it was delirious, almost psychedelic: innumerable patterns, colors

. . . and prices. Lloyd used the cheapest ones, so I began stocking paper I liked, better designs, more expensive naturally, for Lloyd to use for the more important bindings or for custom orders.

Lloyd did make me tear my hair out: despite my written work-orders, he would jot notes in the books, sometimes wrong. And it was not unusual for him to misspell on the spine, most notoriously mangling the title on a handsome leather binding for Steve Sears of his first Civil War book, *Landscape Turned Red,* and the author on Jim Controvich's own copy of his big bibliography of World War II unit histories. I learned later that misspelling is endemic to the binding process, finding it from time to time on British books: imagine, setting all the type up backwards.

Bill Waters was there from the beginning, unpacking the Boston books, and helping us set up. He was cobbling together other freelance work, and gave us a lot of hours; we would have hired Bill any time, but couldn't afford an employee, and his interests lay elsewhere. But especially during our first year in business, he helped us develop our catalogues, both editorially and in tracking down suppliers, and "store-sat" for us when we needed to be away. Tall, good-looking, our unlikely "'Nam vet" was invaluable: reliable, funny, imperturbable, and able to deal with almost any situation, no matter how absurd. During one of our absences, he coped with a leak over the duplicate shelving and a soldier-of-fortune who brought in the magazine of that name; Bill was particularly taken with the Letters to the Editor section, entitled "Flack!"

Finding customers was a different challenge in that pre-internet era, and print advertising and PR the best ways to do so. We already had some names, and sent introductory letters to Ray's list and later to a slightly used list Peter Hlinka sold us, keeping on file for future reference a list of World War II historians brought in by Joe Garabrant. Early on, we obtained the addresses of U.S. Army libraries for our mailing list-to-be, and while few of them were buyers, their referrals were a significant factor.

In an effort to make ourselves better known in New York, we joined two local groups, the British Military Historical Society and the Historical Arms Society, and attended a lot of meetings. That was relatively fruitless, and often boring—a lot of secretive, cheap collectors who didn't want to talk about where they had found things or what they had paid, or even what they had. The high point with the British group was a screening of *Zulu,* one of the best war movies ever, and a real treat in that pre-video and way pre-Netflix era. We took Frank Crocker with us, and sat behind a member who sang along with "Men of Harlech," the Welsh battle song, as the Zulus pounded on their shields.

The Historical Arms Society met in a handsome private dining room at the Seventh Regiment Armory, a historic and magnificent Victorian building on Park

Avenue, and was enlivened for us by the presence of Richard Strich, the Society's secretary. When there was a "show and tell" evening with each member bringing an item from his own collection, Harris, instead of taking one of his Napoleonic sabers, downplayed it, with a Maltese bosun's whistle, a 1732 piece of scrimshaw, real folk art, which had come down in his mother's family.

I found myself running the advertising and the customer list. I started collecting names from day one, and at first would add anyone who asked to our list. Many of Ray's individual customers continued with us for the long term. Ray's list included two military libraries in Singapore, the Imperial War Museum and the National Army Museum in London, several Canadian libraries and a couple in Australia, as well as some obvious stateside institutions. There were several British book dealers, among them A. A. Johnston and Peter de Lotz, so the word started to get around in England.

The joint ad in *Campaigns Magazine* with Jeffrey's "Grenadier Guard" began in July and drew well, and he referred many customers to us. In August our ad started running in the *New York Times* Book Review classified section, then a very extensive listing, over three columns in tiny type. It was a nerve center of the trade; the Book Review section circulated more widely than the paper, and bookstores nationwide could subscribe to it separately. Those tiny ads produced not only customers but book offers. For instance, a couple in Mississippi who had enjoyed collecting the fine nineteenth-century uniform pictorials together started sending us sale lists, then books.

The *New York Times* ad was one of the first and continued the best until the internet era, even enlisting a customer in Inuvik, Northwest Territory. We started with the similar book review classifieds in the *Los Angeles Times* in 1979, and added the *Washington Post* and the two Chicago papers in 1980. Gradually we began to advertise in a number of small specialty publications that came to our attention, probably from browsing at Sky Books. *Military Affairs* was one of the first, and attracted some serious and far-flung collectors, such as our favorite Philippine customer Alberto Montilla. A naval customer told us about *Warship International*, a small periodical for naval historians and devotees. Their classified section, "On Target," was remarkably cheap and drew well forever. Every now and then we would buy a mailing list, but those were never fruitful.

A new customer, Tom Shydler, helpfully suggested places for us to advertise as he had found us only in a roundabout way. A few weeks later, after trying to order from the catalogue a little late, he wrote, *I can see that my comments concerning your need to advertise were misplaced. Please do nothing that will increase the already cutthroat competition...*

The Military Bookman listing in the New York Yellow Pages produced steady calls, either from those looking for an occasional gift or some who might become long-term customers, and eventually I began to ponder how we could arrange to be listed in the Yellow Pages in other major cities. This idea was primarily a reaction to the inept typesetting of the *Los Angeles Times* Book Review section, where we advertised monthly in the classifieds. I don't know what the typesetters were smoking in the copy room, but something always came out wrong, like the address or phone number. I was ready to give up on them after a couple of years, but wanted a showing in L. A., and for that matter in other big cities that didn't have book review sections in their papers.

By dint of many, many inquiries over many months I found an agency that placed Yellow Pages ads all over the country. There was a huge choice of cities, at different rates geared to population, so the Military Bookman began showing up in the Yellow Pages in Boston, Denver, Houston, Philadelphia, Dallas, Kansas City, Atlanta, Seattle, Phoenix and so on.

This was expensive, but enormously successful and in unexpected ways. The listing was found by locals, but also by travelers arriving in a new city who would check the Yellow Pages for bookstores. Sherry Newkirk, an enthusiastic customer in Connecticut, excitedly reported finding us in the New Orleans Yellow Pages. One man came in and said, "I found you in the Chicago Yellow Pages." Unh-hunh, we said. "But I live on the West Side and had never heard of you!" Dealers would shake their heads and say, "Everywhere I go I check the Yellow Pages and you're listed!" and sometimes, disingenuously, "How did you do that?" I would simply answer, "It wasn't easy."

There was always the incalculable: *Dear Sir, I am a postal employee in Denver and through [seeing] your correspondence I was able to obtain your address as well as the knowledge of your very existence.*

Or, plaintively: *A copy of your catalog was seen in a friend's home . . . but he wouldn't let me borrow it.*

Or: *I found your [subscription] questionnaire among the pages of a book I recently purchased.*

Or, two army colonels: *One of your subscribers . . . very kindly loaned me his copy of your catalog. It's wonderful! As [he] said 'For a military history buff, it's like a kid being turned loose in a candy store.*

We increasingly got referrals from specialty publishers in our field, particularly Presidio Press and Battery Press. Guidebooks listed us, even a Japanese guide to New York, brought in by a new customer. Some PR came to us in big general magazines' roundups of New York bookstores, or neighborhoods, or Christmas shopping for men. The Military Bookman showed up in airline magazines, every now and then the *New York Times* (always welcome), the *New Yorker, Town and Country, New York Magazine* again, even *Gourmet* and *W*. A lengthy and well-illustrated article in *Avenue Magazine* was very charming—the writer was smitten with Harris—but it did not bring in anything noticeable.

The most productive was *Gentlemen's Quarterly Magazine*. In a brief mention, the writer said, in his article "Corporate Maneuvers," that young executives on the rise might stop in at the Military Bookman and, for business strategy, buy *Infantry in Battle*. As usual, we had only one copy when he was there, long gone by the time the calls started, and that was extremely frustrating. After half-a-dozen of these requests, I said to a caller, in some exasperation, "Well, I don't know why the writer mentioned that book, the one all the management seminars use is Clausewitz, *On War*, and we do have that in a recent Princeton edition." That became our answer—coincidentally one of the few new books we stocked and could order—and dozens of copies moved out at $35.00 apiece. Later, in 1986, GQ gave us a full-page feature in "Elements of Style," and that issue must have lingered in barbershops and doctors' offices, because we got calls and letters resulting from it for years. We always included copies of the article to new people, with orders and answers to inquiries.

Eventually we had customers in every state except one of the Dakotas. Ray had had some foreign customers, but by the time we were well established, we had customers in every country in Western Europe and Scandinavia (including a Norwegian admiral), with many Canadians and British, as might be expected; when the Wall came down, we enlisted a few Czechs and Poles. We had Argentines (some old Nazis?) and Brazilians, even a professor in Kuwait and a man at the far end of Chile. Many Japanese; several in the Philippines. There were always a few in Hong Kong; one, an American, lived on a houseboat, and told us his business was busting labor unions, so perhaps it was good to be able to put out to sea. Many Australians, including their "West Point" in Canberra; a South African, a number of Israelis. Two Jordanians. One in Panama, whose mail drop was in Miami, which didn't make for speedy communications. An Indian commander had to communicate and pay and ship via his son in New Jersey. One American stationed in Guam was very active; when he came home he seemed to have less time to read.

Two people in the diplomatic corps, he a Spanish ambassador, she an American, were each customers before they apparently met and married on a posting in Honduras. We deduced this from afar and further learned that they played war games together. Once she confused their suppliers and wrote us an irate letter about missing pieces in a new game: *You can imagine the havoc it causes when we set up war games.*

Foreign customers had to be really fanatical and patient to put up with the difficulties: they usually got their catalogues later, sometimes much later. Shipment by surface mail took a long time too. Payment was complicated before credit cards were common, and some postal money orders were unacceptable due to punitive bank fees here; exchange rates were always hard on Canadians, and variable for Brits. It was a bit horrifying to get dollars in the mail, but it happened. Packages to both Italy and Israel had to be registered and were limited by weight to four books, an extra expense for buyers. The Italians really suffered with their mail service, packages often taking four to six months. More than one Italian order came back to us. One Mexican customer had a P. O. box north of the border in Texas.

It is unclear to me how we thought we were going to maintain and replenish the inventory, once we got going. My fantasy had been wandering through New England, as in Christopher Morley's *Parnassus on Wheels,* shopping through all the book barns. We immediately began running a "Books Wanted" box ad in the *AB Bookman's Weekly,* which brought customers as well as offers.

We started going to auctions, at Swann especially, which at that time really focused on books. The presiding auctioneer was usually the genial George Lowry, and sometimes the crusty Edwin Halbmeier. Sometimes we went down on the subway with Herb, who exulted, "I always take a taxi back if I've bought well." Harris knew what he was doing at an auction, but it took me a long time to be comfortable with the process. All the buyers then were dealers, and almost all men, a coterie, gossipy and rivalrous. One exception was the formidable Mrs. Rubinowitz of Fourth Avenue Books. Another was a dealer who was muttered about as a "breaker," that is, one who buys beautifully illustrated books, only to gut them for the prints and color plates. In the '80s the scene began to change as retail buyers started attending auctions, which tended to drive up the prices, and made it harder for dealers to buy.

Auctions would not have been enough to keep us supplied. But you cannot predict what will happen when you open a door on the street. One of the good surprises was the appearance of book scouts. I don't believe we knew there was such a species, but that first summer we learned. Good book scouts divined what a dealer might want, and in their rarified and secretive wanderings, bought books they gambled on reselling.

The word was out and the drums were beating. The first scout had appeared at Herb's in March, the very day Harris first talked to Ray McGuire. Oscar Schreyer was a retired gentleman in his seventies; he was Viennese, with the unique charm that seemed to come with that provenance. Though Jewish, he had been a lawyer of canon law in Vienna. When the Anschluss came in 1938, he and his fiancée walked from Vienna to Paris, leaving behind their families who were too old to escape and died in the camps. Eventually, in New York, Oscar became a toy manufacturer, and it seemed to suit perfectly his gentle, playful, curious personality and his almost child-like sense of wonder. In his retirement, he entertained himself with a little light book dealing for a few select clients, and bought a good bit from us, mostly early aviation and Holocaust material. He offered us unusual early aviation material or antiquarian pamphlets found in Portugal that he would present with a beatific smile. He telephoned his congratulations and laughter, when he received our first catalogue: we had a whopper of a typo in the World War I section: *Judische Fliegen im Weltkrieg,* instead of *Flieger:* Jewish flies rather than fliers.

Oscar probably told Janet Toback about us. A beautiful, serious young woman enamored of books, she was a quick study and would come along to offer three or four cartons of well-chosen books on a little suitcase trolley. She was very professional and had a good eye, and subsequently worked for Jim Carr, an unfriendly dealer on East 82nd Street who bought estates, stashing them in one of the few New York houses still to have a barn out back. The books went into the barn, and Janet ran the books and would set aside titles for us, and call.

Joe Ward began scouting to support his habit, and would show up with a small but choice lot, some probably culled from his own collection. His wicked sense of humor enlivened the transactions.

Joe gave me a hot tip that the Weyhe Gallery, a well-known art bookstore on Lexington Avenue in the 60s, had a stack of Henri Lachouque's *Anatomy of Glory* at a sale price. That book, about Napoleon's Imperial Guard, was an all-too-rare combination of an excellent text and fine, well-selected and richly reproduced illustrations. Although legitimately an art book, with stunning selections from Anne S. K. Brown's famous uniform-art collection, it apparently had not found favor with Weyhe's customers. I hit the road and bought all they had, at least twenty copies, which went out fast. It was always in demand, even after Brown University and then Lionel Leventhal's Arms & Armour Press reprinted it.

Jim Pine showed up with a bag or two from time to time, but seemed at least as interested in talking to Harris about the Yankees as in selling books. Alan Weiner worked with Jack Feldman for a bit and did some scouting for us; Jack was retiring and Alan bought the name Academy Books and moved downtown to West 18th Street, where he had great success.

Howard Portnoy, a cheerful, good-natured Navy captain stationed in Washington, found us in the *New York Times,* and began to accumulate large lots at various book sales there, often from government book sales. He drove them to New York on his regular visits to see family, and always wanted to know what we were paying for each book, pretty tedious, but it was part of his learning process. Howard was one of our Washington finders well into the nineties.

General dealers began soliciting our business. Aaron Popok, in his book hunting, had become friendly with a dealer in Long Island City, George Chinn. George soon stopped in to introduce himself and entice us to his premises, one of the dirtiest bookstores ever seen. We did buy, and George offered us a priceless tip, which he must have developed of necessity: to clean and restore a fine-weave cloth-bound book, he applied a thin coat of vaseline, then wiped it off with cotton; it picked up the dirt and brightened the book like a facial. George was a character, one of the many autodidacts who populated the out-of-print book business— men (almost all men) who, despite non-literary backgrounds and usually with only a high school education, were drawn to the world of books. They often had encyclopedic knowledge and voluminous memories of the books themselves and frequently of the subjects. Diamonds in the rough, possessed by their trade, or calling really, they rarely factored their own time into their pricing equation. Many wrote arcane codes in each book to indicate where they had bought it and what they had paid for it (and who knows, what the weather was like that day), with little regard for the time consumed.

Soon we learned about the Bryn Mawr Bookstores, run by serious, professional alumnae volunteers for the benefit of the college. There were a number scattered around the Northeast; ours was way east in a basement on 79th Street. The books, which had been donated, were always in good condition and reasonably priced. When my errands took me that way, I paid a visit, had a good time with the ladies, and always left with a bag of books. They called us when anything special in our line came in. It was reciprocal; for years we donated the books that were not in our subject from lots we had acquired. The Bryn Mawr Clubs elsewhere held yearly book sales, but they were madhouses the first morning when all the dealers and scouts were scrambling, and after participating in those spectacles in Westport and Princeton that year, we left the fray to our various scouts.

We got a call from a man in Brooklyn who wanted to sell his books. We must have gone on a Sunday; the whole family trailed in and out of the living room that was garnished with about ten pairs of the man's shoes, quite large shoes, neatly paired and deposited around the room. The books were not exciting, until Harris engaged the man in conversation about his wartime service. It turned out that he had been the editor of his unit history, and had about fifteen unclaimed or returned copies, almost forgotten in a closet. He hadn't thought they were anything special because he had worked on the book, but that find made our day worth the effort.

We heard from the Whites, dealers in Asbury Park, and took a jaunt to the down-at-the-heel seashore town with a wonderful but decaying carousel—a productive visit, the first time, because of years of accumulation in our subject. We bought a good bit in the medium-sized, well-organized store, then of course they had more books in their big house—too many, suffocating—and some surly, disaffected teenagers, one of whom was dealing in old jukeboxes. One buy was a nice leather set of Dickens, soon refurbished for my parents' bookshelves. White's became an occasional stop for us when we were going that way, but they never had as much for us again because we had cleaned them out the first time.

A friend in Williamstown, Massachusetts told Second Life Books what we were doing, and they began offering us posters as well as books.

We started buying from Joe Garabrant in Pearl River from time to time. He lived in a neat and extremely well-tended, newish house, and his duplicates and other books for sale were in the garage. The books were always good copies, at prices that worked for us. Joe's house was lined with bookshelves, all World War II books in pristine condition; the only picture in the house was the then-current poster of Whistler's Mother with a machine gun.

Alma Anderson of Salt Lake City immediately found us in the *Times* classified ads and sent intelligent, on-target, purple-ink mimeographed lists, for over twenty years. Good books in excellent condition, reasonably priced. At first I was very frustrated because I didn't get enough of what I wanted, but I negotiated a deal with Alma to buy everything I could if she gave me a head start on the list. Alma was very reserved, we never chatted much; but I could feel her interest, and eventually she sent in a friend who had moved to New York to report on the store.

From England, we received mimeographed lists from P. T. Clarke, well-chosen books, a good bit of military, also dogs, gardening, art, well described and priced. I didn't know if P. T. were a man or a woman. We ordered perhaps half-a-dozen books from each list, for years. I always bought. And we received blue airmail letter sheets from a dealer named Henry Lloyd, with lots of book chat and gossip, along with perhaps eight or ten desirable book offers.

Other scouts would hit yard sales or library sales and send us offers written out on three-by-five index cards, which they wanted returned, marked yes or no.

And just as important, some of Ray's customers who had become ours decided to divest themselves of all or parts of their collections. Joel Keller decided to concentrate on World War I and sold us the rest of his military books; we drove out through the Delaware Water Gap to the Poconos to pick them up. Craig Cassen sold us all his books, most memorably about five feet of the Ballantine Books World War II paperback series, which lined the shelf over the long radiator cover in the front of the store. Charley Woolley, an old crony of Ray McGuire's, drove down from Massachusetts with some beautiful and rare Napoleonic and British uniform plate books, which certainly added tone to our first catalogue. We visited Orson Munn, nearby on 86th Street, who sold us some good uniform titles.

He had an enormous toy and model soldier collection, thousands; I had never before seen "flats," the two-dimensional models.

Ray must have told us about J. S. Canner, or vice versa. Canner was a venerable supplier of libraries, known for bibliographies and long runs of scholarly periodicals. In their warehouse near Fenway Park, they had a lot of Civil War books that they wanted to clear out, many older titles and many in duplicate. Harris sent me off to Boston, so I could combine time in the cold warehouse with seeing some friends there. I went armed with the first volume of Charles Dornbusch's esteemed Civil War bibliography, which was when I developed a love/hate relationship with him, it, and whoever oversaw its production at the New York Public Library. Charlie was out of control and the NYPL apparently exercised no editorial function, allowing him to publish a reference book unpaginated and with the sections arranged in no alphabetical order.

There were many good books at Canner and I bought a lot. We had decided that I should buy odd volumes of the classic two-volume memoirs such as Grant, Sherman, Sheridan, hoping to find the complementary volumes later. Some of those odds were with us for years and years. Well, we didn't know any better then. I bought about six copies of an Iowa regimental history—a lifetime supply.

Canner also had full sets of the *Official Records of the War of the Rebellion*, one hundred and twenty-eight parts, something we never wanted to stock but were happy to order from Canner for several customers over the years. In this huge work, the War Department compiled the orders and reports from both Union and Confederate armies; it was published in the late nineteenth century, about twenty years after the Civil War. One buyer, Mr. Toop, wanted us to send a "dummy" insured package to his brother in Rhode Island, so that he could avoid the New York sales tax. We obliged and sent his brother a box of bricks from the old furnace, insured for about $2000. To our consternation (and theirs, I assume), UPS lost the package and invited us to file a claim. We didn't. But Mr. Toop must have plunged into the books and immersed himself, because we did not hear from him again for many years.

Canner had odd volumes of the *Official Records* too, and when Steve Sears, my old boss from American Heritage days, called me needing the volume covering the Battle of Antietam, I knew where to go. Although the Antietam volume was in demand, Canner had a copy for us. I was pretty pleased with myself, Steve was pleased, and we were even more pleased with his nice acknowledgment in *Landscape Turned Red*. And we were delighted to go to his book launch party in Connecticut, a great celebration, and I won the door prize, a signed copy. Steve Sears became, in the post-American Heritage era, a noted Civil War historian, and we liked being able to provide him with books from time to time. We got several calls as a result of the mention in *Landscape,* one man seemingly taken aback that I—in person—had answered the phone.

When new books came in, they were taken back to the inactive, "dead" files, the catalogue cards retrieved, and the books put out to be repriced and redescribed. Duplicates would be taken to the back, to the shelves behind the curtain. Books for which we had no record were set aside to be catalogued. I had almost immediately developed a system for "wants," writing customer info on the backs of catalogue cards in the dead file, with metal tags to alert us—a laborious but often rewarding task. Any incoming books with want tags would be processed in and set aside up front to be quoted to the waiting customer by postcard, then put in the sequestered quote shelves for two weeks, to await a response, or not.

Harris was constantly reading other dealers' catalogues (especially British) for titles in our subjects, clipping and gluing them onto our four-by-six catalogue cards, adding them to the dead files as reference on pricing and, indeed, their existence.

As books came and went, the file cards moved back and forth in a time-consuming routine. We had a card for every title, and our drill was to pull the card from the active file when the book was sold, take it to check for a duplicate copy, and if there were one, redescribe the book if in different condition, change the book and card prices and refile the card, or file the card in the dead file to await the arrival of the next copy. Ray had passed along ten or twelve full card files; we had perhaps fifty by the time we computerized.

Harris started talking about a catalogue that first fall, and it was obvious that we would have to do catalogues to make it; we could not hope to survive on local traffic and random requests. I shrank from it, knowing better than he how much work it would be, but soon we had to start figuring it out. Fortunately, Bill Waters was available for both editorial and legwork. He visited the suppliers George Chinn had generously told us about, good names: a mailer, Johnson & Hayward, who handled all our mailings, all ninety-three issues; Gene Aretzsky, our typesetter until we computerized; and a printer in furthest Brooklyn at the end of the subway line, who unfortunately did not stock red cover paper. After two Brooklyn catalogues, we changed printers and ever after had red covers. Red, the most military color, was Harris's favorite, and what I wanted for the catalogue. It stood out from the junk mail. *My heart always jumps a little when I see the red catalogue in the mailbox,* wrote George Banister.

A friend of Bill's was hired to type up the mailing list names on the IBM style cards the mailer required. The mailer also required the cards to be filed in zip code order; soon I knew more about zip codes than I had ever wanted to.

Bill and I set an editorial style for the catalogue after discussions with Gene, and Bill painstakingly went through the cards, yellow-marking authors (bold), underlining titles (italic), essentially coding the different type styles to be used by Gene. The different type made the text much clearer in the small type size we chose to pack in more listings. Producing the first catalogue seemed endless, taking about four months, but we were learning.

For each catalogue we chose a mix of subjects, in each case listing all we had in that category, a selection from different periods and areas, working our way through different subjects in subsequent issues. We always had too many books to include in a single issue: too long to produce, too expensive, and ultimately too much for a reader to digest. When we hit our stride, the catalogues contained about 2000 titles in each issue, and that was less than a fourth of the inventory.

To the post office.

Producing each issue was extremely laborious, even after we got our procedures in place, a nit-picking, labor-intensive and lengthy process. Usually it took about two months from when we started until the catalogue was in the mail. Pulling the cards against the books on the shelves provided an inventory check as well: some books on the shelf without a card in the file, some cards in the active file with no book on the shelf—mad scurrying. Misfiled? Misshelved? In the duplicate stacks? Some books were wildly misplaced by wandering customers, or even hidden for their next visit. Endless detail, and always urgent. Harris ran the inventory and did the trouble-shooting.

The editorial end was my job: proofreading the cards—often at home, with my morning coffee and no distractions—before they went to the typesetter, one box at a time, and then the galleys when they came back perhaps a week later. Gene lived on East 89th Street and would swing by for pickups and deliveries. Then all the cards had to be re-filed in the active files, after extracting and noting those that had been sold in the meantime. (We never segregated catalogue books, as some dealers did.) After Gene made our corrections, he brought the page proofs came back for another checking, then again with the "blues," the final checking copy. Then off to the printer, one of a succession, whose performance would always be unpredictable—many misrepresentations, many failures on schedules. "All printers lie," quoth Henriette Johnson, of our mailer, Johnson and Hayward. The catalogues were shipped directly to the mailer, or almost always. Once, they were stupidly shipped to us. Once the mailer called, unwilling to mail the new issue without my say-so, because the printer had used cover stock that was almost cerise, really ugly. I reluctantly approved it because of the time element. The mailers were the most reliable part of the process, but after that we were at the mercies of the post office.

Mail order was completely by mail for the first years, aside from the occasional telegram, telex, or call from someone compelled to reserve a special book. It was, after all, well before fax machines and cheap phone rates, and long before email. We wrote letters and postcards; we shipped orders book rate, when that enlightened policy still prevailed, at the post office, at first charging $1.00 per order. We sent catalogues bulk-rate through the post office, and learned that northern Virginia was almost invariably the first to receive them; the last was the Bronx. Beyond that it was anybody's guess, and we later ran a pool to pick the first reporting area.

We learned packing from Herb, I think. We reconditioned the books, then wrapped them for rough treatment. Harris would demonstrate their hardiness to a new shipping clerk or a leery mail order customer by throwing a well-packed book against the brick wall. On 92nd Street, we were around the corner from a deli that was a good source of boxes. We quickly learned that Tropicana cartons of frozen orange juice were the perfect size, the smaller just right for a four-book order, the next size for six to eight books.

Mailing the orders required a trek with a shopping cart to Gracie Station on 85th near Second Avenue, and a long wait where the post office's finest passive-aggressives presided. Even though we had a mailing manifest already written up, making the load faster to process than one old lady shipping a package to Europe, we got dirty looks from clerks and other patrons.

We had two great mailmen on 92nd Street, known at Gracie Station as Black George and White George. Black George was a lively spirit and a sharp dresser (off duty), and was renowned for the number of days he managed to go fishing. White George was the faithful slogger who probably did most of the work on the route. We almost never saw the parcel post carrier; curiously he always attempted delivery on Mondays when we were closed. We had to be told by the pharmacist up the hill that the guy would only deliver for a price: twenty-five cents a package. He had gotten away with this extortion for years because his brother-in-law was the head of Gracie Station. We left this liability behind when we moved to 93rd Street. After a few years we were shipping enough to sign up for UPS, but trips to the post office for foreign and some other shipments were still a necessary chore.

CHAPTER FIVE

"If I ever want a divorce, I'll just kill Harris."

1977 – 1978

Snow, store, and a dumpster.

It was Thanksgiving time 1977, and Harris was having lunch with his visiting kids at the Greek coffee shop up at the corner of Lexington when the new landlord made his first appearance in our shop. Bad vibes accompanied him, like the silver-nosed gunman's jangling theme in *Cat Ballou*. He told me that he would soon be doing renovations in the building. Under the (as usual) ill-constructed J-51 legislation, owners could get tax abatements for renovating old-law tenement buildings, with little or no protection for existing tenants; it was catnip for a crook like Charlie Fridman.

There were only a few long-time tenants upstairs, among them an older Irish couple who "air-mailed" their garbage in the time-honored tenement way, and a man who looked like a Central European intellectual. Through that November, one apartment had had a flood, one a robbery, and a third was vandalized. The tenants were scared, and Charlie was glad to find them new quarters, not at the same rent of course. He had quickly cleared the apartments and then started in on the two stores. Gus, our buddy next door at Burgess Movers, called early one December morning (we did not open until ten-thirty) to report that someone had taken a potshot at our show window. Amazingly, we had taken insurance on the big pane of glass, and it was replaced by early afternoon. We were shaken though; it wasn't a great neighborhood but it wasn't bad, and it was hard not to attribute this to the landlord. The harassment soon was unmistakable. The heat and water were turned off, so we got in space heaters in the front of the store and kept our coats on. It was a particularly cold winter with a good bit of snow, some of which sifted through the badly caulked show window—and never melted. Soon it was too frigid to work a whole day there. Amy and John Cummings and eight-year-old Mark, my godson, were in from England and came to see us and the store for the first time. What an introduction to the Military Bookman: there we sat with the propane heaters, I in my fur coat—not very welcoming for anyone. Mark was undeterred. He loved the store, but we took refuge up the hill in the coffee shop where there was heat.

The water was turned off, but on again capriciously, and pipes froze and cracked. The leaks started in mid-December, when our German friends Ute and Peter Grauer were visiting for a few days. Peter helped Harris move some books out of harm's way—for the moment. It was the first time Peter had seen a cockroach; fastidious Peter was horrified.

The radiators upstairs were taken out and there were many more leaks: warning shots. We covered the shelves with plastic drop cloths. Workmen were starting to dismantle the interiors above us, and a dumpster arrived at the curb. The demolition was nerve-wracking. Trying to do business in this deteriorating and rather scary environment was absurd, and if the store had not gotten off to a good start we would have packed it in. We started taking some of the more precious books home. In a day or two, there was a break-in through the hall wall, in the only place that bookshelves ran along the wall and therefore where it would do the most damage, hardly a coincidence. Someone had squirmed through a ten-inch shelf and knocked books all over the floor, which then were leaked upon. Some good books had been stolen from the rare book cabinet, two of which were later found in the garbage at the Y up the hill. The adding machine and an electric heater, hardly precious, were taken too. We had never thought of robbery; bookstores were hardly a usual target for junkies or even vandalizing kids. We started moving more books to safe places; Herb was good enough to take us in again, and we put a little sign, "Military Bookman in Temporary Bivouac" in his window. We continued to refugee the more expensive books home. One snowy night, when faithful Bill Waters was helping us schlep books back to the apartment, pulling the full shopping cart up the snowy hill, while we had our arms and shopping bags full of big, beautiful books, he remarked that all that was lacking were the Stukas to strafe us.

We got no help from the Department of Health or indeed any city agency we asked. It seemed we had to sue Fridman. Our lawyer Howard Friedman, principled, serious, and intense, believed that we would find a remedy at law; he told us we had to maintain a business presence in the store to have any claim against the landlord, so most of the books remained there, at risk. The situation had little humor, but it sort of amused me that Howard Portnoy, our Washington book finder, was in town the day that Herb volunteered to serve the landlord with papers, and was agog to go along for the melodrama.

On January 16th, two days after the "burglary," came the denouement. The water had been turned on, gushing through the pipes up to the disconnected radiators above. A flood had been unleashed, and a neighbor knew something bad had happened because Burgess's little neon sign went out. The Burgess guys called us at seven a.m. By the time we got to the store, there were two or three inches of water on the floors, and the drop cloths were dripping. Had it not been for the drop cloths our inventory would have been pulp, and some of it was lost. The little store was a sad and forlorn place.

A few days later, a new customer, following a lead from a bookshop in Queens, walked in to the sorry sight of still-wet drop cloths and realized there were puddles on the floor. And Harris was ready to bite anyone's head off. Undeterred, Phil Haultcoeur asked if we had any medieval warfare. Harris reached under a drop cloth and pulled out Viollet-le-Duc's *Annals of a Fortress,* perhaps slightly damp. He asked if Phil had read it and told him that he should. Phil bought it, but when he came back for more the store was gone.

We were seeing a lot of Howard Friedman during this horrible time, and I was doing a lot of the clerical work for our case at his office, to save money. The movers at Burgess had no inventory, so nothing much in the way of physical losses they might suffer, but Fridman was after them, too. Several days after the big flood, he appeared in their office and provoked Gus sufficiently for Gus to take a swing at him. The villain acted as if he had been hit hard enough to fall down and hurt his back. Harris called Howard, who turned to me and said, "There's been an altercation up at the premises." In the face of phonied-up assault charges, Burgess began looking for another space and gave up any thought of joining us in our lawsuit against the landlord.

We had our day in court February 8th, seeking an injunction to stop the renovations and hoping for some kind of equitable settlement; but anyone who has served on a jury knows that the law and justice are often very far apart. Fridman's lawyer swore that there was no work going on in the building. We hadn't thought to take photos showing the mess, the interiors, the dumpsters, or the flood; we had not anticipated such a blatant lie. The judge chose to believe the landlord's lawyer; Howard thought the judge might have been "touched." It was a real blow to him and he was shaken. The stress, the inadequacy of the legal process, and our very vulnerable position were frazzling all three of us. I said to Howard, "If I ever want a divorce I'll just kill Harris rather than go through a court." One night Harris and I were just too stressed to be together: I went to a movie alone and Harris went up to our local Italian restaurant, Piro's, and helped Peter, already a friend, prepare the veal.

Harris as Modern Major General.

Around that time, Herb ran into Fridman in the locker room at the Y. If we were distraught, Fridman was quite unhappy. Harassment was his modus operandi; he was not used to anyone fighting back, and his legal bills were mounting. Herb arranged a meeting between Fridman and me, figuring that at least that would not come to fisticuffs, and chose a meeting place on my turf to give me an advantage. Summerhouse, one of the first nice restaurants in our neighborhood, was a ladies' lunch place, with lots of watercress and avocados, and strawberry butter for the biscuits. Not Charlie Fridman's scene. It was horrible sitting at the same table with that thug; he acted as if he weren't ruining our business life and, as in *The Godfather*, it wasn't personal. Nevertheless, he made me an offer—meager, but surely more than he had ever paid out. It certainly did not compensate us for the cheap rental contract. I took back to Herb the pita bread with bean sprouts I was too tense and enraged to eat, which he dove into while listening fiercely, raising his head to utter the immortal words: "Dis is broads' food." I took back the landlord's offer to Harris and Howard. Howard, a righteous warrior, wanted to continue the fight; he shook his head saying, "I just want to go into court and hear the judge say 'Mr. Fridman you are a bad man.'" Years later, one did. It was Howard who called to tell us that Fridman was going to prison.

In the midst of this grim time we were invited to a Valentine's Day costume party. The theme was "great lovers of history." We needed a party, but didn't have much time to think about costumes. At the last minute, Harris called Jeffrey Kleinbardt, who then had in stock some British Army uniforms, the real thing. Harris walked into the uniform of a Modern Major General, 1902 edition, as if it had been made for him: the close-fitting, sexy pants with the red stripe up the sides, the gorgeous scarlet tunic with all the trimmings, topped by a fore-and-aft hat. I drew on his mustache. It hardly mattered what I wore in the face of such magnificence, but I threw together something vaguely Victorian, cameos and my great-great-grandmother's paisley shawl, and put my hair up. "There's something about a man in a uniform," goes the old saw, but until you have been confronted with the physical presence, the embodied tradition endowed by the fabric, the gold braid, the tailoring, the plumage, and the medals, the impact cannot be imagined. Getting a cab in the snow was another story.

Harris was living his fantasy that evening, which everyone knew and loved. It was funny and charming, but the splendid reality of the uniform was truly impressive. It took him several weeks to return it, and in the interim he delighted in greeting our dinner guests in full regalia.

CHAPTER SIX

"I always wanted a brownstone."

1978

The new store. Back: Richard, Joe, Margaretta. Front: Tom, Mel, Harris.

We took Fridman's offer because a lawsuit can easily rule your life and inflicts a lot of wear and tear.

And we took it because we had developed a bright alternative. One day the previous fall, the Hungarian super of our building, Mr. Agh, had come to tell me, "I bding leddy to see house." His accent was thicker when he delivered questionable news. I went on red alert, "Is this house being sold?" He was noncommittal—a few Magyar grunts—but eventually we learned, when the store was not yet under threat, that the brownstone house we lived in was going on the market. Before long, we faced the possibility of having all our worldly goods, including tons of books, out on the street.

Harris said, "I always wanted a brownstone." I just goggled at him. But he was right: we had to consider buying that house or something like it; two larger rents would have been hard to handle. Fortunately for us, real estate prices were very depressed because of the city's near-bankruptcy, and that made it possible.

So running parallel to our store crisis with the wicked landlord were negotiations with our good landlord, Leroy Rubin, to buy the house we lived in.

Three years earlier, when we were soon to be married, I had started looking for a rental apartment between my freelance jobs. I was getting into practice reading the classifieds, getting scared, as always, at the prospect of paying too much and getting something only so-so. I saw a few places. One evening I read the stale *New York Times* Harris had brought home and spotted: *93rd St, 5th/ Mad, brnstn duplex, 2 BR, wbf, $575.* That was little more than our two rents combined. "For that rent, it's got to be a slum," I said. Harris, very intense: "Do me a favor, get up there and look at it."

I tried, but the apartment was not yet ready to show, I was told. I cased the block on my way back from "collecting"—signing for unemployment—on West 96th Street. It had to be the "remuddled," battleship-gray number 31—surely not the brownstone with the big beautiful window at 29, which I remembered from my explorations of the neighborhood years before.

But it was 29. I finally got an appointment with the landlord's young agent, who met me at the handsome, decorative, iron outer gate of the vestibule. Inside it was a strange and distasteful, even creepy, scene. In the vestibule, the glass panels of the inner wooden front door had been given a red coating, with a speakeasy-type flap in it, and the grotty light fixture in the hall had a red bulb. In the hall the floors had been painted black, the walls chocolate brown, and the woodwork, later found to be mahogany, many layers of white. The rooms were all locked off from each other with heavy-duty locks, and huge nails were here and there in the walls. In what was to be our living room, a disgusting double bed mattress was on the floor, and cheap, stick-on, marbleized mirror squares covered the fireplace wall. The rather handsome cast-stone mantelpiece was adorned with six or eight half-empty cans of beer; in the fireplace, the *wbf*, was a hot dog grill. That room and the dining room were highlighted by plastic, Japanese, "Tiffany" chandeliers. The tiny kitchen was red and black, with roach-ridden pegboard, and frozen milk and other revolting items were in the fridge. Upstairs the bedrooms were a medley of red and black and cheap, dark brown paneling. The agent had interrupted the evicted tenant in one last tryst on the brown shag rug. In the back bedroom was the frame of a waterbed that had been attached by a garden hose to the shower; the hose was there, but no showerhead. Knee-deep litter included many old Playboy magazines, shoes, and the occasional tennis racket. In the other bathroom, someone clearly on a psychedelic trip had painted large blue and orange flowers on the walls.

But I thought, "This could be wonderful," and couldn't wait to get to a phone to call Harris. I flew down the steps and then scrabbled at the front door to get out—there was no doorknob! I called upstairs and the tenant lazed down to let me out, saying, with a leer, "No one can get out unless we let them." I shot out into the street and found a phone, and Harris was available to come. Back to find the super, Mr. Agh: when could I return with Harris? Not until the evening, he said. But there are no lights, he won't be able to see it. With a rusty chuckle, Mr. Agh said, "Bding a flashlight." I bought the biggest one I could find. Maybe it was just as well Harris couldn't see it too clearly; with a leap of faith, he said, almost to himself, "This feels like a home." Harris had sent me to talk to real estate agents, saying, unrealistically, "Tell them we'd like a brownstone, with a working fireplace, and it would be nice if there were some built-in bookshelves." And there it was.

The house, we learned much later, had been notorious, or at least the top duplex, our apartment. Girls, stolen goods, drugs, the latter available in numbers sufficient, we were told, to have been raided by the feds for narcotics.

The landlord had done a lot for us; they had junkmen who regularly cleared out such scenes for them, although there was plenty more for us to dispose of when they had finished, such as the pegboard and the cheesy maritime painting hanging in the bathroom. When we put them out on the street, they were gone by our next trash run. The landlord's painter, Salvator, didn't speak English and would answer the phone in my absence, "I no spik Eenglish I only paint." Using a six-inch-wide brush, he slathered white paint on everything in his path, so I scurried to pull out nails ahead of him and routinely touched up the messy drips after he left for the day; several coats were needed on those brown and red and black walls. We had the floors scraped and refinished; the parquet that was uncovered was a revelation.

We had been quite content with the apartment and had made some modest improvements, never imagining we would be there for long.

By this time we knew that New York City was perfect for our business, generating energy through the sheer concentration of antiquarian book dealers, fairs, and auctions, to say nothing of writers, publishers, and other book people. Additionally, many travelers, especially businessmen, came to the city and managed to get uptown to see us, sometimes en route to or from LaGuardia Airport. With space at a premium in Manhattan, readers were frequently thinning out their books, providing another source for us. People changed their interests, or died. A continuing supply.

Our neighborhood, where we had lived for four years, had been known almost since it was developed in the 1890s as Carnegie Hill, for Andrew Carnegie's mansion at 91st Street and Fifth Avenue. A landmark for us: Helene Hanff had lived nearby on 95th Street while she was buying books from Marks & Co. in London, a relationship chronicled in *84, Charing Cross Road*. The movie was later shot on these streets at the suggestion of an actress neighbor who appeared in the film. It had long been a nice, residential, family neighborhood, with a few eccentric millionaires, some artists, and a *soi-disant* Russian prince thrown in. Around the corner on Madison Avenue, the stores were a typical New York mix, with the occasional fleeting diversions such as a Haitian art gallery, an African boutique, a gypsy fortune teller. Harris had consulted the gypsy in the uncertain summer of 1975, after a palm-reading friend at Fire Island told him big changes were coming; the gypsy had agreed.

All the practical conveniences were interspersed, including no fewer than seven laundries and dry cleaners, two butchers and several hairdressers. Otherwise: Tony's TV and radio repair, Joe the Greek's excellent pizzeria, the enduring and comprehensive Feldman's Housewares; a Jewish deli (whose kosher proprietor refused to make Harris a cream cheese and salami sandwich); a bar posing as an Italian restaurant (beaded curtain and plastic flowers) where the *New York Times* truck drivers stopped for a beer around 11 p.m. on their way to the Bronx and north. At 92nd, Flessas, a florist in a large corner store with big windows was an ornament of the neighborhood. Farther on, at Epstein's newspaper and stationery store, Mr. Epstein stocked Russian newspapers for the Orthodox priests at Park Avenue and 93rd and the school kids got their supplies.

Across the avenue: a stylish but faded pharmacy standing vacant; a smelly fish restaurant; Patrick Murphy's Market, where there really was a Patrick Murphy complete with brogue, in shirt and tie and long white apron in the old style; a French laundry, with gruff Mabel taking in the work and Lottie doing the delicate ironing in the window; and the small and shabby Hotel Wales with a seedy coffee shop, and some artists' studios upstairs; Nick the cobbler; a custom tailor; Gristede's market where there were few visible customers (most of the orders being phoned in from Park Avenue). The block past 92nd Street included a bicycle shop, a notions shop, a plumber with a bathtub in the show window, and a one-story Citibank branch.

Across Madison, one of the first wave of Korean groceries—a real food revolution—had replaced the liquor store in one of the two buildings that had not been sold to a developer. He had leveled the mid-block houses and emptied a large, rather handsome Beaux-Arts building on the corner before being stalled by the economy.

At 94th Street, the imposing crenellated façade of the nineteenth-century Squadron A Armory rose, a nice military touch. Harris remembered seeing polo games there with his grandfather, who had belonged to Squadron A, a historic National Guard unit. On the other side, there was a grubby French deli and tiny Piro's Restaurant, where we had often consoled ourselves that difficult winter, dragging in at a late hour and saying to Peter Miletic the chef, "Just feed us."

On Sundays we heard the bells from the Russian Church at Park Avenue, and seasonally, the bell of the itinerant knife-sharpener, who walked the streets with his grinding wheel on his back. On sunny days with open windows, we could hear a canary singing in the big building across the street, and sometimes a soprano practicing. Occasionally and always late at night, the girls at the home for unwed mothers down at 6 East 93rd would be bored and set off the fire alarm for a full turnout of Engine Company 22.

When we started to think about buying the house, before the store harassment began, we learned that the side-street zoning was commercial within a hundred feet of Madison Avenue, and Harris, often so prescient, said, "Someday we can put the store in downstairs." "Not anytime soon," I retorted; I was apprehensive that Harris would be able to go back to work after dinner, and the store would really take over our lives. The store was there six months later. The first store had been convenient for us, but this was as good as it gets. Friends joked that we should put a fire pole in the dumbwaiter shaft so Harris wouldn't have to leave the house.

It was an anxious time, but we reached an agreement with Mr. Rubin and counted the days until the April closing, which depended on the unpredictable downstairs tenant, an Armenian shrink, who had promised to leave by the end of March. Harris was struggling to get a mortgage, difficult in our neighborhood then. We were in a business half-life, and moving out of the old store. We had had a storeroom in the basement at 170 East 92nd where we had consigned the periodicals, and when Harris went down with the Burgess guys to empty it, he emerged with my favorite French knife in his teeth, like a retriever. He had taken my best knife to open cartons when we moved in, and I hadn't let him hear the end of it.

We were lamely dealing out of Herb's basement, and a little from home. The shelving and most of the inventory had been moved by the Burgess guys to a storeroom that Richard Strich had found for us on the Lower East Side. The posters were at home, cluttering the living room, and I bought more from Neil Reynolds and sold some to Don Knox, the author.

A few intrepid customers tracked us down in Herb's basement. Mr. Tanaka talked big, and reserved stacks of Americana books for shipment to Japan, but he took with him the precious 1794 Charles Stedman, *History of the Origin, Progress, and Termination of the American War,* the classic contemporary British account. He had asked for a volume discount, and since we were doing little business we agreed. He paid for the discounted Stedman and was not heard from again. Jan Van Weerden, from the Netherlands, amassed a well-chosen pile of World War II books, including all the *Marine Corps Monographs* we had; dense, heavy books, we expected to ship them. To my amazement, he whipped out tiny, folding, nylon shopping bags and prepared to haul them off. He confided that he was going on to a military specialist he knew of in Boston. I told him that we were Ray's successors, so he came back the next day and bought more, instead of going to Boston. And later he sent me one of the magical shopping bags.

We started work on a new catalogue, our third; the logistics were crazy, inventory all over town, Bill editing the cards in Herb's basement and hoping the books were really there somewhere. We were using a new catalogue printer, who was a customer, and the catalogue would also announce our new premises; and it would have a red cover, as did all that followed.

One cold winter night on the way home from Herb's, I noticed a light in the erstwhile pharmacy at the corner of 93rd and Madison, which had been vacant for months. Around Christmas, someone had been selling trees out of it, but we wondered what would be next. Something special seemed to be happening. I knocked on the door and the bearded model-maker opened it: "Oh, it's you!" I exclaimed. "Oh, it's you!" said Ray Sherman, co-founder of the Corner Bookstore, which opened that spring and was to become a beloved neighborhood fixture. Before long, we met his partner and wife, Lenny Golay. The neighborhood was on the brink of gentrification, when most of the laundries would turn into restaurants, Piro's moved into the Jewish deli space, and mine were not the only geraniums on the block.

29 East 93rd Street was an 1890 brownstone house, four floors and a basement. Originally a single-family house, around 1960 it had been divided into two duplexes by a sturdy wall in the stair hall. When we bought the house, we continued to live in the top two floors, and the plan was to rent out the first (parlor) floor soon, but as quickly as possible to convert the ground floor (originally the kitchen and small dining room) into the store, with the basement for duplicate-book shelving and various storage. Naturally, we hired Joe Garabrant, and he did the work with amazing speed—sometimes almost too fast.

In March, the tenant in the downstairs duplex left to buy his own house nearby, and Joe began cleaning out the junk in the basement that memorably included the original clawfoot bathtub, a wine closet, a mummified cat, and the wooden works of the defunct dumb waiter. In no time, he had taken out the inside steps from the ground floor to the first floor, closing it off to make the business separate from the house, and was ready for demolition of a wall in the ground floor. Harris called Mr. Rubin and said Joe wanted to take down a wall; our landlord said, "Mr. Colt, that would be premature." But we came home that night to plaster dust.

Joe really didn't like our house however; it was too old and crooked, not "on the money." He had to be watched so that he wouldn't get rid of old detail, but he did later come up with a great security system for the big parlor window, his only aesthetic accomplishment for us.

We were buying books, naturally, and in the spring we picked up a lot from a dealer on Long Island who was moving to Virginia. A case of World War II K rations was thrown in. We stowed it all in the as-yet-untenanted parlor floor, out of Joe's way. Soon after, there was a break-in through the then-unsecured window in the parlor; imagine how disappointed the thief was to find little but books, and the upper floors locked off. The K rations did not appeal to the thief, nor did the books. He climbed out onto the front steps with his only find, my college Olivetti typewriter, into the arms of an undercover cop.

We closed on the house in late April and Joe could go on unhindered (not that he had been). The store-to-be was down three steps from the street, in a little courtyard, with two windows on the front; the entrance was underneath the front stoop that went up to the house, through an iron gate and then left through a wooden door we painted a blazing, military red. To the right there was a newer black door, with rickety steps under the stoop leading to the basement. The space had the original, Victorian, golden-oak woodwork, some painted white, but the plaster side walls had been stripped down to the brick, which glowed warmly and lent the impression of an old-fashioned store, little diminished by the necessary steel shelving and fluorescent lighting. We took down a wall and threw the space together, aside from a center core that incorporated bathroom and packing table. The bathtub area was walled off and the packing table and water-cooled air conditioner suspended over it. The old oak pantry cabinets were utilized for storage and for reserved and quoted books. The glass-doored, oak kitchen cabinet became the rare-book cabinet, lined with green felt from the notions store; and the kitchen closet, with new shelves, held the ever-growing dead files. The brass speaking tubes were our intercom from home to store. We had to part with the cast-iron stove and the built-in oak icebox. Joe painted the plaster walls white, and we chose cork-linoleum flooring.

I had another idiotic conversation with Con Ed to open the house account; they wanted an enormous deposit; I said, "I don't want to." Richard told me to appeal or threaten to appeal to the Public Service Commission. I did, and we got a happier resolution.

In the Bowery (then the lighting market), we found an antique ceiling fixture for the front room of the store that looked as if it had always lived there, and Richard installed it after he put in new wiring for the lights and air conditioner. On his way uptown, Richard invariably stopped at Papaya King for papaya juice and a couple of hot dogs; once, on his way downtown, he stopped by 170 East 92nd and put glue in the locks, his gesture to Charlie Fridman, the wicked landlord.

We spent a lot of time figuring out the shelving arrangement with a graph-paper floor plan and colored paper shelf pieces, and managed to maximize the space— we were never able to improve on our original design. We left some room on the front walls for posters and prints above the chest-high shelves, and hung folding panel wings over the basement trap door for more poster display. The rest was solid books, although a more spacious arrangement, wider aisles, and more linear feet of shelves than the first store. We traded up for a larger size oak teacher's desk from Richard (leaving the petite one behind at Herb's); this one was painted battleship gray, and Harris stripped and refinished it in the midst of the cacophony of other work going on around him. We eventually created more work space with old golden-oak dining tables and office chairs.

We always had a comfortable wives-and-girlfriends chair, and Richard brought in some little toy trucks for visiting children. I took one down for a little boy who came in with his father, and it was not returned to the shelf. He was a nice little boy and I couldn't imagine he had taken it. Later I found it neatly parked on a low Vietnam shelf where his father had been browsing. We made a cushioned window seat over a non-functioning radiator in the back, but otherwise seating was in short supply— there simply wasn't room for it.

There was a back door leading to a space like the bottom of an airshaft, with walls of varying heights on four sides. After I found that my reject plants would live out there, we created a little garden with deep planters of brick recycled from the ancient furnace. Gardening was all trial and error because it was so dark, a money pit that nevertheless gave us great pleasure. It was a seating annex for the store, in season, and the scene of many after-hours gatherings and parties, and occasionally a business meeting, or a firing.

We called back Circle Signs and the painter produced a handsome twenty-by-thirty inch hand-painted sign with our already-beloved logo, and a small one for the railing by the sidewalk. He was to paint two later versions, one necessitated by the theft of the signs. At that time almost anything was being stolen in our neighborhood: outside lighting fixtures, whole window boxes, daisies and geraniums from the pots, even the garbage can. Bushes were routinely chained to an adjacent strong point. But the signs? The next ones were screwed in through the wall and welded to the railing.

The flooring was put down and Burgess retrieved our shelving from the Lower East Side. After it was reassembled Harris ceremoniously shelved the first book, about Malta in World War II, Ian Cameron's *Red Duster and White Ensign*, in the presence of Howard, who had seen us through our legal marathon. Burgess brought the books in from Herb's basement and from the downtown storeroom we never saw. We worked furiously to get the books on the shelves, and some posters on the walls.

Amidst the pleasurable excitement and hard work of moving, I took a call from a woman at the New York branch of an Argentine bank. Our card files had been unpacked, but the books were mostly in boxes. I was able to tell her that we had a copy of *Coup d'État: a Practical Handbook,* by Edward Luttwak, which John Le Carré had called "a gastronomic guide to political poison." She needed it as fast as humanly possible, but I then had to tell her we did not know exactly when we could send it because we were moving the bookstore. Most people would fall back and be reasonable, but she was most demanding. She could not wait! We could not provide. In mid-June the book surfaced, I called, and she sent a messenger with a check.

In July 1978 there was a coup d'état in Bolivia, but no one seems to have tried it in on the Junta in Argentina. Or maybe the book didn't get there in time.

CHAPTER SEVEN

"I am keeping it in a plastic bag until I hear from you."

1978 – 1979

Harris taking catalogue orders.

After a much-needed vacation we were ready for business in July. The new catalogue was in the mail and old customers were finding us. Even the "poor soul" tracked us down. Ads and referrals were bringing in new customers. Before long, on Saturday mornings when Harris flew down the front stoop at ten-thirty, it was normal to have six to ten regulars waiting on the sidewalk, some from furthest Brooklyn or Staten Island, or even New Jersey.

We were part of Mike Wolfson's Saturday routine; he combined jogging with booking, and arrived with a dampish check folded up in his shorts pocket. Frank Crocker came frequently, and now I had a line of sight from my desk to "Frank's shelf," with a good view of Frank genteelly and humorously grousing about the price of a scarce book, and Harris smiling his little smile, knowing he had the fish on the hook, that Frank had to have that book. It was Frank's "club," as it was for Mike and many of our regulars, especially the Saturday guys, who would offer opinions on chosen books and intelligent discourse on the subject to others browsing in the same aisle. Phil Haultcoeur, who eventually found us again, said it was "*Cheers* without the booze." We were Frank's secret place, but eventually we met his wife Jean and she found that we didn't talk war all the time, and we all became good friends.

It became part of our Saturday mornings to have Philip Kamil come in, peruse the British section, grab a cup of our questionable coffee which brewed too long in the pot under the rare-book cabinet, and then sit down across the desk from me for a visit and to observe the action. Like the Military Bookman, Philip had undergone a transformation, sporting a very becoming beard and looking very Brooks Brothers. Philip was a connoisseur and we always enjoyed showing him any new treasure. He would scan it appreciatively and say, "Nice, but not for me."

When the catalogue "hit," it was always an exciting time. The first big reservation from the Summer 1978 issue was phoned in by George Harris, late on a beautiful summer Saturday afternoon. We didn't know George, and it was fun to have a new customer who started off with a bang. The check didn't come and didn't come— we were loath to disassemble the large order, but figured George had had a couple of gin and tonics after a strenuous day and had forgotten about it. A few weeks later he called again: where were the books? George was a medal dealer and turned out to be a good customer. The first check never did turn up.

Nick was our mail carrier on 93rd Street for a long time. He was a big handsome Polish guy, with bright blue eyes. It was the era of Polish jokes and Nick loved them. He would roll in and say, "Where's my little friend?" Harris was usually ready for him with a new joke, either Polish or post office. We had Polish neighbors who had "improved" their front door, and the law required separate mailboxes or slots for each tenant. So four handsome, brass mail slots were installed in the door—but it was Nick who told us, with relish, that all the mail fell on the floor together.

Nick took good care of us, but there were periods when the mail delivery was seriously unpredictable, often very late or even lost. It really confounded us. We took telephone orders from the catalogue, put books on reserve, and then took them off because checks hadn't come. Naturally the customers were exasperated. One in Kathmandu, who received his mail in Washington wrote: *I was disappointed to hear in your letter . . . that the post office was unable to find the State Department.*

An early visitor in the new store was a bulky Italianate gent. He was not interested in books, but asked what we intended to do about our commercial garbage. Harris, hoping to avoid a mafia garbage contract, was wide-eyed and disingenuous, "We're a bookstore, we don't have any garbage." This stunning piece of illogic defeated the dim "soldier," and he just went away.

In June, in the hiatus between stores, we had gone to New England to the first of a number of Harris's school reunions. We decided to do some book shopping around the edges of the weekend in New Hampshire. Someone

Philip Kamil: "Nice, but not for me."

suggested the Book Farm in Henniker, and it was a bonanza. It was the bailiwick of a professor at the nearby college and a wonderful setting, the New England book barn of your dreams, clean and well-lighted and full of cheap, good books. We were buying so much and so fast we didn't even consult or show each other what we had found. We got to Henniker Friday afternoon and put in a couple of hours, returning on Sunday after the reunion festivities, with two friends and book-lovers, Keene and Nancy Taylor, in tow. Nancy was tall, blonde, smart and warm; Keene was shorter, blonde, always interesting and engaged, and extremely well-read. He was always looking for history and especially Churchill. I had not met the Taylors before that weekend, but there was an immediate connection, especially as they were thinking about going into business together in Washington. That alone gave us a lot to say to each other: the hazards of working with your spouse. Keene and Harris had been friends since tenth grade, with interruptions, and Keene was perhaps the only person in whom Harris had confided his bookstore fantasy. After the reunion, we went to Boston for books, to Brattle, Goodspeed and Morrill, and a new large shop, Avenue Victor Hugo.

We had asked the professor not to ship until we had reopened, and so weeks later, about eight cartons came in from the Book Farm. Harris was checking in the New Hampshire books from the dead files in the back closet, and came forward looking especially intense, cradling a small paper booklet in his open hands. "Did you buy this?" almost accusatory. Yes, I said. "Did you know what you were buying?" Well, I think so. It was a slight, rare Lafayette Escadrille piece for which I had paid $1.25, before dealer's discount. Harris soon sold it to a happy Nate Kaufman for $125.00.

We had incorporated when we moved that summer: Howard Friedman and Melvin Kushel insisted. By that time our partnership had begun to define itself. We both were buying and selling, but I took the initiative in a lot of non-book areas while Harris was concentrating on the books and tending and "policing" the inventory, and on selling them, and organizing catalogue subjects. I was happy to leave Melvin Kushel and the accounting and taxes to him. I developed the advertising, the design and look of our catalogues and the store, the customer records, files, policies, eventually correspondence forms, and did the always-large job of catalogue editing and proofreading. I was the one who usually recognized the need for new help, or systems or equipment.

Incorporation required officers, and I wanted to be Chairman of the Board—it sounded like long lunches and not so much work. Howard and Harris wouldn't let me. I became the President, so that the business would be fifty-one percent woman- or minority-owned, which conferred an inscrutable advantage I do not recall. My being President was a bit tongue-in-cheek, but Harris seemed to think it appropriate. We then had a lively conversation about who should be Secretary, Harris telling me that that title had the most power because only the Secretary could use the corporate seal. Wielding the corporate seal did not tempt me; I rejoined that I had spent my working life avoiding being a secretary and was not about to start. So Harris became Vice President and Secretary and I was also the Treasurer. The seal was not often deployed.

Harris was analyzing the inventory, as always, and we had both quickly realized that we had no market for the scholarly periodicals that came with Ray's inventory. Ray's primary business was with libraries; we intended to focus on people: collectors and readers. Unbeknownst to me, one summer Monday Harris, in his day-off leftover army fatigues, was paring down the inventory and taking stacks of the unsalable periodicals down the street to a handy dumpster near Fifth Avenue. I was outside puttering around in the courtyard when an irate doorman hotfooted up the street to protest, "Your super is putting stuff in our dumpster!" I was truly nonplussed. I looked at him blankly, "We don't have a super."

We had wondered a little about how the neighbors on 93rd Street might feel about a shop on the block. When we were setting up, several ducked in to say hello and wish us luck, one bearing a celebratory bottle of wine. Another was Ken Mathews, a neighborhood landlord, who later traded a little legal help for UPS shipping. We encountered our neighbor to the west, the "Russian prince," Felix, who asked in lofty tones, "Is it all going to be private?" In a later exchange, he had observed my new little garden wall in the backyard, which abutted the extension of his house, and said, "If it leaks, I'll sue you." This was Felix's idea of humor, but having recently emerged from a lawsuit, my blood ran cold.

The new store worked perfectly. There was more space for books and customers, wider aisles; and we gradually added work space for staff. Richard Strich found us a discarded hospital cart, a two-decker, that we didn't even know we needed. It turned out to be invaluable for the active card files; painted red, it belied its former function, and it rolled handily along, taking the files to the shelves when we were working on a catalogue. Richard also brought us an old brass shop bell, hung to ring when the front door opened. A contrasting new accoutrement was an electric pencil sharpener from Bill Waters, acutely aware in his editorial capacity of our need for it. Peter Miletic entertained himself by going to local thrift shops and flea markets, and gave Harris what was later identified as a Japanese naval sword. Harris kept it in the store, for occasions that warranted saber rattling.

Not only did Harris have a new red "hot-line" phone, but another new toy that was a boon to customer service: what was then called a "walk-around phone." This was cutting-edge technology although it was subject to interference from the steel shelving despite the long antenna, but it enabled Harris to take the distant customer to the subject and to read him his favorite shelf.

We needed a new part-timer, Bill having gone on to a career in theater management; he was still available on weekends and helped out with at least one more catalogue. Tom, at loose ends, was happy to come in for a few days a week to file, shelve, pack orders and do post office runs, and generally play court jester. Tom certainly knew the books and some of the customers, but he was about hopeless with anything like physical work, and that was what we needed most.

Tom told us he had been given extra credits by wherever he went back to school, for "life experience." That was something he did not have, living with his mother and working part-time for a gentle bookstore. He got them with the green-card girl he married, who dumped him as soon as she could.

An old friend, Mary Ellen, "Mel," had come back to New York after her second divorce. Mel and I had worked together at Princeton University, and even then she talked about B. H. Liddell Hart. Mel didn't need to work, but she really needed something to do. She started coming in part-time in the new store that fall, eventually four days a week, and more in our absences. She was attractive, clever, vivacious, popular with customers, and fun to have around. She and I, who shared an art history background, worked on the posters together.

In September, we had an opening party for customers and friends, with wonderful music provided by Bill Waters, whose area of World War II expertise was dance music. He had researched it, collected it and taped masses of it for just such an occasion. And there was a door prize—the K rations—the winner drawn by number by our seven-year-old nephew, Ran Barton. Melvin Kushel won, and you could tell he had rarely won anything. Melvin had just missed World War II, arriving in Europe in the immediate aftermath; K rations were about the worst thing he endured. Melvin was so pleased to win, and thoroughly disgusted when he saw the prize; he left it behind. We later sold it, the second drawing having failed to produce a taker.

Although the business was coming back strongly, after the six-month hiatus our finances were in parlous condition: we were being offered a lot of books, and there was the unwelcome surprise of needing a new furnace. We needed some kind of tenant in the parlor floor soon. It was Richard who suggested a psychiatrist, as they seemed to be thick on the ground in our neighborhood. This was a great idea: no machines, not much traffic, and quiet as long as it wasn't a scream therapist.

We advertised the whole floor, envisioning the fancy white parlor as the waiting room and the handsome paneled room in the back as a Freud-in-Vienna office. Various people called or came in response to the *New York Times* listing in July, but said it was too much space; shrinks don't need much of a waiting room. So we had Joe reconfigure the hallway for two offices, with a little waiting room under the stairs—then were told that the bathroom in between, or at least its doors, was in the wrong place.

Then the *Times* went on strike, for almost three months, a landlord's disaster. Our only ad was a sign in the parlor window. We were a little desperate; both Harris and the store were bouncing checks at one point.

Then Sheila Keegan came. She had phoned when the space was first listed, but the office was too expensive and too big, especially for someone just opening a practice. When Sheila walked by in the fall, the sign on the window advertised two offices, the hall having been altered, and that made it possible for her. Wondering with some apprehension what the Military Bookman might be, she was relieved when she saw two women working there. She was hooked by the paneled room, saw the possibilities. She was the only one with the wit to see that the bathroom door could be moved to the waiting room, and the nerve to rent the whole space and sublet the front room to someone else.

Sheila opened her psychotherapy practice in December, the same day our Winter catalogue "hit," and we drank champagne with her and some friends and all went on to Piro's. Eventually Sheila celebrated her new practice with a party; we had a less interesting party of our own, so arrived in the shank of the evening. One of the die-hards still there was the vaguely familiar Brendan Gunning, tweedy, funny, quick, his face a map of Ireland.

Sheila, cute and savvy, was almost immediately a good friend and a consultant of sorts. We joked that we could have cross-referrals: we certainly had customers who Needed Help, and she could prescribe that her over-aggressive types take it out in reading.

Sheila was an active participant in the store's life, hanging out during breaks in her schedule and watching the action, and making lively and funny observations. She had pungent remarks about some of the customers "whose disposable income went for books instead of a dentist," certainly not for their clothes. We often had a "sanity check" conversation with her about bumpy times in staff relationships. It was she who, before long, said we were running a "sheltered workshop."

We usually asked callers "Are you local?" and if so, encouraged them to come in and see how much we had. How many said, "No, I'm in Brooklyn (or Queens)." It always amused me; it was local in terms of our geographic reach, our customer net was cast wide. It was always fun to see first-timers in the store. They were overwhelmed by the sheer amount of the subject on offer. Sometimes they went through everything, taking a lot of time, and then started to leave empty-handed. When we asked if they needed help finding anything, they often said, with a dazed look, that they just had to go away and think about it.

There's a person for every book. Soon after we opened, I began to keep lists of funny and improbable titles that were bizarre to my uninformed eye. Ray's inventory included—the cure for insomnia—*Lead Acid Storage Batteries.* I thought we would go out of business before that book sold. But within two years, the day came: someone plucked it from a Submarine shelf, saying seriously and indeed passionately, "I have to have this book."

UNAUTHORIZED, UNOFFICIAL, AND PERSONAL BIBLIOGRAPHY   -   List No. 1

Polish Ministry of Information - The Black Book of Poland.

Richards and Banigan - HOW TO ABANDON SHIP

Murray - WINGS OVER POLAND

Louise Spencer - GUERILLA WIFE

Merrill - A COLLEGE MAN IN KHAKI

Theilhaber - JUDISCHE FLIEGER DER WELTKRIEGE

Charrington - WHERE CAVALRY STANDS TODAY - 1927

JOURNAL OF THE SOUTH AFRICAN MUZZLE LOADERS ASSOCIATION, 1960

Wesley Stout - TANKS ARE MIGHTY FINE THINGS

MacDonald - UNDERCOVER GIRL

Tennant - IN THE CLOUDS ABOVE BAGHDAD

PICTORIAL HISTORY OF THE MACHINE GUN

unknown - WITH THE VICTORIOUS BULGARIANS

Baldwin -   WITH BRASS AND GAS

Van Winkle - AVIATION GASOLINE MANUFACTURE - McGraw Hill

Livingston - Hot Air in Cold Blood

Hale - By Motor to the Firing Line

Woods - COLOSSAL BLUNDERS OF THE WAR

Prinzing - EPIDEMICS RESULTING FROM WARS

Great Britain, H.M.S.O. - HANDBOOK OF THE TURKISH ARMY - approx 150 p., only 34 printed

Houghton - THEY FLEW THROUGH SAND

Benbow - BOER PRISONER OF WAR IN BERMUDA

unknown - MERCENARIES MANUAL

Hall - THE BALLOON BUSTER

Ralph - WAR'S BRIGHTER SIDE

Watson - A POLISH EXILE WITH NAPOLEON

Rosebery - PEACE OR PESTILENCE: BIOLOGICAL WARFARE AND HOW TO AVOID IT

Herring - TRIFLING WITH WAR

Anon - THE CANNONEERS HAVE HAIRY EARS - A DIARY OF THE FRONT LINES

Williams - AMERICAN CATHOLICS IN THE WAR

Brasted - SOLDIER OF GOD

Irwin and Johnson - WHAT YOU SHOULD KNOW ABOUT SPIES AND SABOTEURS

Whittaker - WE THOUGHT WE HEARD THE ANGELS SING

Metcalfe - WITH CROSS AND SHOVEL

Miller - YOU CAN'T DO BUSINESS WITH HITLER

Semoff - T HE PRICE OF BLOOD

Waters - THE CROSSES OF SACRIFICE (THE STORY OF THE EMPIRE'S MILLION WAR DEAD)

Shuster - THE STRANGLING OF PERSIA

Gorgas - SANITATION IN PANAMA

My lists were compiled of books that had passed through our hands. Issued irregularly to a very few, they particularly delighted Oscar Schreyer and Deborah Harkins. I occasionally shared them with favorite customers, who would laugh through a dozen or so entries but arrive at a title that intrigued them and, suddenly serious, say, "Do you have this now?"

A customer momentum was building, and gradually I was finding new places to advertise. Nevertheless, the majority seemed to find us by word of mouth: a friend, another store, a library.

There were other, improbable connections. Some time after we moved to 93rd Street, we decided the store floor could profit from some professional care. Mopping was not good enough. We called numerous listings in the Yellow Pages, and Michael Rihn was the only one willing to undertake such a small job. Maybe it was the lure of the Civil War books. Mike, a Brooklyn boy, was a Reb at heart, already enamored of the Lost Cause, and he began to accumulate a fine collection of Confederate memoirs, trading floor-polishing for books. He was first on our list when an unusual book in his interest came in. Mike read in his truck, between his maintenance appointments, then stowing his precious book under the seat in a plastic bag. Mike was very compact, dark, and sturdy, with a beaming smile and a very loud voice—I always figured the latter was because he had to talk over the noise of the waxing machine. His Saturday morning visits, before opening time, were always fun, yelling about books over the sound of the buffer.

John Catherwood said he had heard us described on a local radio program, a source we could never identify. A tall, attractive, prematurely balding banker with a sharp, sardonic sense of humor, John was already a seasoned collector, and quickly showed himself to be a serious reader, particularly interested in the massive scale of the Western Front in World War I. He studied all theatres of that war, and would discourse at length on the "millions of men [who] collected and just went at each other," the commanders not understanding and slow to learn, having had experience only in small-scale colonial wars of short duration.

John often came up from Citibank at lunchtime, and would return to his office with his purchases in our distinctive shopping bag, to be remarked on by his colleagues. He later confessed he had desk drawers full of the bags, as he didn't want to go home to his wife, Margot, with them. He was gradually infiltrating the books into the house. On one bank assignment, only one of his colleagues knew where he went on those two-hour lunches; the others suspected a torrid afternoon assignation.

Alvin Wiener, a short, squarish, bleached-blond gynecologist from furthest Brooklyn, wore cologne so strong we could tell from the back of the store when he came in the front door. Alvin was a likable guy, a winningly enthusiastic

Napoleonic collector, fun to deal with. He loved the beautiful, nineteenth-century French illustrated books, as Harris did, and confessed he kept his favorites under his bed. (It's hard to imagine reading those big books in bed; maybe he didn't have enough tall shelves.)

Another voracious uniform book collector, Conrad Biegel, lived in northern New Jersey and, due to post office vagaries, that was one of the last places to receive the catalogue. He never ceased to complain about this, but even when the first-class-mail option became available, he groused about paying for it. Biegel spent a lot of money on good books, but he was so negative it seemed joyless.

A student working nearby as a doorman was allowed to read on the job and we supplied him. Another guy, whom I think of as a doorman, was an actor. Douglas Kahn, as he was known to us, was known to his answering service by his stage name, Irving Metzman. Occasionally we saw him on screen—as a doorman, in *Arthur*—and nudged each other, "There's Irving Metzman."

Our doctor came in for a look, and, surprising all of us including himself, bought a couple of posters. One was a very unusual Spanish-American War, thirty-six inch long lithograph, "A Yard of Heroes," depicting Admiral Dewey and his Manila Bay officers, and the other, a striking and rare Australian World War I poster. Its text read: "Don't Just Stand There. Go and Help." The doctor told us ruefully that it was a message for his wife's numerous family who never lifted a finger during their long visits.

Our former landlord, Leroy Rubin, called to inquire about his World War II unit history, and before long we had it for him. He enjoyed seeing the store when he came to pick it up, and confided to Harris that his real estate group had made a mistake selling the brownstones on the block.

Sent probably by Sky Books in one of their many referrals, Lionel Leventhal was a British publisher of military books, founder of the very successful Arms & Armour Press. Lionel was in New York once or twice a year:

I first heard about The Military Bookman in the late 70's. . . Those were the 'glory years' of Arms & Armour Press and the sort of book that I was publishing was enjoying considerable success.

So I visited, and found a haven of peace, of quality books, of knowledge, and good people. The shop had a wonderful, comprehensive stock—the best I knew of in Britain or America—backed up by an immensely valuable card index with details of the various editions of the books and seemingly every military book ever published. The card index was Harris's pride and joy, his secret weapon.

My visits to The Military Bookman became an important part of being in New York, although I was only able to visit briefly. But I used to end one meeting with a major publisher, catch a taxi uptown, have a very friendly time at the Military Bookman for about an hour, and hasten downtown again.

It was very important to keep in touch with the market, and to know what real people were reading, and I used to discuss books with Margaretta and Harris. . . . I drew inspiration for books to reprint or subjects to publish upon from the store but also from their distinctive, red covered catalogue with their logo on the front, which was always eagerly read. I have to this day a run of them on the shelves behind my desk.

Vigorous, smart, imaginative, Lionel was endlessly creative in his business, and a major networker; we could count on him to give us news and gossip of the trade in England, and from the first he encouraged us to go book-buying in Britain.

Every now and then one of Harris's former Wall Street colleagues would drop in. There was a reasonably priced American World War I War Bonds poster in a simple, bright design, a large blue "V INVEST" on a bright red field, and we sold copy after copy to our Wall Streeters for their offices. Mike Wolfson, a Wall Street lawyer, bought one too. One of Harris's old associates persisted in asking him to write reports, but Harris, ever single-minded, had happily turned the page.

A customer from Queens was known not only for his Marine Corps collecting, but for his style. It was the era of close-fitting, printed polyester shirts with long collars and deep V-necks, open well down to expose a number of gold chains, and an unfading tan. The guy thought he was a hot ticket, and his gray curls encircling a bald pate and flowing into full sideburns found their counterpart in copious gray chest hair in which nestled the chains. He was pleasant enough to deal with, aside from his ego. Mel christened him "Gold Chains" and he was known among us as such to the point that I can barely recall his name. He bought everything and anything on the U.S. Marine Corps, including posters. We had supplied him with most of the books by the time Mel left, and he followed her as a poster customer, although he still came in from time to time. Years later, Mel called Harris and alerted him that Gold Chains was bouncing checks, "under indictment and on the lam."

There were very many Marine Corps collectors, the majority of whom ended their letters with "Semper Fi." We tracked one Marine Corps officer for over twenty years, through various postings and into retirement.

Harris had for years collected histories of embattled Malta in World War II: British airmen's accounts, but those of naval convoys as well. The store enabled him to upgrade the condition of some titles, and he put into inventory his old copy of a scarce British account he had found in Malta many years before, Hugh Lloyd's *Briefed to Attack.* The book was wormed, and we so described it to Richard Garczynski, in Wisconsin, who shared this Malta interest and badly wanted that title. He wrote about the wormholes, and was told that they were minor, didn't intrude on the text. After, evidently, some inner debate, he ordered it, but wrote to Harris on receipt about his bookworm concerns: "I am keeping it in a plastic bag until I hear from you." Harris assured him that, in the twenty-five years he had owned the book, no bookworms had shown themselves, so he assumed they were long gone. *I will take you on your word and open the bag,* wrote Richard.

Ira Karp was indeed sort of fishy, with a pasty complexion, rotund form, staring eyes and a mouth that tended to pucker like a goldfish. He was an idiot savant, and a "close talker," and for a while we were on his rounds when he came in from Brooklyn. Ira collected the Army Green Books, the Official Histories series, but there was no evidence he read them, and indeed he did not seem to be interested in other literature. Instead, he unfortunately talked—close—to other customers who were trying to browse. Sometimes I felt compelled to divert him so the accosted customer could have some peace. Maybe that is why he called me Mrs. Colt, whereas he called Harris, Harris.

David Ballantine, a droll fellow, regularly came in from Bearsville, like a little elf out of the Catskill woods, armed with a brown-bag lunch. He browsed the shelves and talked books and book business with Harris for a few hours. Sometimes his brother Ian joined him. Ian was the creator of the vastly popular Ballantine Books World War II series, small paperbacks on battles and leaders, weapons et al. David was trolling for likely World War II memoirs for Ian to reprint in paperback. He always sent us a funny, newsy thank-you postcard after his visits, often continuing the conversation. Responding to a book offer, a discursive comment on an old postcard of a cow: *Georing [sic] wanted an Iron cross 1st class for Max Schmelling who didn't make the jump because he had the runs. Defiantly Heydte had the award reduced to Iron Cross 2nd class, and this was the high point of the invasion for him. Thank you for thinking of me.*

Roger Bell, in England, signed on for the "Society for Study of the ETO," surely a tongue-in-cheek name to justify his ever-growing collection on the European Theatre of Operations in World War II. He bought selectively but had a fairly rarified wants list. Roger's correspondence was in a class by itself: a series of home-made greeting cards with military themes. Every book offer Roger received from us was the occasion for a celebratory thank-you card, usually concocted of a doctored World War II photo, or his own drawings. He was a great cartoonist, in a Bill Mauldin mode, and his pictures were a treat. One printed Christmas card was embellished with falling snow and a Kilroy face, with holly on helmet, peering over the usual sentiments. A choice example came in after I wrote, sternly I guess, about his recent failure to respond to quotes: a firing squad.

Keith Melton, the owner of "McDonald's of Ogden," was a collector of espionage posters, and sent in orders from Utah written on a coupon for a free Big Mac,

Clai Marshall.

shaped like a burger. A real collectible. Someone remarked that I should collect the stationery we received from customers: anything from their wives' flowery notepaper, Dellwood Dairy note pads, a note sheet with pig cartoon titled Hogwash, a cartoonish Napoleon captioned "I'm in complete control..." There were letterheads such as Banzai Motor Works; NSP Veterans Group, an incarcerated veterans group in the Nebraska State Penitentiary; Ministers to Rodeo; Aggressive Christianity Missions Training Corps; Free Love Ministries; Moliballistics; Foundation for Mind Research (they wanted Hitler's speeches); and City Liquidators. A return address in Japan: "Flying Leather Gifu Head Quarter – Wanted/Original W.W.2 Jackets with the USAAF insignia." Several made their own: Collector of German Military Insignia, and the Carl von Clausewitz Memorial Institute for Strategic Studies (with an Executive Secretary and a membership of one).

A history teacher in Arizona, Glen Frakes, signed up and began, amazingly, to buy many Western Frontier titles for and through his school library. He seemed to do better at getting funds for books than a number of well-known institutions on our list, and when he became the Librarian, said he would do even more. He ran up over $3000 in purchases for the school in the years he was a customer.

A Bermudian, Coralie Frith Powell, was reading about nineteenth-century British wars relating to her family's history. For some reason, the mail between New York and Bermuda, both letters and packages, was notoriously slow and rough. Mrs. Powell was very patient and understood the realities. The progression of her requests was interesting and we had had a fruitful exchange for several years. That winter, she decided to treat herself to a fine classic, a six-volume set of W. F. P. Napier's *History of the War in the Peninsula*, in tan calf with gilt spines, and was in great anticipation of their arrival. Then, bad news: the books were received in shocking condition, several volumes disbound from being shaken around in transit. It was obvious to her and to us that they had not been properly packed, and the damning part was the post office clerk's note on the package, per Tom's say-so, "Rattle OK." This was the end of Tom's brief career as a shipping clerk.

At just this time, Harris's local godson Clai Marshall, who lived nearby on Fifth Avenue, wanted an after-school job to earn money for various teenage accoutrements, such as a skateboard. Perfect. Clai was a skinny kid, with longish curly hair that wreathed his head like a light brown aureole; he didn't seem to have much stamina, which we ascribed to his following his languid girlfriend's vegetarian diet. But he was intelligent, wry, conscientious, and very observant, very aware of the customers and what was going on around him. When I took a call from someone whose package had not yet arrived, there he was, unasked, at my elbow with the post office shipping log.

I had my wrapping nook where I would stand and watch the piles of books build, separated with typed labels that were to be applied to the final package. Each book got a little TLC. If they were cotton fronts they got a wipe down with Vaseline and a cotton ball to bring out the color and get off the grime. Bent ends got Elmer's glue and India ink to the edges, and if it was leather, Harris took out the magic elixir (sheep's lanolin) and we would work that into the surface to "feed"? the book. Each book was wrapped in a page or two of the New York Times and I might stop to read the occasional article. The book then got corrugated cardboard that had to be fitted perfectly including protecting the edges . . . The last part of the process was the Kraft paper off a big roller, then I applied the paper tape that came out of an old [dispenser] that had to be filled with water.

Clai was there through the hot summer before we signed up for UPS, and Harris, arms upflung, would send him off to the post office with a "Banzai" straight out of *Tora Tora Tora*. Clai always came back from hauling a full shopping cart with his curls completely wilted, and exhausted. I revived him and everyone else with tomato sandwiches from upstairs, five or six slippery sandwiches going downstairs on one plate.

One day I came back from an errand and found an unknown guy sweeping up out front, and once again heard that *Cat Ballou* music. Harris had bought Charlie's sob story: just out of Riker's Island jail and needing bus fare to go to Baltimore. Charlie showed up from time to time over the next few weeks until he found the chance to snag the ever-victimized Mel's wallet from her invitingly open handbag. Melodrama—mug shots—no resolution. Clai later spotted Charlie near the subway at 96th Street and ran back to tell us, to no avail.

Another time, a couple who were clearly not book lovers prowled around the store. Harris signaled to Mel to at least close her handbag, sitting by her feet—one of them was stooping low ostensibly to browse the shelf next to her—but she was

Harris, Luther, and protesting UPS man.

oblivious. Harris took up position with Peter's sword. They got the message and beat a retreat.

By September, Clai had had enough of shipping, or had decided to concentrate on schoolwork, and we finally had enough shipping to enlist UPS. UPS was another, better world, a man in brown came and took the packages away. Carl, our first driver, made it look easy, with a particular flick of the wrist as he maneuvered the hand truck; so easy that a supervisor followed him around from time to time to see if he was working hard enough. Guys named Max and Joe and Billy and others succeeded him, all pleasant, good-natured and fun to deal with. Even when confronted with huge stacks of parcels during heavy catalogue ordering, they were cheerful, after mugging their horror and dismay for the camera when face to face with our record pickups.

UPS was not infallible. Complaints ranged from *The dog ate the package left on the porch* to non-delivery of a precious, signed World War I memoir of the 4th Fighter Group, *Mr. Tetley's Tenants*, which had been entrusted by UPS to a neighbor who then lied saying he did not have it.

The packing table was briefly manned by Harris's son who was living with us at the time, but then we had a series of after-school kids, recruited by Clai, with Clai occasionally reappearing when he had cash flow problems. One summer, Mel volunteered the son of a French friend, a handsome and charming young man who lent a cosmopolitan flavor. He was going on from the packing table to his grandmother's for a family holiday, and when asked where she would put all those people, and he said, winningly, "It is, how you say, *un château*."

Sent by Clai, Jesse Mentken, then in tenth grade at Clai's school, certainly did some packing, but was quite good at the never-ending filing, both book and customer cards. He mentally collected the odd mailing list names he was filing; Rick O'Shea, Nicholas Nicholas, Mr. Broaddus and Wiley Sword were his favorites. Jesse was a dear, funny, quaint kid, he reminded me of Charlie Brown: the way he walked and the odd questions going through his head, which he verbalized on his arrival. Jesse was with us for several years, both after school and as a summer job, and had his own idiosyncratic take on the store, which he wrote up for a school essay. In due course he brought in his younger brother, Oliver, who was with us through his high school years. Oliver was wry, smart, observant, and very reliable.

Nevertheless, I mused to Sheila that it would be a relief to have shipping clerks not at the mercy of exam schedules and other teenage priorities, which often seemed to fall at catalogue time. Sheila's friend and ex-colleague Brendan Gunning was between careers, and she hesitantly suggested him. Brendan came for a summer and we all had such a good time that he came again, two years later, for a five-month stint. Brendan was funny, playful and naturally gregarious, and I think we all assumed we would be friends because of Sheila, but soon we knew each other very well. Brendan did the packing but also cataloguing, sometimes in the peaceful backyard with a stack of books, and put in time shelving duplicates in the basement.

An old friend, Sandra, and her husband Peter Francis were in from London, and phoned to say, without much notice as usual, that they were coming to see us. I turned to Brendan, sitting there with a card file on his lap, to brief him on these people dropping in out of the blue, and his eyes grew large: "I think I know this woman." It slowly dawned on me that Brendan and I had met years before; I had gone with my then-roommate Ute to one of Sandra's many parties when they each lived in New York, and had met Brendan in her West Side garden.

After Brendan departed for a new job, we had become used to having another part-time, semi-adult, "old child" as Harris had called him, around, someone who could give us more consistent time and attention than the kids, although we continued to have work for Jesse and Oliver and their successors. We were casting about and putting the word out to our network.

A friend of Bill's suggested Michael O'Rourke. Bill, who knew him well, had serious reservations, saying that he was about the smartest and funniest person he knew, but . . .

Michael was militantly gay, militantly leftist, and came to us in an election year, in the fall of 1980. He began his tenure at the packing table where he held forth on innumerable subjects while working. If you wanted to know which generals and field marshals and warrior kings were gay, Michael was your man.

And he was happy to spell out the reasons gay employees were superior: they could live on a small salary because of no family obligations and didn't lose time for children's schedules and illnesses. They were trustworthy, frugal, loyal and true, he maintained, and quoted some study to prove it.

Michael was extremely intelligent, well informed, verbally agile, with a sense of humor like no other. Harris listened tolerantly to his politics for a while, but as the

Reagan election drew closer and Michael more voluble, was heard to tell Michael, dryly, that the packing table was not a platform for his political beliefs.

The business always required more staffing. I was ever on the alert for part-timers, and an old friend from my days at Time-Life, Jean Stratton, was building a freelance career, and helped us out putting together one catalogue. That involved a lot of time on one's feet, at the shelves. Maybe it was too much for Jean, as ever in her spike heels; she genteelly fainted back in the Nineteenth Century section and was fortunately caught by Bob Puk, former Marine. We sent her home in a taxi, and she was back the next day to resume.

Mel continued part-time, resolutely making her own hours: no Saturdays, when we were almost always busy with local customers. She wanted her weekends in Southampton. There were always many mail inquiries and Mel dealt with a lot of the correspondence. Then and now, there was a convention referred to as an SASE—stamped and self-addressed envelope—sent with a customer query, as a courtesy and to put on the pressure for a reply. When it seemed better to send a catalogue, I couldn't bring myself to throw away postage and just pitched them in a desk drawer. But Mel wanted them and took batches home to the penthouse, and steamed the stamps off.

Michael was brilliant and capable but wildly erratic in his habits, and the only person who ever got away with reading the *Times* at his desk. Nevertheless he had quickly grasped how we did things, and we all enjoyed him and got along with him, so we took him on full-time after about eight months. The four of us had a good time together, and without our quite knowing how it happened, the "class trip" became an institution. There seemed to be a number of good war movies in those few years: *Breaker Morant, Gallipoli, Das Boot, Officers and Gentlemen,* and others. The restored version of Abel Gance's epic, *Napoleon,* was shown for only a few days at Radio City Music Hall, and it was a natural for us. We would go off to a movie after the store closed, and have a burger afterward, for troop morale. Mel reciprocated one year with a Christmas party in the penthouse and an Easter brunch with an egg hunt amidst the lilies on her terrace. The climax of this particular period was the Broadway production of *84, Charing Cross Road,* which was our class trip Christmas treat for 1982.

Michael was nothing if not entertaining. He had traveled widely and was frequently wined and dined at the latest new restaurants, which he would critique for us. His stock of arcane information was vast, and his Jesuit schooling shaped his dialogue. He had an art history background and, strangely enough, had worked for the same odd woman who had been Mel's and my boss at Princeton University.

Michael was knowledgeable and helpful, good with store customers and on the phone; many of our regulars enjoyed his irreverent ways and were drawn to discuss various topics with him. Michael quipped that every soldier who had survived the Burma-Siam Railroad and every Jew who survived the Holocaust had written a memoir. He gossiped pleasantly if a bit maliciously, deliciously about some customers, for instance constructing little riffs about "Connie and Bea" after Conrad Biegel had come into the store with his equally dour wife, Beatrice.

At that time, we piled up incoming books, with the catalogue cards in them, in great stacks on the floor, awaiting a quiet interlude for a pricing session among the four of us, which Harris intended to help the junior members know and learn to evaluate the books. The lure of books on the floor was irresistible for many customers; I would say, to no avail, as they went through the piles, "Those aren't for sale yet, there are plenty on the shelves." Michael held a certain fascination for a local psychiatrist, who probably wanted to study him. The shrink had the unfortunate habit of heading for the piles of incoming, not-yet-priced books and pawing through them despite our objections. Once Michael saw him coming, scampered to a shelf, any shelf, and pulled a common book and put it on the pile; the shrink bought it!

When it was Michael's turn to pull the cards for a catalogue, he would smoothly wheel the red file cart to the shelves, intoning, in the manner of a French waiter, "chocolate mousse, crème caramel." It always made me laugh.

On Tuesday mornings, the phone was always busy because "they" had been cut off from the source for two days. And by this time, our regular customers had learned that they should call to reserve the books they wanted in a new catalogue because of the competition, although there were always some who were amazed that anyone else in the world might want the book that they coveted.

Taking catalogue reservations was frantic. The phone didn't stop because at that time we had only one line. There was one "master copy" of the catalogue, usually in Harris's hands. He was by far the best order-taker, often suggesting and selling additional books by pointing out related titles the client might not have noticed, or describing some that had come in since the catalogue was assembled. The customer's requests by author and page number would be found, the book would be known to be available, or else marked R for reserved, or X if sold. Once off the phone, the order-taker would write up a reservation sheet and hand it off to someone who would drop down to the basement to pull duplicates first.

There were so many phone reservations that it behooved us to know exactly what was in the basement. Since calls came in thick and fast, we couldn't always be saying to the customer, "We might have another copy," and then running downstairs to check. So a new routine was added to the mix: counting duplicates for the catalogue, as soon as we received the advance copies. Now we had the extra help to go through this elaborate ritual: two people in the somewhat grubby and cave-like and, in season, cold depths, one to read the shelves and the other to annotate the master copy of the catalogue. It had to be done fast, before the calls started.

It did pay off, and on one occasion with laughs. A scarce and wanted book then was by Fairfax Downey, *The Indian-Fighting Army*. We had two copies of the first edition (the reprint was even more scarce). As soon as the catalogue hit, one Western Frontier customer called, practically breathless, to reserve it. Within the hour, the second copy was spoken for. Then, apparently, the second buyer called his friend and collecting rival, our first caller, to crow about his coup. The first buyer called us, in consternation and ready to be angry or upset and I, amused, was able to assure him we did, in fact, have two copies.

CHAPTER EIGHT

"I saw this great machine gun book the other day and thought of you."

1978 – 1980

Joel Block, faithful scout.

We started to explore new book-buying possibilities. For fun and curiosity, we went with Richard Strich to an antiques show on Long Island, and found a few books. I bought some World War I "car cards," small, oblong posters used in trolleys. We always had a market for the U.S. Food Administration posters, handsome images exhorting those at home to save food and eat right for the war effort. We sold many of them as "kitchen pictures." One of the car cards was "Save a loaf a week, help win the war." Richard promptly bought it from me, before I realized I wanted it myself. When I told him, he sold it back. The image of a mellow, crusty loaf of bread hung on our refrigerator.

Richard took Harris off to the big gun show in Columbus, Ohio, because there were always books for sale too. I stayed at home with Richard's big black dog, Kate; she was as full of personality as Richard, and good company. Harris returned shaking his head at the large range of lethal merchandise and the bizarre people buying and selling, but otherwise with little to show for the long road trip.

Richard knew my penchant for funny titles and happened on one he brought to me: *Who's Who in Baton Twirling.* It still makes me laugh. I had the book propped up on my desk to amuse passersby, and one woman sat down across the desk from me while her husband browsed. She became transfixed by the book, finally asking me if she could look up someone in it.

It so happened that we bought several large aviation lots around the same time. William Guthman, a noteworthy Connecticut dealer in military and historical Americana—weapons, accoutrements, uniforms, documents, some folk art pieces, fascinating stuff—was known to us by reputation when he called Harris about John Cuneo's collection. Bill was acting for Cuneo's widow, in Westport, Connecticut. Cuneo had written two excellent books on the early German air force, and a very good one on Col. Robert Rogers and his Rangers, of French and Indian War fame. Harris went up to Westport to see the books; Cuneo's collection was a wealth of material, fine early aviation. We often saw Bill in his booth at the Winter Antiques Show, and would hear from him occasionally, usually about Von Steuben's army manual. Bill either needed a copy or had one to offer, and copies of the classic how-to for the Revolution went back and forth. There were many times, in fact, when I wondered that books ever reached the readers, there was so much horse-trading among dealers.

On a less-exalted level, I took Michael in a rented van to buy a very large aviation collection in Yonkers. That was a mixed bag, many good books but a great many cheap pictorials. The woman in Yonkers asked me what to do with her other books, and I suggested giving them to charity, being so obliging as to provide her with an instant appraisal for a tax deduction; she turned around and tried to sell them with that document.

There was hardly a book in the Yonkers lot that did not contain relevant and interesting odds-and-ends, ephemera. "There's plenty here for your collection, Margaretta," Michael said. Surrounded by collectors, I was not immune to the virus. I found myself gathering the extraordinary variety of curious items culled from the books that passed through our hands, discovered as we checked them in. Up until then, my things-found-in-books collection fit into a cigar box—I had to take over a desk drawer. The staff had become aware of this proclivity and were on the alert for new oddities.

In my collection, the sentimental favorite was a receipt from Helene Hanff's bookshop Marks & Co., 84 Charing Cross Road. One early American military book yielded a letter dated September 12, 1842 from a young officer at an American Artillery barracks, with a contemporary, hand-colored drawing, very stylized, of a mounted cavalry officer; I framed it. To me, the most amusing was a mimeographed order from Gen. Alexander Patch. In late 1944, his 14th Armored Division was engaged in fierce fighting as they approached the German border. Patch was fulminating about their unmilitary language, which sounds straight out of a movie script.

Both the Cuneo collection and the Yonkers lot included civil aviation. Non-military was not of use to us, but just around this time we heard from Bartlett Gould, a retired schoolteacher in Massachusetts who dealt in civil aviation books. After an initial conversation setting ground rules, we started sending all the civil aviation books and inquiries that came our way to Bart. He reciprocated with

copy   HEADQUARTERS
                              SEVENTH ARMY
                              APO ### 46   Séverne, France
                                                            10 Dec 44

FROM: Commanding General, Seventh Army
TO: Commanding General, 14th Armored Division
SUBJECT: Radio Communications

1. It is hereby directed that you will take immediate steps to rectify radio
communication procedures within your command.

2. For your information, the following list of radio procedure violations was
monitored in the period 0001 to 2400 8 Dec 44 by Seventh Army Radio Monitoring
Service:

            3d Infantry Division   116 violations
            36th Infantry Division   146 violations
            45th Infantry Division   178 violations
            14th Armored Division   768 violations

3. This headquarters realizes the number of radios in an armored division
to be far more than the number in an infantry division, but such a number of
violations in a single day is not to be tolerated.

4. For your information, appended is a transcript of a recorded radio communication
in your command, timed 0824, 8 Dec 44, apparently between a tank company commander
and a tank commander:

            Foodray 18, where the fuck are you.
            Foodray 6, passed line B 20 minutes ago.
            Foodray 18, that's a good answer to another question, where ar
                            you now.
            Foodray 6, 200 yards east of 645.
            Foodray 18, how's the weather up there
            6, pretty cold
            18, that's too bad why don't you move up where it's warmer.
            6, being held up by small arms fire and an anti-tank gun.
            18, where is anti-tank gun.
            6, that's the trouble, we can't see it.
            For Christ sake, that's why you get $175 a month. Get up and
                find it.
            Yes, sir, captain, sir. My mother told me I should go to
                college so I could get to be an officer.
            Never mind the bullshit.
            Roger.
            Roger, out.

5. The only words in this entire communication that bear any relationship to
correct radio procedure are the words "Roger" and "Roger out."

6. You will report to this headquarters no later than 2400 12 Dec 44 what steps
you have taken to correct this situation.

                    (signed)   Alexander M. Patch

                               Lieut. Gen. U.S.A.
                               Commanding

the military aviation, which he did not want. At first Mel mindlessly sent Bart
some unexamined items that were shabby or defective, but we got that ironed out
and some very congenial trading and back-and-forth took place for about five
years. The Yonkers lot particularly resulted in shipments of dozens of boxes, in
installments—possibly a little overwhelming for him. But we urged him to take

his time, and he regaled us with stories of his own book scouting through New England. We never met but felt as if we knew him; the ongoing correspondence was literate and delightful.

Lenard Stutz, an early customer, was a gentle, scholarly man who became a friend as well. He gave Harris a charming French children's book on Napoleon, and was buying at auction before many private people were. When we visited him, we saw in his bookshelves his auction purchases with the auction lot number bookmarks still in them. This little quirk came back to us poignantly when he died very young, and we bought his military books. More than one customer confided to Harris over the years that his wife had been instructed to sell his books to us when he died.

Well-known Marine Corps writer, Col. Robert Heinl, author of several of the Marine Corps Monographs among other works, did not offer us his library, but we learned that he had extras of his Korean War title, *Victory at High Tide.* We ordered six signed copies from him, one of which was inscribed to the Military Bookman. That was only months before he had a heart attack and died, on a flight near Haiti. Heinl had been head of the U.S. Naval Mission there during Duvalier's dictatorship, and he and his wife had written a book about Haiti; one way or another he had made some enemies. After his death, Mrs. Heinl stated her belief that Papa Doc's wife had put a voodoo curse on the Colonel, with strange and bad emanations that struck him when he was in the vicinity.

Carmen Perrotti's long-term plan was to retire from cold Massachusetts to Florida, and he was starting to pare down his library. He offered us his World War II cruise books, naval unit histories of individual ships, so we finally met him when we picked up the books, and drove a full station wagon to New York. Carmen recommended some of his favorite bookstores along our way, and in one we were introduced to the Japanese woodcut prints of their turn-of-the-twentieth-century wars, which we bought and sold for a while. Cruise books were never as much in demand as Army units, but the Naval Academy, which rarely had any money for books, placed a big order when we listed Carmen's lot, so we did well with it.

A major collection that came on the market was that of Charles Bremner Hogg Jackson. An omnivorous collector of militaria (uniforms, swords, helmets, decorations etc.) and related books, Jackson had left his enormous holding to the Smithsonian, with the understanding that they would keep what was right for them and sell the rest. Much of the militaria and the important books went to auction, and one of those books found its way, circuitously, to Harris's collection. Jeffrey Kleinbardt, for whom Jackson had been a major customer and therefore a major loss, had helped appraise the militaria and put us in line for the lesser books. Jackson had wanted everything, even relatively humble publications, and remnants of that lot were in the store basement for several years, to be mined for inventory, for my ephemera collection (the 1842 soldier), and by our military-minded nephew, Ran Barton, who visited from time to time with his parents Peggy and Randy.

Mel and I went to buy books in the East 70s, an address that turned out to be a converted carriage house. A number of these remained on the East Side, in the side streets east of Fifth Avenue. Built to serve households on Fifth Avenue, they were distinguished by the tall, arched doors still to be seen in the facades. In this case the former stable floor had been turned into a mini-museum with handsome wood-and-glass display cases for the man's model soldier collection, and the related uniform books. The soldiers were spectacular and made more of an impression than the books. I wished Harris had gone with me, but he and Brendan saw them when they went to pick up the books.

There were some sour buying experiences. A dealer in Portsmouth, New Hampshire called Harris and described a lot of military he didn't want. He represented it as being in good shape and including a bunch of unit histories. A big lot, he'd send it down in a van after we sent a check for $2000. In good faith we sent a check for what turned out to be a load of mostly junk. When Harris tried to break the deal, the dealer refused. We shipped the books back with the same trucker, and he wouldn't accept them. We were stuck. There weren't many usable items; I cannot remember how we got rid of the dross.

We soon got screwed again. Nick Romero, a young guy in California, was one of our first mail-order customers. He bought modestly for five or six years, mostly Napoleonic books, and had been particularly excited to order Lachouque's *Anatomy of Glory,* when I found a supply at Weyhe. To our surprise, Nick wrote that he wanted to sell his books, and sent his list, asking for a $500.00 down payment. Given our relationship and knowledge of what he had bought from us, we sent the check; the books never came. I wrote repeatedly; he had moved from his address. This fraud was particularly offensive coming from an established customer, so I made inquiries with the Post Office about mail fraud, but it seemed they regarded that as a crime perpetrated only by vendors, not individuals. These two episodes led to stricter policies all around. No pre-payments, for one thing.

We had become acquainted with search services. Oscar Schreyer searched for ballooning and Holocaust books and a few other things for his clients, so his delightful visits combined buying and selling. A good number of searchers were listed in the *New York Times* in the section where we advertised, and there were many more: a book lover's best hope of finding a scarce and wanted title before the internet. A search service, usually by mail, would reserve for weeks our book, which might or might not be taken by their customer. Then they would invoke a dealer's discount, adding who knows what markup and fee for the buyer. Meantime we were tying up a book that was likely to be wanted by one of our people. It added layers of complication for us and often no reward, and soon we found we could not oblige. Donan Books often visited us at the first store when we weren't so busy, but the process was just not viable for us as time went on. But turning the tables, the Book Ranger, a search service in Greenwich Village, had accumulated some military that he did not want, and called us in to buy. Richard Chalfin, in business for years as the Better Book Getter, was the searcher who really worked hard at it, covering the many New York shops on his motorcycle. We accommodated Richard because he was willing to play by our rules.

We started to combine book buying with our social travels, and our Washington friends, Keene and Nancy Taylor, were a regular destination. They often went to the local bookshops or auctions in Bethesda with us.

But how melancholy to buy from a moribund business. Our first such encounter was just across the Potomac. A dealer with a Civil War specialty in his small shop had died; we walked in, unknowing, and introduced ourselves to his wife. She said, "Well, do you want to buy a bookstore?" and burst into tears.

One of our first dealer friends, Carl Pugliese, whom we had visited regularly in Tuckahoe, called to tell us he was not well enough to continue in business and wanted to sell his military books to us. Brendan and Jesse went with Harris to pack them up. Carl was better known as a military artist and illustrator, and was very much involved with the Company of Military Historians, a well-known group devoted to American military studies. He was a quiet, unassuming, knowledgeable man and always comfortable to deal with; and he had been a memorable part of our start in the business.

We had lots of referrals from Sky Books, which carried new books on military subjects; their focus was on the hardware, that is tanks, aircraft, guns, ships and such. They tended to attract the heavy-breathers, the wannabe mercenaries (and probably some real ones), readers of *Soldier of Fortune* magazine, as well as those with more historical interests. If the strange ones made their way to the Military Bookman once, they usually didn't return; we were too tame.

There was considerable overlap in subject matter, but the emphasis was different. We did have tank and artillery titles but usually sold off gun books that came in to specialists like Joe Garabrant or Rutgers Book Center.

There were many books at Sky that we would carry on a second-hand basis, so when Sky's manager showed up in his little red sports car with bags of books of that ilk in the trunk, we bought them. With his second lot, Mel smelled a rat, got suspicious. The books were too new, and all Sky material. Harris called Sky's owner, Bill Dean, whom we barely knew, and alerted him to possibly missing inventory. Bill checked, called the police and once again we were asked to set up a culprit. We bought a few more lots from the manager; Mel played her part well. The sting worked and the manager was arrested at his apartment. Bill Dean came in to reclaim his books and reimbursed us, but that was all the thanks we got.

There were other times when we were offered stolen goods. A guy arrived with a large lot of Army Second World War official histories, the big green books. Harris suspected him, his manner, the price, or something, and waved him off. Another time, a customer and sometime-dealer came in and perused the shelves, then claimed his ex-wife and mother-in-law had stolen his antiquarian armor books when he was in the hospital and sold them to us.

Sometimes it seemed as if we were a marketplace or exchange for all kinds of odd items. Someone sorting out an estate brought in several boxes of lead ships, the scale models of various fleets and famous ships originally used in Navy war games. We called in Bob Schepps of the Soldier Shop to have a look. He opened a box and inhaled, and pronounced them rotten. Lead ages, like everything else, and these were no good.

A customer sent us photos of a pilot's chair and other accoutrements from the "ready room" of the U.S.S. *Enterprise*, the renowned aircraft carrier of World War II. He didn't expect us to buy it, though it was an amusing idea to play with. We posted the photos and description on our trusty bulletin board, but it found no takers. We suggested that he donate it to the Admiral Nimitz Museum in Texas, and he eventually did. Perfect.

Generally we did not take books on consignment, feeling that one should put one's money where one's mouth is. But once in a while there was an item that was not quite our subject; or good, but the seller wanted too much; or a long shot. Occasionally this worked, but we had one set on consignment for so long that the owner had died before we sold it. Another consignor had moved and we couldn't find him to pay him when the book sold.

On the other hand we often took pictorial items on a consignment basis; some sold and some didn't. Years before, Carl Pugliese had given us a great quantity of the huge series of the Company of Military Historians American uniform plates. These pictures were regarded as authoritative studies, but they were relatively cheap. Listing them was a chore and they were a big handling and shipping and bookkeeping nuisance, and not profitable enough to warrant the effort. They became ours when we bought Carl's books and we ended up fobbing them off on Jamie Delson, who, after all, was all about soldier figures. We had some splendid but rather gaudily framed Austrian uniform plates by Trentsensky hanging around for years; when we gave up on them, the consignor couldn't be bothered to pick them up and we sent them to a thrift shop.

Mrs. Mitchell Siporin, widow of an Official Artist in World War II, wrote to us about his books, and some of his war art. Some of Siporin's works were reproduced in the Fifth Army official history. We bought the books, and took the art, from the North African and Italian campaigns, on consignment. It was not without interest, but it was really the tag ends of his work, and went nowhere but back to Mrs. Siporin.

Michael Robinson, whom we had known since he was briefly one of Herbie's many partners, sold himself with his looks and tony British accent, and a good line of chatter about his book expertise. He became head of the rare books department at Brentano's, and in 1980 acquired an interesting lot from the Troy Public Library. He arrived expecting us to take two important Wellington titles off his hands; his asking price was exorbitant, but we agreed to take them on consignment. The jaw-dropper was *The Funeral Procession of Arthur, Duke of Wellington.*

R. Ackermann, a London publisher in the mid-nineteenth century, produced a number of folding panoramas of historic events and exotic sights. This one documented the Duke of Wellington's funeral in 1852. The Great Duke had been the British victor in the Napoleonic wars and then a major force in British politics until his death. A state funeral probably only exceeded in grandeur by Queen Victoria's included representatives from each regiment of the then-huge British Army, the Lord Mayor and many other officials, and the Sovereign. Artist Henry Alken depicted it, regiment by regiment, on a sixty-six foot long lithographed and beautifully hand-colored set of panels (each over a foot long), one copy of which was stretched around the wall on the ground floor gallery of Wellington's residence, Number One London. Connoisseurs of British Army uniform pictorials could ask for no more. It was absolutely spectacular, but not that uncommon.

Since it was overpriced, the panorama was with us for several years, entertaining customers and friends when we unfolded the stunning soldier panels, and then wowed them with the extra foldout of the huge catafalque carrying the casket that was cast from the guns captured at Waterloo. We listed it in catalogues, but we knew it was too expensive, and Michael wouldn't budge on the price, so we just enjoyed having it in the store. Philip Kamil knew enough to buy one elsewhere. Then we heard that Brentano's was in receivership and, although in all likelihood they would never have known that we had those two books, Harris called the lawyer in charge. The man was conditioned to harassment by creditors, very suspicious and guarded, but finally Harris got through to him that we would probably have money for him if he agreed to lower the prices.

We repriced both books appropriately, and both Wellington books sold soon after. We were sorry to part with the *Funeral*, but it was going to a good home with a favorite customer, and Brentano's needed the money.

We continued to buy posters from a few dealers who visited, at auction, and by happenstance. Considering that they were a sideline, an amazing multi-national variety passed through our hands. Some favorites became permanent decorations for the store: I had immediately bought the well-known "Books Wanted" poster by Charles B. Falls—a "full-sheet" size, thirty by forty inches—of a grinning Doughboy standing against a black background, balancing a huge stack of books. It was one of a number done for an American Library Association campaign to collect books for the troops during World War I, and we acquired several more of the series for the store. From his World War II poster collection, Michael Wray had given us, as inspiration, a well-muscled Uncle Sam, sleeves rolled up and hammering a "V" on an anvil, "Volume for Victory." Along the way, I collected a few World War II War Bond Christmas posters, jolly seasonal Santas, a shivering penguin ("Save Coal"), and a nice July 4th Uncle Sam. Later I found a quintessential illustration, the original sheet music of "Over There," combining the all-American talents of George M. Cohan and the young Norman Rockwell. After I found and framed it, we bought and sold several more. Lloyd Gayle, our binder, found and gave us a large, battered bi-plane model that was permanently parked atop the aviation shelves. It was Richard Strich who brought in a toy helmet, World War I style; somehow it became a ritual for Mel to don it the first of each month, feign a trance-like state, and predict the next month's receipts. Someone else brought in a stage prop, a Napoleonic bicorn, which usually sat above the appropriate section—better than a shelf label. Once I coerced Harris into posing for a photo wearing it, and another time he wore it to a costume party.

We were continually offered collections, and between that, our finders, dealers' lists and catalogues, and other sources, we never ran low on books, which had been an initial concern. By the mid-eighties if not before, our inventory fluctuated between eight and ten thousand titles or more, with duplicate copies of many in the basement. We turned the inventory yearly and on a day-to-day basis it was never the same makeup. Some subjects were stronger if we had just bought a certain collection, or sparse if they had just been in a catalogue. There was ebb and flow. In retrospect, it amazes me to think what we, especially Harris, had in our heads about availability, rarity, demand and all the variables. Sometimes Harris would go to the basement for duplicates, and stay down a little longer, surfacing with other titles that he thought were not on the shelves, by some processing error. He was usually right.

In our buying, we liked to find things we hadn't seen before, the more esoteric and obscure the better. There was continuing interest for us in the unpredictable variety of what came along. There were always books that we hadn't seen or known of. I loved to find titles such as *Merovingian Military Organization* or *The Ottoman*

Steam Navy. But I came to think that there were some books like *Guadalcanal Diary, The Battle is the Payoff,* or *They Were Expendable* that should be burned in the street to make them scarce. Bestsellers in their day, we never had to buy them, they just seemed to crawl in under the door. We always had more than enough.

In contrast, a dealer from out-of-town offered us one-and-a-half sets of the Third Army *After-Action Report*. It had the charisma of Patton, the monumentality of a tank, and enough information to choke any scholar of the ETO. It was published in Regensburg in 1945, we understood, in an edition limited to one hundred and eighty-two copies, and was stamped "Secret." In two volumes, thirteen-by eighteen inches, each about six inches thick, it was the ultimate source on Patton's army in 1944 – 1945, when it swept from Normandy through France to the Rhine.

During the lifetime of the Military Bookman, an improbable ten-and-a-half copies passed through our hands. One was in Ray's inventory, with a pending purchase order from a Canadian library. Subsequent sets were sold to libraries, but the majority to private customers, and fast. I don't think we ever had to list it in a catalogue. The odd volume, volume one on Operations, was sold to a young doctor and Patton fan who could not afford the full set.

We were aware of the new publications and in a few instances stocked new titles. When we opened, we met Dick Gardner, of Nashville, Tennessee, who was fervent about unit histories. Dick was in the process of quitting his "day job" to go into the business of reprinting them in limited numbers, performing a service for vets who had lost or never had their copies. At first we carried some of the most in-demand units; it was good to be able to offer the reasonably priced reprints to the vets who wanted them.

We received a mailing about a new, privately published translation of Gen. Erwin Rommel's treatise on tactics, based on his World War I experience and observations, *Attacks.* We could never find enough of this classic, usually known as *Infantry Attacks,* in any translation, so were glad to carry the new version. It appeared to be a one-book labor of love, and we sold hundreds of copies over the years without any idea of who "Athena Press" might be.

Jeffrey Simpson and I had become acquainted during our time at American Heritage Publishing Company, and it was an enduring friendship. Tall, red-haired, socially adept and urbane, Jeffrey was a writer, and author among other pictorial and social histories, of *Officers and Gentlemen,* a fine book of historical photos of West Point. We decided to carry it in the store, and it was one of the few new books we carried over the long term; West Point collectors regarded it as a must.

Eventually we started carrying Bill Guthman's book, *March to Massacre,* a study of the early years of the American army. We were buying them from Bill, so they must have been the remainders.

We always had someone waiting for Donald Morris's *The Washing of the Spears*, the book on the Zulu War; it was finally reprinted in 1986. Don would stop in whenever he was in the city and sign any copies we had. He was a journalist and teacher, and this book his main writing achievement; he loved to come to a place where the denizens knew what he had done.

Vantage Press was a vanity publisher, that is, one accepting manuscripts from writers who could not find a commercial publisher. Vantage performed the publishing functions for a fee, and printed whatever number the writer wanted, marketing it modestly by mail. The military titles, almost always memoirs, were routinely offered to us, for instance. We never bought from Vantage, but innumerable Vantage war memoirs came to us second-hand; they sold to our market, which appreciated the special stories and information.

AMS Press, a library publisher, began doing reprints of some multi-volume British military classics, and for that purpose they had bought a set of Oman's *History of the Peninsular War* from us. It occurred to Harris to see if they would undertake a reprint of the much-requested and scarce *West Point Military History and Atlas of the Napoleonic Wars,* by Esposito and Elting, which had been published in 1964, probably in a small edition. We had an impossible-to-supply backlog of requests. AMS didn't know the book or its cachet, but we convinced publisher Gabe Hornstein, and they did reprint it, in a somewhat smaller format. I believe it worked very well for them; they gave us fifty copies at the outset, and we ordered many more. Harris's catalogue tag line was, "Thank God for this reprint!" The demand didn't diminish: Lionel Leventhal, the British military publisher, got on the bandwagon and did another reprint in 1999.

Usually, when magazines were part of a lot, we left them behind. There were exceptions. The short-lived but excellent British uniform periodical, *Tradition,* was desirable complete or even in single issues. I bought a run of the *Illustrated London News* for 1939–1942 ten blocks away on Madison Avenue, and it sold quickly. We took a bound run of *Fortune Magazine* for the war years and sold it immediately—but it had to be shipped to Peter Mayer, a regular customer especially for "science and industry" subjects, in Austria. The only shipping that was reasonable was "sack mail," uninsured by definition. We sent it off with our fingers crossed. On a visit to Brattle Book Shop in Boston, I found that they had stacks of *Life* Magazine and sold individual issues. We regularly ordered the two issues with Patton covers for his devotees.

And for fun, we sold the fabulous Military Bookman T-shirt. The store logo lent itself to enlargement, and as soon as I had a chance, I searched out a place to order a small number of T-shirts—the rare first edition in white—mostly for the kids we knew, and ourselves and some friends. A few years into the new store, I discovered a source that would accept orders for as few as three dozen T-shirts. We ordered them in "catalogue red" with the logo and the name. At first I ordered S, M, L, which seemed to fill the bill. But after we supplied the kids, including Jesse and Oliver, there were few takers for S, and eventually we went on to carry XL and even XXL for our bulked-up armchair generals.

The T-shirt traveled, and our loyalists delighted in flaunting theirs in exotic places. A friend wore his trekking in Nepal, and the photo record appeared in our tenth anniversary catalogue. The shirt stayed in Nepal with the Sherpa. There were T-shirt sightings in Malta (on the cousins), and in select London pubs. A photo on our bulletin board showed a T-shirted customer, Sarah Gilmer, in a Georgia riding ring with her horse Tilly (named for the seventeenth-century field marshal).

When we moved the store to 93rd Street, we developed a new stable of finders. A sparkly, diminutive lady in her seventies, Mrs. Irma Kochenthal, was a volunteer at the Brick Church Bookshelf and Fair, a yearly fundraiser, at 91st and Park Avenue. Mrs. K. regularly combed through the books contributed for the Fair and arrived with little lists for us; she never let us pick them up, preferring to trundle over our selections in her shopping cart. On her visits we were treated to tales of her extensive travels and New York activities. Mrs. K. also volunteered as a poll-watcher so we always saw her at the Church of the Heavenly Rest, at 90th and Fifth Avenue, where we voted. She was a delight and a breath of fresh air.

The Lichtenbergs came in to introduce themselves on a day when we were not in the store, and Michael talked to them. Dan and Anne were retirees, a genial couple who enjoyed booking together, and they were known (to us) as the "Golden Age book scouts." They covered Westchester County and farther north, and obviously enjoyed the hunt and their visits to us, arriving periodically with a station wagon loaded with boxes. After we bought, Anne and I would have a little chat while Dan ran the books we had rejected downtown to sell to the Strand Bookstore. There were only two breaks in their fifteen-year visiting cycle, when Dan had hernia surgery, a book dealer's hazard.

George Chinn showed up occasionally with an armful of books, a little pushy, not used to our being so busy. One afternoon, he brought in a copy of Capt. John Thomason's well-known Marine Corps memoir, *Fix Bayonets!*, and asked a ridiculous price. Harris said, no way; George persisted, relentlessly, telling Harris how scarce it was and how our copy was way underpriced. Harris said, "Wait a minute," dropped down to the basement and came back with three copies. He told George he could have them all for a low price. George shut up. Probably he and some other dealers were surprised and a little jealous that we had rather quickly established ourselves and were becoming well known and successful.

A dealer whom I shall call Jabba the Hutt drove in once a year from the Midwest for a decade or more, bringing lots of good material. Since he took up so much space, blocking an aisle, we mandated that he come on a Monday when the store was closed. After a while only Harris had the patience to deal with him, because the buying was so laborious: book by book, Harris would give him a price, and he would sit and debate whether he was getting enough, consulting the elaborate penciled coding he and other dealers put in every book showing when and where he had bought it and how much he had paid. He would say, "Oh, I can't let it go for that." On others he got more than he expected. He never seemed to factor in all the time this took or to figure out the totality of what he came in with and how much he left with, and realize he had made a good profit.

We never knew Murray Levine as more than as a voice on the phone, calling from Queens with indifferent book offers. Alternatively he sent verbose, over-elaborate descriptions of common books, written in a blue ballpoint scrawl. We sent him our catalogues for years so that he could learn what we were looking for—but he rarely came up with anything unusual. Obviously he loved the hunt, whether in Queens, Florida in the winter, or Schroon Lake in the summer, and was more than reasonable about what we paid him. He could be sweet, too, once apologizing to me for his rambling write-ups. He was certainly persistent, and sometimes his whiny voice set off desperate evasions and whispered "I did it last time"s as we decided who was "it" that day. Murray was a World War II vet, and he had served in the 2nd Air Commando Group in Burma, hazardous duty; we often asked him to come in to the store and tell us his story, but he never did.

How many women have been told, affectionately, "I saw this great machine gun book the other day, and thought of you." Only a good book scout would come out with a line like that.

Jim Pine, a scout even when we were at 92nd Street, by then had a shop, but still came in with books, for old times' sake and to talk to Harris about the Yankees. Dick Snyder, Jim Gray, Edwin Friedman, Hank Frank, George Hayward, et al.—Melvin Kushel suffered recording the sheer number of checks we wrote, many of them for small amounts. Eventually we had to ask our scouts to make appointments; it was just too much to deal with more than one or two a day in the midst of normal business. We waved them off entirely in peak catalogue season.

A few of them weren't worth the time and aggravation. One guy habitually brought in junk and then would argue to have us buy things that were shabby, common or otherwise useless to us. I wouldn't deal with him. Harris sometimes fobbed him off, giving him books from the basement that we were going to get rid of. He was unpleasant and never learned, and Harris it seemed was not able to tell him not to bother; maybe he nurtured the unlikely hope that the guy would come up with something worthwhile. Never happened. What a waste of time.

On the other hand, a local super recognized a good set of the classic Douglas Southall Freeman's *Lee's Lieutenants* left out in a hallway and figured out where to take it.

Another guy who could have been a super or a street person showed up one afternoon with an armful of odd volumes of some good sets. We gave him a check and then one of us dropped down to the basement to look at the same titles in the duplicate stacks. This nervy S.O.B. had sneaked down there, grabbed the books, came up and presented himself in the store and sold them. Outrageous! A quick phone call to the bank; he made a scene when the check was refused.

This little episode made us more vigilant from then on. I sat at the front with an angled view of the front door under the stoop, so I usually saw who was coming. Once, from the corner of my eye, I saw someone pass under the stoop but not come in to the store. I alerted Harris, who leapt to the iron gate under the stoop and locked it, then locked the red door, effectively creating a cage for the miscreant when he came up from the basement. The "perp" knocked a bit desperately on the door; Harris, very rough, and probably rattling the Japanese saber, "Who is it?" "I'm the Con Ed man!" Well, that never happened again; they must have put a red flag on our file and the meter readers always checked in with us before descending to the basement.

CHAPTER NINE

"She's on strike."

1981

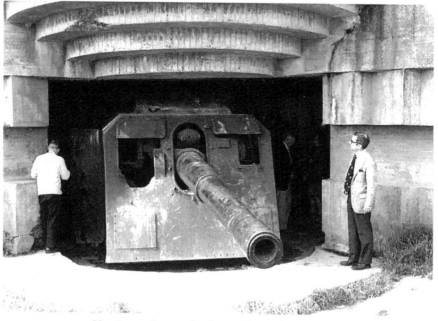

Harris at a German bunker, Utah Beach, Normandy.

In early 1981 I spotted a small ad in the *New York Times* travel section for Stephen Ambrose's tour "From D-Day to the Rhine . . . In Ike's Footsteps." It wasn't hard to persuade Harris to sign up, and we started talking about adding on time at each end of the tour. Harris wanted to see his London cousins, the Stricklands, and we were counting on seeing Amy and John and Mark Cummings, in the north. My friendship with Amy dated from our days working together and for Steve Sears at American Heritage in the sixties. She had married an English businessman.

Ambrose, a professor at Louisiana State University, was already well known—in our circles—as Eisenhower's official biographer, and the tour was well planned, including landing in Normandy at dawn on June 6th. There were to be talks by Col. John Eisenhower, Ike's son; Maj. Gen. Sir Kenneth Strong, Ike's brilliant intelligence chief; British historians Ronald Lewin and Michael Foot; French Resistance members. Forrest Pogue, a U.S. Army historian and the official biographer of Gen. George C. Marshall, would be traveling with the tour. There would be stops at the invasion beaches in Normandy, the Bayeux Tapestry and several cathedrals, Rommel's headquarters at La Roche-Guyon, and after Paris, World War I battlefields, Bastogne and the Ardennes. The last stop was Stuttgart, where Rommel's son and his naval aide Adm. Friedrich Ruge were scheduled to speak. This was perfect for us, because straight from the tour we could visit friends, Ute and Peter Grauer, who lived nearby. Ute and I had shared an apartment in New York for two years in the sixties, coming together for the most practical reasons: I couldn't pay my rent alone, and she needed somewhere to live. We were not strangers for long, we found much in common, and our friendship continued after she went back to Germany. We had traveled together, and visited back and forth.

It was in my mind to call on several book dealers in London with whom we had done business, especially Henry Lloyd, our first British correspondent; Julian Browning, who had visited us at the Military Bookman; Doug Blann of Landmark Books, who had been calling Harris to place large orders for over a year; and perhaps Peter de Lotz, the preeminent British military book specialist, whose occasional catalogues Harris devoured. It was a priority to see Lionel Leventhal, who was eager to show us his Arms & Armour Press and his antiquarian bookshop, Ken Trotman Books.

We landed in London at dawn on what looked like a lake, and arrived with the milkman and the sun at the cousins' in Ealing, where we received a warm welcome. Harris and Richard were first cousins and had spent time together in their teens; they resembled each other only from the back, the same Maltese proportions. Richard was somewhat brusque, and almost soldierly in his bearing. Jilly was pretty, warm, vivacious; their three children were eighteen-year-old Dominic, tall and handsome; red-haired Candace, eleven; and Harris's godson, freckle-faced Edward, ten. All were lively and bright and hospitable. The Stricklands took us in to their family and provided our base for a week, as we ranged around London. Harris prided himself on navigating the Underground and I was happy to let him figure it out; then, as on later visits, our destinations were in all directions. Ironically, that year we did not know of the naval specialist right by the tube station in Ealing.

We spent a somewhat tedious first day in New Malden with Doug Blann who had a large shop with mostly new books, but had been buying "exotic" American titles from us. Despite our relationship, he was very uptight, and indeed bland; dealing with him was like pulling teeth, no fun, and it all took too long.

Henry Lloyd's chatty, newsy letters about the British trade had charmed and intrigued me, and we headed off to meet him in the Inner Temple the next day. We got pretty confused but a friendly barrister took us part way, telling us some history of the Knights Templar. The entrance at 5 King's Bench Walk gave us no clue, but then we saw The Bindery in the sunny, pleasant basement. Henry's main business, there in the midst of the legal establishment, was binding law journals, but there was a small, densely packed entrance hall, full of law and military books. Henry proved to be a handsome, open-faced gentleman, who had served in the British Army in India during World War II and afterward as a hydraulic engineer, but had recently gone into both legal and military books. He had excellent material, pricey, but so much we had never seen. On a high shelf I spotted the distinctive red British Official Histories of World War I, which we almost never saw in the States. Harris was more in a "looking mode," but I started pulling them down, checking the prices and stacking them on a table. "What are you *doing?!,*" said Harris. "I want to buy these." Eventually, we were all crawling around on the floor to see the lower shelves. Afterward, we repaired to a pub where Henry stood us a round.

A quick look at the Temple Church and then by tube to Julian Browning in Holland Park. In a pretty row of wedding-cakey buildings, Julian's flat was on the top, with a little terrace. He was quite friendly, not with the reserve we had initially met in New York; we had coffee and chat, then books. I found a nice U.S. Infantry manual with a Confederate imprint. Where had it been since the Late Unpleasantness?

Next day we did more booking before we headed north. Francis Edwards, a long-established and famous antiquarian bookstore, was a must. Marylebone Street was fairly chichi and Edwards was ravishing; its handsome, carved wood facade opened to a paneled and leathered front room and then a long, skylighted gallery with a balcony and two floors of shelves. But it seemed on the wane; the inventory was not as good as I had expected, or as pricey, or as full. In the Strand, we stopped in at some stamp dealers for Harris, on our way to the famous Simpson's-in-the-Strand (where Harris had never been). There we treated ourselves to smoked salmon, vintage port et al., and felt we were really in London. Then along to the storied Charing Cross Road. It had been the center of the London old-book trade, as Fourth Avenue was in New York, and Number 84, though no longer Helene Hanff's beloved bookshop, Marks & Co., commanded our special attention. As we discovered, the trade spilled over into Cecil Court and Great Newport Street, around the corner. We had a good time poking around, and of course we found some books.

After Charing Cross Road, on to Euston Station, where we took the express train north to the Cummings's, near Preston, in Lancashire. The train ride seemed long but it was a sunny June day, and I said to Harris, "I hope you realize the fatted calf is being killed." What a welcome! Amy was a marvelous hostess, combining American with British amenities, including the knock-up-in-the-morning tea tray. Amy had blonde, short, curly hair, a beautiful smile and a full-bodied laugh, with a great sense of humor. John was short, with receding, russet hair, merry brown eyes, and a gentle sense of humor. The Cummingses had thought of everything wonderful to entertain us, including a memorable, if rainy, day touring in the Lake District. We stopped in to see twelve-year-old Mark at his school at Sedburgh, little knowing that there was a great bookshop in the town. We took a long pause for a five-star, sybaritic luncheon at Sharrow Bay, and climaxed our touring day with tea at ancient Sizergh Castle, home of other Strickland cousins.

Amy had found us a bookshop (the first of many) to tempt us. Mr. Sankey and Broadhurst Books in the resort town of Southport, on the Irish Sea, was our first real English bookstore experience, and for me remains the paradigm: a four-story house full of the books which had flowed in from generations of local families, cycling through or resting on their way to their next owners. Effervescent Amy and Mr. Sankey treated our visit like a social occasion, it was all very cordial. We were entering *84, Charing Cross Road* territory. The antiquarian books were sequestered in the office, presided over by ancient Mr. Broadhurst, whose suit was holding him up, as Amy said. We had a good time, again so many titles we saw only rarely or not at all, well-made English books, even when in the smaller format required by wartime restrictions. Book post was cheap, so they mailed off that batch.

Back in London, Harris went off to visit Peter de Lotz for an afternoon, and I opted to see an old friend. Harris returned somewhat starstruck, excited. Although our tour had begun, there were free times in our schedule, and we took an afternoon in Hampstead to see Lionel in the Arms & Armour offices with the enigmatic address. Lionel, ever-gracious and welcoming, was delighted to show us around. He had acquired the Ken Trotman name and antiquarian military bookshop after the founder's death, feeling it should continue as an entity. He led us through a warren of buildings to the Trotman office. Then to visit Peter—a mecca for the militarist. Peter de Lotz had been at it a long time; after a few years at Francis Edwards, he had gone out on his own. With his growing family, Peter lived in and did business from a large house in Hampstead, not far from Lionel's offices. Tall, dark, clever, acerbic, he knew he had the primo stuff. Most of two floors of large rooms and the hallways were shelved; the books were always very good copies. Peter covered all periods, pretty much as we did, although not much Americana, or uniforms, and no antiquarian books. Naval was in the downstairs hallway, the Holocaust in the living room, and on and on. We romped through it, but I think we spent the most time upstairs in the back room. We were not allowed to buy from the top shelves: they were duplicates and even when we asked nicely, they were off-limits.

All these finds presented a logistical problem, and I called Lionel from Henry's or from Peter's; he kindly provided the crucial information that made it and our future British buying viable: the name of a freight consolidator whom we used for many years. We asked the dealers to mail to the consolidator in Essex and when our purchases were accumulated, they were all shipped together as a lot at very reasonable cost.

The D-Day tour presented a rare opportunity to visit not only historians but participants, and in places where the history had happened. We had met our D-Day group and we found some very pleasant people, including some veterans, several of whom had family members in tow. There were a couple of Air Force vets, dashing pilot types; Stuart Butler, a charming and youthful Californian, was one of them. Well-known author Merle Miller, who had been an editor of *Yank* magazine during the war, was collecting background for his book *Ike the Soldier*, and we quickly became acquainted with him and the Pogues. We started with a walking tour through "Ike's London." That night we had dinner with the Leventhals and told them about our tour, and Lionel, ever on the *qui vive*, said, "*the* Stephen Ambrose?" We lived in a rarified world. The next night Steve seated us with reserved John Eisenhower at dinner before he spoke, thinking he would be comfortable with book people, who wouldn't ask tactless questions about his parents. John was quietly charming, and looked so much like his father, who was about the same age in 1944; I could understand why my mother had a bit of a crush on Ike. John's first, fine book, *The Bitter Woods*, was about the Battle of the Bulge, and was always wanted in the store.

When we met General Strong, Harris took the opportunity to ask him about the SHAEF (Supreme Headquarters Allied Expeditionary Force) Intelligence reports I had given him. He captured Strong's attention but the General immediately asked if they were the "Most Secret," distributed only to the high command. They were not, but still pretty special. In the course of our book-buying life we never saw even an odd issue of this series.

Of our days in England, visits to the Imperial War Museum and to Southwick House in Hampshire stand out. The latter was SHAEF headquarters in the months before D-Day, and Forrest Pogue spoke to us in the room where the difficult D-Day decision had been made.

There was a bonus in Portsmouth before we embarked for France: a stop at the magnificently maintained H.M.S. *Victory*, Admiral Lord Nelson's flagship. Only the British do things that way: the *Victory*, an eighteenth-century ship of the line, was still in commission in the British Navy, though in dry dock. On the deck there was a simple, highly polished brass plaque, "Here Nelson Fell," and below decks, another, "Here Nelson Died." Stirring.

All along the way, Steve provided knowledgeable and interesting commentary, occasionally in dialogue with Dr. Pogue, and interspersed with remarks and questions from the group.

We took a dreary night ferry—not an LST—landing in Cherbourg in the grey dawn of June 6th, and found coffee and croissants in the village of Ste.-Mère-Église. It had been the scene of a disastrous night landing by some of the 82nd Airborne, who had been dropped off target, landing in the Place and in the nearby swamps. The town had changed its yearly festival to June 6th, and the *autos timpanants* (bumper cars) were being set up in the Place while we went to visit the small Norman church. The town's ancient escutcheon had after the war been emblazoned with a parachute, as on two stained-glass windows that commemorated its deliverance and the American sacrifice. For the holiday, a dummy of a paratrooper was suspended from the steeple by his chute. Merle Miller murmured, "Life imitating art . . . or vice versa."

We were driven through the *bocage* country; the dense hedgerows that had held up the Allied advance had to be seen to be comprehended. At a railroad crossing, an ancient hero was discovered. Accompanied by his little black dog, and on crutches, he wore a beret, a three- or four-day growth of beard—and his D-Day medal. He described, in almost-unintelligible country *patois,* how he had rescued by boat and ferried out the paratroopers who had missed the drop zone and had landed in flooded fields: "No one died."

We went on to wide Utah Beach; it would have been a long run on the broad sands to find cover but fortunately the beach itself had been lightly defended and had few visible reminders of the war. There was a small "home-made" museum in a leftover pillbox; many local people were visiting the invasion beaches that weekend, and a few old jeeps and other military vehicles restored by hobbyists wound in an impromptu procession for the occasion.

In Bayeux that afternoon, we saw, all too briefly, the ancient tapestry, which recorded the successful cross-channel invasion in the other direction in 1066. We were swept on to the Mairie for a reception that was far more than anticipated. The setting was a beautiful, stately room, with brocade walls, crystal chandelier, portraits, Louis furniture. The Mayor, in riband and seal, of DeGaulle-like stature but much better looking, received us with champagne. To the surprise of all, including Steve, he presented each of the eight veterans in our group who had come through the D-Day beaches with a medal of the town, and a fine speech honoring their service. It was truly moving; everyone was thrilled to the core.

Next day, the British beaches and the museum at Arromanches and the manicured American cemetery high above Omaha Beach. Our veterans laid a wreath at the monument and we were all quite impressed by how many

French people were there paying their respects that day, and how many other commemorations there were. Our whole D-Day experience was more emotional than I would have imagined, and it continued to be. We wound our way along the pastured cliffs to the Big Red One marker (First Infantry Division) then down to the 351st Regiment marker on top of an almost impregnable German pillbox.

Steve provided a picnic on Omaha Beach at the base of the First Division memorial. We learned that Forrest Pogue's D-Day duties had been conducting after-action interviews for the Army's study of the Omaha Beach landings. Low-key and southern, he spoke most eloquently on the beach. Then Harris passed around the copy of *Omaha Beachhead* he had had the foresight to bring—not having known that Dr. Pogue had been a major contributor and would sign it for us there.

Harris was in his element, and there were great scenes as he used the maps in the book and led some of the vets to the sections of the beach where their units had landed. Daisies and buttercups bloomed in the craters and ruined landscape of Pointe du Hoc where the Rangers had gone up the fiercely defended cliffs to take the German position. Stuart Butler, a veteran of the Pacific air war, started showing us construction features of the pillboxes.

Harris loved talking to the vets, whose reactions to the tour experience varied. Some of them were expansive about their memories, perhaps for the first time, triggered by being there. Others had read about the war to a greater or lesser extent. There were those who did not want to be told about their war, by Ambrose or any other historian. We certainly had not signed up to find customers (although we did acquire a few), but it was clear that these latter vets were not interested in reading about their war either.

Steve Ambrose spoke at length some evenings and supplied plenty of information on the bus. On occasion he treated us like a college class, asking us to speculate about the viability of a 1943 invasion (dubious), and trying to fit some observations into his preconceived ideas. He may have been trying to provoke debate, but it didn't fly with the vets or the serious readers, like Harris.

We enjoyed hanging out with Stuart, the tour's organizer Peter McLean, and Moira, Steve's wife and occasionally Steve, although he was often too busy answering questions or holding forth. We had many an after-dinner drink and good talk with these people and Dr. Pogue and Merle and others of the group.

On June 8th, we set out for Paris and stopped at "Pegasus Bridge," so-named for the emblem of the British unit that had liberated it. Steve briefed us on the bus, telling us about how some of the British 6th Airborne under the command of Maj. John Howard had landed three gliders with absolute accuracy to seize the bridge over the Caen Canal and hold it for the Allied advance from the beaches. The gliders landed on a dime, and those troops were almost the first Allied soldiers in France, arriving at 12:16 a.m. on June 6th. We got out of the bus near the café on one side and crossed the bridge to the far side, the landing area. Ambrose was running on, in his professorial way, about Howard and the drop, and the two of us wandered off along the canal toward the bridge. There we were approached by a brisk but diffident British gentleman who, despite grey hair, brown tweed jacket and walking stick, had a decidedly military air; he had seen us from the café on the other side. He asked, "Anyone here from the 6th Airborne?" We introduced ourselves and he responded, "Major John Howard." I know my jaw dropped and I stared at him as if he had—again—dropped from the sky. We immediately took him over to the group and interrupted Steve.

Howard's practice every June in the days around the sixth was to hang out at Monsieur Gondrée's café on the other side of the bridge, and wait for other British vets to come along.

Howard became voluble and told us several good stories, including that of Gondrée digging up the champagne hidden from the Germans, buried in the dirt of the kitchen yard, to celebrate the Allied arrival and La Libération. And he told us about "Rommel's asparagus," bristling thickets of stakes that were being installed along the canal to thwart just such landings. By luck this had not yet happened by the bridge, but the holes had been dug and stacks of the poles lay along the bank. Around dawn on June 6th, well after the Germans at the bridge had been subdued, along came a crew of Italian workers whose job it was to erect the stakes along the banks. They were informed of their new POW status but not confined; and their reaction was . . . to continue putting in the stakes. "Stupid buggers," Howard said; he told them it was beside the point but they said, essentially, "You're here now, you may not be here tomorrow and we have a job to do."

This chance meeting was the genesis of Howard's collaboration with Ambrose on the book, *Pegasus Bridge,* and Howard became a featured speaker on later Ambrose tours.

We went on toward the Château de La Roche-Guyon and as we rolled across the rich and verdant June plains of Normandy, Steve growled, "You can see this is great tank country." The handsome old Duchesse de la Rochefoucauld lived in decaying splendor in the historic château, which had been appropriated by the Germans for Rommel's headquarters. The housekeeper told Harris that Rommel's staff had been quartered in the stables.

Harris and I took a day off from the tour in Paris to pay our first visit to Librairie Pierre Petitot, the military book specialist in France, and to find René Johnson, a militaria dealer where Harris had shopped as a teenager. Harris bought a Napoleonic saber for the collection he had started at Johnson's. Somehow we also managed to work in the Musée de l'Armée and a little shopping for me.

The tour went on to Reims, meeting Maj. Gen. Sir Kenneth Strong and Lady Strong at the school that had served as SHAEF headquarters in May 1945. We had met the Strongs in London, and the General was a most memorable figure; never handsome, in his last year, his looks had condensed to one refined down to his intelligence, to an appearance totally cerebral.

The German surrender was signed at SHAEF headquarters on May 8th, the Allies represented by Gen. Walter Bedell Smith, Ike's chief of staff, with General Strong as translator. Strong was the last survivor of that occasion, and it was his first visit since 1945. He spoke to us in the SHAEF war room, and although clearly frail and quite deaf, his recall was vivid and deeply felt. Everyone was spellbound. He spoke of Ike as "kind and friendly" and added that Bedell Smith supplied "a little iron in his soul." Eisenhower was down the hall from the surrender room, "very soldierly," but would not meet the Germans; he felt that they had needlessly prolonged the final stages of the war, at great cost. Hearing General Strong speak at Reims made a deep impression on everyone.

Afterward Lady Strong changed Sir Kenneth's lapel decoration to the Légion d'Honneur for the anticipated reception by the French. Alas, the French blew it. Memory was long in Normandy, but it had signally failed in Reims. The Strongs were philosophical. As Lady Strong left our bus, she said gaily, "Don't do anything I wouldn't do!"

We had time to visit the overwhelming Cathedral, its windows a casualty of World War I, and drank the *vin de pays*, champagne, with Stuart in the café across the Place. Later, crossing the Meuse River, Virgil, a vet, opined, "The last time I saw that river I put a Bailey Bridge across it."

On the way, we had an encounter with World War I: Verdun, where we stopped at the haunting, appalling Ossuary—the repository of all the odd bones unearthed, mostly by farmers, in the killing fields of the Western Front—and the huge, sepulchral fort at Douaumont. Luxembourg City was our base to study the Battle of the Bulge. We visited General Patton's grave at the regimented American cemetery and then the very different, sylvan, German one nearby; Bastogne and the formidable, in military terms, Ardennes landscape; St. Vith; Malmédy, scene of a massacre of American POWs; and Remagen, where the Allies took the first, critical bridge over the Rhine. Finally in Stuttgart we heard from the Germans: Manfred Rommel's recollections of his father, and those of Admiral Ruge, Rommel's naval aide, were fascinating.

After two weeks of intense travel, we had a few relaxing, beautiful, non-military days with Ute and Peter near Stuttgart, sitting in the sun drinking wine. We left Ute holding the bag—that is, the sword—when Harris was not allowed to carry it on the plane. We went on to Malta, to visit Harris's mother's family, more Stricklands: aunts, uncles, and cousins whom he had not seen in years.

1981 was a watershed year for us. We had our first experience buying books in England. We opened our poster gallery. And we took our first move toward computerizing some aspects of our business.

After two years, we were fed up with Sheila's psychiatrist tenant who was using the parlor space inappropriately, for assignations and as a guest room. One night we heard someone downstairs and Harris descended, a sword at the ready—to find an equally alarmed woman, ready for bed. Another time, the tenant stupidly left the big window open for air one summer night and was wakened by someone stepping in and onto his stomach.

By this time too, I wanted the front room for a poster gallery. So we renewed the lease for Sheila's office and she got rid of her tenant. Sheila said, "Now you can take the wall down." That had not occurred to us, but when Sheila took her vacation that August, Joe Garabrant, the deconstructionist, dismantled the wall with relish. A big messy project: although a recent addition, the barrier separating the upper duplex from the rest of the house was plaster and the dust permeated the house. The side of the mahogany stairway and banister were revealed, and Harris began to strip the wood in his spare time amid the comings and goings of Sheila's Monday patients.

We had the gallery set up by fall and had all that extra display space and a large flat poster file, as well as a desk. There were still posters in the store, but they served as a preview to what could be seen upstairs in the beautiful, bright room.

The mailing list and how to handle it was a constant preoccupation for me. As catalogue production costs were rising, especially that of paper, we had realized that we should limit the mailing list to real buyers. It was a continuing debate though, Harris not wanting to charge for catalogues. Eventually we had hit on the scheme of sending a sample issue, with a form inviting a two-year subscription, for a modest cost; the cost tended to sort out the sheep from the goats. In the course of two years we would have listed all our subjects, and the subscriber and we should know if we were meant for each other. We would continue to send catalogues to buyers at no further cost, and drop those who were not buying. There was no resubscription. (I do admit that "John G. (Muzzleblast) Gotzen" was kept on the list for years past his active time; I just wanted to see that name on the printout.)

We also listed "wants" for subscribers, as part of the service. These titles were either from their own lists, or for books in the catalogue that they had tried to order but had missed out on. Listing wants was time-consuming; we didn't want to do it for deadbeats or tire-kickers.

Our mailer's requirements—names and addresses on individual IBM-style computer cards, filed in zip code order—were cumbersome to say the least, with changes of address coming in on a regular basis. Quickly, I had realized we needed a duplicate customer file in alphabetical order, to find people by name. A change of address meant two unfilings, two new cards, two refilings. Boring and labor-intensive. Jesse became the main tender of these files, and he would sit in the corner observing all that went on. On a particularly manic afternoon, he said, almost to himself (he lisped a little), "They should make a movie of thith plathe." Mel immediately began casting; Dudley Moore was a shoo-in to play Harris.

It was undoubtedly in one of those frenzied catalogue periods that I brought Harris a banana for lunch. It was swamped with paper; and its silhouette, a black shadow of its former self, was discovered an indeterminate time later in a thorough cleanup, an indelible mark on the corner of the desk. There had been so much paper on top of it that it never smelled.

In the lulls between catalogues, we worked to record customer spending on the alphabet cards. Jesse called this "taxi dispatch"—a rather hilarious undertaking, three or four of us sitting with segments of the files on our laps, entering color-coded numbers on the cards as I read them out from the sales log. Over-elaborate but effective.

Since the customer files were my bailiwick, it is perhaps not surprising that I was the one to start thinking about a computer. What really pushed me over the edge was the threatened mandatory use of the nine-digit zip code. What a nightmare. It was a situation crying out for a computer.

New personal computers were appearing, and Mel and I had come upon a small sales office on Third Avenue that looked promising. When I first broached the idea Harris was dismissive. Luddite that I was and am, the last thing I had ever expected to be lobbying for was a computer, but as I agitated, he tuned me out. I decided to skip work to get his attention. Michael told me that Stuart Elenko came in that day and asked where I was, and Harris told him, "She's on strike." Stuart cracked up, "I love it!" Harris caved in one day, came grumping upstairs in the evening saying, "Where are you going to put it, it takes a whole room." He had gone to IBM school in the sixties when computers were huge, and we all remembered the IBM display at 57th and Madison, all those big machines with the cards sorting madly, right in the window.

Well, we got the computer for the mailing list from a nice salesman named Jake at a short-lived store called Computer Era, and I can't begin to remember the make, it was probably obsolete by the time it hit the desk. We named it for Jesse because it was he who had done so much of the filing. The program was very

Margaretta and the computer.

restrictive and inflexible, as were the people who serviced it, Jake having left almost as soon as he sold us a computer.

"Jesse" kept modest customer records, and printed shipping labels (which had previously been typed). It produced the mailing list on a wide-carriage dot matrix printer—always a big hassle to align the paper properly—and the printout went off to the mailer, who sliced it up into mailing labels to be affixed to the catalogue. Some customer dissatisfaction was alleviated as the program allowed us to offer first-class catalogue mailings for an additional fee, although there were those who seemed to view our modest charge as a rip-off rather than a service, and despite their frustrations wouldn't ante up the five bucks a year.

We took turns doing the customers' data entry, using the information they provided on a questionnaire included in the Winter 1981–82 catalogue. A customer could give us two addresses, one for catalogues and another for packages if necessary, and could designate six areas of subject interest. Of course some customers checked every interest option or tried to write in their own definitions. (Questionnaires don't often ask the questions you want to answer.) We needed answers on some: I wanted to know, for example, how they found out about us. Some questions were just to satisfy my curiosity, such as age, occupation, how many books owned and from how many sources, and especially: how did you become interested in your subject.

In each customer record there was also a "comment" line that we used primarily for our own codes such as tire-kicker, quote-dropper, reservation-dropper (particularly heinous), unredeemed check bouncer (even worse). Also: cheapskate, picky, SS tendencies, questionable dealings, edition or d/j freak, and other sins and misdemeanors in our particular book dealer's canon. The computer made it easy to track customers' buying activity, and if someone had not bought in those first two years, they were dumped.

Reading the customers' responses in the questionnaires was entertaining in various ways. Some were unrealistic in their expectations about the books, the mail, the shipping—no surprises there. Bright-eyed, wiry, little Dan Weinberg of Abraham Lincoln Books was visiting from Chicago when this was in process, and I reacted aloud to one comment, "You never seem to have anything for me anymore." I said with some asperity, "They don't realize that the more they have, the harder it is to add to it! " Dan, burst out from behind a shelf exclaiming, "Yes, they just don't get it!"

"Jesse" was a vast improvement, but as soon as we had it we knew it could be better. And Harris started dreaming about putting the inventory on a computer.

CHAPTER TEN

"What's your five-year plan for the Military Bookman, Margaretta?"

1982 – 1983

Brendan, Harris and part of one Kiralfy shipment.

Brendan came back for another sojourn that spring, bringing his own brand of playfulness to the proceedings. He was fun to have around, and neither he nor Harris had lost touch with his inner child; when Harris told him he was talking too much, he went into a mock-huff, and took a vow of silence. That lasted about ten minutes. He was detailed to the dead files to list wants. The first thing this Virgo did was make labels and scotch tape them to the file boxes; the files were ever-expanding and their labels soon out of date. "A–AZOY" remained his monument until eclipsed by the computer. Brendan left again in the fall—the book business was not for him—but stayed in our life.

A few weeks before we went to Europe the previous spring, we had seen a huge collection in the Bronx, undoubtedly the weirdest we ever visited. Alexander Kiralfy, who had written a small book on naval strategy, had spent the rest of his life assembling books with the ambition of rewriting the history of the world. Right after he died, his strange daughter had come to the store to offer the books, with some unusual and ultimately unworkable conditions. She convinced Harris to go to the South Bronx to see the books.

Kiralfy had lived in one of the big, old, once-fine apartment buildings on the Grand Concourse, in 1981 a very rough area. Ms. Kiralfy told Harris to dress for it. Off he went in his beloved army fatigues, probably unshaven, to meet her. As they went into the apartment she played out the charade for the neighbors that her father was still alive. "Hi Dad, I've brought you a visitor." She was convinced that the apartment would be burgled (unlikely, nothing there but books) or trashed (possibly) if the neighbors knew it was unoccupied. Harris came back shaking his head at the quality, quantity and logistics and wanted me to go see it too. It was horribly fascinating: bibliomania at its most rampant. Full bookshelves lined every wall, creeping into the kitchen and bathroom, climbing over the doors, and then forming bulwarks around every piece of furniture, beds and chairs surrounded on three sides, and apartment and books dingy and dusty, uncleanable. And there were several dust-clogged dioramas crammed with lead soldiers, furious depictions of Kiralfy's favorite battles, almost unintelligible actions, perhaps realistic portrayals of the chaos but unattractive, shabby, and covered with dust. It was a wealth of books, in every subject, but the great majority were not for us.

Kiralfy's obsession had alienated and perhaps physically displaced his children and his wife. His daughter clearly hated him for this uncontrolled passion. But she was crazy in her own way: her conditions were that the books be removed all at once, in one day, and that she be paid in cash. It was not hard to walk away from that one.

And in due course, as we should have expected, the books showed up. A man with a trucking business, but a love affair with books, had met her conditions, and was wholesaling lots by subject, nine months later. Mel and I took a jaunt to Long Island to see the books, mostly boxed and in his garage. We made a deal to buy in installments over several months; even with our subject sorted out, there were still more than we could digest, spatially or financially, all at once. So we got the books we wanted after all, in lots of thirty or forty cartons every couple of weeks (pasta cartons, too big for packing books, on which the seller had ruined his back), each installment filling up our little courtyard over most of the summer that Brendan was working with us. We were lucky to have the extra help. We sent Mel on that year's Ambrose D-Day tour, so she was gone for several weeks in June. She brought back a rusted-out tank part found on a French battlefield, which took up residence on a store windowsill.

We were loaded up with books, but that fall, we traveled again in Europe, to Gomera in the Canary Islands (no bookstores) and then to France. We had less than a week in Paris and, despite being with friends, we did some booking. Buying in Paris was always heady—well, Paris is heady! Our first stop, the most serious visit, was always to the Librairie Pierre Petitot, the long-established military book specialist on Boulevard St. Germain. A charming space with handsome woodwork, and the many leather volumes were gems in a beautiful setting. They carried new books as well, and the old books were on open shelves, in contrast to many continental dealers who had listings on catalogue slips, which necessitated requesting books as in a research library. Monsieur Petitot was gone by the time we first visited, but Madame and their two daughters, chic and petite Parisiennes, were in charge. They sent us on to Librairie Historique Clavreuil on a picturesque street on the Left Bank, and we discovered others in our wanderings. Harris found a new militaria dealer, on rue de Miromesnil, so we carried a sword to London: a short one, a sapper's sword, which fit in the big suitcases we used.

On to London, as much for social as for book reasons, but we visited Maggs for the first time, and some general stores, probably Piccadilly Rare Books and Chelsea Rare Books. The latter was a particularly attractive, bright place, with a friendly older proprietor, Mr. Bernard, and there we found, among other things, Churchill's fine, four-volume biography of his illustrious ancestor, *Marlborough: His Life and Times*. Maggs Bros., a long-established antiquarian book dealer, occupied a handsome town house; much of the military history was in a jumble in the dingy basement, remnants of collection upon collection from Victorian times on. The curator had carved out a corner and tried to civilize it, but the most intriguing sections were the dustiest. We realized that that basement was like an archaeological dig, and required more time than we had on that trip.

Ute Grauer, who worked for British Airways, flew in from Stuttgart to see us for a day or so. She was staying with Sandra Francis, who also worked for an airline, and made good on her offer to get us desirable hotel reservations, for the first few days at Brown's and then after the weekend at the hard-to-get Stafford. Sandra, small, dark, and wholesome-looking, was an operator; she must have known everyone in the travel business. We had high tea at Brown's Hotel with Ute, and she was curious to tag along while we did a little light booking interspersed with shopping, from Liberty to the Burlington Arcade. We went to Brighton for the weekend because the Strickland family had moved there, so it was a family visit, with booking and the Royal Pavilion thrown in. There were a number of shops for us in Brighton, most in or near The Lanes, the medieval warren of small streets where various antiquarian businesses clustered. There was an unwelcoming naval dealer in nearby Hove with whom we never did connect despite several tries. We contented ourselves with Holleyman & Treacher, Kokoro and others. On a very wet Monday morning, Richard dropped us off at a Malta stamp specialist, a sour-smelling shop I was only too glad to leave, even in pouring rain, to walk to the train station. We returned to London and, soaked for the day, went straight to Peter de Lotz. Peter plied us with coffee as we stacked up the books, then in late afternoon drove us in to the Stafford Hotel, a delectable Frank Crocker recommendation tucked away in secluded St. James's Place. The Stafford was an intimate, warm antidote to a cold and clammy day—Frank had told us there was even a cat near the fire. We made quite an entrance, with a call as we were checking in, multiple messages from dealers and friends, Peter talking nineteen to the dozen and collecting from us an accumulation of books that we had checked there, along with most of our things, a swirl of activity. We were shown to our room and realized, "Oops, we checked a sword too." An American-style hot shower and a drink warded off a cold, and we were set to meet Amy and John Cummings and Sandra and Peter Francis for dinner.

When we returned to New York we had to face certain realities. I was realizing that the posters were a separate arm of the business, indeed a separate business. My enthusiasm for the posters had not abated, but mostly in vain had we tried to interest book customers in the related pictures. Most customers were not visual, or seemed to have tunnel vision, heading straight for "their" shelves without a glance at the walls. It required almost physical effort to grab a tank customer, pointing, "Look, look, here's a great tank poster!" Sometimes this worked. We showed the posters with related subjects in the catalogue, with some success. New York walk-in customers bought, but typically had little wall space; a "kitchen" U.S. Food Administration poster and one more were probably enough.

We were having a lot of ups and downs with Mel. It was all too clear that her mind wasn't on the books. Clear to us if not to her that she had lost her interest and was no longer engaged. She was making a lot of mistakes and ignoring things that needed attention. She was preoccupied with her third divorce and new boyfriends, and obsessing about her net worth with her morning coffee or planning her next fancy party.

We developed a proposal for her to buy the poster business, which she did enjoy, and run it under the aegis of the Military Bookman. It would be a separate but related enterprise in our parlor, already the poster gallery. The negotiation was painful and prolonged. Mel bought the poster inventory and we gave her the list of poster customers, wall space in the store and space in the catalogue, with a very nominal rent on the parlor for that year. She went off on an extended trip to South America, not quite realizing that she would return to a different situation, in denial that we could do without her.

In the interregnum between Mel and whoever came next, we left Michael in charge in the store, while we joined my parents for a long-planned week in the South. On our way to Charleston to meet them, we stopped in Atlanta to see friends, and it oddly happened that we were offered a collection there, just at that time. We called on the sellers, but I think they weren't quite ready to act—maybe it freaked them out that we appeared so quickly. So that came to naught, but instead we paid our first visit to Yesteryear Books, which was a great shop with a history specialty and had a lot for us.

We met my parents in Charleston and Harris had phoned a Charleston customer we knew, Charlie Peery, for a hotel recommendation there. Charlie invited the four of us over to his handsome old house near the Battery to see his remarkable collection, almost all on the Confederate Navy. My mother especially loved seeing the house. Paintings and memorabilia overshadowed the books, which were many and rare.

In the midst of our sightseeing, we found a couple of hours in Charleston and much for us at a good bookshop, Harpagon Books—and later a few odds and ends in small shops in Savannah. Even in such charming places, before long it would cross our minds, "Wonder what the bookshops are like here?" We were immune from the hunt only in the Caribbean and the Rockies.

It hadn't taken us long to start combining booking with pleasure travel or vice versa. A few years earlier, we had been with my parents in New England, browsing in an antiques shop, and Harris spotted the distinctive wing insignia of the Lafayette Escadrille on a small pamphlet coquettishly peeking out from under a shawl. A little treasure. He struck. Once in the car, my father asked an obviously satisfied Harris about it. He was shocked at the anticipated markup; my mother was thrilled.

In the meantime, Michael was understandably a bit frazzled by a week alone in the store, complicated by a catalogue deadline or mailing list crisis he had to handle. Finished for the day, Sheila found him one night sitting on the bottom step in the house, head in hands and needing a sympathetic Sheila shoulder, moaning comically, "I need a drink." On our return, our priority was to find a fourth person, this one full-time.

It was in these circumstances that John ambled in one evening. He toured the shelves, and on his way out, used his perhaps well-worn but charming line, "If you ever need someone to work in a military bookstore . . . " "Sit right down here," I said, and the interview process began. John was wearing his time-honored Navy bridge coat, and I said, "I have a feeling you came by that coat honestly." We had not yet advertised to replace Mel, but we desperately wanted to fill her slot before she came back from her travels, so that she would have no illusions of returning. It had already been too difficult to dislodge her.

We interviewed others but John seemed like the answer. He had put in time at the Corner Bookstore and who knows where else; he was a real book person, often spending his spare time browsing and scouting in other bookstores. (He later found me Christopher Morley's two books about bookstores, *Parnassus on Wheels* and the *Haunted Bookshop*.)

The second interview, with the three of us, was light-hearted and got pretty funny when I asked him if he were Catholic. (I had felt surrounded and a bit overwhelmed by all of Catholic upbringing: Sheila, Mel, Michael, Brendan, Bill Waters, and even Harris. It was a little too much for me when at several of our festive gatherings they sang "Tantum Ergo.") A totally illegal, irregular, irrelevant question but John just laughed.

John was attractive, tall, slender, with a shock of prematurely graying hair, glib, and a closet misogynist: a good talker, a good storyteller, who was eking out a living in New York trying to make it as a writer. We never inquired too closely into his circumstances. He had done his military service in the Navy and naturally gravitated to the naval books. He made himself the naval curator, which was great; we liked it when someone cared enough about a subject to take charge of it. He had a real feel for the books and was good at chatting up the customers and pretty good at selling.

Other areas of his responsibilities were shaky; he was a Virgo, but could not seem to file the catalogue cards right or get the bank deposits right: pretty important duties. Brendan had explained to me that Virgos love and need order and precision, and he shuddered when I told him of John's shortcomings. I don't remember about John's balancing the checkbook; Harris and Melvin probably suffered through that aspect.

We had many a gin-and-tonic stoked evening with John and Michael, both unattached. During the summer, we routinely kept glasses and a supply of the ingredients in the little garden out back, and after the store closed, someone would make a run upstairs for the ice. Eventually we would wander off to Hanratty's, an old Irish pub at 98th and Madison, which did a great burger. The talk was good too; both were entertaining and it was an interesting mix. John was a great one for philosophical ramblings and projections. He often got around to needling me, as President, "What's your five-year plan for the Military Bookman, Margaretta?" I had never lived my life that way and certainly not our unpredictable business life. Eventually when he asked, I said decisively, "Less work and more money."

Our staff problems solved, for the moment, and Jesse the computer making that aspect of the work lighter, we began to think about more buying in England.

Our British buying in 1981 and 1982 had been rather haphazard, but very successful, so we entertained ideas of regular and more premeditated buying trips. We started talking to Amy Cummings about helping us with research and arrangements, identifying likely sources, and making appointments for us. It would have been hard and time-consuming to try to set up such an expedition from here by mail, or worse, very expensively by phone, with a five-hour time difference and with dealers with erratic hours. Amy and John were delighted to help us figure it out, and Amy overjoyed to be part of it. She and especially John, who traveled a lot on business in England and knew great places to stay, had a lot of input on mileage and lodgings. We invited Amy to go along with us for the ride, to see the fruits of her planning. It would be September, with their son Mark away at school and

John working. We looked forward to time with the irrepressible Amy, who offered a wealth of information and laughter.

We and she had Sheppard's invaluable bookstore guide, and later Mark sent us its counterpoint, Driffield's, an anonymous, cranky, mischievous and hilarious guide, the writer's comments on the shops he had visited as a book scout. We had come to know, or know of, various military specialists, almost all one-man-bands, working from home. Those we saw by appointment, and the general bookstores in the usual business hours. There were always more shops than we could fit in.

Some of our customers seemed to have the fantasy that "buying in England" involved some secret underground repository, where one could say, "I'll take a box of eighteenth-century wars, and half-a-dozen Indian Mutiny." In fact, every book was hand-picked, handled and chosen by us. In the general shops, the job was finding the titles right for us, sometimes in sections that might not be obvious; for example, T. E. Lawrence, Lawrence of Arabia, could turn up also in literature, biography, or travel. At the military specialists', all the books were of interest, so it was a matter of selection and price. Book buying was a treasure hunt, particularly in England, but it never failed to surprise me, both here and there, when a large, even pretentious place turned out to be full of not much, while a tiny place could be a bonanza.

In truth, the trip planning was hard work, painstakingly put together. Each year we targeted a section of the country where we had not been but perhaps knew of a military specialist or two, or someone with whom we had had dealings. (One of those I wrote was P. T. Clarke, whose lists I had been buying from in the late seventies, but I got no answer.) Amy and John plotted it out for us. Amy, Sheppard's in hand, made preliminary phone calls to general shops, querying military stock, getting other suggestions and referrals, checking shop hours, weaving in the specialists, and planning a delightful itinerary from lovely country house hotel to traditional inn. We tried always to include a castle hotel to nourish Harris's rich fantasy life. He and I pictured Amy, ever charming and curious, making inquiries and appointments like a social secretary.

We decided to open a British bank account, because it was elaborate, expensive and time-consuming to send bank drafts to so many dealers. Working on that premise in 1984, we set out, ranging through the shops, piling up stacks of books along the way, and blithely telling the dealers (skeptical or trusting), "We'll be opening a bank account when we get to London and will send a sterling check." Naive of us, to say the least. No British bank wanted any part of us because we had no assets in England. This was embarrassing and more than inconvenient. Fortunately we lamented to the sympathetic ears of the Stricklands. And how lucky, Jilly's brother was with Midland Bank, and vouched for us, so we were able to open a checking account and fulfill our commitments. This made our buying much easier—and cheaper—over all those years, as well as being a great convenience for our British customers.

We never went with a budget. We often had to lend the store money for a couple of months before the cash started flowing in from the big buy. Each year there was a different exchange rate to bear in mind as we shopped. Philip Kamil watched the exchange rate for us, urging sometimes, "Go now, it's cheap." One year the pound was down to a dollar, months before we were going; I toyed with the idea of buying pounds for the next campaign, but no . . . it didn't make sense.

The store at 29 East 93rd Street.

We never went to England with want lists; we knew what was wanted. But we usually read the basement duplicate shelves before we went, to try to internalize a "don't want" list. There was always so much that was new to us and that was exciting. Harris and I approached buying differently: he sensibly looked at contents, bibliography, author, before he perused the text. I found myself looking at the middle of the book first, feeling as if I could assess its quality by the look of the text on the page and by reading a paragraph here and there.

Thanks to Lionel, we had the freight consolidator to whom the dealers shipped, and we gave each dealer a sheet of very specific packing and shipping instructions, often disregarded. There always seemed to be one delinquent dealer holding up the whole shipment. Urgent communications from the shipper sooner or later resulted in completion of the consolidation. Thanks to this method of shipment, the shipping charges were relatively cheap. The dealer discount in England was ten percent, and our mental rule of thumb was that the discount covered the shipping. Then one glorious day (never rainy), one to two tons of books on a pallet would arrive curbside on 93rd Street, then filling the front of the store until we could get them down the trapdoor to the basement. We tried to rally some extra helpers to unload, and sometimes a customer would walk in on this, pick up on the excitement and volunteer; once Melvin, our accountant, was there and lent a hand. What fun, like Christmas, because by then we had half-forgotten what we had bought. In early days, I was overambitious and silly enough to catalogue some noteworthy books on the spot in England, or to send lists to the store of what we were buying, so that we could get them listed in the forthcoming catalogue before the lot arrived at the store. Once, with a delayed shipment, this resulted in a vast game of "concentration," with stacks of books all over the floor, to fill catalogue orders already received for books just coming out of the boxes. Madness. I gave that up soon enough.

We almost always went in September, getting into that routine because it was a quiet time in the store, our off-season, between catalogues. We started in the country, saving the pricier London specialists for the end. We usually spent about a week in London, seeing Peter de Lotz and Victor Sutcliffe, and other "militarists," lunching with Lionel, visiting some large stores and especially Maggs.

Several times we flew in to Manchester, so much easier than Heathrow in the early morning, and with the smiling faces of the Cummingses to greet us. Then we would rent a car and hit the road, usually on the left side, Amy a bit white-knuckled in the back seat. Amy always marveled at how intense we were about the hunt. In vain, and increasingly wistfully, she would point out a brown marker for a historic house here or there, but we usually didn't let up, aside from a pub lunch, until the end of the day. We could visit the local cathedral or church and the old part of town after five, when the shops had closed.

Then there was the challenge of finding our way, taking turns driving, the navigator with the big Ordnance Survey book of maps on lap, remarking the straight stretches of Roman road and occasionally exhorting the driver to stay left. We almost never got lost in between towns but in towns we often did, and the one-way patterns and pedestrian streets were confusing and impenetrable. In Colchester, we gave up, parked the car near the pedestrian center and walked. Kendal was like the Indianapolis speedway; on our second circuit we spotted the bookshop, but had to do the circuit again to figure out where to get out of the pattern. It was such a struggle to get to a bookstore in Norwich that we didn't arrive until it was closing. When we did get where we were going and found a parking place, the "pay and display" meter was a new IQ test. Part of the fun was the picturesque addresses, some of which we had been writing on air-letter sheets for years. Many houses had names rather than street numbers. One found one's way from the bottom line to the next one up of the multi-layered addresses: county, then town, then village, maybe a road, then perhaps a house with a name. Jordans, near Pitney, Langport, Somerset; or Lantern Cottage, The Drove, Twyford, Winchester.

Military history was an honored subject in Britain and there were numerous specialists, usually single practitioners. We learned soon enough that they generally worked from "private premises," always by appointment. They sent out lists or occasionally did book fairs. They were all chatty, if not gossipy, being alone most of the time, wanting to know where we had been and whom we were seeing. Real social calls, many of them. Some of the specialists were bookmen, and had chosen their subject. Others came to it by way of a military career, much like the "reading souldier," Col. Robert Monro. These visits to specialists were interspersed with stops at general bookshops, most of which had respectable military and naval sections, as determined by Amy's queries. They were typically in old, often picturesque houses in the center of town. I imagine some of them had been bookshops for generations.

In 1983, we were just getting our feet wet. Arriving on Sunday in Manchester, via a shuttle from London, we had our jet lag with the Cummingses. It was a shock to get up from a nap on Sunday and find John and Mark and Harris watching American football, just becoming popular there; I felt as if we hadn't gone anywhere. Next day, we again visited the charming Broadhurst shop in Southport. Mr. Sankey didn't have as much for us this time. We had been there rather recently after all, and it took a while to "refill" subjects that had been heavily bought out. We also went to Amy's more local shop, Halewood, in Preston. We had been cautioned about it, and it was a mess, very disorganized, and we worked hard in the disarray to spend over £1100. Spending a lot was a sign of success, especially when the books were as cheap and numerous as those were. It was a workout, handling, looking, evaluating, so many calculations, currency conversions, and decisions. Then we took to the road, with many pangs leaving Amy behind, as Mark had come down with food poisoning at a family wedding and had not gone back to school. We had to go it without the pleasure of her company and without her to brief us on the shops and talk us through the roundabouts. We had a little, bright-orange Renault, so at least the Brits could see us coming. We arrived without incident and with a certain sense of achievement in Hereford, where the Red Lion turned us away but the Green Dragon took us in, and were in time to visit the Cathedral and its ancient *mappa mundi.*

When people think about buying books in England, they think of the "book town" Richard Booth created in Hay-on-Wye, a pretty village on the Welsh border. He had several shops there himself, and other dealers clustered in the town. Naturally enough, we planned it into our first trip and then several more times over the years. It was interesting but rarely exciting; the Booth shops were rather dirty and ill lit. Dealing with the Booth people was never pleasant; they were a surly lot who seemed to take out their resentments in the careless way they packed and shipped the books. We put together a large lot, and then fished in the other shops. The Hay Cinema Bookshop, in a former movie theatre, bright and pleasant, was the other big one, but there were many small specialists. That part was fun, because although we may only have found a half-dozen things here or a dozen there—usually in crossover subjects—it added up to a productive time.

Peter Eaton's establishment, "Lillies," had gotten a lot of press in the States as the largest bookshop in England, with a million books, and since we were going that way it was a natural. Lillies was a huge Victorian house on extensive wooded grounds near a pretty village, Weedon, in Buckinghamshire. Seeing a cottage roof being thatched in the village was more memorable than the books. They had quantity rather than quality, the best stock having been siphoned off to Eaton's shop in Holland Park in London. We did just as well or better in the considerably smaller Weatherhead's in nearby Aylesbury. Both were near our picturesque inn, The Upper Reaches, built around a water mill, in Abingdon.

The White Hart Hotel in the pretty village of Dorchester-upon-Thames was an easy distance from Oxford. We did not have much luck in the Oxford shops: too humanistic, too many classics, and precious little military aside from the occasional Greek or Roman. We wandered through the University colleges and walked into the Bodleian Library—an exhilarating moment. We visited Blackwell's, the venerable Oxonian book mecca, and found a few things. They had recently moved their antiquarian division to a hamlet outside of town and thither we went. Fyfield was an astonishing place, exactly like the feudal village that I had studied in school: the squire's house, the church and the manor house disposed around the green. Blackwell's was installed in the fourteenth-century manor house, and we were directed upstairs to a large, handsome room with fine woodwork, a big sunny window, and a refectory table that surely has doubled in my mind to forty feet long. The aroma of antiquarian books that have spent one or two centuries in a damp climate without central heating scented the air. The snobbism of the help did not diminish our pleasure, and we were brought the titles we asked to see. Harris, unawed, opened a large and ancient tome and bent down to the centerfold to inhale with relish. We chose a couple of wonderful eighteenth-century leather-bound books, one a treatise on strategy.

It was a rich and memorable experience in book buying, and we were loath to leave and face the weekend traffic to drive to Brighton. The supercilious Blackwell's clerk gave us directions he said would connect from the M-road to London to the M-road south to Brighton: an interchange as yet unbuilt, a dirt exit ramp to nowhere, mocking us. Consequently, we got almost irretrievably ensnarled in the Home Counties around Cobham and Chobham, with no one to question except a few locals who had been in the pub too long. We did not reach the Stricklands until after nine; Richard was unsympathetic.

We visited the bookstores we knew in Brighton and heard their anxieties about a man purportedly wanting to corner the out-of-print book market and opening the

Quinto chain of cheap and junky out-of-print bookshops, and the bad threatening to drive out the good.

We drove to London, and were cocky enough about our driving to keep the car. We immediately set out for the History Bookshop, in Friern Barnet, and got so lost that we didn't get there before closing. It was something like ten miles as the crow flies, but London was laid out in cow paths from village to village; with no grid system there was no correcting by going around the block. We called from a phone box, but the bookstore people were very grumpy and wouldn't wait for us, so we gave up and turned the car in at Victoria Station, never to attempt that again. In London, we always stayed in Mayfair, so central, the hub of the Underground, with dealers to visit in all directions. We saw Peter de Lotz, always a big buy, and Maggs Bros. Ltd.

Maggs was another order of magnitude—one of the great antiquarian booksellers of London and the world, since the mid-nineteenth century. Ensconced in a grand house on Berkeley Square, its setting was perfect for the contents. Maggs had a strong military specialty, much of it down in the somewhat grubby basement. Some good sets in our subjects were in the handsomely shelved main floor which, furnished with antiques, looked more like a fine house than a shop. On our first visit to the curator's office, we were shown his desk chair—uncomfortable, he said—which had been captured from a Russian general's tent in the Crimea.

Philip Kamil and his wife were in London and we met them for dinner near Sloane Square. Philip was becoming addicted to London and was very soon also to Maggs.

All in all, we had seen about fifteen dealers in ten days. We did the paperwork for the shipper and sent the store a list of payments to be made to the vendors before we went off to Malta for a week to see Harris's family, and then on to Rome.

Mary Strickland Di Rienzo was Harris's favorite aunt and we were fond of her husband Giacchino and enjoyed him too. Giacchino, a little dandy, had been in the Italian consular service in Malta where they met in the 1920s, but they had lived in Rome after their marriage. During the war, doughty Auntie Mary had been part of the "Rome Escape Line," sheltering escaped Allied prisoners of war in a walled-off room of their apartment (reached only by a plank from window to window). Mary was, I suppose, an "enemy alien" in Italy, being Maltese and British, and a force to be reckoned with at any age.

Harris had visited the Di Rienzos in Rome several times in his teens. They had moved back to Malta in about 1960. Harris thought they would enjoy visiting Rome again with us, and wrote to invite them.

Mary answered with great excitement; they had just been talking about going to Rome and she was not up to the trip, but Giacchino, a spry seventy-eight, would go, and would welcome our help with some business.

When they had moved to Malta, the Di Rienzos had stored Mary's ancient family silver in a Roman bank, which had its vaults in the Alban Hills. They had now determined to sell the silver, "for the comforts of our old age," and asked for our help. They were set on its being sold in New York, in spite of Harris's advising it would fetch more in London or Rome or Malta, because they wanted to keep it secret from the rest of the Malta family. For months before we arrived, Harris kept asking them to attend to documents or permits necessary to take the silver out of Italy. In vain, we realized when we saw them; Mary had her 1929 inventory listing what she had taken from Malta to Rome when she married, that was it. Obviously they wanted to avoid bureaucratic complications and would risk our taking the silver with us.

When we got to Rome, it was fun to see Giacchino on his native turf; he had a new spring to his step—Harris said he was pawing the earth—and was chatting with everyone he encountered, having missed his native tongue in Malta. I resented a little the time being taken from our sightseeing by the silver caper, which was more elaborate than anticipated; but it took on a life of its own, with its own fascination. The first order of business was to go with Giacchino to the tiny bank branch to show his passport and request the silver be brought in from the vaults. Returning a few days later to collect it, the three of us gathered with the bank clerk in a booth much like a tailor's changing room in size and amenities, unpacking a black foot locker and an almost as large wooden box, digging through newspapers from 1960 to retrieve the gorgeous and remarkably untarnished silver, piece by elaborate piece. The nasal-voiced female clerk was reading the items off a paper tape resembling a grocery checkout receipt, as I repacked more efficiently to fit most of the swag into the big suitcase and a bag Giacchino had brought. We hauled it back to the tiny rooms at our so-so *pensione* Jumbo, where Giacchino had insisted on staying for old times' sake. (It was near the Via Veneto, where he had liked to sit at Caffé Doney and look at the girls.) In our cramped room at the Jumbo, Harris made a precise but informal document listing the inventory: several pairs of candlesticks, a Baroque tureen, a teapot which had belonged to the first English governor of Malta, a commemorative platter incised with an allegorical battle scene, three or four trays, eight service plates with armorial devices, sugar bowls, coffee pot, and a chocolate pot with a topknot and cloven hooves. Giacchino signed the paper, entrusting the silver to Harris to sell, as I managed to repack almost all of it into the foot locker. Giacchino, the quintessence of passive aggression, sat and watched us do it all. Then we went forth to have a glorious time in Rome, looking at menus for the *porcini* mushrooms Michael had ecstatically told us would be in season, and finding a large brass finial for the newel post in our hall that Harris had recently refinished. Giacchino entered into it with delight, showing us his favorite places, starting with the Pantheon. We got sidetracked to buy a fluorescent-yellow duffle bag for the chubby, lovable tureen, which needed its own conveyance, and was cushioned by our laundry. It was all a little crazy: the plan was just to check it all through to Paris, hoping that it wouldn't be inspected, and that we wouldn't fall into the hands of the watchdog office of *La Ricchezza Romana,* which had to clear antiques exports. I naively thought that if we were stopped, we would just hand the bags off to Giacchino, but when departure day came, he left Rome hours before we did. We were nervous, but there was a helpful diversion at the airport check-in: a rather dangerous-looking man who had been refused entry to the country jumped to the front of our line and Harris, pretty tightly wound by that time, had a bit of an altercation with him. As a result, none of the *carabinieri* or airline staff looked at anything else and they even forgot to pull my ticket. The flight was uneventful and it was a great relief when the old suitcase and the dazzling duffle—more than twenty kilos of overweight luggage— popped up on the luggage carousel in Paris.

In later years, we usually stayed on the Left Bank because it reminded Harris of his youthful sojourns in Paris. I had started out at the grand hotels of the Right Bank, and on this occasion I had persuaded him to stay at the Hotel Meurice; after all it had been the Wehrmacht's headquarters during the war, so it was history. It was good timing too, because of our bulky and precious baggage; we would have needed an extra room for it at a tiny Left Bank hotel.

We stayed in Paris for what turned out to be a week; we had to extend our stay because Harris was feeling rotten, probably from "silver stress." Ute was flying in for twenty-four hours to see us, and we told her we'd meet her at Librairie Petitot at one. Finding it closed that morning, we went on to Librairie Clavreuil. By the time we met Ute, we had spent thousands of francs at Clavreuil. They had two classic British sets, Napier on the Peninsular War and Fortescue's massive history of the British Army, at very reasonable prices due to lack of French interest. We spotted them immediately when we went in; other books there were found more laboriously, through the catalogue slips. The three of us went to Ute's favorite brasserie for lunch, then meandered along on the Left Bank finding small bookshops and buying a few things here and there. She always took interest in what we were choosing. As usual, we put together a package, often some aviation books, at Les Arcades, on rue de Castiglione, near the Meurice. We took Ute back to our grand room at the Meurice before dinner that evening to pick up the *porcini* mushrooms I had brought her from Rome, and unpacked the splendid silver for show-and-tell. After she left the next day, Harris's militaria dealer, René Johnson, took us to see a retired military book dealer, Monsieur Roulleau, who was selling from his apartment. He was a charming man and, from the little we saw, he had wonderful books. Alas, we quickly learned that not only would he not ship, but he wanted to be paid in cash to avoid taxes. It was a short visit.

We had twenty kilos of silver from Malta, 2800 pounds of books from England, and more from France, to show for our travels, and the books, which arrived in December, sold more quickly than the silver.

November was replete with melodrama: Mel's scene when Harris told her we would not be renewing her lease, and a computer crash. But by Christmastime, we felt like a celebration. Inspired by a Southwestern turkey-dinner menu in *Gourmet Magazine*, I decided to have the store Christmas party at home, telling Michael and John they could bring "dates." Michael invited Sheila, and John invited Philip Kamil. We included Rita and Mike Wolfson who accepted with alacrity, and Jean and Frank Crocker, who were tentative. Frank was already sick, but rallied, and it was a happy surprise when they appeared. The margaritas flowed, all were in good form and Michael was at his hilarious best.

CHAPTER ELEVEN

"In the library . . . real cats were splayed out across the pages"

1984 – 1985

Amy Cummings in Lancaster bookshop.

The Colts in Berkeley Square

Before her departure, Mel had arranged a small show of World War I art at the Military Bookman. She had cleared it with me, but it had slipped my mind, and I was startled when the consignor came along to hang the exhibit. Peter Hastings Falk was a dealer-cum-art historian who had acquired the art remaining in the estate of Lester Hornby. In the course of his long career, Hornby had been one of the American Official Artists on the Western Front. There were to be several small shows of his work, in two galleries and with us, running in New York at the same time. The war art, mostly etchings with one naval watercolor, was reasonably priced and attractive, and Peter had prepared a sales brochure that we mailed to our list, so our work was nominal. There was a joint ad for the shows, and that brought in people who may not have known about us, always a good thing. The art did remarkably well, from the mailing and in the store too. The customers included several institutions, most notably the Australian War Memorial. Michael had quite a hassle with an unpleasant neighborhood customer, semi-dealer loudmouth, crass and pushy—he seemed to think he was entitled to the gallery frames Peter had provided to show the prints, at a dealer's discount to boot. Michael ever after referred to him as The Pig. The Pig was the kind of buyer who always made you feel you had made a pricing mistake when he sprang for something, and I didn't enjoy selling him anything I particularly liked, memorably a scarce early edition, nicely rebound by Lloyd, of Sun Tzu's *Art of War*.

The Hornby art sold out, and then Peter found another cache the next year, and it sold too. Around the same time, a man who worked at the Soldier Shop brought in an unusual watercolor by the great French war artist, J. O. B.—atypical because it depicted a French *poilu* attacking a German trench in World War I, not J. O. B.'s usual period. It was expensive but we took it on consignment, and it sold quickly. These successes made me think that war art was still a viable commodity for us.

Not quite in the same league, a commercial illustrator, Adrian Osterling, who lived in the neighborhood, came in to talk about doing war paintings on consignment or commission. Why not give it a try? Adrian had painted on spec the usual stalwarts: Winston Churchill, J. E. B. Stuart, and George Patton, and some aerial combat scenes. They were surprisingly successful, and at least two customers commissioned more than a few from Adrian. One, an Italian businessman working in New York, was a veteran of the North African campaign and had been buying the relevant books, then wanted several paintings to reflect his experiences in the Desert War. Another was a Marine who ordered several combat creations. Adrian obliged. And I commissioned one too, for my father's seventy-fifth birthday, of his Confederate grandfather in uniform, in front of Springdale, the Barton family house in the Shenandoah Valley. Adrian gave him a dueling scar—ridiculous—amended—and the beautiful house was a little too much on the Tara scale, but Daddy was pleased.

There were always new book sources. On a brief visit to friends in Litchfield, Connecticut, they found us a book fair. Another time, I cajoled Harris into combining a pilgrimage to a special greenhouse in furthest Connecticut with a party in Wilton and some book-buying. The bookstores were nothing special but the greenhouse was intoxicating. We built an extended weekend into one of Harris's Massachusetts school reunions, flying to Worcester and having dinner with the Controviches and then following Jim's leads to some small and obscure shops between there and Boston. One looked unpromising, the books falling down in the shelves, nevertheless had a lot for us. Another, in the back of beyond, had ridiculously high prices for a "garage dealer"; it was hard to imagine who his customers were. We visited Michael Ginsberg and Western Hemisphere, two non-military specialists, and each had material for us. We had dinner in Boston with the Perrottis, and a lively conversation about Norman Prince, a World War I aviator who had attended Harris's school. We did the Boston shops. We had visited Brattle Book Shop a few years before, when they were in temporary quarters following a disastrous fire in which they had lost everything. They were rising like a phoenix from the ashes with the help of their many friends, including Anne S. K. Brown, whose curator had sold her duplicates to Brattle: a fine assortment from the famous uniform book and print collection later at Brown University, and we had pounced on them.

We never knew what might turn up. Sy Reit, our "first author," whom we hadn't seen in some time, called to tell us that, when clearing out a closet at the behest of his wife, he had found some things left from his wartime service in the Army Air Force and thought we might be interested. What had come out of the closet was several large volumes of original photos of aerial reconnaissance of France and Germany in 1944 and 1945, an amazing compendium which was very exciting, perhaps unique. Since Sy had been involved in putting it together, he did not quite grasp its very real historical value and was amazed at the size of our check.

A long weekend in Wilmington was a chance to try several shops in Bryn Mawr and again the Baldwin Book Barn. There was a potential new source in Wilmington: Peggy Barton's mother read the local paper thoroughly, and sent us a clipping about Holly Oak Books, an established shop that had moved in to town. On our next visit, we went downtown to check it out. The proprietor was not there, but a just-arrived, large, and as-yet-unpriced lot of military beckoned from behind the counter. What timing. Harris decided to stay over and the next day he made the acquaintance of the inimitable Mort Rosenblatt. A former merchant seaman with the beard and vocabulary that went with it, Mort was another knowledgeable and autodidact dealer, a chain smoker with a raspy voice, a real character. His shop was well organized and fairly large, and his prices were usually viable for us, but the negotiations were half the fun. Mort became a regular stop and I visited more often than Harris, as I was more often in Wilmington to see my family; maybe that's why Mort once said, "Margaretta is a more aggressive buyer than Harris."

We went to Washington twice, once for an auction and once for a new venture of Lionel Leventhal's. These visits always included Second Story Books, and the Taylors, and at least once we took Keene Taylor with us, and all pawed through unsorted piles on the floor of their warehouse in Alexandria.

To promote his books and military books in general, Lionel developed a special, one-day Military Book Show as an adjunct to the American Booksellers Association annual show. That first time, he invited us to participate as the only out-of-print dealer and military specialist, and because the show was in Washington that year, it was easy to say yes. We visited ourselves on the Taylors again, and had an intensive day at the show. I made a large poster, a muddy photostat of a photo of the store; blown-up and hand-colored, so that it looked decidedly antiquarian, like an old postcard; and we took catalogues to give out. We saw a lot of our Washington customers there and who knows, maybe met some new ones. One was Gen. Charles B. MacDonald, Army historian and author of a number of the "Green Books." He also had written an excellent book on the American Army in the ETO, *The Mighty Endeavor*, and needed another copy. We quoted it to him as soon as we got back to the store. The show was also an opportunity to make ourselves known to military book publishers who had not heard of us, and they began to refer customers to us as a source for their books that were out-of-print.

And we went to a different kind of auction. Harris's many attempts to interest New York silver dealers in the Maltese hoard confirmed his previous certainty that there was little market for continental silver here. We had not wanted to put it at auction, such an uncertain prospect, but we got lucky. Sotheby's curator was British and had some knowledge of Malta, having gone to Worth School in England, which had a number of Maltese students. The lot was well placed, and mostly well described, in a June auction of continental silver, which we attended, hearts in mouth. It did nicely, the tureen was the star, and it was a substantial total for Mary and Giacchino.

Around this time, a unique book source made his first appearance. Book scout extraordinaire-to-be and sometime writer Joel Block found us and his calling because his daughter lived across 93rd Street from us in the early eighties. Joel came in unobtrusively and began with extensive browsing, then started coming in with a few books every so often. Soon he would arrive with a couple of shopping bags, having lugged them over on the bus. Joel liked to think he worked undercover, going so far as to pay sales tax on his purchases when he could have gotten a resale number and bought tax free. He was paranoid about being taken for a scout (although he usually had one of our catalogues in his pocket), and paranoid about his sources being discovered; he was deeply shocked when he found me shopping at Jim Carr's, one of "his" stores.

Joel honed his craft; he studied our subject and scrutinized and usually read every book he brought in, more thoroughly than we ever had time to. His bookmarks would show particularly interesting passages he thought would sell the book; the tiniest defect was pointed out. He began to scout for other specialists too; he loved the game, and like most book people could not pass up a small store, thrift shop, library sale, or yard sale. He persuaded various friends, including naval historian Paul Silverstone, to take him to out-of-town sales or remote bookstores (like the one in Hillsdale, so deep in the woods one could not always find it.)

Joel sold mostly to me, and I developed a game played only with Joel. For every book he brought in that had a "want" on it, I would pay him an extra dollar, doubling up after five wants. He brought in small lots but nevertheless frequently earned these bonuses. And as time went on, Joel prided himself on bringing in significant items we had never seen before. Sometimes he would call from a phone booth on the street, "This is Joel, calling from 'the field,'" to check a title in our records, before buying it for us.

Buying Pamela Sneed's books was a different story. Pamela had flowing tresses and flowing garments and looked like the Greenwich Village artist she was. In the course of her career as an illustrator, she had collected and used for research a large number of uniform and illustrated histories, many of them nineteenth- and early twentieth-century publications. Pamela began schlepping in a heavy bag of big history and uniform pictorials every few weeks, and in the course of it we became friendly. For her, it was probably a bittersweet, gradual parting with the books, and there was a dramatic progression: the books became older, scarcer and grander as the months went on. The finale was a dazzling copy of Édouard Detaille's *Cavaliers de Napoleon*. The artist had been the premier French military painter of the late nineteenth century, and Harris's favorite. Detaille's stock-in-trade was scenes of the Franco-Prussian War and the Napoleonic Wars. It is curious that there was so much French glorification of their armies after their disastrous defeat in 1871, and that they maintained their illusions of *la gloire* in the face of it. This book, however, was the rather scarce 1895 selection of Detaille's paintings of French Napoleonic cavalry, and I had found a copy of it, bound in buckram, for Harris at the Soldier Shop the Christmas before we were married. In our time at the old store, a much nicer copy, with a handsome, three-quarter-leather binding and a hand-colored frontispiece, had come in from a couple in Mississippi who had also sold us their collection in installments; and the better copy went home and the lesser copy into the store. Pamela's was a probably unique copy of a very limited edition of twenty-five numbered copies, each with a watercolor sketch by the artist on the half-title page. But this had a dazzling, gilt-leather binding replete with Napoleonic motifs, red moiré endpapers, and the bookplate of Enrico Caruso, the great Italian tenor and Detaille contemporary; and it had three copies of each plate, on different kinds of paper, one copy of each plate hand-colored. It was breathtaking in its beauty and rarity, and it was tempting to think of Detaille as a Caruso fan who had prepared this copy especially for him. Pamela brought it in on a day when my parents happened to be in the store, so they were privy to my dealings, the process and the excitement. Needless to say, Pamela's copy went upstairs, and the Mississippi copy went into inventory.

Sheila's Fourth of July picnic was already a tradition when we met her, and she was a great party-giver. At first, the picnic was only three or four couples, and took place in a secluded corner of Carl Shurz Park, overlooking the East River. The core menu was always the same, with Sheila's heavenly fried chicken, potato salad, and corn bread. Hauling the food and drink was a production, and the variables in the weather and the lack of running water also figured in the easy decision, after a couple of years, to move the picnic to the Military Bookman. Eventually, the guest list grew to include the store staff, some favorite customers, and mutual friends. The backyard was pretty and fun, just big enough, and if the weather were sweltering or rainy we retreated to the air-conditioned store. The big desk was cleared for the mouth-watering picnic food, Harris stocked the bar, which was set up on the packing table, I made the guacamole and the dessert, and Bill Waters brought his home-made cookies. We cleared the other tables for action (not always simple), and decorated with the foreordained red-white-and-blue crepe paper, flags and balloons. It was usually a long-running party, occasionally with a few people hanging out on the front steps.

Ah, the front stoop, always a magnet. One of the banes of our existence was its attraction for students of the local private schools, who gathered there at lunchtime in good weather. Most notoriously, the French kids from the Lycée Francais, a block away, were living the stereotype of the ugly French: arrogant, rude slobs. They would move only very grudgingly if someone wanted to go up the steps to the house. Their litter was legendary. We complained to the school many times; Harris once did a demo, taking a lunchtime's garbage and cigarette butts to the Lycée and dumping it on the Dean's desk. I, frustrated and disgusted beyond measure by another day's garbage, called to vent to another administrator. That didn't satisfy me; I tore off a six-foot-length of computer paper and with red magic marker wrote: "The Lycée Francais had lunch here." It and their leavings festooned the stoop only briefly, long enough to amuse some neighbors, before the administrator came and whisked it away. No real respite came until the school moved many blocks away.

Tall Brian Markham was the last of our "after-school" packers, and when we took the traditional photo of a huge UPS load with its packer, I had him hold the yardstick for scale. Brian was the son of an old friend of Sandra Francis's, did a few innings at the packing table, the first that July, and continued to turn up in school vacations and short bursts in the summer when he was available and the packing table not occupied.

He was spelled in August by my godson, Mark Cummings, fifteen by then, who came from England to stay with us because Amy and I wanted him to experience some semblance of an American summer job, in this case packing books. We all enjoyed that, because Mark was so interested in the subject and the store, and during Mark's month, our nephew Ran came up for a long weekend and helped pack, transferring much of the book dust and newsprint to himself via the vaseline

Mark, Ran, Michael, John, and Harris at West Point.

treatment. We took this particular time for a "class trip" to West Point, Michael, John, Mark and Ran and a picnic on a bright summer Sunday up the Hudson. We saw the Academy's Museum and the spot where the Great Chain had stretched across the river to block the British fleet during the Revolution. Next day we took the boys to Sky Books, where Ran was shocked at some of the merchandise available, such as *The Anarchist Cookbook.* "You wouldn't think they'd be allowed to sell this," he said. Before Mark went home, he and I had our own expedition to the U.S.S. *Intrepid,* which had become a museum on the Hudson River.

The illness of Frank Crocker, who had become such a good friend through being a customer, had shadowed our year, and he died in late August. We went off to England with heavy hearts.

Mark had gone home in late August, and less than a week later we met in England. Harris and I flew into Heathrow and, after the usual rental car hassle, drove straight to meet all three Cummingses in Cambridge. It was a sunny, lazy Sunday afternoon, and there were crew races on the Backs, viewed from the lawn of a well-positioned pub where we had bangers and lager. A treat for Harris and John, little guys who had coxed crew at Princeton and Cambridge respectively.

Next day, with Amy in tow, we visited four Cambridge shops. G. David was tucked away in a secluded passage beside St. Edward's Church. Galloway & Porter was nearby, and Deighton Bell and Jean Pain were along Trinity Street, across from the colleges. Enjoying the special feel of a university town, we wandered through some of the colleges and saw glorious King's College Chapel before hitting the road for Bury St. Edmunds. The Angel Hotel, a venerable coaching inn dripping with ivy and flowers, faced the gardens and the ruins of the ancient Abbey, and the inn offered dinner in the vaults of the thirteenth-century wine cellar. Around the corner was Graham Scott Books, with a strong history section, and another smaller shop, and between them it was a productive as well as charming stop. From there it was a pretty drive east to Halesworth, where Amy in her inquiries had discovered Patrick Quorn Books. Pat, a foxy little character with ginger hair, specialized in a handful of subjects, among them jazz, I believe, but was very strong in ours. It was a gold mine of reasonably priced, solid stock. We had fun, a great time, and worked from 11:30 until late afternoon, Amy making a run for beer and chips. It was not hard to spend over £2000. We paused briefly in Framlingham, where I had visited Amy and John when they were first married, and later little Mark too, at Cherry Tree Farm. We saw the nearby, overgrown airfield, where units of the American Eighth Air Force had been stationed from 1943 to 1945. Our success with Pat Quorn had left us no time for the Ipswich shops, and Amy took us that night to Dedham Vale, beloved by John Constable and captured in his many landscapes. A pretty and gracious country hotel, a hilarious and superb dinner after a full day's work, and probably the first and only time I asked a chef for a recipe. The next day threatened rain and we went on to Colchester, where Castle Books, a few blocks from the foursquare Norman castle, was in the midst of a pedestrian area and parking was tough. It was an charmingly crooked old shop, with history up under the roof and down some precarious steps—a good lot, a garrulous dealer, and a rush back to the car before the rain. After a pub stop at Maldon, Amy had an appointment for us at a completely contrasting place. The famous Foyles Bookshop of Charing Cross Road had an antiquarian arm at Christina Foyle's country residence, the ancient and picturesque Beeleigh Abbey. I noted a "ghostly lady" and Amy noted:

The peacock sitting on the garden bench greeted us [and] the hilarious initial greeting by the Hollywood type-cast housekeeper in her apron and our entrance through a large kitchen with birds' aviaries on the counters, and a cat's tail hanging out of the lower AGA oven, and then going into the library with the refectory table and the various books' cradles on it and the windowsill, several of which had real cats splayed out across the pages. We went up to the large attic where all of the antiquarian private books [for sale] were on display accompanied by a rather sweet effete young man who was so pleased to see anyone under 80. We heard all about Christina Foyle and her famous literary lunches.

Our visit yielded several antiquarian treasures, but more amazing was the place and the denizens.

We went on to Canterbury, "the holy blissful martir for to seke" and also books. We traversed the rainy downs and as we topped the hill under heavy gray skies, the Cathedral was bathed in sun. The hotel was boring and its restaurant looked as if it had been decorated by a multiple personality, but it was welcoming and the food good. After dinner, we visited friends of Brendan's, who lived in a half-timbered Tudor house in the country nearby. Our host told us that the blackened timbers of Heron Manor were recycled in the fifteenth century, from ships that had been tarred against the sea water. It was a dream by moonlight.

The center of Canterbury was full of crooked little houses, and there were three shops to interest us. To visit the Chaucer Bookshop in Beer Cart Lane was worth it for the nomenclature, although we spent less than £200; we found a few books in a shop that was focused on coins and medals, and almost none in the third. We made our pilgrimage to see St. Thomas Becket's tomb, but were surprised and excited to find that of the Black Prince, Edward, England's war leader in the early part of the Hundred Years' War. The magnificent tomb was crowned by a gilded effigy of the Prince, and splendid replicas of his accoutrements were displayed nearby. We took a more personal pilgrimage to nearby Blean. A few years before, I had been antiquing with Amy in Connecticut when I fell in love with a splendid, conceited turkey named Ermintrude, an extraordinary, prize-winning turkey who flourished on Tilekiln Farm in Blean in 1830, and was memorialized in a tavern-sign-type painting. Paraphrasing our customers, I had said to the dealer, "I have to have that turkey!" Tilekiln Farm or road seemed to have mutated into Tyler's Hill road and there was no sign of an old farm.

The handsome, old, seaside Imperial Hotel in Hythe was our last evening with Amy, who departed for home the next morning. We missed her infectious laugh and her merry and informed commentary from the back seat. She was spared our next stop.

Lewis's Bookshop in Folkestone had some military, but—like a blessing or a curse —they had more at home. The house was a mess, overflowing with books, good and cheap but an ordeal. Book accumulation on this scale is a disease, even for a dealer. I sat on the stairs going through stacks of books piled on every step, finding among other things a little Indian Mutiny treasure for Philip. It was physical as well as intellectual work to spend over £400, but we got a lot for it. We had great expectations of nearby G. Marrin Books, which listed World War I as a specialty, but it was disappointing and a bit uncongenial. Somehow we found the energy to go on to Hastings, where we got snarled up looking for Bohemia Books, which was listed as an aviation specialist but had ceased to exist, and a hard time finding the fabled Howes Bookshop, ensconced in a Victorian schoolhouse. Howes was a tonic after the chaos of Lewis's, wonderful, a perfect setting, perfectly organized books in excellent condition, easy to work in. The somewhat schoolmasterish proprietor, after we spent almost two hours and how many pounds, kindly led us to our hotel; we must have complained a lot about getting lost in Hastings. The Beauport Park Hotel was set in pretty gardens; Amy and John's planning was right on, tranquility after another intense day.

In the morning, Battle was a must. About six miles inland from Hastings, it was the battlefield in 1066, and the town grew up around the huge, long-ruined Abbey built by William the Conqueror, which overlooked the field. We went on to Tunbridge Wells, which had the combined virtues of Hall's Bookshop and tea with another Strickland aunt, Richard's mother. And thence to Brighton to see the Stricklands again, this time staying in the mid-Victorian splendor of the Grand Hotel. It was a wedding cake of frosted white, layered with cast-iron balconies, and the interior had the old grandeur, with magnificent marble and a crystal-chandeliered lobby and a particularly handsome cast-iron staircase.

A month later the Conservative Party convened in Brighton, and an IRA bomb targeting Margaret Thatcher and other leaders exploded in the center of the Grand Hotel. The staircase survived the blast, and Mrs. Thatcher made her way down it to escape the disaster. Perhaps six months after that, a very discreet NYPD officer in plain clothes paid us a visit in the store. At the request of Scotland Yard and Interpol, they were interviewing anyone who had stayed at the Grand in the months previous to the bombing, to inquire if the guests had noticed anything "out of the ordinary."

Jilly Strickland's work took her near Lewes, so we went along in convoy on Monday and she had a look-in at the bookshops as we got started. The little old town had two shops as picturesque as their names, Bow Window Books and the Fifteenth Century Bookshop, with charm to spare but only a couple of books for us. We were more successful at the more prosaically named, tiny, but equally attractive A. J. Cumming: we bought a whole shelf. We were not far from the castle, high on a hill, with views of the town toward the coast. On to Guildford, to the venerable Thomas Thorp Bookshop, in the High Street, our first visit there but not the last. More significant was the establishment of Charles Traylen, down the hill and around the corner in the handsome Castle House. We must have bought a lot because Mr. Traylen took us to the Jolly Farmer pub before we went on to London. Dutch courage to face the perils of traversing Hyde Park Corner.

As usual I spent the first morning in London making appointments while Harris went to the bank to check on the transfer. For some reason it had taken us a few years to get around to Victor Sutcliffe, in Tooting Bec, south of the Thames. Harris had been studying his extremely scholarly lists, brought in by a customer, for years. When Harris returned, I said, "I talked to Victor Sutcliffe, and we're going there this afternoon. He sounds really nice, and young." Harris said flatly, "He can't be young." Victor's listings were so knowledgeable that Harris was positive he was quite a bit older. Victor was in fact young, or at least younger than we were; he had more time to read than we did I guess, and had been at it longer. Tall, curly-haired, humorous, with a pipe and a studious air, Victor was always a pleasure, in person or by letter. This was the first of many delightful visits in Tooting Bec. Victor would open a bottle of wine, and we would talk books as we read the shelves. He had refined his military focus to pre-1914, and his inventory was small but choice, with many scarce and rare titles. After a year or two we met his delightful wife Anne-Marie, and their children, and then it was a social call as well as business every year. There was a period when young daughter Theodora took phone orders in Victor's absence.

Victor drove us part way back and we walked over Westminster Bridge, through the parks, and back to the hotel in Mayfair. That evening we had an important rendezvous at Simpson's-in-the-Strand: Keene and Nancy Taylor, giddy with excitement and jet lag, on their first visit to London together.

We finally made it to the History Bookshop and it was pretty good, though not cordial. Some dealers greeted us as colleagues, others perhaps as competitors. In Charing Cross Road that afternoon, we visited the relocated and reconstituted Francis Edwards and some smaller shops but didn't find much. Up the Northern Line to Hampstead, for a full and successful day with Peter de Lotz, with a lunch break with Lionel and a foray to his Ken Trotman Books, where we ran up a £900 tab in less than an hour, then returning to Peter's for our grand finale. Peter always interviewed us about where we had been and volunteered to pick up the books we had accumulated around London and deliver them to the shipper with his own lot. Victor fenced with him, offering to deliver our purchases to Peter. This was a game; as Victor said, "He wants to see where you have been, he never would let *me* into *his* house!"

Harris met Mary and Giacchino's representative to turn over Sotheby's check for the silver, with a sense of accomplishment and relief, a load off our minds. The next day was a Saturday, a real day off. We bought nothing but a crock of Stilton cheese, and spent the day with the Taylors, mostly at the Victoria and Albert Museum; we were with them having a drink at the King's Arms in Shepherd Market when the news came that Prince Harry had been born: instant celebration.

On Sunday we flew to Paris. I was very dubious about the Left Bank hotel Harris had booked; it wasn't listed in any guidebook. Harris said he expected to be there about ten minutes and wouldn't take the luggage out of the cab until I approved it, but it turned out to be charming, newly redone and very French, and close to our bookshops. We went to the Jardin de Luxembourg and watched children encountering a hilarious talking robot. The next day, we first visited a new militaria purveyor, and carried a Napoleonic sword to the bookstores: more eloquent than a business card to announce our interests. We didn't work so hard in our week in Paris, but we managed to spend a ton of money. There had recently been a major book auction there, which included a great number of uniform pictorials, and apparently Petitot and Clavreuil had split it up between them. We bought so much at Petitot that the Petitot daughters took us to lunch. And then we bought a lot from the same auction at Clavreuil—big decisions, I noted in my

Harris and new sword, rue Saint-André-des-Arts, Paris.

diary. As usual, we stopped in some lesser but pleasant shops like Librairie Jules Verne and Les Arcades, and we went to a couple of toy stores to look for lead warships for Ran (and Randy).

On the last morning, I bought a baguette and croissants to take to Ute and Peter, along with the Stilton, which had been cooling on our hotel windowsill. Our week with them in Germany was vacation, with a trial run at a big Stuttgart bookshop, Müller und Gräff; we found a few cigarette-card albums, always good.

When we returned to New York, we seemed to be increasingly occupied with personnel problems instead of books. The ever-fluid shipping department required a lot of supervision. Beginning that fall, Caldwell Luther Dowling, a big, easy-going, street-wise kid, sometime musician, floor-waxer and junior entrepreneur, manned the packing table for a number of months. Luther cast an interested eye on the "silver vehicle" footlocker, and we gave it to him for his music equipment. After about six months Luther thought he'd try the Coast Guard, but didn't like it enough to continue: too cold on the Great Lakes. He returned from time to time from his various ventures to fill in his and our schedule; he and Brian were there together during a particularly busy Christmas season, one big black kid and one big white kid photographed with stacks of UPS packages which were also over six feet tall.

Luther was succeeded by Desmond Brown, a nice young man who lasted about seven months, and was on hand to pack our biggest single sale to date. It was still a part-time job, and it was understandable that these guys would go on to better opportunities. But the turnover was exhausting.

In the meantime, we had begun looking for a computer programmer to revamp the Jesse computer and eventually to create a system encompassing customers and books. After about two years with the Jesse system, we were dissatisfied and wanted to improve it. It was a great asset but we had worked with it enough to know it could be much better. We made inquiries and were interviewing programmers—then not so easy to find, or affordable. It was very early in the game for small business applications. Every now and then, we saw some forgettable, or maybe just very expensive, person, often geeks who seemed to enjoy being obscure. We were getting nowhere.

On another front, someone connected me with Terry McNally, a cute, smart, very professional young woman who was supplementing her variable income as a singer in the chorus of City Opera with free-lance proofreading. I still had to read and edit the catalogue cards, but when the galleys came back from Gene the typesetter, Terry took over.

Stuart Elenko knew what galleys were (even if he couldn't spell it): a preview. In between visits, we heard from him: *Hi. I miss the action of being there. Hope everything going well for you. As usual – we are one step ahead of the sheriff. I will be coming by – or calling you... When's the next catalogue & can I see the gallies!! Please!*

The volume of other paper work was such that even with two full-time people, I wanted other part-time help if we could find it. Before I could put out the word to our network, serendipity kicked in.

The retired librarian looked at first sight ideal. Michael told us she had stopped in in our absence; she lived right over the hill on 93rd Street, and was interested in some part-time work. We needed to correct the disarray created in the card files by John, and after that we wanted some help on cataloguing. I phoned and arranged for her to come in the next week, in the afternoons. The day she started, I was down on West 23rd Street buying a used IBM typewriter; we planned to set up a work space for a cataloguer upstairs in the former poster gallery. When I returned, there she was in the front of the store, properly dressed for business in a gray knit suit and clearly loving being there. I introduced myself and sat down at the computer to see what orders had been processed, chatting away to her. She was reading the card files on the red cart under the ceiling light, almost at my elbow. A few minutes later, I saw from the corner of my eye that suddenly she was throwing file boxes on the floor—in fact she was having a *grand mal* seizure. There was no mistaking it even though none of us had ever seen it. The excitement must have been too much for her. Michael was hysterical, dithering around—John was at a loss—Harris hovered. I found myself putting a ballpoint pen between her teeth (as one has heard is appropriate) and telling someone to call 911. Meantime thinking "what the heck next???!!!"

First the police came, then the medics, who took her to the hospital. They told us that such an episode was harder to witness than to experience and that she wouldn't remember anything. We were all wiped out, but she was not so affected. Nevertheless, we (I) had to tell her she couldn't come back.

I tried again. The previous summer, hoping to learn more about describing the rare books that came our way, I had signed up for a one-week, intensive course at Columbia University Library School's rare book program. I felt an affinity with Claire Boos, a "classmate" from the publishing world, and we kept in touch; and it occurred to me she might know some editorial type looking for part-time work. Claire produced Chris Busa, another writer-to-be, a good-looking guy in town for an indeterminate time from Cape Cod. Chris was with us for six months or so, and helped out in myriad ways as needed: packing, cataloguing new books, pulling cards. The military literature was a revelation to him; he read Clausewitz, among others, and later spoke of his stint as "like a year in graduate school."

On a December Sunday, Sheila and I went upstate to Duchess County where she had discovered someone who made spruce Christmas garland, very bushy and fresh— perfect for our Victorian house. She had ordered yards of it for her office and our stairway, and then she and I went off in a borrowed station wagon on a clear, crisp, cold day, the snow blue-shadowed in the standing reeds. We loaded up garland, well-scrutinized Christmas trees, some presents and even a few books found at an unpretentious antiques mall, and as the wintry dusk was falling and the sun setting through the mysterious snowy woods, we wound our way to the Rodgers Book Barn in Hillsdale. Cider simmering on the cast-iron pot-bellied stove scented the air, and it was warm, cozy and conducive to reading, and buying. I put together a boxful before their closing, when we headed home to Harris who was happily watching football. He had to interrupt the Giants game to help me wrestle with tree and garland.

John was hard working, but not necessarily doing what we wanted him to do. He seemed to spend a lot of time in the basement, and engaged with customers sort of selectively; he was resistant to some of the ways we did business. It was a bit wearing, but perhaps not enough to let him go. After a couple of years he was a dubious asset. When he was going to Chicago to visit his family that Christmas, I began to fantasize, only to Harris and maybe Sheila, that he would feel like being closer to them, and wander into Dan Weinberg's Abraham Lincoln Book Shop and exercise his time-honored line with the same success he had with us.

Caramba! He did and he had! Then it was The Long Goodbye, interminable: we started interviewing for his replacement in January and John did not leave until late February.

When John told us he was leaving, we talked to Chris about joining us full-time, but were not surprised that he had defined a different direction for himself. After returning to Provincetown some months later, he kept in touch, that fall sending us cranberries he had picked in the Cape Cod bogs, wrapped in a cranberry-stained letter meditating on "military red, blood red, the color of the cover of your book catalogue."

We decided to venture into advertising John's full-time position. Our hiring had been serendipitous and catch-as-catch-can up until then. We listed the job in the *New York Times's* large Help Wanted section, and got plenty of response. Almost too much, we didn't yet know how to control or filter it; once I found myself talking to a legally blind job applicant who tried to convince me that her disability did not disqualify her.

Ultimately, the most appropriate candidate, because of his lengthy bookstore resume, was Jason Duberman. A large, lumbering man with a skimpy mustache, given to tired, plaid shirts and greasy stuff on his hair, he seemed good-natured and realistic. Jason lived alone, or rather with a cat that terrorized him and attacked his treasured H. L. Mencken books; he seemed powerless to do anything but complain about the cat. Jason's bookstore experience included his own shop, which had failed, so he was accustomed to retail if not business. He was a bookman, not an aspiring anything-else. However, there was a very long and trying learning curve.

Harris had talked among others to Melvin Kushel, our accountant, about wanting a computer upgrade and also an entirely new computer system and needing a programmer. Eventually Melvin had a name for us. When we met Dave Liebman, I think we instinctively felt we would be in good hands. Dave was definitely not a geek, and communicated well with earthlings. He was easy-going, likable, and cute, with curly hair and an irresistible chuckle—and always interested, curious, when confronted with a new situation or a problem to solve (not that it was ever a problem for him). He had the gift of listening well, and observing the business happening around him. I think we became his hobby; he certainly wasn't making money on us: hours and hours after work and on Saturday afternoons. I believe he liked the challenge of creating this then-new small business system, with its complicated requirements.

Dave was as generous and giving as the first group, Computer Era, had been tight and negative. First Dave improved Jesse, to tide us over; this also allowed him to see and understand a lot of what we needed in the customer files. The Jesse remake, which took some months, also allowed us to get to know each other.

That spring Chris left us and New York, and somehow, maybe thanks to Claire, we quickly found another part-timer. Lewis had a publishing background, which I always felt comfortable with, and which sometimes proved better than a bookstore background: bookish, but nothing to unlearn. And publishing experience was naturally helpful for catalogue preparation. Lewis was preppy, nice-looking, had a good sense of humor, knew history and was interested in the subject matter. He was willing to work, and fell in with our systems readily.

When we had visited Paris the previous fall, our timing was good because of the recent auction of outstanding uniform books, almost all French and nineteenth century. The most spectacular, at Clavreuil, was the rare and monumental Alfred de Marbot, *Costumes Militaires Francais* in three beefy, red morocco volumes. The mid-nineteenth-century set, when complete, was comprised of four hundred and fifty hand-colored plates on the period from 1439 through 1815. We had had some of the individual plates and they were very fine and of a size worth framing; that and the fact that they had been issued over eight or ten years made a complete set a rarity.

We must have been feeling our oats. The set was very dear, but I said to Harris—or he said to me—"It would be nice to have this once." It was indeed nice, but a bit sobering when we and it got to 93rd Street and we considered how hard it might be for us to sell a $7500 set. It was a big leap for us.

None of our local uniform aficionados fell for the Marbot, although the other French acquisitions, still expensive, but less so, were selling well in the store. We listed it in the Spring 1985 catalogue with other splendid uniform offerings, the fruits of our fall travels. Our fingers were crossed, but the lot was doing well. With remarkable speed, we heard from the Acquisitions Librarian at the Australian Defence Force Academy, in Canberra. She sent a huge order for most of the big-ticket uniform titles, including, oh joy, the Marbot. We were ecstatic, and confirmed by return mail that we had reserved them.

Some time later, we received a very revised purchase order, significantly reduced, from a different librarian. It did, happily, still include the Marbot set. I fantasized that the over-excited first librarian had been led away and was lying down in a darkened room, under restraint.

Purchase order in hand, our next challenge was the shipping. It would have been scary to entrust such an important and precious piece, going so far, to the post office, even if it had been possible to insure it properly. There was no international UPS or FedEx at that time. Other dealers who routinely shipped such pricey items carried separate insurance policies to cover such shipping, but this sale was an anomaly for us. We were all puzzling this when Harris had the inspired idea of calling the Australian military attaché at their embassy in Washington, ostensibly for suggestions but probably hoping for more. The attaché, a colonel, was more than gracious, he was enthusiastic and accommodating. "Just send it along here to my attention and I'll put it in the pouch." While the pouch was probably more like a container, one still envisioned a big brown leather sack or a duffle bag. Whatever it looked like, the books went along to Washington by UPS, then safely and quickly to Canberra, the colonel's alma mater.

CHAPTER TWELVE

"Who the boss?"

1985

Harris and Lewis at the dead files closet.

The customer variety was vast. There was a professor in Oman. There was a prison guard who came in on Saturdays from Staten Island. A man who had been a pilot in the Berlin Airlift found us. Referred by the Marine Corps Headquarters, a couple at a plantation in Buka, Papua New Guinea, wrote for the Marine Corps Monograph on the savage Bougainville campaign, which had taken place in their "neighborhood." How exotic, to be sending the book to Bougainville.

Nancy Graham had been a flight instructor during World War II and was one of the first female helicopter pilots. She became a regular customer, for aviation books, naturally, but "Whirlygirl" had to be tracked from her perches in Florida in the winter, to Vermont in the summer, with interludes in Charlottesville, Virginia. She often stopped in New York on her seasonal migrations, and like the birds which targeted Central Park a block away, she found us. In between she had long phone calls with Harris. In Vermont, she was friendly with a nice, tweedy, older gentleman, William Pagenstecher, and they found they had us in common. He was from St. Louis, and a collector of fine, early Americana books. On his way to to his summer sojourn in Vermont, it was his habit to stop in New York.

We did business with some very specialized libraries. The huge Mormon library of genealogy in Salt Lake City—"the Mountain of Names"—bought obscure, family-history related items; many of the small Revolutionary War local histories published privately or by historical societies were their meat. The Society of the Cincinnati, in Washington, was an organization devoted to the

American Revolution, with a fine library that included papers of its founding veterans. The Hoover Institution on War, Revolution and Peace, a right-wing think tank at Stanford University, had been on Ray's list and continued to buy from us. Some Army and Navy libraries ordered, but we often had great difficulty getting paid in a timely way. We did a good bit of business with two libraries at Fort Bragg, those of the 82nd Airborne and the Special Warfare School, but not without problems. On one occasion, six weeks after reserving two books totaling $25.00, they called to say the library couldn't afford them; a few months later they executed an order for over $600.00. The U.S. Cavalry Museum at Fort Riley, Kansas, was for some years a good and relatively easy customer.

Norwich University, a military college in Vermont, spent very little, but once called to buy a very impressive antiquarian book as a gift. The library at Angelo State University, in Texas, was a regular, good customer for twenty years, remarkable for being hassle-free for us.

We got a kick whenever we received an order from the Library of Congress or the New York Public Library, both of which we perceived as having everything. The Army's major repository, the U.S. Military History Institute, was at Carlisle Barracks, Pennsylvania. We had paid a call on them after a few years in business, when we were visiting friends in the vicinity, and were overwhelmed by the collection. We never imagined being able to provide them with anything, as they seemed to have it all. But we did. We mailed catalogues to the American Battle Monuments Commission at Flanders Field and the Meuse-Argonne cemeteries, and each gave us many referrals. Their main office and library in Washington, which did buy, was impeccable to deal with: responsive, quick, with not much paperwork and fast payment. The Imperial War Museum was a steady customer, sending small orders on blue air-letter sheets, but they added up; we were to address catalogues to the "Keeper of Printed Books."

Libraries often were tough; one had the impression of bland functionaries who didn't care about either the books or the merchant's real-life needs. Even later when the government libraries got credit cards, there were still the flakey and inconsiderate purchasing agents to deal with.

Often the level and quality of business we did with a given library depended on the acquisitions librarian—like a good cook making a restaurant. Gordon Chappell, a National Park Service librarian, bought for himself and for several of the libraries in California; that compounded the difficulties of getting paid, but he was a good customer. We had a great relationship with the Naval War College library after Bob Schnare arrived, and with the National Defense University Library at Fort McNair in Washington when Susan Lemke took over. Susan was a consistent and enthusiastic buyer for twenty years. She bought beautiful books and took such delight in them that they might have been for herself. At the University of Kansas, Richard Ring was a regular buyer of World War I books, especially unit histories. Emory University had some special collections and interests that we could serve, and it was easy to do business with Emory after our friend Sandra Still became an acquisitions librarian there. Sandra was about the only librarian for whom we filed wants, because we knew she would respond. The University of Texas at El Paso was good from the beginning but only got better when Tom Burdett, already a private customer, became the curator at the S. L. A. Marshall Collection. These personal connections, with the understanding and appreciation of the other's requirements, made for productive and enjoyable relationships.

Susan Lemke was a particular delight to deal with. She loved the books, and especially enjoyed dealing with Harris. Once or twice she visited the store, so we had a "visual" and so did she—always good. She bought when she had the money, and on one occasion she had a nice chunk she hadn't expected, a sum she had to spend before the end of the fiscal year. She called Harris for suggestions, and he happily sold her a splendid antiquarian book. Susan told us she was so excited about it that she ran it all over the library to show it off.

Some odd organizations were heard from: the U.S. Pike and Shot Association, the Council for Abandoned Military Posts (acronym CAMP), the Fortress Studies Group, the International Hoplology Society, the Aircraft Carrier Study Group, the Lighter-than-Air Society.

I collected some curious business cards in my desk drawer: Aviation Nose Art Researcher, Stevedoring Consultant, Custom Painted Pilot Helmets, Military Exotica, City Liquidators. The two-sided Japanese and Chinese cards were my favorites. Philip Kamil had a camel logo. It was tempting to think that "Ernst & Whinney" were lawyers, but they were accountants, which also works.

Businesses came to us for a variety of reasons. Occasionally they wanted corporate gifts for their executives, the usual being a nice leather set or a signed copy of a general's memoir. Management seminars wanted titles on group leadership, strategy, tactics. A crony of Bill Blass came in looking for a gift for him and returned to buy a fine illustrated book on French military bands, for a uniform-inspired line. Pantone, a company that produced color studies and guides, was interested in uniform books for different reasons. Simulations Publications, designers of war games, when those were history-based board games, had obvious needs. We were an occasional resource for the theatrical costume company, Brooks-Van Horn.

Law firms had clients who were plaintiffs in asbestos cases, whose condition stemmed from their naval service. The lawyers needed *Jane's Fighting Ships,* a massive annual compendium giving the rundown on every warship in service: plans, sections, elevations, presumably showing where the asbestos might lurk.

An F.B.I. or D.E.A. agent, always undercover in one guise or another, was often out of town on assignment and impossible to reach when one of his wants arrived. He artfully altered his appearance from one job to the next, with subtle changes that produced real deceptions, so that each time he visited there was mild confusion. Harris usually recognized him; I did not know him as well, so was never quite sure.

Mr. Stanley Soika came in from Queens several times a year, and collected small uniform pieces, illustrated handouts of uniforms, insignia, and decorations. Mr. Soika was very shy, with a sweet smile; he never talked, and always brought his own manila envelope for his purchases, which I teased him about. We had not at first paid much attention to these little easy-to-overlook folders and pamphlets, not even cataloguing them but pricing them cheaply and putting them together in a shelf box in the uniform section. It may be that Mr. Soika's interest made us more alive to the value of this ephemeral material.

Rear Adm. William Cockell was a good mail-order customer for British naval classics, when he was not at sea. When we were in Malta in September 1983, we read with great interest in the local paper about his leading the search for the "black box" from the Korean Airlines flight 007, shot down by the Soviets after it wandered into their airspace. It goes without saying that we sent him the clippings from the *Times of Malta*.

We saw foreign businessmen and tourists, the occasional celebrity, and many business travelers who paused on their way to or from LaGuardia Airport. Chris took an order from Richard Nixon's office. A Colonel with the Russian U.N. delegation stopped in. A Brazilian diplomat was a regular for a few years. Chinese and Indian military representatives, our own United Nations. An Australian general, a big, bluff man, came in often while he was posted in Washington, and we continued to hear from him —less often —after he went home.

Rupert Allason, sometime British M.P. and a prolific and well-informed writer on British intelligence under the nom-de-plume Nigel West, was a regular, coming in whenever he passed through New York en route to Bermuda or London. He bought everything on his subject that he didn't have, the ideal customer. When former MI-5 agent Peter Wright published a memoir, *Spycatcher*, it was for a time banned or "unavailable" in England. Rupert called from London and asked us to mail him one posthaste. We bought it at Doubleday's in midtown, but Harris left it in the cab coming home; the Corner Bookstore had to order it for us.

Michael got a kick out of selling the key biography of Sidney Reilly, by Robin Bruce Lockhart, to the writer who developed the TV series, *Reilly, Ace of Spies*.

Government historians such as Richard Kohn and Sheldon Goldberg for the Air Force and Eliot Cohen at the Naval War College were collectors, although most academics seemed to rely on their institutions' libraries. William Gardner Bell, a retired Army historian, heard about us from Forrest Pogue and sold us his own books. We continued to get referrals from Steve Ambrose, and after we had met John Eisenhower in London on the D-Day tour, he started buying when he was working on his Mexican War book and others. Jim Bloom found us in 1978. He was a tax consultant, but was beginning to follow his military history interest and write about it, and became one of those with whom Harris had lengthy conversations; Jim especially liked, as I did, the little British *Special Campaigns* and similar series that we found in England.

Actor Ed Herrmann bought some posters. Dave Hill, manager of the "Pretenders," was buying a lot of aviation books. Paul Newman's office called for a book on Stillwell; I toyed with the idea of delivering it myself. Joel Grey stopped in for a look.

Glen Patterson, a local regular, was a Patton devotee. All Patton books and only Patton books. Well before he had enough, we learned that he was an arborist, working in the city. A couple of years earlier, Lenny and Ray at the Corner Bookstore had run a campaign to raise money for street trees, Callery pears, on our blocks of 93rd Street. We had contributed, but the planting scheme had not included a tree in front of our house, because the sidewalk was narrower there. One November day, when our neighbor Felix, our "local prince," and I were watching the migratory birds dive in for the berries on the Boston ivy that glorified our houses with fall color, he and I became friendly. We conspired to share in putting in our own tree on the sidewalk in front of our houses. One might think that such a contribution would be welcomed by the City, but it was hedged with bureaucratic hurdles: we needed a permit, and a New York City forester (I didn't even know there was such a person) had to approve it. The forester was hard to get because he was out of the office looking at trees most of the time. When he was finally reached, he took a tolerant attitude about the sidewalk width and we got our permit. Then there were only certain acceptable trees and planting methods. Glen was able to enlighten us on the process, and when we got the permit and redid the sidewalk, he got the skinny little tree and planted it.

In the spring my parents visited, and my mother could not resist a new little antiques shop right across the street. She came back excited at finding a piece for us for our dining room, so I went back with them. But what I focused on was a smallish, dark oak, partners' desk, not terribly expensive. The size was perfect for the store, where the increase in staff had led to Harris's working across from me, scrunched up on the wrong side of the front desk. My discovery led to a fracas between the proprietors about the desk's cost, but resulted in the addition of a good work space for Harris, who would have been willing to continue to labor in discomfort against the flat side of the old desk.

Herb Weitz had seemed energized by our beginners' enthusiasm and drive. This lapsed after a while, and in the early eighties, he turned to the production of fine bindings, finding by luck a large lot of old, finely cut tools used for gilt-stamping, establishing the workshop in his basement, and doing the sales pitch upstairs. Herb did the talking and others did the work. They turned out handsome books, from classic bindings to those with "frills," such as inlay of various sorts or pictorial leather. Herb became the binder to the stars.

For Harris's fiftieth birthday, I had Herb bind a loose set of rare and beautiful French uniform plates and text by Horace Vernet and Eugene Lami, *Collection des Uniformes des Armées Francaises, 1791 à 1824*. Harris had bought the plates and text, with his father's help, when he was a teenager, both of them fibbing to his mother about the price. The binding job was complex, two volumes, the text to be interleaved with the plates, and the three of us sat with our heads together over it to collate it. The dark red leather was the same on each volume, but the tooling differed, on one volume Napoleonic iconography, the famous bees, on the second, the fleur-de-lis of the Restoration. Herb's creations were very expensive, and we couldn't do much business with him aside from giving him the occasional referral. He was still selling some books, and bidding at auction for a few special customers. One of them was big spender and loud talker Wink Jaffee. Wink, a former New Yorker and commodities trader, had made his fortune and moved to a ranch near Aspen, Colorado. Herb was willing to share the wealth in this case, and Wink began ordering some fine pictorials and rare books on Roman history from us. Jaffee certainly wasn't easy to deal with, very abrupt and high-handed, and on one occasion did not come through on a $5000 reservation. A big black mark in his record.

At the other end of the spectrum in collecting, Carl Harm, a large rough man, had a wholesale business as a supplier of street vendors: glasses one week, scarves the next, perhaps whatever fell off the proverbial truck. A strictly cash business. He came in with wads of cash from his vendors, and always bought bags of the cheap World War II books, quantity not quality. Harris could never convince him to upgrade to the really good titles; Carl was, after all, attuned to quantity, not quality. He spent thousands of dollars with us in just a few years, and I had visions of vast rivers of cash flowing through the underground economy. Then it transpired that Carl wanted to sell all the books back, obviously using us as his laundry. We declined; his accumulation was not desirable because it was all common books, the kind we always had in plenty.

With my background as a picture editor, I usually handled the uniform-plate books, although Harris was very knowledgeable and enthusiastic about them too, having collected them since his teens. Nevertheless, I was loath to answer a summons to see a significant collection in Scarsdale one summer Saturday, but the unpleasant, indeed arrogant, owner would have it no other way. The collection was tantalizing, magnificent, huge, and it was clearly out of our league. We couldn't afford it; we couldn't digest it. Conceivably we could have bought it in installments, but that was not an option. The man was selling the books to finance his new passion for antique musical instruments, of which a number were on display. He had called me in just to admire; he certainly already knew, as I told him, that the books should go to auction. I sent Jason and Harris to look at the books some months later, at the viewing before the sale at Phillips, just for "education." The consignor's expectations were grossly inflated, and it gave me a certain perverse satisfaction to see many lots not meet his reserve and go unsold.

I was in the dead-files closet as Harris bustled back with an elegant, red-haired woman, whom I saw in my peripheral vision. Hot on their heels, Lewis went by, mouthing to me and pointing, "Arlene Dahl." The titian-haired movie star still looked like a star, still lovely, and flawlessly turned out in a chic, *café au lait*-colored suit. She was looking for books on the Danish Resistance in World War II and Harris was happy to find her several. He was just intent on helping the customer find what was wanted—he needed to be told after she left who she was, and then it registered.

Harris enjoyed dealing with unusual requests. He led a man wanting flag illustrations all through the store, patiently extracting books from across the spectrum of periods and subjects, putting together a shopping bag full for the happy buyer. As the man was reaching for the doorknob, Harris said, as if it had just occurred to him, "Wait!" He pulled from the oversize shelf a rare (and expensive) Civil War book on Union Army flags and standards. The customer had to have it.

Telephone customers provided equal variety and interest. There was a veterinarian who called from his office, with animal noises in the background; an Aussie on a sheep station in Boolcoomatta, interested in World War I aviation and starved for books. Neil Howell, who worked at NASA in Houston, knew his own customer number, bestowed by the computer (a feature which made filing wants much simpler for us). It was fun to work with Neil, who bought a lot by telephone in conversation with Harris. Once Harris was checking in books when he called, and mentioned an incoming book he thought Neil would want, but said suspensefully, "Oh, there's a want on it . . . Number 695." Neil, excited: "That's me, that's me!!!"—as thrilled as if he had won the lottery.

The Jordanian military attaché in Washington had a name to conjure with: Timoor Daghistani. What a charming and attractive man, and from the start a good, serious customer. Having had a British military education, he was particularly interested in British military history. He bought a lot in the store and from catalogues, but he responded very irregularly when we quoted to his esoteric wants list. This was frustrating, to have an unusual book for someone who wanted it but was too busy to answer, and at the same time keeping it from someone else who might snap it up. I sent him, I guess, a few chastising notes. On a subsequent visit with his pretty wife, he brought a box of Godiva chocolates to apologize. What a diplomat.

It was interesting to read the customers' questionnaires when they subscribed. One man listed his occupation as "grasscutter." Was it a summer afternoon and he was feeling oppressed because his lawn was too big? Was he retired and feeling that that was all he was doing? Or was it really his business?

Another listed herself on the questionnaire as "book junkie." Mary Elizabeth Braun was, instead, our Helene Hanff. She found us in a small mention in the *New York Times* travel section, about the time a friend had noticed her *new obsession with World War II*. A favorite correspondent who bought by the box, she was an omnivorous reader who worked through all the books she bought and shared her thoughts about them with us. Her collecting was not limited to World War II, although she appeared to be of that generation. By the time we had arrived at a reasonable price for Wellington's Funeral she was ready to buy that. We were blown away that this customer who had been with us for only a year sprang for such an expensive and significant piece, without seeing it. She wrote to us after it arrived, *It knocked me over.*

When we got beyond "Mr. and Mrs." we were "Dear Friends" or "H. C. and M. C." and she was "Your faithful client, M. E. B." Harris sort of monopolized her the way Frank Doel did Helene. It was hard to say whether they had long chats interspersed with lengthy orders or vice versa. We all loved her letters, from her home in Beverly Hills and elsewhere. Her extensive travels included World War II tours to Europe and the Far East. She wrote to us even on the road, and gave us her reactions to not only the books but the battlefields and numerous other places she went. She wrote from Bruges after visiting Arnhem, "the bridge too far." A postcard came from the bridge on the River Kwai. We were in her mind in these special places, I think, because she knew we understood the import of what she was seeing. But alas, she never came to New York, although she always vowed to—just like Helene Hanff.

The eighties was the time of the Japanese boom, and there were many Japanese businessmen in New York, with a noticeable number coming in to the bookstore. They were always very courteous, and one found oneself returning the little bows in spite of oneself. (We had always had mail-order Japanese customers, and it still seems curious that some would address the "Militaly," others the "Miritary" Bookman. Is it a northern or southern accent?) One young man took an interest in some of the handsome woodblock triptych prints of the Russo-Japanese War, which he may have been familiar with at home. Their production was a minor industry at the time of the Sino-Japanese and Russo-Japanese wars. Artists created thousands of such images ranging in quality from crude to sophisticated. I tried always to have a few in stock because I liked them and there was interest. We often did not know the precise subjects, so on one particularly specific image, I asked the young man if he could translate the caption for me. It turned out to be inscrutable to him as well, as the writing was an antique form, much I guess like gothic German. Trying to relate, I heard myself saying how much I liked the "woodbrocks" and enjoyed dealing with them, while slightly bowing. He took no notice of my gaffe, probably sounded okay to him.

Another Japanese customer on his first visit was so serious, even grim, that it was hard to approach him. We realized later that his English was scanty. He was a little fellow, so short that I did not want to stand up. (I am five feet eleven inches in bare feet.) He made his determined way around the store and was in the back for hours until the end of the day, when everyone else had left. Harris and I were sitting at the desks up front when he emerged and asked Harris about the possibility of a discount. Harris said, "I don't know, you'll have to ask the boss." "Who the boss?" he said. "She is," nodding to me. The little man swiveled his head to me, then back to Harris, "You kidding?!" No, Harris shook his head. Back to me. I just nodded. We all laughed.

The next day he returned, much more at ease and having a good time. I felt I could ask him about a curious Japanese print on the wall. It was a series of panel views framing a mountainous landscape, all with soldiers and horsemen. He conveyed to me in very rudimentary English that it was a game, combining two folk tales or legends, one about a soldier-prince on a quest. The game was played by progressing around the board in movements governed by a throw of the dice or some counter (much like Monopoly); he said that if one player caught up with another in the same square "it's kiss my ass." I can imagine the look on my face. Who taught him the little English he knew?

Who The Boss, indeed?

It was hard for many male customers, or even female, to grasp that I was It. I had followed my husband into a male-dominated business, the out-of-print book trade, specializing in a subject with a ninety-five percent male clientele of a largely right-wing, reactionary, old-fashioned mentality. There were a couple of local naval historians who were insufferable, so macho and full of themselves—but perhaps they were obnoxious to the rest of the staff as well.

Regular customers were usually not a problem, once they got used to the idea, but some men did not even register the sound of a woman's voice. "Sir, I'm talking to you," I said to one. It was beyond the imagination of some that I could be the boss. I worked with a telephone customer who ordered several books, and in his letter he was full of compliments: *Again, it was a pleasure dealing with a person with exceptional customer consideration and a clear-cut professional approach. I am sure your supervision [sic] must be very pleased with your work.* He signed himself as "Director, Quality Control" for an aerospace company. I had occasion to respond and signed myself as "President."

It is possible to be oversensitive. People would call and say, "I want to talk to someone about ----." I would say, "I'm someone, talk to me."

I could not help but notice that many customers would say, "Harris had such and such a book" as if Harris had done all the buying and evaluating. There was a perception among some that I was just the manager, and I *was* the manager, but I bought at least as many books as Harris. There was not a doubt that Harris had command of the inventory, with all the books in his head, to an astonishing degree from our many sources.

Harris never made me feel less than a full partner, and when we had incorporated, I had become the President. It made sense in a number of ways, aside from the tax advantage. Harris was the partner with the business background, but I was a willing learner, and it was as if, after he off-loaded on me a lot of business principles and practices, he blanked out on that aspect, aside from the accounting. It freed him to develop his extraordinary knowledge of the books and to be the amazing salesman he was. I did run the business and he respected what I did. When he said I was the boss, he meant it, but I believe it also amused him to surprise, test, and provoke people with it. And it was a good out for him at times. Harris and I had plenty of differences of opinion, freely aired before staff, and sometimes customers.

A later associate, Emily, occasionally referred to me as "she who must be obeyed." Other employees, mostly male, were attuned—well, if they weren't they didn't get hired. We did interview applicants who obviously didn't get it that a woman was the boss, and a couple of them slipped through the cracks. Gay men seemed to be more comfortable with a female boss. It is curious and amusing to think that our staff, in such a macho business, was, over time, largely gay, indeterminate, or female.

Soon after Jason came along, Michael was beginning to deteriorate; his alcoholism was catching up with him and he became more irresponsible and erratic. (Around then he had lost his apartment and had no place to keep his two huge cats named for Church Fathers, Augustine and Aquinas.) In early August he disappeared for about a week. Harris found him and pulled him out of one of his haunts, a gay bar on Third Avenue, and brought him home to stay with us for a week. We valued Michael and were very fond of him and tried to salvage him, not only because we had a business trip to England planned that we didn't want to cancel. He seemed to pull himself together, and we went off to London with our fingers crossed.

We were flying out on a Saturday night at nine, and Harris had me biting my nails: he invited the store crew and our neighbor Felix, and Sheila, who was house-sitting for us, for after-work cocktails, and sat there shining his shoes, barely having started to pack. Amazingly, we caught the plane, and in the early morning met Amy at the Heathrow car rental. We had chosen to campaign in the West Country that fall. We logged 1400 miles and thirty-nine shops, a wonderful mix of books and sights, in remarkably good weather. We had a leisurely drive south to New Milton, and a leisurely lunch before jet lag kicked in. The Chewton Glen Hotel, on the south coast, was very fashionable, with a chic and cosmopolitan crowd there for Bank Holiday weekend—more well-dressed women than I had ever seen in one place in England. Overnight, the valet polished Harris's shoes again, and not to his liking. We walked to nearby Barton-on-Sea in the morning (I "collected" English towns named Barton), and later found disorganized Ashley Books, in the Old Tabernacle Church in Bournemouth, open on the holiday, and staffed by ladies who reminded me of my friends at the Bryn Mawr Bookstore. In New Milton we managed to buy only eleven books from an arrogant, unpleasant man reveling in his own inefficiency. We drove through New Forest and saw its ponies and a little Nelson museum, which displayed what were said to be the Admiral's baby clothes, including one pink bootie. In Southampton, we found several dozen cheap but good books at Cherringtons, then drove past the castle and the Titanic memorial. In Winchester, two shops and another few dozen books, and after closing we paid our respects to Jane Austen and King Canute in the Cathedral. Lainston House, another country-house hotel, was exquisite, and only a few miles down charming back lanes to Henry Lloyd's new home, a cottage in the village of Twyford. Outside London, a normal domestic feature was a garden shed out in a long back garden—a novelty for Yanks. Many of our "country" dealers used their sheds for books, and Henry used his for a small binding operation, where he repaired or rebound some of his finds. As before,

Henry had excellent books and our dealings were cordial; we had a good time with him and his wife afterward at the Bridge Pub.

We saw Salisbury Cathedral only from a distance, and we detoured for a passing look at the fenced-in Stonehenge, which Harris had never seen.

We pressed on for a mid-afternoon appointment near Gillingham, at Woolcott Books, an Amy find. Jack St. Aubyn was another British Army officer, a colonel, retired to a farm not far from Shaftesbury. Chickens were pecking in the farmyard as we were pecking at the shelves, and we put together a large lot, he and Henry making up for the rather slim pickings in the small general shops.

Shaftesbury, high on Gold Hill, was a familiar sight for Masterpiece Theatre fans. The town seemed, however, very real. The Grosvenor Hotel was traditional in the best sense, and full of flowers. When we met gregarious Amy at the bar, she was chatting up the local farmers.

The next day, a gorgeous one, we had promised ourselves some sightseeing. After doing our duty, finding an armful of good and cheap books at a charming little shop near the hotel, we saw the Abbey ruins. A pretty drive to ravishing Sherborne, another town that grew around an abbey, all golden stone and equally PBS-ish. Amy wanted us to see Thomas Hardy country, and we headed south toward Dorchester. On the way she was nattering on in the backseat about the Cerne Abbas Giant—"very rude, very rude." Harris's eyes were rolling around in his head as he tried to understand what this might mean, and I speculated aloud about the rudeness aspect. Then we saw him, a chalk figure cut in the hillside outside town, and indeed gigantic in every part. The village was particularly charming, and we found a wonderful pub. We were headed west parallel to the coast, and reluctantly passed up several seaside towns, clogged with tourist traffic. We did penetrate Sidmouth, a pretty town with red cliffs and a bookstore. We only netted thirty books; Harris said it was fished by St. Aubyn. We had hoped for a real cream tea, but at five p.m. we were too late.

We were booked at Combe House, near Gittisham, and had a way to go. Back roads shrank to lanes. A magical, late-afternoon drive through what looked to me like an enchanted wood, the late sun slanting through the clearings under the trees, led into curving, tall, densely hedgerowed lanes, and at a sharp, blind bend a huge and menacing shadow was coming our way—was it a dragon? No, a hay baler. I had to back up a New York block to find a gap in the hedgerows so it could get past us.

Combe House was seemingly set apart by our journey through woods and lanes; the imposing Elizabethan manor house on a hill felt like a hidden, mysterious place. Gorgeous, huge trees with long shadows punctuated the hillside in the late sunlight. The house interior was handsomely paneled, a little down-at-the-heel, but the stately dining room and the food were impressive. Our morning wakeup call was a bellowing bull and a yelping sheepdog herding cattle across the lower sweep of the greensward.

Amy's queries had pinpointed Max Powling, another private dealer, and we found our way there, past Exeter, near Newton Abbot, down a little lane to an old bungalow: a little confusing but we were on time. The Powlings were lovely people, and books and begonias were all over the house, the stock for sale upstairs. Max had only just been listed in the Sheppard's guide and he seemed ill-at-ease at first, probably not used to customers coming. We got past that and worked hard and found a lot, then were free before four, in time to pursue a Devon cream tea; at the Duke of Clarence back in Exeter, the clotted cream lived up to expectations. We saw the Cathedral, and happened upon a Laura Ashley shop with a blouse Peggy Barton wanted. Torquay was not far, and the Imperial Hotel was glamorous, on a hill overlooking the water and with the feel of an ocean liner. All the rooms had balconies and sea views, and the gardens were delightful, day and night.

We came down to earth down the hill the next, rainy morning: a miserable store in town, a filthy mess run by a slutty woman. We were there less than ten minutes. The weather cleared on the way to Brixham where there was a nice shop and nice people, and we put together a decent couple of boxes. At Dartmouth, we took the car ferry, and Amy rushed to provide Cornish pasties from a vendor on the dock to sustain us for the crossing of the River Dart. Pasties in hand, we saw the Royal Regatta from afar, and arrived in Devon. It was a beautiful drive over the hills and down lanes to little villages on bays, eventually to St. Mawes, to the pretty, seaside Tresanton Hotel. Perfect planning: it was Saturday and there weren't any bookshops for us in Cornwall.

The next day, a sunny Sunday, we dawdled and detoured our way to Taunton. We did manage to get down to some of the picturesque and therefore tourist-thronged tiny fishing ports, where the narrow lanes were clogged by caravans. In little towns like St. Austell and Port Isaac, there was parking only at low tide. We saw the dramatic, ruined Tintagel Castle from the heights, perhaps the best way to preserve its sense of Arthurian mystery. The moors, covered with heather, were suitably moody and overcast.

The magnificent and well-named Castle Hotel in Taunton encompassed parts of a Norman castle on an even more ancient site. The baronial dining room starred a rolling cheese cart with sail-like labels; it looked like an armada. Its flagship was the production of a gentleman whose retirement activity was a singular cheese from one cow. The town had a decent bookshop, and then we had an appointment at A. A. Johnston, an old, established name in military books, at the Old Chapel in Pitney. By then Johnston had mostly new books and what was old was expensive, not worth a repeat.

Amy had talked to dealers in nearby Somerton, a nice couple who said they wouldn't have much for us, but knew a retired Brigadier who sold books from time to time. We found a few things with them, and they explained to us that the Brigadier was not entirely well, had been depressed since his wife's death, and saw people only occasionally. They called him, then said Brigadier Clarke declined. It struck me, I said in a rush "Is that P. T. Clarke?"—and the phone rang, the penny having dropped for the Brigadier as well. He had heard the name Colt and our horseman logo and our former business dealings came to him. He invited us over for tea, book talk, and some reminiscences of India as well as a little light book buying. At eighty-eight, he was sharp and lively, wore a monocle, and was taking snuff and sneezing into a paisley handkerchief. Amy engaged him in conversation about the recent BBC series, *The Jewel in the Crown;* he did not think much of it. We went out to his book shed in the back garden, leaving Amy to admire a large, gilded figure of a camel and rider. We bought a few things and he waved us farewell from his garden gate. Amy later sent him some special Kendal mint-scented snuff.

Next to me on the desk is a special copy of the slim book, a British official publication, *Paiforce: The official story of the Persia and Iraq Command, 1941-1946*. It is a bit worn, and the name P. T. Clarke, in pencil, along with three page numbers, appears on the front endpaper; the numbers refer to mentions of his service though he is not named. Tucked in is a copy of Clarke's obituary, and a note from a British dealer who sent it along to us, knowing that we had dealt with the Brigadier. We didn't know until we read the obit that he had had a long and distinguished career in the British Army in the Near East and India from 1917 into the 1940s.

Next day we headed east toward Glastonbury and Wells, and Amy ruminated in the back seat, as we were approaching a town oddly enough called Street, that she went there with Mark and John from time to time to buy them shoes at the outlet stores. You would have thought Harris was a bargain hunter, we had an instant diversion from course and he bought three pairs of shoes, a record for him. It was a pleasure to see him treat himself, he didn't do it often enough. After that, he was dumping his old shoes in wastebaskets, starting at the posh Royal Crescent Hotel in Bath, where he said feelingly of his black pair, "I always hated those shoes."

There was a cluster of bookshops in Bath, nothing noteworthy, but since they were all together it was like one good stop. In Devizes, the military specialist was gone and we bought only a handful of books in another shop in the High Street, but in Bristol we found a lot of good, solid stock at William Georges, a large and attractive shop. We were amazed to see the 1843 steamship S.S. *Great Britain* in drydock on the waterfront.

We were done for the day and made a beeline for Avebury to see the truly ancient standing stones, wandering among them without restriction. We climbed the earthworks for a better view of the cows grazing among the huge monoliths that dwarfed the village, which was set along an axis bisecting the stone circle. It was one of the most impressive sights in England, so mysterious. There seemed to be more cows than visitors, but the scale of the site overwhelmed everything. When we returned years later, there were buses and parking lots and tickets. Not the same.

We passed the famous White Horse, carved in the chalky hill near Uffington, on our way to Abingdon. That evening, we rendezvoused with John Cummings at the Upper Reaches, that sweet inn, and prepared to surrender Amy. We wanted Amy to see Blackwell's at Fyfield Manor next morning, and we parted there. It was not so rich for us that year, but we bought, and once again had a run through the Oxford shops, which yielded a few odds and ends. We stayed in an East Horsley hotel I diagnosed as schizophrenic: Tudor with a California addition. It was very handy to part-time dealer Graham Palmer in Ripley, and we visited him that evening. Graham had come in to the Military Bookman when he was in New York on business. He was a cocoa broker (who knew?) in the City of London, and collected and was beginning then to sell World War II books. Later, after he retired, he started producing lists; we were buying from them and again visited him at his house near Guildford, commuting distance from London. Graham was fun, very opinionated and gossipy.

We shopped in Guildford and then went on to Brighton for the weekend, not, however, at the ruined Grand Hotel. We visited our usual haunts in Brighton and Tunbridge Wells on Saturday, and had a family Sunday with the Stricklands. Then, a long way to London via Eastbourne, a hard-to-find and unproductive stop; and once again to Howes, in Hastings, where again we did well. Another busy day, but we started off with a full day in London, a telephoning and accounting-for-the-shipper morning and then the afternoon at Victor Sutcliffe's: a pattern emerging. The next day was mostly play: Ute arrived from Germany in time for breakfast, and we went looking for a raincoat, to Burberry where she helped me choose one much like hers. We had lunch at a great pub near Berkeley Square and the two of us went on to Maggs.

We usually did not go to the theatre in London after a full day, but bowed to Ute's wish, and our friend Sandra Francis chose the play. The four of us had decided to have a cocktail hour, with smoked salmon and Stilton, rather than a rushed dinner before the theatre, and Sandra and Ute met us in our spacious room. We told them about our travels and, like a kid, Harris showed Ute and Sandra his new shoes, all lined up. Sandra could be counted on to pick something *outré* at the theatre, and this play was about an English-educated Russian intellectual trapped in the Russian Revolution. Fairly tedious: the most memorable moment, for us, was the intellectual's meditating on his uncertain life, and his previous life in London: "I miss English shoes." This brought down our particular part of the house, to the mystification of those around us.

We wanted to visit Pat Quorn again, so we made a day-trip of it, by train to Ipswich and then a local to Halesworth. Pat met us, and we went to the shop, where we thought we were being selective but spent £1400. Pat and Lorna took us to a paragon of a pub, the Queen's Head, for lunch and we sat outside on a cloudless day. It was a stunning déjà vu experience for me, Amy and John having taken me there on my first visit to them when they lived in Framlingham almost twenty years before.

Back in town, the next day we went to Peter Eaton's shop in Holland Park for almost nothing, and then to G. L. Green, the naval dealer in Ealing. Mr. Green had a faint Long-John-Silver aura, and our dealings were friendly. We continued to buy from his mail-order lists after he moved away from London.

We had an unusual appointment on Saturday. Ian Sayer had been a good customer, with seemingly no budget, for some years; he knew by then that we bought in England and invited us to visit him in Hounslow to buy his duplicates. He was a young, trendy, self-made guy with a transport business, but was amassing an extraordinary document collection, concentrating on the Third Reich. We took a lot of his duplicate books off his hands, and then he displayed his treasures, clearly enjoying showing them to people who knew what they were. He had just published his first book, *Nazi Gold*, and was continuing to research and collect Nazi documents.

On a nice Sunday, we went down to Greenwich by boat, to see the magnificent Royal Observatory with its ancient navigational devices and the brass meridian set into the terrace, and then the equally wonderful National Maritime Museum, with the clipper ship *Cutty Sark* in dry dock nearby. Later, wandering through the Market, we found Anthony Simmonds, a fine maritime dealer. We had known he was there, but it was a surprise to find him open on Sunday, and frustrating as by then we had little time. As usual, we spent our final day with Peter de Lotz, who then gave us a lift downhill to see Tom Donovan, also in Hampstead. We had had correspondence with Tom but had not before had time to visit him. A young guy, he dealt out of his apartment, and had a small but decent stock. He revived us with coffee, and we put together a good-sized stack. Tom was to become a regular stop, and in between visits we bought from his lists.

That night we had dinner at the Gay Hussar, celebrating appropriately the end of a stimulating and successful trip. We went off to Italy the next day, happily ignorant that our bank transfer, without the proper coding from our doofus branch bank in New York, had not arrived in our London bank account. Our big transfer of liquid assets had fallen into an ocean of pounds and dollars and was sloshing around, sinking unrecognized, not channeled into our account. We returned from Italy to find the staff frantically trying to field queries from British dealers. Our checks were bouncing all over southern England.

We came home to a bigger problem than the transfer, which was soon straightened out. While we were gone, Jason and Lewis had inherited the whirlwind that was Michael. Within an hour of our arrival, I cornered Jason and questioned him closely, and it seemed that Michael had really gone off the rails. We, with great regret, had to fire him.

CHAPTER THIRTEEN

"You all look as friendly as you sound."

1985 – 1986

Jason, Harris, Robin, Lewis, and Margaretta.

Once again personnel problems dominated our thoughts. By the time we let Michael go, Lewis had been with us part-time for five months, and he had fitted in quite well. It was natural to offer him Michael's job, as he had taken to the store and our way of doing things, better, in fact, than Jason.

Next, another shipping clerk. Harris went out to canvass our friendly neighborhood merchants among whom there was a rotating subculture of part-time workers. Scott, at Feldman's, had no one to suggest, but Julian—Patrick Murphy's Market then being in its Cuban period—sent Ismael Medina to see us.

The morning Ismael came to apply for the part-time job, he politely introduced himself to Harris, and asked, "Are you the boss?" "No, she isn't down yet," Harris said, with a mischievous little smile, I am sure.

We all took to Ismael, a fine, good-looking, young man who paid attention to what was needed, very conscientious. He seemed to like the books and the store, and was a natural although none of us knew it yet.

At about the same time, Stuart Elenko called me. Stuart was a very active customer, cranky, funny and charming in his own way; he was usually phoning to order or to ask for the advance galleys of the new catalogue if it included the Holocaust. But this time, he was calling about his daughter Robin, a college student, to see if we had some work for her. I recognized the compliment, but hesitated. Stuart could be difficult. With his usual aggressiveness, he urged me to hire Robin, but he seemed to feel my misgivings. He said she was a lovely girl, "She's nothing like me, she's like her mother." Robin was indeed a lovely girl, a delight—willing, smart, light-hearted but responsible. She did almost everything we all did, filing, quoting, eventually cataloguing and occasionally packing. Working at the Military Bookman was extra education for this young woman from the Bronx, a "wider world," she said, such a variety of people, such an eccentric business.

Alas, in six months Ismael got an offer he couldn't refuse, a full-time job as a maintenance man in a large building around the corner. We understood and he left with mixed feelings, and came by to say hello from time to time. By luck, Luther reappeared and was with us again for a while; he knew the drill and that was a break, no training.

After six months I was quite dissatisfied with Jason's performance: he was slow at everything, no good at the physical work and the methodical attention needed in pulling cards for the catalogue, which required a lot to time on one's feet at the shelves. He was disorganized and lazy, and not good at taking direction. And he did not seem to be picking up on pricing or knowledge of the inventory. Harris and I really went at it about Jason; after about nine months I was so fed up I wrote Harris a memo, sometimes a good communication tool when we were at an impasse. My dear partner was often too tolerant and always said, of anyone, "He's coming along," even when their shortcomings were driving him crazy. In this case Harris was right. After a slow and bumpy start, Jason did come along, and eventually was as close to a real manager as anyone we ever had, sensible and reliable, if still lazy. He eventually took charge of the Holocaust section and later the Civil War too. We had always had a decent, representative Civil War coverage but were well aware of the long-established top-of-the-line competition. Jason, over time, improved that section of the inventory.

And we finally embarked on the long process of a new computer system. In the course of it, Dave Liebman transformed our business life. Starting in 1986, in many conversations and observations, he essentially learned how we ran our business. He came to understand our needs completely, and cobbled together software that was very much more useful than any other programs we looked at, even years later. But first, the hardware decision: Harris was set on getting IBM "because they would always be there." Dave met us at the IBM showroom at 40th and Park Avenue to see the new color computers, very exciting. I stood out on the sidewalk afterward, the possibilities of the extra dimension of color exploding in my head.

1986 was a banner year for the Colts: in March we saw Halley's Comet in Barbados; we celebrated my parents fiftieth anniversary in Bermuda in June. And there was more to celebrate: the store's tenth birthday in July. We planned a party and did other things to commemorate the occasion.

Gene Aretzsky's designer who worked on our catalogues was a whimsical and talented guy named Michael Harmon. Ever since we had visited A. A. Johnston in England, and probably even before (when found in a book), I had admired his bookmark. "Mark the place for your military books," it said, and there was a map on the other side. I shamelessly copied this idea, in red, and Harris sketched it out, but Michael made it delightful, creating a map presided over by a smiling sun, with a curvaceous Statue of Liberty, the World Trade Center, a playful Library lion, and other landmarks on the way uptown, all the way to 93rd Street, where our logo marked the spot. Customers loved it, and some tried to cadge a handful.

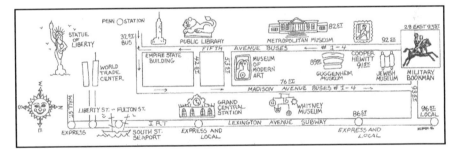

In the Summer catalogue, we included a photo album at Lionel's suggestion, a very popular one. It showed staff, past and present; favorite customers; Gene Aretzsky and Terry McNally, our catalogue "enablers"; Amy, "British Book Scout"; and Joel, "New York Book Scout." Joel was sort of pleased to be included but fretted that it would blow his cover.

As presents for our best customers, we designed web belts (red, naturally) imprinted "The Military Bookman 1976–1986," or alternatively, red playing cards with the logo and dates: limited editions for our elite. Robin and Penelope, a friend of Brian's who was with us part of that summer, helped me send out these presents with little notes. The recipients were delighted: *I wear my belt with pride.* M. E. B. deserved both, and wrote, *I will wear my T-shirt and web belt while I play cards!* Roger Bell's thank-you was the most noteworthy, and a pun on a Pacific battle: a Polaroid of himself as a shell-shocked G.I. in a helmet, and around his forehead the belt, captioned "2000 yard stare on bloody BELLeliu (caused by a belt in the head)."

Jim Bloom wrote, *Liked the pictures in the catalogue. I figured you guys to be much older. No doubt, I sound much younger than I might appear. You all look as friendly as you sound. Thanks for the belt. For your twentieth, I suggest you send your regulars shelving to handle the overflow.*

Of course we had a big party. For the invitation and the sign, I did a logo alteration, changing the Reading Soldier's book to a birthday cake. The party, for staff, local customers and friends, was in the store

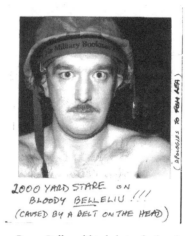

2000 YARD STARE ON
BLOODY BELLELIU !!!
(CAUSED BY A BELT ON THE HEAD)

Roger Bell and his belt in the head.

and back garden decorated for July 4th, and the 5th, the birthday. It was a full and festive weekend, with OpSail in New York Harbor and the usual fabulous Macy's fireworks. On the afternoon of the July 5th, the caterer at Bremen House, a remnant of the old German neighborhood, called at the last minute to say he couldn't provide the party food—at all. I had to beat the bushes for edibles; many nearby shops were closed for the holiday weekend, but I crawled under the metal shutter of the now-Irish Rory's Deli around the corner to plead for whatever he had, and then took a run to Third Avenue where I found an Italian deli, which made up the difference.

There was a great turnout: the staff, many customers; the Wolfsons, Mike sporting The T-shirt; Philip Kamil; Jean Crocker; Sheila of course; Mrs. K and Joel, our favorite scouts; Lloyd the binder; Howard the lawyer; Gene the typesetter; Lenny and Ray and others from the Corner Bookstore; Brendan Gunning; Bill Waters; Joe Ward and Dan David, by then entrenched at Sky Books; Rory and his family from the deli. Michael O'Rourke divined we would celebrate and came unbidden, and was his best, hilarious self. John called from Chicago at the height of the festivities. Randy, Peggy, and young Ran Barton were there; Ran retreated into a book after a conversation with Russian Orthodox Brother Isaac, a part-timer at the Corner Bookstore, got too much for him. The party went on till all hours. A great evening, and music courtesy again of Bill Waters.

It was fun having the girls around that summer. Robin pitched in with whatever was needed. Once, in the absence of the shipping clerk, Harris asked her to sweep at the end of the day. Robin said, "Which end of this thing do I use?" The Jesse computer had a ubiquitous command: "Press any key to continue." Robin always hit B for Barry; she had a big crush on Barry Manilow. Penelope was smart as a whip, and a quick study, and I used her talents on the catalogues. Another girl worked for us later, after Penelope had gone off to Greece. A good group, better than most of the boys, but they were a little older, or just more mature. We noticed that Richard Chalfin, the book scout, came around scouting with greater regularity, and soon he began taking Robin off with him on his motorcycle.

1986 was a great year for buying too: we were offered a series of small, good collections, relatively easy to handle and process. In February, we went to see Joe Garabrant and bought a large lot. In March I visited and bought a naval collection in Greenwich, Connecticut.

In April, a new source presented himself. Sy Getchburg, based in Elizabeth, New Jersey, scouted on a large scale. Sy had a day job, but he had the book bug. He had many books in his house, but the military was stashed in his mother-in-law's basement. Off we went on a Sunday, and it was cold, a miserable day spent in our coats in a dank none-too-clean unheated basement, with Sy occasionally making a run to Dunkin' Donuts for coffee. The books were many, not dirty, and reasonable, so it was worth the trip. Sy even had an aerospace section so we thought we'd give that a try. Thoroughly chilled, we came back on the bus around dinnertime, and made tracks for a cozy French restaurant for some restorative onion soup. Through the eighties, Sy called regularly, and we tried to answer the call in warmer weather.

On a snowy day in April, at the invitation of Stuart Pyhrr, of the Metropolitan Museum's Arms and Armor department, I went there to look at books. The late curator, Stephen Grancsay, had left his enormous library to the Museum and we were to have the unique experience of buying from it. What a kick, to buy from the Met! The whole side gallery in the Arms and Armor section had been closed off and shelves installed to accommodate the collection. The fine antiquarian books had already been taken to auction (that got away from us), but there was plenty for us. I bought about two hundred volumes, solid history, mostly Medieval and Renaissance, "my" subjects.

The compellingly named César had presented himself in the store, and offered himself and his van for hire, to pick up collections we had vetted and bought. Our shipping clerk would go along to pack and load the books, but our understanding was that César would help load too. It was too much for one person to do. We sent César and Ismael off to Sy Getchburg's for that lot and then for the naval lot in Greenwich, and later, with Luther, to pick up a collection in Larchmont. César didn't like exercise, and Ismael complained that César was lazy and wouldn't help with the boxes. At a later date, I went with them to buy a collection out in the mountains of north Jersey. The house was built into a mountainside, the books in a dampish cave-like room. I think I did more hauling than César, who had to be urged on.

In May we combined Clai Marshall's graduation festivities at Skidmore College in Saratoga Springs with an expedition to Vermont. We stopped at a couple of shops in Albany, checked out the bookstore in Saratoga, and after the graduation drove north to Essex, to take the short but magnificent ferry ride across Lake Champlain, Adirondacks behind us, and Green and White Mountains ahead. We were buying most of a collection from the widow of Civil War historian Stephen Z. Starr, who lived near Stowe. Dan Weinberg of Abraham Lincoln Book Shop had been there first and extracted the Civil War books; he may have recommended us to Mrs. Starr for the rest of the history. We got more Churchill than we had ever had, and, after Mrs. Starr checked with her children, a later installment of some fine books on Roman history. The rented station wagon was so full it wouldn't go over the mountain to Stowe, so we drove the long way around. We worked our way south in the beautiful spring through Vermont and New Hampshire. We needed to have everything we bought along the way (except a few plants) shipped.

It was off-season, so some inns and bookshops were closed. Before we went I had made some calls, working from a New England bookstore listing I had sent away for, to plan our stops. I was talking to a most helpful bookman in Vermont for some suggestions. "After seeing you," I said, "we'll go over to the Book Bear in Marlboro." "But that's me!" he exclaimed. The compilers had switched info in the

The Book Farm, Henniker, N.H.

list. Subsequently we found the more reliable pamphlets put out annually by the dealers' association in each state.

We went to a shop in Rutland, the Haunted Mansion in Cuttingsville, Pleasant Street Books in Woodstock, a couple in Bennington, and two book barns in Henniker (our first one was the best). We swung by East Chatham, New York, to Librarium on the home stretch.

Then in June, Harris and Luther went around the corner to Fifth Avenue and 98th Street to collect, by hand truck, in several runs, the aviation books of the late Paul Parker. Paul had been a dapper, cheery local customer and neighborhood activist, who often stopped in at the store just for a hearty hello. His tall, lean figure, in fedora and Chesterfield coat, was a familiar sight as he tore down the many leaflets disfiguring lamp posts (only signs for lost pets survived Paul's purges). Paul had collaborated on a physically huge monograph on a World War I fighter plane, and his books included a full run, twenty-six volumes, of *Cross & Cockade*, a serious periodical for World War I aviation buffs. We took the set on consignment and finally sold it about eight years later. Paul's fine book collection had been large before we came on the scene, so he had been only an occasional, but memorable, customer. Richard Strich had brought in the hand truck, bright green, brand-new, and found on the street. It certainly was an improvement on the shopping cart and he knew it, looking pleased with himself and happy to help us. This may have been the last of Richard's thoughtful contributions: things we didn't even know we needed over the years. He died not long afterward.

Soon after, a lot came in which had been pending for several years. George McMillan had been a Marine Corps combat correspondent, and had written the sought-after unit history of the First Marines in World War II, *The Old Breed*. Appropriately, he lived not far from Parris Island, South Carolina, the Marine Corps boot camp. When he first wrote to inquire if we would be interested in his books, he didn't have a list; it took him quite a while to make one up, and he then sent it to us and a few other dealers. Our offer was the best, but one of those dealers came back to him, and offered $50.00 above our bid. George called it like it was —tacky—and accepted our offer. Ten boxes arrived.

In July, I visited a small collection on East 79th Street that had several noteworthy books on knights: one was a magnificent piece by Hans Burgkmair, *Landsknechts at the Triumph of Emperor Maximilian*. The original art was produced in the early sixteenth century; and the various partial but lavish reprints of that album recording the Triumph were scarce, as was pricing information. I asked Ute to make some inquiries in Germany about its value; Lewis's and my sense of it turned out to be correct, it was "worth" about twice the amount we put on it. But, as Harris often said, a book is worthless until it is sold. We priced it for our market;

and to our surprise, it and another Landsknechts book were very shortly sold to Stewart Pyhrr at the Met, right around the corner from its former home. I wrote Ute, *We always have mixed feelings about selling a beautiful book fast, would like to have had it around for a while. . . This is the second book we have sold to the Met this month, which is I feel some kind of landmark in our business life.*

Later that month, I went to see a large uniform book collection in Larchmont. Russell Schneider had been a good customer and was retiring to Florida; he thought he shouldn't take his nice books to that humid place. I combined my visit with lunch with a Larchmont friend, Diane Elliott, who knew the Schneiders from their church.

As if this weren't enough, in September we had a very productive time in England. We flew into Manchester, got our car, and rendezvoused with John Cummings at a pub called the Tickled Trout, near Preston, so that he could lead us home to Amy and Mark. For this visit to Halewood in Preston, Amy had called to check on their hours and say we were coming. They opened specially for us on Sunday, and the rascally proprietor had pulled out the good military for easy viewing amid the chaos; there was more than a suspicion that he had jacked up the prices. We chose judiciously and Mark went with us to take notes, and we bought a hundred books. I was fighting a bad cold, and the next day, Labor Day, I slept late and emerged to find Harris in the middle of an enormous bank-transfer hassle. It was a holiday at home, but he was able to reach Lewis and laid the problem off on him. We went on to Southport, to Broadhurst again, very civilized in comparison to our Preston stop, and good hunting.

Amy had scheduled a visit to W. B. McCormack, in Lancaster, an attractive city in the local, gray stone—and a handsome shop, with many antiquarian books and a most pleasant proprietor. We found twenty-two books for £465, which suggests the high quality of the stock. After a pub lunch, we parted with Amy, who had broken the news that due to an impending trip of their own, she could not travel with us. We went on to Carnforth Books where we found an unusual and interesting lot of reasonable books, under the aegis of a prissy proprietor. We were not finished there until after four, and had hoped to visit Ewen Kerr Books, in Kendal. We phoned the new owner, Brian Peet, who was more than agreeable about staying open for us. It was a pretty drive to Kendal, but the traffic pattern once there was crazy. We finally found the appealing shop by the bridge. Mr. Peet gave us coffee and treated us very well, and we kept him there until seven. We had a rainy drive in failing light to Lake Windermere and did not reach Michael's Nook Country House, in Grassmere, until eight. We were more than ready for a drink and the excellent, perfectly served, and rather pretentious dinner, but were interrupted by a call from Lewis in New York, who had been grappling with the

New York bank. Our host was very put out that business was interfering with the precious pace of Dinner.

The next day was beautiful and brisk, and we drove through the Lake District to Cockersmouth, with glimpses of Derwentwater and Bassenthwaite Lake, many sheep, snug farms. We reached Whitehaven at noon, only to find that the bookstore was closed on Wednesdays. All we accomplished there was to ascertain that Lewis had straightened out the transfer to the British bank. In Carlisle, a town of red stone, we saw the Castle and Cathedral, and a small but remarkably good shop, the Bookcase. It was cheek by jowl with a little crafts shop where I bought a hand-made pepper grinder: a very fine grind it turned out to be, like English rain. In a residential area, we visited Mr. McRoberts at Maurice Dodd Books, a private house full of excellent stock. His less important books were very reasonably priced, which made it conducive to stepping up for the special ones. Leaving Carlisle at rush hour on our way east out of town, we went looking for Hadrian's Wall, and took off on a B road to run parallel to it. Stopping once to walk through a pasture to see it at close hand, we were all alone and the wall wound over hill and dale into the distance in the late golden sunlight. We ran out of wall and time just at the turn for Langley Castle, a very imposing and stark Norman tower and our shelter for the night. It was interestingly converted but really oddly decorated, as if Laura Ashley pink and blue sprigged fabric and white wicker could tame the austere stone walls and fortress proportions.

I woke early due to the uncurtained Gothic window and collected our book notes to send back to the store. We got a good start to go north to Newcastle upon Tyne. It was a pretty drive, and for once we found our way in the town and were right on target. The main attraction was Steedman Books, on a grand, neoclassical street near the imposing Theatre Royal, and not far from the castle. We had a good time, finding some very nice and then, in the back room, some fine books. Steedman sent us on to Frank Smith, an aviation specialist in a suburban area. High prices, but we bought. We turned south toward Durham and York.

Durham was spectacular from a distance, the cathedral and castle close together on a steep hill, crammed into a tight meander in the river. We found our way through several unexpected roundabouts, parking fairly close to the University Bookshop, having tea at the Almshouse, and then climbing up to the cathedral: so monumental, so stark, so Romanesque, with not too many later accretions. I was astounded to find the tomb of BAEDUS VENERABILIS, the Venerable Bede, England's first historian, in a side chapel.

It was easy to get to York, but as usual a struggle in the tangle of streets once in the old town. Amy had booked us into a handsome Georgian mansion called the Judge's Lodgings, and we had a large room on the second floor up a long flight of stairs, with a breathtaking view of York Minster. That evening there was no hint of Yorkshire pudding on the menu: the proprietor was French. But the Minster was illuminated and we could see the bats flying. York boasted many bookshops, some quite specialized. They were fairly close together, in clusters, one attractive and good shop after another, so it was possible to accomplish a lot in a day or two. Quite by chance we started at Taikoo Books, a travel specialist. We had learned to check the travel sections in general stores and at specialists. There is a genre of travel books that are not as they appear. For example, Frederick Burnaby's *A Ride to Khiva,* certainly described an interesting 1876 journey in an unknown land, but Burnaby, a British officer purportedly on leave from his posting in India, was really prowling around central Asia, checking out the extent of the Russian penetration and interests in Turkestan, and trying to assess the threat to "the Jewel in the Crown." At Taikoo Books an older couple, who turned out to be the proprietor's parents, were store-sitting while he visited a collection. It amused me that the father was all for waving us off—no, no, no military—but the mother was welcoming. It was just as my parents would have been. She somehow knew better and watched with excitement and pleasure as we piled up about £1300 worth of books.

In Fossgate, we found two shops for us, then browsed up the Shambles, found a pub lunch and on over the bridge for two more shops. Very many books. We were worn out and saw no prospect of the classic roast beef and Yorkshire pud Harris had so wanted, so again spent the evening at our hotel. The next day, a Saturday, we had plenty of time for the Minster, seeing the damages from the terrible fire two years before, and Morris dancers in the square. It was a short drive to Lincoln and we detoured to see some Roman ruins, arriving at the White Hart Hotel by the cathedral in the midst of wedding celebrations. The town was pretty and sunny and the cathedral magnificent on its dramatic hill.

We did not fare so well in Lincoln. On Steep Hill, in an extremely picturesque bookshop, we put together a large stack, and then the dealer said he did not ship. In another shop, although we were obviously buying, we could not see the antiquarian books without an appointment. We had dinner at the bottom of the hill at the nine-hundred-year-old Jew's House Restaurant, because the hotel was busy with weddings. When we got back from dinner, the staff was sweeping up the confetti. There was a celebratory afterglow of flowers the next morning. Being Sunday, it was a day for the cathedrals and not books. A sunny day and a flat and uninteresting drive south as we tried to discern the difference between a marsh and a fen. We were heading toward King's Lynn in Norfolk, but detoured to Ely, which we found particularly interesting and tranquil, the cathedral harmoniously melding its several periods, with a glorious Gothic chapel. We were staying that night in a place Amy had chosen for its location, because the next day we were finally visiting the elusive A. A. Martin nearby. Congham Hall was a mellow country manor, and I lingered at a huge bowl of sweet peas in the living room. We were in time for tea and then drinks in the dreamy garden. In the morning I wandered in the kitchen gardens.

Tony Martin had done time at a number of London shops before he went out on his own, and we had heard a lot about him, but he kept moving Woodford Books a little farther from London. He was tired of the city and, I guess, a bit reclusive. We had bought from his lists, and we finally caught up with him in Norfolk, in a pretty stone house on the green in Docking. He was as friendly in person as he had been in correspondence; I do remember the particular chill, despite a beautiful September day, of a book room in a stone house.

We had planned to go on from Tony's to the shops in Norwich but once in the town were confounded by the traffic patterns, arriving only at closing time at the shops, near the cathedral. We were turned away from the books, but not from the cathedral and cloisters. We went on to a favorite hostel, the Angel in Bury St. Edmonds, for two nights, our base to visit Graham Scott again and then Pat Quorn in Halesworth. Another very full day. Then we made for Cambridge. Richard Brown had recently bought the Ken Trotman enterprise from Lionel and had relocated it to the outskirts of Cambridge, where he lived. We were there for several hours, entertained equally by good books and Richard's wife and little girl. In the town we visited some of our usual shops, and Galloway & Porter had the most for us. The insidious Quinto had taken over Jean Pain's space. We went again to King's College Chapel before the difficult drive to London.

We had our usual first day in London: phoning, accounting and lists for the shipper, laundry, and Victor Sutcliffe. Philip Kamil was at large in London, and knew we were going to see Victor; and there came Philip up the walk when we were in Victor's book room.

The next day we headed down to Greenwich—by train this time, only a fifteen-minute ride—to see Tony Simmonds for naval books, and a couple of other shops that had escaped us the year before. We even found a few books in a second-hand sort of place in the Market. Then a breakneck run back to meet Richard Strickland at the National Youth Theatre where vivacious, red-haired daughter Candace, an aspiring actress, was performing. We had dinner with Candace, sixteen and pretty and excited, then drove with Richard to Brighton. It was a melancholy visit because Richard and Jilly had split up, and her warm welcome and effervescent personality were so absent. Everyone was depressed, and the next day was a cold and rainy Saturday; Richard deserted us for a golf game and it was hard to get a cab to go to our bookstores. Holleyman and Kokoro were, as usual, good. Harris and I then parted ways, he to his Malta stamp dealer and I to the Lanes. On Sunday

Richard took us to visit godson Edward, fifteen, at Worth School, over some twenty miles of country roads. To arrive in time for mass, it was a white-knuckle drive, Richard having several close encounters with cows. Worth was impressive, neo-gothic buildings in a sylvan setting, and Edward was a presence in the school choir. His voice hadn't changed but he had grown five inches since we had seen him. We talked to him about visiting us in New York the next summer. It was late when we got back to our digs in London.

We called Lionel and were invited to lunch and then to see the remains of Arms & Armour Press. Lionel had sold out to another publisher, but he and the offices had continued in Hampstead for two years. In the meantime, Lionel was busy and energized, creating a new imprint, Greenhill Books, which among other titles later did short-run reprints of Napoleonic classics. Lionel was as usual in the vanguard: the economics of the new publishing possibilities inherent in these small editions were soon to affect the business substantially.

We went on to the Aviation Bookshop, and were there too long as Harris tried to interest them in buying from us in some kind of contra-account arrangement. We were overtired, with a long day ahead of us: we took the train to Winchester where Henry Lloyd met us and carried us off to charming Twyford for a friendly lunch at home before we got down to business in the chilly book shed, with a little sherry to keep off the damp.

Next day to Maggs, where we raked through some dusty and unmarked treasures in the basement, setting aside stacks to be priced for our consideration. We went on to new territory, King's Road, booking along the way.

Sandra Francis was determined to see us, so we had breakfast with her before going on to Peter De Lotz who gave us coffee in the fancy new kitchen we had helped pay for. It was four o'clock before we knew it, and Peter delivered us to Tom Donovan, where we bought fast, revived by a little sherry. Peter was good enough to collect us and drive us to our hotel, a boon after an exhausting three weeks of buying. On our last day we went back to Maggs to select from the newly priced books, did our own shopping, most notably Stilton and smoked salmon to take on to Malta to the cousins. Back to regroup at the hotel and there was Philip Kamil. We convened and debriefed in the hotel's attractive library room, which we hadn't known was there. Rush hour traffic to Heathrow was harrowing and we were the last on the plane. Air Malta was the Third World: safety procedures before takeoff featured crew members walking up and down the aisle carrying the life vests and masks, with no demo.

Roger Strickland and family met us at that late hour, and carried us off home, where we drank champagne until the wee hours. We had planned to go on to Paris after Malta, but there were two terrorist bombings in Paris just then, and security became very tight. It seemed an unpleasant time to be there, so we stayed on in Malta. Then, although we were only changing planes in Paris, we had to change airports and therefore needed to obtain a special French visa. That took about a day at the usually sleepy French consulate in Valletta. The bureaucrat reminded me of my autocratic French teacher: severe questions as she precisely placed the visa revenue stamps on our passports, a paragon of inefficiency as she took all the necessities in and out of several drawers. It was sad to be missing Paris, and made for a very long day going home.

We returned to find all in good order, and with a lot of inquiries engendered by an article in *Gentleman's Quarterly*, in the September issue. It was the most intelligent piece ever done about the store, by a young woman, Lisa Henricksson, who had taken the time to hang out and get some idea of what was happening. It was the best kind of "advertising" for us, and the ripple effects were felt for years.

We were hoping that the British consolidated shipment would come by early November, but the persnickety bloke at Carnforth had procrastinated in mailing our lot to the shipper for so long that they sent it on, finally, without his books, and he had to mail them separately. The big shipment did not arrive until Thanksgiving.

In early November, Tom Donovan from London was visiting New York and the store. He was there when Eldred's, a Cape Cod auction house, called us, like an afterthought, late on a Tuesday about a Friday auction, military with many books. Over dinner with Tom at Piro's, we discussed it and decided we had to go.

We made a memorable, last-minute run to the Cape on Thursday: tie-up on the Grand Central Parkway, missing the morning plane, getting connected through the Boston shuttle to a Hyannis flight, renting a car, racing to the auction house to look at the books in the afternoon, breathless. The cataloguers had fixated on the objects—uniforms, decorations, weapons and accoutrements—of the large and remarkable collection, and neglected to describe or lot the books as they deserved to be. For us there were quantities of good stuff, especially on uniforms, including many of the Moritz Ruhl late-nineteenth-century small books with superbly detailed color lithograph folding plates of various armies. But much was badly lotted, most egregiously a set of the Austro-Hungarian official history of World War I, described as lacking one volume which we easily spotted in another lot. Next morning at the auction, Ray McGuire, long back from the Caribbean and back in business, was there with his "banker," Charley Woolley, but we blew them out of the water; there was no other book competition to speak of. After arranging to ship our massive buy, we sallied forth to a few bookstores, the big one fetchingly named Parnassus, and antique shops. On the Cape, the antiques seemed to be mixed with books in an appealing combination, and I found our first copy of the sheet music of "Over There," the one we framed for the store, and some other cheap and irresistible sheet music, "The Caissons Go Rolling Along" and "Anchors Aweigh" which brightened up the catalogue. It was late autumn, bittersweet was climbing over the fences, fires burned in our small inn, and many places were closed for the season. But we had friends to see, including Chris Busa, who was by then involved in starting an arts magazine on the Provincetown scene. It was a treat, a stolen weekend we hadn't expected.

Around Thanksgiving, as the Cape Cod books were being logged in and processed and the first catalogue calls were falling on us all at once, the British books came. Some of the Cape Cod books were a challenge; Michael had known German, but as I wrote Ute, *No one but the two of us even knows that Verlag is not an author!* We were working hard and late, and it may have been then, either by "presidential decree" or by a meeting of "the board" that the store agreed to send us out to dinner whenever we worked until eight o'clock or later. It was invoked many times.

Early in the New Year, we had a special "class trip." We heard from a former neighbor of fond memory: she and I had, in earlier years when she lived next door, trained up the wisteria on the front of her house, and she and Harris had scavenged together for firewood; when a tree was cut down on Fifth Avenue, she had come running. She was a script supervisor and had just worked on the movie of *84, Charing Cross Road,* and sent us tickets to the preview. It all came together, the movie having been shot in our neighborhood where half of the story happened.

CHAPTER FOURTEEN

"Do you have books on World War II?"

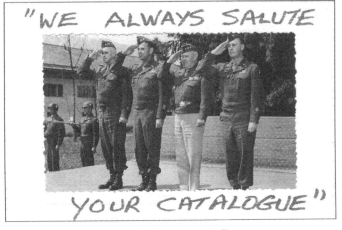

An order from Roger Bell.

It was H. L. Mencken who said something about no one losing money on underestimating the intelligence of the people. It was a surprise to have a phone call from the corner of 92nd and Third, "Where are you?" "We're between Third and Lex at 170 East 92nd—you can't miss it." They did, I saw them breezing by. How many came into 29 East 93rd Street, with two signs outside, one at the sidewalk and the other larger one on the wall, saying, "You're hard to find." "Well we're right where we say we are, at our advertised address."

Many of these wanderers had stopped at our neighbors, the Corner Bookstore, to ask where we were? How many roamed, disregarding the two signs, up the front stoop and rang Sheila's bell? One, on a Monday when we were never open (and in fact were not there), was rudely insistent. Sheila, interrupted in session with a patient, told him we were closed. He responded, "But you don't know who I am!" "It doesn't matter who you are, the store is closed."

One strange regular, Jonesey, who read, often in the garden, but very rarely bought, had the nerve to call the home number on a Monday with some hare-brained query. Harris, climbing down from a tall ladder where he had been cleaning woodwork, was not cordial. It was not the only time we got calls at the home number, especially when a new catalogue was in the mail, as if they thought we slept under the desk or had the master copy hanging around our necks. One man, late on his Christmas shopping, pursued us up our front stoop on December 23rd at six p.m., when we were more than ready to start our holiday.

Any retailer can corroborate that the full moon produces some bizarre queries and behavior. And that you never know who or what might walk in the door. Even before we opened, our then-five-year-old nephew Ran Barton was in the store when a lady strolled in off the street and asked if we had any books on clocks. He was incredulous, "It *says* Military Bookman."

Is this a library? Maybe that was a legitimate question, old books, no cash register, aside from our carved wooden Polish box (a Polish cash register?). But one clueless visitor browsed for an hour and then came up front and asked to sign out his selections.

Do you have books on World War II? How many do you want.

Do you have any books for sale that aren't on the shelves?

Do you buy books? Well, we don't print them or steal them.

We have no record of that title, it sounds like fiction. *It's a fiction novel, yes.*

Are you just a store that takes orders from time to time?

Do you sell rosaries?

I'm a member of your club. Well, no, there is no club, you are a catalogue subscriber. There is a Groucho Marx answer for this one.

And: *Can you make a living at this?*

Michael later asked me if the caller sounded young; no, I said, he sounded dumb. "I'm looking for a book by this guy eye-bid." Confusion. "That doesn't sound familiar, how do you spell it?" "i-b-i-d." Light dawns. "Oh, you saw that in a footnote." "I saw it in a book, yeah." *Ibid*, the repository of all wisdom. Usually intolerant Margaretta carefully explains what it means, gets off the call and cracks up. Harris sallies forth from the stacks, calling her an intellectual snob. Oliver, fifteen-year-old shipping clerk, leans out of his nook: "Does he want the companion volume by *op. cit.*?"

One entitled guy bulled his way in on a Monday when we happened to be there with Dave and the computer, and chose an expensive book. The check bounced and bounced and bounced, despite our leaving messages at all three phone numbers listed at his Long Island estate. When pressed, an officer at his bank confided that some people keep an account with a small balance just for this kind of con. Another check-bouncer particularly offended me because I had worked closely with her to find an appropriate, and expensive, poster for her boyfriend. She worked in a law office and must have known she could get away with it. I was sounding off to Howard Friedman, and he offered to write a lawyerly letter for us, which produced results after many increasingly nasty messages had failed.

It was fine with us when browsers came in with small children or dogs, as long as they were well behaved. The dogs were better behaved than some of the children: I found a young boy at the computer in back, using it as if it were a game, while his father benignly looked on. The probably overtired child of a preppy doctor and his trophy wife had a tantrum in the middle of the store, which they did nothing to mitigate or remedy or remove.

There were visits from a sinister rock musician with LOVE and HATE tattooed on his knuckles. I gave him a wide berth. There was a creepy, strange cab driver who occasionally took his break browsing in the store. Once I came uptown in his cab, realizing along the way that it was he, and feeling him assessing me in the rear-view mirror and it wasn't pleasant; finally he asked if I worked at the bookstore. We were almost there by that time.

There was a not-too-tightly wrapped customer, who always handled, not gently, all the good books, and then bought one for $7.50, and who despite our remonstrating, was up on a chair; he lost his balance and pulled the shelf down with him.

One man came forward with his choices and Jason, seeing the prices in the books, thought that they had not been properly processed, and started maligning Harris as he checked the prices in the computer. The would-be customer got edgy; he hadn't realized we had the prices on file, and had been in the stacks with his pencil, busily changing them to what he thought he could get away with.

I took a call from a woman looking for a particular naval book; but she had no specifics, no author, no title, not even a war. She told me it was blue. When I told her we had about twenty shelves of naval books and most of them were blue, she called me a c--- and hung up. I was shocked enough to repeat, more or less, the exchange, managing to shock Luther too.

Often we had to be mind readers. A man called asking for a book on Napoleon's Imperial Guard by Lacocky. I was perplexed; then it came to me. I said, more to myself than him, "Oh, Lachouque," giving it the correct French pronunciation. "Some might say it that way," he conceded, condescendingly. I couldn't help myself: "Well, the French do!"

John Catherwood was browsing in World War I and hanging out with Harris in the back, when they heard a man telling me that he had a contract to write a volume for the Time-Life Civil War series, then in production, and wanted some basic background books on the war. Harris sort of muttered and he and John waited with bated breath, and perhaps some apprehension, for my answer, which they expected to be scathing. There was a pause while I presumably tried to moderate my response, then was very restrained and asked what period, subject or focus. He had no answer. He was a cheap writer for hire, he didn't have to know anything.

We gave short shrift to one mail-order customer who returned books too often: he didn't like the page layout, or it was "too text-oriented." We did take returns if the condition was not as described, or if someone had inadvertently bought something they already had, but certainly not for editorial or aesthetic reasons. He was advised to shop locally so he could examine and then choose.

Over the years, it was not uncommon for our collectors to be attracted anew to the same titles and then to find they had bought duplicates. It easily happened; sometimes there was a different dust jacket or a variant title of the same book, which we tried to note in the catalogue. *I hate to be a pain but would like to return a duplicate copy of An Apache Campaign. I did not recall that I had previously purchased a copy from you in June 1994, and of course, another copy from you during my recent trip north. The memory is going . . . as are the knees.* He enclosed a photo showing both copies. The customers were usually embarrassed but we took their returns without demur.

Col. Russell Bowen took no such chances. A collector and bibliographer of C.I.A. and other intelligence materials, he traveled with his catalogue files in the trunk of his car so as not to buy duplicates. His colleague, Col. Walter Pforzheimer, also amassed a huge espionage collection. Bowen imagined their competition to be fierce, and on receipt of the Winter 1988 catalogue sent a frenzied telegram: OWNERS LIVE UPSTAIRS 2ND FLOOR, DLR TONIGHT, RUSH RUSH. Colonel Bowen bought a lot but was never known to respond to a quote on a book he had requested. His record was finally marked "don't waste stamp."

One bibliomaniac lived in Washington and was a very active member of the Society of the Cincinnati. He bought a lot, but confessed to me that his wife forbade him to bring more books home, and then so did his secretary, to the office. Finally he rented a room at the Society and filled it up. Perhaps recognizing that he should no longer buy for himself, he visited us several times, purportedly shopping for the Society, which was on our mailing list and from time to time ordered from us. He reserved stacks of books to be quoted to the Librarian; it was clear to us that the Society would already have them, not uncommon books, in its venerable collection. And they did. This was a lot of fruitless work for us, so after once or twice we refused to do it. Eventually, our relationship was terminated at his request (and to our relief) after a testy exchange about our unwillingness to send things on approval.

Michael was outrageous, but often on target. To troublesome customers, he was polite, but after the door closed behind them he would say, "Shop elsewhere!" How we wished we could say that directly to some of them. Our mantra was not: "The customer is always right." In the life of the store, we put up with a lot of difficult people, accommodating some unusual situations and requests, but managed to make them understand how we needed to do business. Some however were beyond the pale: one man wrote us at the outset of doing business that he wanted to negotiate a big discount because he anticipated buying many books from us.

This kind of correspondence just made me tired; I wrote him that he should start buying and when he had a record we could talk about it. At times, I wrote the letter I wanted to write, then tore it up—and then wrote the letter I had to write.

Two arrogant big spenders treated us all badly. They were cavalier in their dealings with us, rude to each of us at different times, nit-picking; their records in the computer had all our bad codes in multiple. Harris, the most patient and accommodating of men, finally told each of them that we did not want to deal with them anymore, saying to one in a letter that his attitude was "hostile and unfair." They were shocked; I don't think that had ever happened to them. There are some people whose business is just not worth the aggravation.

We received a sputtering letter from someone dropped from the mailing list for not buying. Jason had explained, offering to list his wants. *My special requests will go elsewhere as it would be hippocratic [sic] of you to accept same when I am not even worthy of your catalog . . . your arrogant New York city snooty attitude makes me glad I left.*

Another customer, a lawyer, threatened to sue when through some snafu we couldn't provide the book he had reserved. An outraged man in the Netherlands was hampered by the language barrier and acute frustration that the books he wanted had been sold; he cited legalities, obligations, "rules of buying and selling." But a customer in Norway, on receipt of a rare and much-anticipated set on Russian Army uniforms—seven volumes, and we, disgracefully, had not collated it—was distressed to discover that it had missing plates: *This is a grave disappointment, though not a catastrophy . . . I would be glad if you could look into the matter. I hope you can solve this mystery.* Another, when we couldn't find a misshelved book, *I want you to know if you come across this book in 'Mediterranean' or even 'The Balkans' or quite possibly the Zulu Wars, you will find me still quite interested.* Reasonable and unreasonable.

It always shocked me when dealers stiffed us. An established dealer in Michigan, Brian Russell, didn't pay us for a several hundred dollars of books, shipped in good faith: never made good. Alan Culpin and his wife were dealers who moved a lot (no wonder) and apparently made writing bad checks a business practice. We called when their large check was returned by the bank, and Culpin's response was, "That's your problem!" Getting payment was a lot of work; the check kept bouncing until we finally communicated directly with their bank manager and managed to get it paid. They traveled in England too, and who knows how many dealers they victimized; one of our British regulars was still enraged years later.

There were some libraries that were more trouble than they were worth. I have never understood the library discount; to my mind, there should have been a surcharge for all the elapsed time and the paperwork. We briefly did business with several small colleges, who seemed to order one $15.00 book at a time. A couple of months could go by while we held the book for the purchase order, did the invoices, often required in quintuplicate, and then waited for payment. We would have been better off donating the book. They didn't seem able to send a petty-cash check. We politely stopped doing business with those institutions. Among that number, amazingly enough, was the U.S. Marine Corps Historical Center, which had us waiting for months for a purchase order for a $20.00 book by Charles and Eugene Jones, photographers with the Marines in Korea. The Joneses themselves always wanted copies and the Marines had been pleased to find the scarce title. Finally, in a fit of pique, I sold it to a local customer and dropped the Marines from our list. Later most government libraries got credit cards and the situation became dramatically different, but it still depended upon a person to follow through, and the Marines later struck out again.

Large library orders were sometimes no better. A new American museum in Normandy, Le Mémorial, placed a big reservation with us and took nine months to transact. Then they were surprised that some books had been sold, then lost the refund check in the shuffle and asked for a new check. Maybe this was just incompetence, but in subsequent dealings, we asked for prepayment from their American fund-raising committee. The Mémorial later got into financial trouble, apparently defrauded by its president, and a well-known autograph dealer who had also had problems with them told Harris the guy had been running it as a scam.

We got strange, long, hand-written letters from a man at the U.S. Armor School Library at Fort Knox; it was impossible to tell if he were inquiring for himself or the Library. I conducted a fruitless exchange as he would not recognize how we did business, or explain his purpose, and at the same time wouldn't leave us alone. We wrote the Chief Librarian for clarification and he had to call him off.

There was someone to misunderstand anything, no matter how much I refined the verbiage in the catalogue and correspondence. There were numerous time-consuming exchanges with people who thought we should do business their way and not ours:

I would very much like the [scarce French Foreign Legion] books which you noted for me, but you must understand I am just a blue collar working man who is about to go on Social Security and I just cannot afford those prices! If you could manage to price them at an amount I can live with I would certainly appreciate it! Also can you send books out on approval? Investing this kind of money on books I may read once is not very practical.

This letter was noted "jerk" and his next letter, equally dense, "the hell with this." Both went to the bulletin board.

MRS. JOHN J. McCLOSKEY, JR.
~~108 WESTWOOD CIRCLE~~ 2600 Barracks Road
CHARLOTTESVILLE, VIRGINIA 22901

The Military Bookman
89 East 93 Street   October 3, 1994
N.Y. N.Y. 10128

          Dear Sirs,
          Perhaps you can help me find
information on a man, who was with the military
during World War II, perhaps overseas as well as
the U.S.A. and was in a Hot Air Balloon.
          His name is Paul McCullough,
I could have the wrong spelling and his middle
name could begin with a J. He never married.
He lived in St Louis Missouri, at least for a while,
I know of about 1940-1945. He died in Tucson,
Arizona in a cheap motel.
          I feel, during the Second World War,
there were not very manny Balloonist so that is
why I'm taking a chance on you that he could
be, at least, mentioned in an aviation history book.
          I would appreciate any help you could
give me and I thank you in advance for reading
my letter   Sincerly
                        Mary McCloskey

          SASE Enclosed
P.S. Perhaps he floated over France.

*Sometimes a customer would be so long in the bathroom one felt a
bit uneasy—then would emerge laughing and say, "I love the one
about the . . ." It was often this, one of the all-time winners.*

In the store on 92nd Street, we had hung a bulletin board near the front door,
for postings of obscure and specialized organizations, toy-soldier shows, Civil
War shows, book shows. In the new store, the only space for the bulletin board
seemed to be in the bathroom, over the toilet, and there we posted complimentary,
strange, outrageous, and funny letters and a few apropos cartoons. As Jesse sagely
wrote, *For some a bookstore is a bookstore and a book is a book. The letter of request
for a book on toothpick holders still stands as one of the classics.*

The *New Yorker* used to have, in the small spaces at the ends of the columns,
snippets titled "Letters We Didn't Finish Reading." A handwriting analyst could
have had a field day with our incoming mail. There were some letters I didn't even

want to open, I could tell from the writing they were strange or weird. Off-the-wall requests and offers abounded, and the best ones made it to the bulletin board, a changing assortment with some perennial favorites.

Tell me everything about yourself. I am a HITLER hobbyist.

I have an old Bible. What is it worth?

I am interested in locating soldiers' ghost stories from the Civil War.

I would <u>love</u> to get a book.... About <u>World War 1 ace Frank Luke</u> ... I'm a <u>Mormon</u> and would like to know if there are any other books about Mormon aces. . . . If there are any <u>Mormon</u> General & Admirals I'd be interested <u>also</u>, OK?

I have enclosed a picture of a 40MM gun crew. I am interested in purchasing a book that has the picture in it. I have not seen the book, but have been told about it. . . .I am the sailor wearing headphones and standing near the base of the gun barrels.

In WW2 I had a 'Janes' book of ships from the 30's . . . I lost it on a ship that went down. Do you have any 'Jane's' book of ships for those years.

Recently, Mark Cummings sent me DVDs of a British sitcom set in a bookstore. A great sitcom idea—I often felt we were living in one—but most of it was very contrived and not germane. The dealer reminded me of Herbie but with less energy. But it was worth viewing the whole thing for one episode: the dealer, who preferred to read, smoke and drink rather than sell, was approached by a customer who wanted a book marked £3. He wanted to pay only £2 for it; after some back and forth, the dealer examining the book, they settled on £2.50. The dealer took the money, tore out the first fifty pages of the book, then handed it over to the flabbergasted buyer. Later in the episode the customer returned, almost begging for the first pages. For a wonder, the dealer had them in his desk drawer, pulled them out, and said, "That will be fifteen quid."

Harris had the perfect technique for hagglers. For a book marked $30.00, for instance, the customer might say, "Can you do better?" Harris would take the book, look it over, check the price, brush the spine approvingly with his hand, and say, "Well, it's a nice copy, I could probably get $35 or $40 but I'll settle for $30." What answer is there to that?

One regular Saturday browser was always irresistibly drawn to the stacks of books set aside to be quoted, and not available for sale: over 8000 books on the shelves, but those were what he wanted to look at. He had to be shooed off innumerable times—the lure of the forbidden. When we would take his name and offer him the next copy, he usually failed to respond.

One always aggressive and rather annoying, though luckily not frequent, local customer really pushed me to the brink in 1994. He came in with a review copy of my book that he had purchased at the Strand, deeply discounted of course, and asked me to sign it. The tyranny of manners, as Michael had frequently remarked: why didn't I just tell him I would only sign copies bought from the Military Bookman—or inscribe it "for Harry, too cheap to live."

Customer vagaries were many and beyond predicting.

Please mark . . . to deliver to Rear of address. We normally never answer front door.

Any change can be credited to my account. All of twenty-one cents?

Our Philippine customer, Alberto Montilla, ordering in the midst of the considerable upheaval of the 1986

After our first, there were a number of convict letters over the years. "Please waive all costs as I am on a very limited budget." Even when the requests were reasonable, we usually didn't answer, having learned from experience that the inmate would have trouble paying or take forever, or that the prison would not let him receive a military catalogue. One determined inmate's intermediary was his mother, who received his mail and sent us checks. One we didn't answer was this unsigned letter from a Florida State Prison.

revolution that toppled the Marcos regime, was concerned more about his shipment than the politics. *Please see to it that the boxes are well wrapped (preferably in plastic), as these will be arriving here during the start of our rainy season and sometimes parcels do get wet.*

A Turkish customer asked to have his package mailed using a variety of stamps for his collection.

Someone sent us, unsolicited, a bunch of books, most of it landfill.

In 2000, an erratic customer sent in our recently discovered refund check from 1988, asking to have a new check. Sighing deeply, I offered him a credit.

Paul talked to a caller requesting a first edition of Julius Caesar's work on the Gallic Wars. Paul described the several antiquarian editions we had in stock, but the caller was set on the first. Paul was nonplussed; he could not determine whether the inquirer had any clue about translations, editions or rarity. He refrained from asking whether the man wanted vellum or papyrus.

A veteran customer and I were discussing his intention to purchase a 1702 first edition set of the Earl of Clarendon's monumental work on the English Civil War, which we were bidding on for him at Swann Galleries. I was describing the set and the binding, and speculating on where the books had been all these years, and through whose hands they would have passed. He astonished me by saying, "Oh, I never like to think of anyone else owning the books before I did."

A man on the West Coast fretted about books described as "uncut," that is, never opened, never read, the front edges of the pages joining two pages at the outer margin. Somewhere along the way, this had become an asset, a real plus, in the book business. Not to him! We had a nice set of an unusual title, and he called to inquire if it were really uncut. It horrified him to cut the pages, they were then all ragged and irregular, and even when he had taken such a book to a bookbinder to be cut, he was unhappy with the result. In vain I regaled him with my pleasure in reading an uncut Jane Austen, with a silver letter opener in hand. I could tell he shuddered. He didn't buy that scarce set that he wanted.

Terry Dotson was a disabled vet in Arizona and we gathered that a large chunk of his disability stipends went for books. He bought a lot from us in the fifteen years he was on the mailing list, but his dense and tightly written, long orders in ballpoint pen were difficult to decipher. He wouldn't call to reserve before sending the order, so many of his choices had been sold before we heard from him. At first we filed those as wants for the next copies to come along, but his lists were not only voluminous but hard to read, and we couldn't make him understand the effort involved. He wanted attention.

Joseph Moran couldn't call: he was deaf, and he lived with his sister, who couldn't walk. There were elaborate instructions for dealing with UPS, to be put on the label. Dealing with Mr. Moran had other demands; he couldn't afford everything, so there were lists of variables when he ordered, sort of one from Column A and one from Column B. One of his always-courteous letters was so tortured we couldn't figure it out:

I would suggest that if I send the list of books from the first or second or later choices before buying them, either you or your assistant will check off the list of books that you have or cross out the line of the books that have been sold and send the copy to me but you may keep the original one. . . . If I send the list of books in the future, please do not send the books without paying for it.

Humanity is divided between those who see the doughnut and those who see the hole, and we had plenty of each, most noticeably those who appreciated our efforts to list their want—*Thank you for remembering what I wanted!*—and those who complained bitterly about the modest $3.00 shipping for such a book.

I am astonished at the Bookman's long memory and am grateful for the service.

Bless your heart! I had requested Irving's Dresden *quite some time ago—and you didn't forget!*

The knowledge you have of the thousands of books passing through your hands never ceases to command my profound respect. Whew! Are you a speed reader? I'm usually afraid to skim for fear I might miss a clue.

The many customer aggravations were more than offset by the interest, appreciation, and enthusiasm of the majority of those we dealt with. The pleasures of our business were the ongoing relationships, both local and distant—recognizing the handwriting on the envelope or the voice on the phone. Jacques Lacasse, an eclectic reader in Montreal, was always pleased when I recognized his distinctive voice. Oscar Messina's gravelly voice was one I would still know.

We thought of particular customers when the perfect books for them arrived, or noted and discussed with them when their interests evolved or changed. I was talking to Neil Howell, who had been a Marine Corps collector exclusively, when he started ordering in a very different subject; I said, "That doesn't sound like you." He sounded amused and guilty at the same time, "I hoped you wouldn't notice!" On occasion, we had the pleasure of helping a one-time customer pinpoint the ideal gift: I dealt with a woman on the West Coast, suggesting a Christmas present for her boyfriend. It must have been a success: she was a florist, and sent me a poinsettia. We all had our special customer friends, local or afar. Harris had ongoing and lengthy football conversations, even off-season, with Bernie Hill, in New Orleans, and one Christmas Bernie sent us a box of pralines.

We watched some customers' children grow up—glimpses of them on Saturdays—or heard about them and where they were going to school; Neil Howell consulted Harris about New England prep schools. We received family snapshots, once even of the customer's azaleas, and requests for photos of the store. Mothers came in with their kids (mostly boys) wanting books for school projects, or for their burgeoning interests; usually the endless series of aircraft or warship or tank books were good introductions, or illustrated histories such as American Heritage books or the Time-Life series or the Ballantine Books. The Osprey *Men-at-Arms* paperback series of uniform pictorials was another good starter and there were plenty of grown-ups who wanted them too.

We conspired with some wives for gifts for their husbands. We knew that others objected to their husbands' collecting because we had to ship to office addresses.

I wouldn't want the old woman to find out about this! (That missive went straight to the bulletin board.) *My wife thinks I have too many books now, and therefore to avoid any hassle . . . I have them sent to my office.* I couldn't understand this: there were many worse things the guys could be doing with their time and money.

Correspondence and calls were often very personal, even intimate. Customers confided in us about why they wanted a certain book, where they kept their books, how their interests developed. There was a back-story on so much collecting. Some of it felt like a confessional—a very private, even secret story, of interest to no one else they knew. We heard about new bookshelves, even a new library addition. Sarah Gilmer, in Georgia, bought seventeenth- and eighteenth-century history including some fine antiquarian books. She named her horse for a seventeenth-century field marshal, Tilly—sort of an in-joke that few of her acquaintance would share—and later disclosed, *Don John of Austria is now one of my idols.*

We received a catalogue request from a man aboard the U.S.S. *Ranger*, a supercarrier. Pretty straightforward, but on the back of the envelope was a charming little sketch of the ship with a couple of planes going up, captioned "Somewhere in the South Pacific."

I read anything I can get my hands on dealing with this subject. As a basketball coach I began reading about strategy in battle as a grounds for learning game & coaching tactics.

I know mailing money is risky but it's quicker than checks or M.O.s. Please continue to mail me catalogs. I am not rich, yet, but when I graduate college I will fix that.

I would wish your computer to know me as a resident of Cork! It is there that the small hall to my library is being made redolent of the 11th Hussars (and of course of the famous CHARGE) as a result of my discovery when we raided attics in London that I had inherited the oak chest the 11th had taken to the Crimea, containing 36 velvet 'holes' for their sherry glasses, and still containing as well the 19 remaining glasses HRH Prince Albert, their Col., had presented to them . . . As well as drawings and other stray and dusty bits and pieces of the regiment's past. It is in Ireland that I look forward to reading your catalogues. . .

Though I have never had much desire to be rich, every time I receive one of your catalogues, I realize that there are certain advantages to wealth. Like being able to buy all the great and rare books in your catalog.

Customers sent us Christmas cards. One wrote, after the usual sentiments and his signature, *A very satisfied customer.* Jim Garzillo, an eclectic reader in Brooklyn who rarely came in, sent a classic Santa in an Air Force jacket painting a model plane. *How do you like the card? I do not think Santa is painting a 'B' model '17' looks more like the 'A' to me . . . and also the USAAF was not sending bare metal forts over the fatherland till late 1944. Enough picking of nits. Maybe next year I'll look for card where Santa and the Elves are going Over The Top or some such seasonal greeting. Anyway, to another fine year of book collecting . . .*

Prussian Grenadier watercolor, a customer's homemade greeting

We received shakily written letters from old generals, on generals' one- or two-star flag letterheads, wanting to read about their wars or buy. Adm. John H. Morrill wanted multiple copies of his World War II minesweeper memoir, *South from Corregidor.*

We heard about wives and ex-wives: *Now that my life is getting rearranged— ex-wife remarried and my new lady friend a lover of books & my library—it is possible I'll get back to pre-Napoleonic studies.*

Don Ellis, who had been flogging the U.S.S. *Enterprise* ready-room chair, wrote a few years later, *Now fully retired I am exercising my right to* **wallow** *in military history . . . and enjoying it.*

There was plenty of humor in the correspondence.

From the wilds of Arizona, a customer, ordering: *UPS delivers to the Mission regularly so the agency knows where it is. Fort Defiance, after all, consists only of a school, hospital, service station, 1000 Indians, 200 whites and about 500 goats.*

I'd like to thank Margaretta for the quote on the tank poster. I've not returned the polaroid simply because I am very tempted and may yet break down and buy the damn thing! (Hopefully some other madman will snap it up and save me from myself!)

Sorry, Robin, there was a time when I would have killed for a copy of "Armed with Stings" but interlibrary loan had gotten a lot better since then.

Enclosed is a check for (sob) $238.00, to cover the cost of the War at Sea set by Stephen Roskill about which you recently notified me. It's days like this that I wonder if snorting cocaine wouldn't be a less expensive form of recreation than naval history.

Often, customers latched on to one of us: perhaps whoever picked up the phone on their first call. Some asked for the guy with the English accent: Harris had a distinctive accent, prep school with a faint British overlay from his mother, which he had struggled to drop. It was natural that many wanted to talk to Harris for his expertise and voluminous knowledge of the books, and later Jason developed his own following for the Holocaust and Civil War books.

There were always customers for sub books. In one catalogue listing Naval we had enough for a separate Submarine section, and I had a long conversation about the caller's order and interest, which had reached such a level of intensity that he was building a large-scale model of a sub, maybe twenty feet long, in his backyard. I listened, fascinated by his obsession. The next call I took was from another sub fanatic, and he ordered a number of books, although missing out on some to the previous caller. I mentioned then the preceding conversation with the man with the backyard sub. "Oh," he said, with heartfelt yearning, "I *envy* him."

It was so satisfactory to supply an esoteric request. On the other hand, some who threw out a rare want, like a challenge, were capable, when the book was offered, of exercising us and then not buying.

It was fun to be able to introduce a customer, near or far, to a category of books that, unbeknownst to him, was just what he wanted. I conducted a lively correspondence with a Missouri George Bush, who wanted information on Russian and German Imperial uniforms. I recommended the Moritz Ruhl series, and with deep skepticism, he ordered. The feedback was great: *I was overwhelmed by the book. If someone had asked me to . . . describe the 'dream' book that I wanted to further my research on Imperial Russian Army uniforms, I could not . . . ask for anything better than this book. It is just exactly what I was hoping it would be and more.* George always gave me his reaction to what he bought, and thanked us.

Finding and supplying a special book for a customer took on a different dimension for veterans or their families.

One Korean veteran took umbrage that we did not list his war in every catalogue, and that when we did we called it the Korean Conflict: after all, an undeclared war. He was immune to the explanation that there were simply not enough books to run a list in each issue, and cancelled his subscription. He felt that he had fought a forgotten and unappreciated war.

But another Korean vet wrote more than once of his appreciation: *Boy, you folks made my day.* And: *I think I am glad I found you.* And: *I still cannot get over my luck in getting the 2nd Infantry Division Korea 1953 history from you last year. To live it and then read it in a book is an experience you cannot explain to someone who hasn't had it happen to them.*

In 1998, from Virginia Williams: *I am seeking information on the 84th Division in WWII . . . especially of Co. F, 334th Infantry. My fiancé was killed serving with them in the Bulge.*

A veteran of the 103rd Infantry Division: *Thank you very much for helping make an old life just a little bit fuller.*

Explaining his interest: *Was part of WWII myself so it really doesn't affect me as historically and romantically as W.W. I. The latter is a childhood hobby . . . and the former a duty to our country. I just don't have that much interest in it.*

A daughter, ordering *The Bitter Woods* by John Eisenhower: *You've made me happy because I will be able to give my father a truly significant gift that just may bring a few tears of joy and memory to his eyes. It was during the Ardennes Offensive that he was captured and sent to a German prison camp . . .*

Julie Hinton's husband had been a POW in a camp for downed aviators in Barth, Germany for fifteen months. Her husband had previously owned a copy of *Behind Barbed Wire*, by Morris Roy, essentially a unit history, published just after the war; but, a sad familiar story, he had lent it to someone and never got it back. Julie found out about us and wrote in 1979 to see if we even knew of the book. We filed the request, having seen the book once or twice, and four years later were able to offer it to her. She had been just about to write again (did she get some non-postal transmission?) and was thrilled enough to write a two-page letter then, and again after she had given the book to her husband. The excitement of the brown UPS truck, hiding the book in her mother's room, inviting the neighbors in: *My Valentine's Day worked like a charm and I had 'it' wrapped in a Fanny Farmer candy box – it looked very authentic . . . he was shocked and nearly speechless – his first words were 'who had it?'* How rewarding it was to be able to provide this. I believe that was the last time we saw that title.

In 1991 we received a remarkable letter, very clearly written, from Beatrice Snyder who spoke for herself:

My husband was stationed at Fort Huachuca with the 10th Cavalry, and we loved it very much . . . I have heard that there is a book . . . written by a Col. Glass . . . I have passed the century mark but my spirit is still young. How I loved the Cavalry!! And still do!

Two weeks later:

I have been surprised once or twice in my life but never have I been more astonished and surprised than yesterday when I received that wonderful gift. I longed to get this book . . . I hope I don't wear out the pages looking for familiar names. If this envelope bulges it is because I can't get all my thank you's in it!

CHAPTER FIFTEEN

"Just write the book, someone will want it."

1987 – 1988

Dave Liebman, Harris, and "Oliver."

On New Year's Day, we did some strategic planning, expecting 1987 to more or less follow the pattern we had happily established by then. We wrote to Ute and Peter Grauer, proposing that in September we add a week of buying in Germany to our anticipated British two or three weeks, with Ute or both of them helping us plan and going along, mimicking our trips with Amy. Ute was with us for a few days in January and we talked about it. But a couple of major developments made this a very different year. Our world changed.

Dave put together a computer system for us that we started using in 1987. Like children, we, or at least I, expected it to arrive on a "Christmas Morning" day, all shiny and new, but instead it was like a present that arrived with "some assembly required." A lot of assembly. It took well over a year, I think; inevitably there was a lot of trial and error as we all refined our ideas. That summer it seemed agonizingly slow, Dave adding in functions and testing them, one at a time, the development of the system. It was out of the question for us to input the book records, by then probably 50,000 entries, so simultaneously the seemingly endless data entry process went on as we subject-coded every card and sent out one or two card-file boxes at a time to an unknown "service" in Long Island. Harris had developed the coding, in consultation with the rest of us in several after-work long evenings, usually ending at Hanratty's. There were over three hundred subject codes, as most books fit into several subjects and each could have as many as three codes. We added more codes as the occasion arose over the years. Robin did a lot of this precise and thoughtful work before the cards went out. How lucky we were to have her for the transition.

Dave had found a data-entry service near his home, and he ferried the files back and forth. He never would tell us who they were as we (I) were constantly in a rage with them: they made a great many errors and somehow, incredibly, lost all the Ps. A whole file box of Ps! We did a certain amount of checking the computer data entry against the cards when the files returned—all we had contracted for was their double-checking author spellings—and many entries were a mess, and almost had to be recatalogued. The customer records were transferred smoothly from Jesse to Oliver, with the exception of one good customer, who fell between the cracks—but found us again soon enough.

We all fretted a bit about the unfamiliarity of the computer, and Robin thought we would miss a certain sense of security of having the cards in our hands for so many of our routines. It was exciting and scary at the same time.

We kept the card files for quite a while after we had fully converted, before recycling them as scrap paper. The cards contained a nostalgic element. Some of them old and a bit mealy, the handwriting our staff history, one after another: Bill's red and yellow markings on Ray's original cards, Mel's Catholic school handwriting, Robin's coding, prices in the distinctive styles of our changing cast of characters.

The initial program design was used and tinkered with and adjusted to our real needs which we could not entirely define until we worked with it. When we saw how one thing worked, we could imagine what more it might do. In the meantime we were running the store with the card files as well, the two systems in tandem. A crazy time, especially with no Ps! How did we cope with the usual active-to-dead-to-active rotation of the cards in the normal course of business, the increase in paperwork, how did we know what had been entered or what had not? Even after the data entry was completed, there were still many features that Dave, so admirably cautious, added in one at a time, which were tested by use before we moved on to the next step.

Dave was endlessly patient and calm and accommodating, as we thought of new tricks for the computer to perform. It was always fun to see him when he ambled in on Saturdays to deal with our list of requests or problems that had arisen. Bagel and coffee in hand (he didn't like our coffee), he was ready for all our questions. He was always there for distress calls. I think we were his hobby. This was, after all, a very early small-business application, and a new challenge for him. Dave gave us more than we had imagined and then we had a hard time paying him for the job.

Dave gave us a lot of extras: he gave Harris, for the computer in the basement, the solitaire game, but even more insidious, "Minesweeper." Like any addict, Harris got lost in this game, would go downstairs for a legitimate reason and think "just one little game." We lost track of where he was. Someone dispatched downstairs to fetch him (or just visiting, like Michael Wray) would get sucked in and disappear too, until I would call down the heat vent.

This system could handle a network, gradually added in, not the solo machine of the Jesse years. We named this system Oliver, for Jesse's younger and smarter brother. Jesse was singular, but Oliver eventually was quintuplets: five networked computers. We had a program in which the customers interlocked and interacted with the books. When we brought up a customer's record, we could go straight through it into the book files and sell the books into the individual account, or reserve books or list wants. There was a "secret" comment page hidden behind the main record, for miscellaneous information: phone numbers, peccadilloes, credits, or very confidential observations. The staff was instructed *never* to go into it when the customer was standing there—it could be embarrassing.

There was a way to list a customer's rarified interest—as arcane as Flying Wing, Powder Monkeys, B-29, Dazzle-Painting—which we called the Shadow File. It could be worthwhile to make short lists for those designated, for instance, for submarines or poster books, or humor, because we now had the capability of putting together the interested customer with the books. Pat Wirtz, in Illinois, had found us in early years and it didn't take long to figure out that he collected humor, verbal or visual, of all periods. I tried to remember to quote him anything new that came in, and when Oliver came along, it was easy: I just sent a printout of the book record. Pat always responded, and usually bought, spending thousands on his subject, all reasonably priced; he must have had a fascinating collection.

When new books came in, we instantly knew which were wants: the entry was orange. (I told Dave I wanted reveille to sound when a want came in, but Oliver was not up to that.) Oliver color-coded books in different states: in stock, green; out-of-stock, yellow; on quote, blue; with wants, orange; on reserve, red, the colors instantly revealing the book's status. It was just what I had imagined standing outside the IBM showroom on Park Avenue. The color changed as the book's status changed, for instance when a reserved book was sold through the customer's record, the sale was recorded in the customer record and the book record changed to yellow, for inactive.

The books could be coded to fall into any of three subject listings, which made for great flexibility in the catalogue. The coding could be deployed to present books in different contexts and with more exposure, sooner. For example, Margaret Bourke-White, the famous war photographer, was coded for "Women in War," "War Art and Photography," and "World War II Russia."

As we became used to Oliver's capabilities, we made the catalogues more interesting, to us at least, by culling small but distinct subjects out of large. The catalogue could cut a slice through our usual chronological presentation and put books together for a new look, a fresh presentation. Common books sold better in good company, too. More than a few times, we noticed regular customers buying books they had seen many times on the shelf or in the catalogue but had not gotten around to, because the book was shown in a new context.

We could extract a category such as Pirates and Privateers from the larger naval listings. Cavalry could be separate, or grouped with Animals in War. China or Poland or India or Balkans could

Melvin and Harris playing, not accounting.

be shown in a chronological cross-section. War Art, from Goya and Velazquez to Picasso and Louis Raemaekers and David Low, as well as poster books and art and photography did well as a separate subject. In one issue, Photography added up to three catalogue pages, over a hundred books, a surprise to us. We usually listed Music, Literature and Humor together. Segments of popular subjects such as Napoleon vs. Britain made a fresh look at the familiar. We bought one lot of Castles, enough to list separately—once, just Crusades. War Crimes included the Holocaust, the Armenian genocide, the Bataan Death March, My Lai and other atrocities and often ran with Law and Military Government. Medicine took on perspective when interspersed with the many memoirs of doctors and nurses. Science and Industry sold better when highlighted, and could include company histories like *Fuller Brush at War* or Chrysler's *Tanks are Mighty Fine Things*. One category that made for fascinating reading was Volunteers, Soldiers of Fortune and Mercenaries: Italian *condottieri,* the Lafayette Escadrille, William Walker in Nicaragua, the Knights of Malta, American volunteers in the Spanish Civil War, and various low-lifes in the Congo and Angola. Another that always did well was Women in War: warrior queens, Florence Nightingale, Joan of Arc, Gertrude Stein, reporters, spies, nurses, Anne Frank, the unnamed women of Bletchley Park, *The Lady was a Terrorist,* Tokyo Rose.

I was still doing some business in the Japanese war prints, mostly with a few local customers and one in Chicago who went for the naval scenes; Brendan bought a couple for his new apartment. I liked having them around and usually bought only two or three at a time from a Japanese print dealer on Lexington Avenue. She and I both liked the war scenes, but not "bruddy" (bloody) ones as she said. She had pointed out to me the importance of nature, terrain and the weather in Japanese art—as in warfare, come to think of it. Indeed the weather was always a factor, even a protagonist in the best of those scenes: combat in the snow felt cold, rain fog and wind were integral in the images, and the water in naval scenes was active and alive.

Russell Spurr, a writer based in Japan and author of a book about kamikaze pilots, *A Glorious Way to Die*, came in to the store bearing a portfolio of Japanese triptych woodcuts of the Russo-Japanese war, all together back-to-back in one folding strip. There were perhaps a dozen, by different artists and apparently of different battles, but a collector had put them together as an album. I knew we could not sell it as a single item, but I bought it, taking the chance that I would be able to take it apart. It was sort of scary, so I took the portfolio to my friendly Japanese dealer, to see if she had some magic way to separate them, something perhaps to dissolve the exotic glue. The prints were only attached to each other on the edges, and she simply inserted her little finger and gently pulled them apart. How silly I felt.

On another visit, she showed me a handsome, privately printed art book by Nathan Chaikin, of Japanese triptych woodcuts on the Sino-Japanese War. I bought a copy for our own reference and decided we should try it in the store—a great war/art crossover. The author had donated his many extra copies to his favorite little charity, so I started buying five copies at a time from them. The book sold, gradually, dozens of copies. This went on for years, and finally my contact at the charity said, "I'd like to ship all these books to you, these boxes are just in the way here." So we paid what we wanted to for them and continued to sell them.

The books kept coming. I dreamed, sometimes, of cascades of books, a kaleidoscope of color. There were a few visits to Mort in Wilmington. Lewis and I went to see Sy Getchburg in the spring. Our regular finders made their regular visits. We combined a Connecticut party with a few greenhouses and a visit to John Toland. Best known for his World War II books, *The Rising Sun* and *Adolf Hitler*, John had decided to part with a substantial number of books gathered for his various projects. We went back in June to pick them up in Danbury, bearing a Military Bookman T-shirt, promptly appropriated by his daughter. For the occasion I wore a shirt Bill Waters had given me, in the style of a rock concert shirt, "Adolf Hitler's European Tour" on the front, and on the back a list of Hitler's campaigns.

Out of the blue, the Chicago Art Institute wrote to ask if we would be interested in arms and armor books, then sent us a packet of xeroxed title pages, duplicates they were deaccessioning. I hadn't expected much, duplicates after all, but they were scarce arms and armor titles; not only had we never seen them, we could not find any auction records for pricing guidance.

I made an ignorant offer; nevertheless about a hundred and fifty books arrived. There were lavishly produced limited editions of the turn-of-the-century's great private armor collections, many with rich duotone plates. Bashford Dean titles, the von Kienbusch collection, Trapp on the Armory of Churburg Castle, Meyrick, the multi-volume Laking, and many less rare but still infrequently seen studies. I took my time with them, putting them out by the half-dozen, thinking all the while that we could finally have a real showing of this small, scarce, elitist subject in our catalogue, rather than our usual dozen or so common titles intermingled in the Medieval list. It was not to be. Serendipity struck. By some ESP, Nick McCullough of Sotheby's arms and armor department strolled down 93rd Street for the first time ever and discovered the Military Bookman. This bad-boy curator was said to have fired an antique gun in a London sales room and perhaps he had been exiled to America. On several visits, Nick vacuumed up the rare books as fast as they hit the shelf. Nice turnover, but not much left for the catalogue.

It seemed likely that Peter Finer, a British arms-and-armor dealer, heard about us from Nick. Peter appeared in time to gather up some of the Chicago books, and made us a regular stop for some years when he was in town for the big Winter Antiques Show. Alas, we never had another lot comparable to that from Chicago.

Mike Mullins's interest in, and involvement with, the Civil War had only increased. He was writing a column for *Civil War News* and by this time knew all the regular writers and dealers and historians, and he was working on a Civil War regimental history himself. In April, I was not in the store the morning Mike paid his seasonal visit to borrow Civil War books for a show. Mike and Jason were chatting about Mike's alliance with Tom Broadfoot, a well-known Civil War dealer and publisher, to reprint obscure Civil War memoirs, and Mike told Jason about his latest proposal, a rare Stonewall Brigade memoir he had found: *Recollections,* by Randolph Barton. Jason, truly shocked, told Mike that it was my great-grandfather's memoir and that I had been planning to do something with it. Mike, I was told, went white. Everyone thought I would be really upset, and Jason was too much of a coward to tell me, so Harris did that evening, over a drink. But I wasn't upset. I had been procrastinating for years and I knew I had taken a chance that someone would steal a march on me. In my previous history jobs and then especially at the store, seeing the Civil War interest and the many reprints of that literature, I had become increasingly convinced that the Barton story would find an audience. I hadn't worked on it because I wanted to take time to try to fill in some gaps in the sketchy and anecdotal *Recollections* and, if possible, learn more about Barton's large family in the war.

In fact I was relieved that it was Mike, a friend, who had found it. When Mike came back to the store two weeks later, I told him this and said I would like to be involved, and Mike, dear man, responded, "Consida yaself involved!" He talked to Tom and then I wrote Tom with my ideas. A gracious correspondence ensued. Tom said to Mike, essentially, "Back off and let her run with it." He told me to see what I could discover, keep him informed, and send him a sample chapter. So I began to work on what became *Defend the Valley.*

Harris was apprehensive, and I think a bit jealous, of my time being taken from the store. The summer of 1987 was already more than full: my parents were moving and I wanted to help, and not one but two teenage godsons, Mark Cummings and Edward Strickland, were coming from England for overlapping visits. We were in the midst of a fraught and complicated period in the store. And there I was, wanting to start a book! But I really thought I could knock off the reprint in six months or so. And I had to do it.

I wrote to my aunt, Louise Barton, in Baltimore, for the addresses of my father's cousins, hoping that among them I might unearth the original photos used in *Recollections*, or stories or odds-and-ends to supplement the slender text. In short order, my aunt called to say she had a "box of old lettahs, and the first one we pulled out was from Mrs. Robert E. Lee, regrettin' they couldn't come to the weddin'." The hair rose on the back of my neck. I was too astonished to say, "How big is that box?" but waited in great anticipation.

I cajoled Harris into going to Virginia with me for a hot July week before Edward arrived, to Richmond, Charlottesville and Winchester for the first time, doing some book-buying as well acquainting myself with the historical resources there. It was fun and sort of a vacation, as we had already reluctantly decided we couldn't leave the store long enough for a buying trip to England that fall.

At the Virginia Historical Society, I found intimations of more papers: transcripts of a battle account, written with total recall, by Randolph's brother Robert, and of four wartime letters by Randolph. There was no indication of where the originals might be, and the librarians were secretive and possessive. I had written, flying blind, to "Occupant" at Springdale, the old Barton house near Winchester, and she called the store and then tracked us down in Richmond, inviting us to stop in when we got to Winchester. This was thrilling for me. That house had been in my mind's eye for years. At least as important, that was my first of many visits to the Archives at the Handley Library in Winchester, which was to be my greatest Virginia research resource, and its archivist Rebecca Ebert a faithful ally. In the Archives, I found the war diary of an uncle, Frank Jones, who served in the Stonewall Brigade and was killed in 1862. Aunt Louise had told me to see cousin Ann Barton Brown, who lived near Winchester, and we visited Ann and her husband Stuart and I told them what I was doing and what I was looking for. They didn't seem to respond, so it was all the more astonishing when, a couple of weeks later, they sent copies of a much-wanted photo of Randolph in uniform in 1863, and his Appomattox parole.

In Winchester, someone said to me, "These people went away and took their history with them." I searched for distant cousins and sometimes bothered innocent people with likely names. I was also looking for the originals of some documents that I had found only in transcript, and photos I had seen reproduced. There were many blind alleys, and in some cases I was chasing my tail looking for papers that had already migrated to the Handley Library Archives.

I wrote to my father's other cousins, hoping they might have photos or letters or memories of their grandfather Randolph. They did not have much but encouragement to offer (one grumbled, "They have all those things in Richmond"), but cousin Eleanor Thomas, the beagling lady in Baltimore, called to tell me that her son Cal, in Staunton, Virginia, had a bunch of family papers. Then, my aunt introduced me to another branch of the family, Robert's granddaughter Dudley Lalley, who wanted to talk to me about her grandfather's memoir. This was more than exciting; from his battle account I already knew how well Robert wrote. I went to Baltimore in August to see these ladies who held new dimensions of the story in their hands. Dudley promised me a transcript of Robert's memoir.

Dudley suggested I also get in touch with another granddaughter of Robert's, Edith Barton Sheerin, in Albany, and sent me the copy of their grandfather Robert Barton's 1862 daguerreotype. I ripped it open immediately, and Jason said, "Omigosh, he looks just like your nephew!" And he did.

In the midst of all this, we made time for some excursions with Edward and Mark, the godsons. Felix invited us to dinner in his splendid house next door. We took a weekend up the Hudson to see the World War I air show at the Rhinebeck Aerodrome and saw Marilyn Monroe double features (Edward's obsession). We took a day trip to Philadelphia for both Independence Hall and the U.S.S. *Olympia* and a submarine moored in the Delaware River. On the bridge of his flagship, the *Olympia,* Admiral Dewey's bronze footprints memorialized his stance steaming in to Manila Bay in 1898 to rout the Spanish fleet.

By mid-August, Harris was writing:

Margaretta and I are most disappointed to have to inform all of our English friends that our September trip has been cancelled.

After over five years of procrastination, we began in February the computerization of our large bibliographic data files, both active and inactive. Our inevitable doubts were well founded. The software program which we designed is functioning, the hardware is excellent – but the data input, which of necessity had to be contracted outside, has been atrocious, not only inaccurate but in some cases lost altogether. We are staying home to mop up the mess!

We will miss the more-or-less left hand driving, ordnance survey at the ready, the Underground map in one pocket, the pub lunches, the harrowing experiences (for all) of electronic bank transfers that didn't "take," the opportunity to contribute to the U.S. trade deficit – but particularly, the annual pleasure of seeing you.

Take heart – we are temporarily crippled but the prognosis is good. When we are back on our feet, we will return to the books, friends and pleasures of the Old Country.

It wasn't as if we were at a loss for books. Offers continued to come in, and there was one lot I felt confident in buying sight unseen, but it backfired. A historian, director of a prestigious library upstate, offered us his own military books: some really unusual and scholarly titles. There was so much happening that fall, and we thought we could make an offer without visiting, for books with that provenance. Ordinarily we would have sent a down payment, but we felt safe in sending César and Andrew the shipping clerk off in the van with a large check for the full amount.

It was a disaster, and terribly disappointing. Despite the seller's representations, many of the books—the best titles, naturally—were not in good condition and, much worse, very many of them were scored, underlined, and with red and blue pencil at that. Unforgivable! Irredeemable! I was outraged, sort of; Harris thought we should probably let it go but I wanted to pursue it. Since I had negotiated the buy, the onus was on me to call the seller and tell him how difficult it was to be rejecting very many of the books as unsalable, and to try and work out a refund. It was an ordeal. The seller, understandably embarrassed, waffled, saying he had had the books in boxes for years and perhaps he did not remember what he had done to them, but he knew we knew he had handled them to make a recent list. It took a lot of work to figure out how to make this "right." We ended up returning five boxes of books as unfixable, for a refund of almost a third of the purchase price.

Interleaved with all this was the complicated time in the store, as we were adjusting to the computer and its ramifications and the chronic staff changes. Robin left us for law school, and we gave her a farewell dinner party with staff and Sheila and Richard Chalfin, "Better Book Getter," whom she had been dating. We missed Robin and I think she missed the store; she stayed in touch. Then, another piece of luck. An interesting Australian woman, working her way around the world by doing free-lance data entry, among other things, came along at the right time to work on a large and less urgent category of cards, the technical and field manuals, that Harris hadn't wanted to entrust to the clods on Long Island. So she would waft in several afternoons a week and spend some hours at the computer, by then in the back closet where the dead files had lived.

This was the nightmare year of five shipping clerks. After Luther left again, wild-haired Willie was with us for six weeks or so. He disappeared as soon as the catalogue hit and he was expected to pack more than a dozen orders a day. Nice, steady Ed developed health problems. In May, Ismael came back, but left again in the fall for an extended family visit to Puerto Rico. Andrew, the excitable epileptic, was good but lasted only three months or so. No one ever got fully trained and each required so much supervision.

Robin Elenko.

The fabled "box of letters"—smaller than a shoebox but containing over seventy Civil War letters and some relevant photos— arrived from my aunt. It was great good luck for me that this all coincided with the arrival of Oliver. As I was beginning to work on the letters, I had lunch with Jean Crocker and told her what I was doing and hemmed and hawed about using a computer. Jean said emphatically, "Margaretta, you'd be a fool not to use a computer!" Dave, ever generous, put a Word Perfect program in Oliver, and later brought in upgrades. It was an initial struggle; on beautiful October weekends when we should have been walking in Central Park, Harris and I, thigh to thigh in front of the new computer, endeavored to understand the esoteric language that seemed to be inherent in any computer program. In retrospect, it is unimaginable how this complex undertaking could have been accomplished without a computer.

My modest reprint was mushrooming into a very large project, and Harris was perhaps understandably perturbed when I went off hither and yon, to Baltimore and later to Staunton and Appomattox for a few days. Cal Thomas had invited me to visit; he said he had "about a suitcase full" of family papers. "Come on down!"

Harris gave me a really hard time on the eve of my trip to Staunton, as if I were shirking the store. I thought about it as I flew south over the gorgeous autumn-dappled Blue Ridge, and when I came home I said, "I've been playing your game with you for all these years, now I want to play my game, and I would love to have you play too." He relented, and then when he saw what had come out of Cal's suitcase in Staunton, especially a tiny letter that Randolph Barton had received when a POW at Fort Delaware, and how, with all the documents I was finding, the story was taking shape, he became a convert and a staunch supporter in countless ways.

All of this was fitted in around the demands of the store. Our routine came to be that at 5:30, closing time, I would turn to my transcribing and writing, and Harris would start the computer backup (a lengthy process then), work on the day's sales report, and make one or two runs upstairs for drinks, plying me with bourbon, like a real Southern writer.

I started transcribing the documents with the easiest handwriting, and realized that the Military Bookman correspondence had helped prepare me to deal with many specimens of penmanship, if not nineteenth century. But I got used to it, returning repeatedly to puzzling words that came clear sometimes years later. Harris entered documents then known to us only in transcripts. He later took dictation as I read, with great difficulty, the crabbed, lawyerly hand in a legal brief that had been folded tight for one hundred and twenty-seven years.

Dave found us a printer who could take a disk copied from our catalogue program, to produce a catalogue: cutting edge at the time, not many small printing companies had the technology. KNA Press happened to be in Kennett Square, Pennsylvania, about a twenty-minute drive from my parents' home. Dave and I drove down to talk to Dick Taylor at KNA, and then Dave dropped me off at my parents. This was the beginning of our only "happy" relationship with a printer: really professional people, good to work with. It helped that we knew each other; I often went to Wilmington with the dual purpose of checking the layouts and having a family visit. Once on the train returning, I sat next to a man immersed in a World War II book. I remarked that he liked military history. "It's my passion," he said. "It's my business," I rejoined, and carded him.

By the fall, we had to admit that we couldn't produce our holiday-time catalogue—we were straddling two systems—and reluctantly sent a Christmas letter, in green ink, telling our subscribers that the usual issue would be postponed.

Soon after, we produced our first computerized catalogue. With the card files, we had spent weeks selecting the cards from the files by subject on the shelves; proofreading and editing, sending them to the typesetter; proofreading again, and finally off to a printer, who in an indeterminate period of time would produce the booklet. A two-month process. In the meantime, the book catalogue cards could be in any of eight places: active file, dead file, catalogue file, binding file, reserve shelf, on the side to be quoted, on the side to be refiled, or in new book processing. Imagine the confusion.

The computer allowed us to select the subjects we wanted to list, enter their codes in the catalogue program, and, after hours, to run the program that chose the books for the catalogue. Then we started shelfchecking and proofing from printouts, but that didn't take too long; then, after making corrections and updates, we reran the catalogue program, cut a disk and sent it off to the printer. After some back and forth, the catalogue would appear several weeks later. The new system allowed us to produce more issues each year. Going up to three issues a year had been a big push when we started doing it in 1980. By the time all the

Oliver systems were functioning, we were able to do four issues a year in 1990. We still shelfchecked and proofread until the pace of five catalogues a year in 1997 made it spotty.

That Christmas I succumbed to the temptation of ordering a big wreath for the beautiful parlor window. Our Greek florists over on Lexington Avenue made the wreaths themselves, and they got quite carried away. The wreath was handsome, but a good bit larger than I had ordered, institutional size. We hung it out, not easily as it was so heavy, and went to work. I was planning to photograph it later for a future Christmas card. About noon, our Polish neighbor's scowling face appeared at the store window, and he motioned me peremptorily to come outside. He had cornered a thief bearing the large wreath on our steps. Just hold on a minute please I said, and called Harris from the back, and 911. Harris grabbed Peter's sword and, closely followed by Andrew, the volatile shipping clerk, rushed out to confront the thief and keep him on the stoop. I reported the crime to the police and went off to meet a friend for lunch at the Colony Club and dined out on the story. The police were busy with a happening on 86th Street and did not arrive for about an hour. The perp was really happy to see them: "That guy wanted to beat me up and the other guy was gonna cut me with that big blade!"

There was some satisfaction in seeing a perp caught, although he was out again stealing wreaths by the end of the day. The police had plenty of crime to contend with: in the night, drug dealers ran their business from the phone booth next to the Corner Bookstore, and a rippling descant of car alarms down the street signaled a wave of break-ins.

In late January, when I went to Wilmington to check proofs on the first KNA catalogue, I took along Randolph Barton's little ninety-page memoir. Dick Taylor had a new toy, a scanner, and we both wanted to see how it would cope with the typeface of the 1913 book. Pretty good, but uneven—there were many passages I had to correct, or reenter, but that was so much easier than entering it all myself.

Once again, we had word of mouth to thank for a part-timer. ShaRene Barnett was a skinny little high school girl who wanted an after school job. She was on full scholarship at Riverdale, a very good school in the Bronx—a bit of a commute for a part-time job. She was sweet, serious and about the smartest person who ever worked for me: practical, efficient, retentive and clear, quietly taking in everything going on around her. Sometimes I said to Sheila, "She's the only grownup here."

ShaRene wore something different every day, seemingly never the same thing twice: she could wear her mother's clothes, and her hairstyle changed from week to week because she had a cousin who was practicing hair-dressing. In the brief time she worked for us, she evolved from a skinny kid into a slender young woman.

She was scrupulous, detail-oriented and very conscientious, so we set her to shelf checking for the catalogue; I still have a printout on which she noted, "Harris says this book is here but I haven't actually seen it."

Hoping to improve our shipping department, we made the job full-time, and hired someone sent by the New York State Employment Office. Gineau the Haitian, whom Jason dubbed the Voodoo King, was decidedly strange. Once he found an injured pigeon in the backyard, which he tied to the packing table and later took home, he said, to his kids. He was indeed eerie, and always borderline hostile. The only exception was when Amy came for a visit; her friendliness and charm cracked his carapace of negativity and ill will.

One of the burdens for a small business was jury duty. It was a chunk of staff time every two years. Somehow I was called for jury duty far more often than Harris. (Nick the mailman had once, at Harris's request, disposed of his summons.) For four weeks that February, I was sentenced to Grand Jury—a murder Grand Jury. It was harrowing; we heard two of the more notorious cases of the year, and a variety of "standard" murders. I was able to absent myself for two days, when I took a train to snowy Albany and received a warm Southern welcome from cousins Edith and Charlie Sheerin. They were excited about my expanding book project, and Edith took a very active interest. She had said that she had too many Barton papers to carry on the train, "more than a grapefruit box," and there they were, in brown grocery bags all over the dining room table. We had dinner on our laps in the living room, and a great time sorting through several generations of documents—but still not the elusive original of Robert's memoir. I read Civil War letters all the way home on the train.

In what was to become a yearly ritual, I went to Virginia in March, in the lull when the Spring catalogue was at the printer. It occurred to me that it would be fun to take my seventeen-year-old nephew Ran with me for a few days, back to his roots. Ran was history-oriented, and riveted by his resemblance to Robert Barton. He was a fine companion, and we met Edith's brother Bob Barton who came over from West Virginia to see us. Bob had done the transcript of his grandfather's journal, one high school summer; his grandmother paid him five cents a page, not bad for the forties, I guess. Ran and I did some research "on the ground," and in the Court House records. The death records Ran perused had a certain macabre fascination for him, one listing the cause as "gravel"; but he couldn't stay awake checking for Barton references in a lengthy diary in the Archives. After Ran had left, I went to see another cousin, a descendant of Barton uncle Frank Jones. I suspected she had, somewhere, a photo of Frank I had seen reproduced, and when I drove up to the old house, there she was, sitting on the side porch in the thin sunshine of early spring, with a box of letters on her lap: Frank's wartime letters home. At that moment, Frank was on his way to becoming a significant character in the book.

Later that week, in their mother's house in Richmond, Bob Barton and Edith found Robert's original memoir, handwritten in a legal journal, and Bob said to Edith, "Get this to Margaretta."

Two weeks before I went to Winchester, there was a scene in the store. Lewis, separated from his family, unhappy and drinking too much and who knows what else, was tightly wound and had developed a hair-trigger temper. He had already blown up once, at Harris, who in his usual way was willing to overlook it. When he blew up at me for some trivial remark, it was once too often, it looked like a new trend. That was it. Lewis had been terrific in a lot of ways, with a lively interest in the books, hard-working, and with a good sense of humor; it was too bad.

We usually listed a job in the *New York Times* Help Wanted section, later trying the *Village Voice* after getting nowhere with a *Publisher's Weekly* ad or a notice at the Columbia Library School. Listing our phone number meant taking a lot of calls that were mostly worthless, so after a while we just asked for resumes. Sheila was privy to some of them, and on one she wrote, "Wack job of the first order."

We had two interviews with one man; in the second it was clear he didn't understand he would be working for a woman, so that was no good. He chose several books and was allowed to take them, saying he would send a check; he never did. We were interviewing for a while. All in all, we must have had a hard time finding a replacement for Lewis because after several months we settled for Arthur. He was a goofy-looking young guy who had worked for Sky Books, so he knew something of the subject. But not enough else. He had no attention span, no follow-through, and couldn't be bothered to learn. He was not relating to the systems and he made Dave nervous; Dave was afraid he would tinker with Oliver.

In June, I had an appointment to meet someone clearing out a large apartment and selling a naval lot, up on Riverside Drive near Columbia University. It was a big old building, and I was left cooling my heels in the marble lobby for well over an hour; the seller never did show up. But my project was so much in my mind that I began writing the first chapter while I waited. I did go back to see the books the next week, but we didn't buy them.

By summer, most of the old letters had been transcribed into the computer. The two memoirs had been entered in the computer, and Robert's read against the original journal and mostly corrected, though there were still indecipherable words. I sat confronting a huge amount of material, in many disparate chunks, stymied about how to handle it. I was stalled, but Harris got me moving again. He pieced the documents together chronologically, so easy with a word processor, and it was immediately apparent that that was the right thing to do. I started working on a sample chapter for Tom Broadfoot.

At dinner with friends, I was teased a little about my obsession, and as the evening went on someone suggested, half in jest, that I send an Author's Query to the *New York Times*. Those little column fillers in the Book Review section made curious but interesting reading. We all laughed, but next morning I thought, "Why not?" and sent one off, then didn't think any more of it. We were away on the July weekend that the query ran and I didn't know it had until Oscar Schreyer, who had spotted it, called. So did a reporter from the Winchester paper. Hard on their heels I heard from a distant cousin at the other end of Long Island, and, within ten days, a letter from eighty-eight-year-old cousin Frances Jones, in Winchester. The Long Island cousin was fascinated by my project and the bookstore, and took to coming in to the store when he was in town, and then upstairs with us for a drink after work. One night in a cab back to Penn Station, he found himself with a Sikh driver. Having served in Burma and India during World War II, he started speaking Punjabi and they had a great conversation all the way downtown. The driver wouldn't take the fare.

Argosy Books called us about a large French Foreign Legion collection that had been seasoning in their warehouse in Brooklyn, and Harris went off to look at it. It was certainly more on that subject than we had ever seen; usually we had at most two or three shelves. With French Foreign Legion books, there was always a large percentage that were odd, fictionalized and romanticized. The majority of the lot, and the subject, was in French, always a hard sell for us as even our most devoted Napoleonic collectors rarely read French. Nevertheless we knew we had to buy it, but we probably paid too much; it was difficult to assess how we did with such a collection, because it lingered. We put out the most saleable items, but much remained languishing in the basement. We did have one interested French reader at the time who would regularly descend to the basement and rake through the aging typical-French white-covered paperbacks, and then we would give him a lot price. Gradually all the books went away.

A friend took us to see a Mrs. Fredericks, who was selling her late husband's books, a small but interesting collection. We quickly realized that he had been Pierce Fredericks, a journalist and teacher, and author of a book we saw frequently, *The Sepoy and the Cossack,* and another about the Americans in World War I.

We bought a naval collection too, mostly British, with some old and unusual books, many of which were new to us. Horatio Hornblower was a character we had grown up with, eagerly seizing on the *Saturday Evening Post* when it was running C. S. Forester's serialized adventures of a British naval captain in the Napoleonic Wars. Even Harris, confined at boarding school, had access to the

Hornblower stories and he loved them. The Hornblower books were among the few fiction titles we carried in the store, for sentimental reasons, and because they were our generation's Patrick O'Brian, giving a good picture of the era. Then C. Northcote Parkinson's *Life and Times of Horatio Hornblower* came in with that naval lot, detailing Hornblower's career as history, in a scholarly way. Harris got very excited—maybe Hornblower was real!—and took the book upstairs, indeed to bed with him. Quickly, a footnote reference didn't ring true, and he couldn't wait until morning; down he went in his skivvies to the store, where we then had a long run of the British *Navy Records Society* publications. The reference was a phony; Parkinson, tongue deeply planted in cheek, had produced a sophisticated spoof, *convincing and delicious,* as Harris wrote in the catalogue.

As soon as Gineau had put in six months of lackluster performance, the time necessary to "merit" unemployment compensation, he picked a fight with Harris and got himself fired. But it really was a happy day, because by then, Ismael had come back from Puerto Rico and had stopped in to say hello. We knew he was working at Feldman's, and after we fired Gineau, Harris conducted a raid. Ismael rejoined us, full-time, that fall. And soon he became "Ish"—that was what his little girl called him, and it stuck. He said with some annoyance, "I don't want her to call me Ish, I want her to call me Daddy." Little did any of us realize what a fine, productive, long relationship it would be, how much his skills would develop and how close we would become. He matured into the job and made it so much more than it was to begin with, more than we ever expected. Thereafter our only shipping aggravation was the notorious Pete, a/k/a José, who took over our UPS route and never got promoted from it. I fought with him, Jason fought with him, even Emily later fought with him, and every merchant in the neighborhood complained; but it was classic Peter Principle, and he was on the route for over twenty-five years.

That fall, I sent the promised sample chapter to Tom Broadfoot. Tom had it vetted by Mike Mullins and Gary Gallagher, a noted Civil War historian, who were enthusiastic, he told me. In the same letter, Tom added that he would not be publishing it (or anything else for a while, Mike later said. It seemed Tom had bitten off more than he could chew in reprinting the massive *Official Records.)*

I was really thrown, having felt that Broadfoot's wanting to publish the book helped me justify the project to Harris. I didn't know whether I was supposed to look for another publisher then, or what to do next. Harris said calmly but decisively, "Just write the book, someone will want it." It was what I wanted to hear, the moral support I needed.

Harris was giving me plenty of practical assistance too. He helped me understand military questions and undertook some research. He had not been a student of the Civil War but he got quite caught up in it, and later embarked on two related projects, writing articles on the 1862 Valley Campaign and the White Flags at Appomattox. He had become interested in the Valley Campaign when he transcribed Frank Jones's diary and on my trips to the Shenandoah, he had me clocking mileage of marches that Frank had described. When I was "approaching" Appomattox in my writing, I said, offhandedly, "See if you can figure out what happened with these white-flag stories." He was on it like a terrier, and expended great interest and energy on these projects. The articles were intended as appendices but were not included due to the length of my manuscript, and unfortunately were never published. Harris also compiled the family's service records for the book. And it was Harris who thought of the title, *Defend the Valley,* such an important contribution and one that everyone loved.

It was an exciting time. I had a lot of feelers and inquiries out, so I never knew what might come in the mail or who might be heard from or even walk in the door. A couple of barely known cousins sent precious old photographs, and a box of Confederate money arrived in the mail: the "family fortune," courtesy of Dudley Lalley.

Harris was the only child of an only child, and his head was spinning with all my new family connections, but he welcomed and coped with unknown cousins who called or showed up. Customers who came to know what I was doing offered leads or tidbits of information. Steve Sears, by then a well-known Civil War historian, had been my editor at American Heritage, was a sometime customer and was very encouraging. We had a lot of "shop talk" and it amused me when he offered, among other advice, "Don't go to the National Archives if you can possibly avoid it." I did. Steve told me later that, knowing how fanatical I was about research, he thought I would never get the book done. Mike Mullins made some key connections for me with several Civil War historians and researchers, and on his visits to the store I regaled him with my research finds and he loved hearing about my progress.

The two of us needed a break, and in October escaped to Portugal where we couldn't read the language and didn't darken the door of a bookshop. At home our social life shrank as I devoted myself to the Barton project, and I all but stopped reading the Sunday *Times* as I sequestered myself in the parlor while Harris watched football. I pulled myself out of it however, to campaign with a couple of neighbors, out on the cold street with petitions, against a projected sidewalk café at our corner, too noisy too late already, the sidewalk too narrow—feeling strongly about it but thinking "I don't have time for this!"

CHAPTER SIXTEEN

"Is the boat in yet?"

1989

Colts checking in British books.

The Colts at the ideal pub, Cartmel.

More cousins showed up. Cal Thomas came in from Staunton on business and stayed with us, then got fogged in and stayed an extra night. As usual we went to Piro's. Cal was a second cousin, but I had found thirds and fourths, to say nothing of the "removeds," some around the corner on Fifth Avenue, and another nearby on 96th Street.

As with cousins, there were always new and repeat customers and sellers. We had a repeat at the Met: Stuart Pyhrr called us again to buy books.

When the store was on 92nd Street, a local, Second World War unit history aficionado was a brash young fellow named Mike Rivkin, an insatiable collector of only those titles. He was an accountant at City College, and a very active buyer for a while, before abruptly disappearing into his career for about ten years. When he returned, very prosperous and with a car and driver, he was the Comptroller of Brooklyn College. He was again avidly amassing unit histories, but after about two years, turned around and wanted to sell his whole collection back to us for fifty percent of retail. Harris was all for it and I was not; by the late eighties, our unit history business had fallen off, so I thought it was too much to pay. Harris's decision to go ahead with the purchase occasioned the major fight of our partnership.

We had talked about the offer and I didn't like the whole thing: Rivkin struck me as a bit of a flim-flam guy, and Harris's motive in buying was in some measure to thwart a competitor. Our partnership had never included unilateral decisions of any magnitude, and I had been perfectly clear in what I said, so a day or two later when Harris told us in the store that we were buying Rivkin's books, I went up in flames. I was so mad I don't think I said more than "WHAT?!" and slammed out, not even taking my keys with me. Sheila had to buzz me in upstairs.

I was still beside myself, though in the store, the next day, Saturday, when I found out in the nicest possible way that Harris was giving a surprise party for my fiftieth birthday: my family appeared in the store window. It was a lovely party, beautifully planned, and I was amazed that he had such a capacity for deception. And I was perhaps somewhat mollified. Nevertheless, in the following weeks, I returned to the Rivkin subject and kept working Harris over. Finally, he threw up his hands, "All right, all right, if I don't make our money back in six months, I'll send you and Sheila to Mexico!" In due course, he acknowledged that he owed me the trip. I "won" the bet, though didn't collect on it for years.

Some time later, Mike Rivkin was indicted and tried for misappropriating funds from Brooklyn College.

In the meantime, we were trying to replace Arthur. It is unsure why we put up with his incompetence and inattention for so long, probably because it had been so hard to find anyone when we found him. ShaRene had been such a help that perhaps Arthur's shortcomings were not so evident because she picked up the slack. We had given him a very critical six-month review, and to our surprise he said he wasn't interested in the job—"I knew after two weeks"—and resigned. On top of that, he tried to collect unemployment. Sheila told me how to fight that, as it would have raised our rate, and I was successful.

Jason had come into his own, aided immeasurably by Oliver which saved him physical effort and some thought, and he began to function as a manager when we needed it. Sometimes this went to his head and he started thinking he was the boss. When Arthur departed, we abandoned our idea that the "fourth person" should know how to do almost everything in the store, not just pick up the phone or meet the walk-ins and deal with preliminaries, but be able to buy books and cope with any situation that might arise in our absences. Our expectations for the fourth person had been scaled down since we had a hard time finding committed book people. By this time we wanted someone more like a reliable clerk. We listed the job with the New York State Employment Office.

I was still seeing Claire Boos, my friend from the rare book course, and one day over lunch the previous fall, she had listened intently as I described my growing Civil War research, then said a colleague of hers from Crown Publishing, Sandra Still, was working on her own Civil War project. As I came to a certain point in my project, I wanted to talk to Sandra as I had reason to think our interests might intersect; Claire took umbrage at this, feeling I was treading on Sandra's toes. (Come on Claire, it's a big war.) Furthermore, she said Sandra had visited the Military Bookman and had met me.

This was news to me: I certainly had no recollection of meeting Sandra, and that was embarrassing. So I procrastinated in calling her, but eventually braced myself and did it, intimating that we had met. It turned out that we hadn't, but Sandra played the game and we made a lunch date. She would come to the store and have a look for books to reprint, and then we'd talk Civil War. I was upstairs in the parlor, my workroom, pulling out material to show Sandra when Jason called to tell me she had arrived. When I walked into the store, Jason was on the phone again, taking the first call for our freshly advertised job opening and describing the position. Sandra popped out from behind a shelf saying, "I know someone who would be perfect for this job." During lunch at Piro's, we talked about our projects but she kept coming back to her friend Emily Katt who wanted to move to New York and had so many merits, including bookstore experience, that I said repeatedly, "She's too good for us." At Sandra's insistence and with great skepticism, I interviewed Emily by telephone from Minneapolis, and then urged Harris and Jason to do the same. We all but hired Emily sight unseen (Sandra thought to tell us at the last minute that Emily was kind of normal looking.) Ten days later, Emily flew in for an interview on a Saturday, followed by a memorable dinner at Piro's. She started on Tuesday.

Emily's first question about her duties was, "Should I come in early and dust?" I just laughed, and probably said something like: we traffic in addiction, a little dust doesn't matter. Emily hit the ground running and while there was the inevitable learning curve on the subject matter, her financial background made her a great companion for Harris in doing the store numbers. We teased her about the time she slipped a cog, after analyzing best-selling subjects with Harris; her face very serious and intent, she said, "We should buy more Marine Corps books, they do so well." We would have if we could have; their scarcity was what made them so much in demand.

Emily was diligent, rarely sitting still. She had a very good memory for the customers, and she was pretty and piquant-looking, slender and fair, and had many local fans. Her telephone manner, very intimate, captivated many a caller. I sat across the partner's desk from her and I often couldn't tell what she was saying to them; it could have been a 900 number.

As often happened, a phone customer wanted to stick with whomever had helped him first. Allen Schreck drew Emily on his first call. His subject was espionage and intelligence, hers too, and he would buy any imprint of the Military Service Publishing Company, a semi-official publisher which had produced many military texts. Between his avid interests, and, maybe, her manner, he managed to spend over $14,000 in the two-and-a-half years both of them were with us. Mr. Schreck, alas, died. And alas for us, around the same time Emily moved on.

A few months after Emily started, ShaRene's home situation changed, and she had to leave us rather abruptly. When her life settled down, she wrote:

I would like to thank you for giving me a chance to prove myself as an important part of the team at "The Military Bookman." I came to you as an inexperienced tenth-grader; yet, you saw that I had potential. For this, I will be forever grateful. As I regard my employment with you as one of the most enriching periods of my short-lived life. My hiring enabled me to have a new outlook on the path and success of my future. So now the store can add 'encouraging a young black teen to strive for success' to its long list of achievements.

Patton was one of our favorite movies, and it was my luck to take the first call: "This is --- ahem --- George C. Scott." Well, it certainly was, no question about that voice, and given his two famous roles, as Gen. George S. Patton and Gen. Buck Turgidson, one tended to snap to attention. He sent a large first order by mail, and quite a formal letter, to "Gentlemen," apparently typed himself. After his first phone order he always asked for me, and then it was "Mrs. Colt" and "Dear Friends," signed "Geo. C." He seemed to be reading up on General Stillwell in Burma, which would have made a good movie. He was all business, very mannerly but no small talk. I never got around to asking him how much he had read about Patton; and I never had the nerve to tell him my fantasy of his appearing in a Military Bookman commercial.

A film writer came in looking for material on the B-17, "Memphis Belle," which survived twenty-five missions over Germany. We just happened to have a wartime booklet published for the War Bond campaign plugged by the Memphis Belle on its return to the States in 1943, a nice piece of ephemera for him. The 1990 movie bore little or no resemblance to the history.

A tall, handsome, impeccably dressed Parisian businessman with a world-weary air came upon the scene in the late eighties. Jean-Claude Damerval visited New York, and the store, on a regular basis, and communed with Harris back in the World War II stacks. I admired his Hermès ties. He usually bought handsomely also, but on one occasion he left Harris carrying only a small shopping bag. As soon as the door closed behind him, Jason started razzing Harris about not selling so much to this good customer who had no budget constraints. Harris listened, a little smile playing around the corners of his mouth, and at the right moment tossed a wad of cash on Jason's desk. He had introduced Damerval to the small but potent Pamphlet 20 series and sold him everything we had in stock.

Dr. John Clark, in Canada, was only interested in the Holocaust, and so he became primarily Jason's customer, and eventually everybody's headache. He wrote gracious letters and was very pleasant on the phone, except when he was negotiating a lengthy extension of his reservations, or denying that he did so. It was hard to complain about someone who spent thousands over the years, just on the Holocaust—but we did.

Chronically short of money, Dr. Clark, a forensic pathologist in the Montreal coroner's office, would come up with one story after another for not coming through on time with payments. He had always maxed out his credit card, and one time used his roommate's. One tale involved someone crashing through the picture window of his house, which required an expensive repair, meaning another delay on his payment. The notes in his record said, "For many years one absurd and far-fetched story after another, I think he takes them from the crime reports." After ten years, he just disappeared: not even a forwarding address.

Another creative procrastinator was Harlan Hanna, of the Hawaiian Photo Studios in Tennessee. One reason after another for delaying payment on a reservation. The best was one summer when he "got bit bah a spahdah, was all swole up with abdominable pain."

Bill Wilson, from Florida, was in New York regularly, and called a lot in between. He was a little guy, about Harris's size, and also cute. His wife had a small bakery business and Bill often brought us cookies and so he became "Cookie" to Harris. Bill was primarily interested in aviation, but also in Americana.

Phil Haultcoeur wanted naval history, but also actively collected Military Law and Government. We had only a few customers for the law books, which usually came in with collections, not of our choosing. Phil got away with a low price on Gen. S. V. Benét's *Treatise on Military Law,* an important mid-nineteenth century work, and Harris complained about it to him for years, probably because Phil was crowing about stealing a march on Harris—but in truth we didn't have many customers for that subject and Harris was probably glad to see it go. He usually put the law books aside for Phil's regular visits, sometimes as much as half a box. Typical of Harris, he did not "share" this information, with us or Oliver, where it should have been listed in the Shadow file. Harris sometimes operated independently of the rest of the business.

Deborah Harkins brought in her friend Vincent, who was interested in the Civil War and was fascinated by the colorful and scandalous Union Gen. Dan Sickles. Vincent couldn't get enough of the flamboyant Sickles, the "Yankee King of Spain," whose checkered career included controversial service in the Civil War.

Bill Smith, an old friend, first became interested in the idea of collecting World War II when he visited the 92nd Street store. Bill moved a lot, and was mostly a hands-on buyer, shopping wherever he was. But by the mid-eighties, he "needed" the Military Bookman, and started buying from the catalogues and talking a lot to Harris.

We always had a lot of customers for the fine, nineteenth-century pictorials that we kept finding here or abroad. Bill Muir, a New Yorker, was a steady customer for them for years when he lived in the city. Then, in the nineties, he sold his very successful business and retired at an early age to Florida, where he started a militaria business, Grande Armée. Although he still bought, the immediate, visual temptation was not right in front of him, so we did not sell him as much.

Another developing regular was a perennial student/computer geek/foodie named Arnold Brown. He began stopping in at the end of the day on his way to a Russian lesson with an old Russian lady on 96th Street. Arnold was tall and large, and his moon-like, unthreatening face, edged with a frizzy beard, would appear imploringly by the outside light after we had locked up and I was at the computer writing. He was sometimes armed with treats, like Krispy Kreme donuts, then a novelty. I would let him in, and he would apologize and thank me and head back to the armored vehicles section and talk with Harris. Soon he took to sitting down for a little chat with me; he was very articulate and witty.

Bill Hurlbutt, a salesman who came in regularly from Chicago, usually found time in the late afternoon to get uptown to the store. Bill was a good customer for Napoleonic pictorials, and always hung around to schmooze at the end of the day; he never said no to coming upstairs for a drink, and then to Piro's for dinner. Bill was very involved in the Napoleonic Historical Society; he sent us a photo of himself in the uniform of the British 42nd Regiment of Foot at a reenactment at Waterloo, and it went straight to the bulletin board.

When I saw the 2007 movie *Charlie Wilson's War,* about the Texas congressman and party boy who got serious about aiding the Afghans when the Soviets were running over them in the eighties, there was something tickling around the edges of my mind. The movie intrigued me enough that I bought and read the book. Then I strongly urged it on Judy, who was a close friend from our first days in New York when we were both working at Time-Life. Judy was a little bundle of energy, smart, blonde, cute, with not a shy or reticent bone in her body. After a stint as a *Life* Magazine reporter, which honed her inquiring mind and encouraged her willingness to ask anybody anything, she was for years a history teacher back home in Neosho, Missouri. Around the time I talked to Judy about the Charlie Wilson book, one of her former students, the manager of a club in Lufkin, Texas, sent her a copy, which he had asked Charlie Wilson, a member, to sign for her. Judy, who wrote a column for the Neosho paper, got very excited and wanted to interview Wilson for the column, because the National Guard from Neosho was about to go to Afghanistan.

Charlie Wilson, an affable guy, called her; and Judy told him that the book had been recommended to her by Margaretta Colt who used to have the Military Bookman in New York City.

"Oh, I remember that store, I bought books from them, and also a great painting of the defense of the Alamo; I had it copied for friends and constituents."

And then I really remembered him: the quintessential tall, good-looking Texan, even the hat, and an easy, friendly manner. He found us after visiting the writer of the book, George Crile, who lived right across 93rd Street. The painting, "Travis's Line," by illustrator Gary Zaboly, showed Colonel Travis's legendary sword-drawn line in the dirt, which he asked his men to cross if they were willing to stay and die at the Alamo. Gary had brought it in on consignment and the painting had not been there a month, but when Charlie appeared I knew it was for him. It was almost laughably perfect: the painting seemed to have conjured up the ideal buyer. And I remember thinking, "He's been under investigation, I hope the check clears."

Charlie bought books too, and from time to time, one of his staff, "Charlie's Angels," called, looking for a present for him, and we had instructions to call them if something special turned up.

Another Texas politician, Frank Tejeda, came on our scene about the same time. Frank was a decorated Marine, and was serving in the Texas State Senate when we first knew him. He came into the store a number of times—what a nice man. He went on to the U.S. Congress, and had less time for books, but there was some suspicion that his secretary didn't follow through on our offers.

And a Texas collector named Jenkins Garrett gave us a try about this time. He came in and, with Southern manners, introduced himself, and I, struck, said "Mr. Garrett, I met you in Texas in 1970 and you were good enough to give me a glimpse of your collection." Naturally enough, he did not remember the young picture researcher in Texas for a book project, but I distinctly remembered his immense collection of Texana documents, one of which we had reproduced in our Texas book. Mr. Garrett, visiting New York, was leaving no stone unturned, but we had nothing for him: Texas history yes, but nothing uncommon and no documents.

The same month, on what felt like the last day of winter, I drove down to the Shenandoah Valley, as usual in a car borrowed from my parents. The Blue Ridge was very sharp and clear in what was becoming a familiar landscape. I made my regular calls, using resources only available in Winchester. I had found a good general bookstore, Rainbow's End, not far from the Library, and always rounded up a box or two, to be shipped to New York. It was a regular stop on every visit.

But the highlights of this spring were making the acquaintance of two wonderful women. Miss Frances Jones, eighty-nine, was my distant cousin and "pen pal" found through the *New York Times,* and a primary source who had known some of the protagonists in the book. I later stayed with her on my visits and we enjoyed discussing what I was finding and questions arising from it, day by day. Elizabeth Engle, only seventy-nine, was a local historian and family connection delegated to let me into the unoccupied family house where the Frank Jones letters had surfaced. She and I were both hoping for more; and there was much more, among the treasures sixty more wartime letters. She and I sat together, hip to hip for several hours, excitedly digging around in a dresser with drawers of family papers—a bonding experience. Elizabeth was an ongoing "consultant" and a connection to Winchester's old guard. Later I found still more of Frank's letters elsewhere, and finally his photo; as in so many cases, my picture researcher's compulsion to find photos I knew existed led to finding unexpected papers, and then eventually the photos.

When I drove back to Wilmington, I had a date to meet a friend of my parents who was ready to sell her late husband's military books. The books were okay but what really attracted me were vivid hand-colored prints that had been extracted from an 1817 British book by William Nicholson, *History of the Wars Occasioned by the French Revolution.* A number of them were framed on the living room wall, a handsome display. The uniform figures were mostly victorious British and Allied generals, a little primitive but heroic, and Napoleon looking rather thuggish and with a pronounced five o'clock shadow. The visual appeal of the twenty-two plates made it unusual to find the Nicholson book complete; the text was interesting but unfortunately worthless without the plates. Those however were not for sale

I returned from my week in Winchester to a sofa full of personal mail. Harris as usual had left the sorting to me because I had a lot of "book mail" then. There was also a preliminary invitation to what sounded like a grand weekend at Sizergh Castle, the Strickland family stronghold near the Lake District which we had visited briefly in 1981. The July weekend was to celebrate seven hundred and fifty years of the Stricklands at Sizergh. There were to be a garden party, a ball, and other family occasions. How exciting! "Of course we're going!" I said. No, said Harris, categorically. Maybe he thought he wouldn't know anyone. Harris had been known to introduce himself as the American Indiscretion, his Strickland mother having married a Yank. Before too long we decided to structure our twice-cancelled British buying expedition around the gala weekend.

Then Jason broached to us the possibility of his buying for the store in England in June, hitting places where he could go by public transportation. A typical New Yorker, he did not drive. He proposed visiting the general London shops, easily accessible, and leaving the specialists to us, and then going by train to York, where there was a concentration of shops. Jason loved spending our money and looking important, but the buying did make sense. We had always done so well with the British books, and this might make up for the lost opportunities in the two years we had been unable to go. If we and he went in the same time frame, back to back, we could utilize one shipping consolidation.

Amy had visited us for a week in May, and it was fun to plan our trip in person. But this year our visit was sadly different; John Cummings had died the year before, and we missed his warm welcome and friendly interest, and his puckish sense of humor.

We started at Amy's and made our usual call on Mr. Halewood, even to his warehouse, and again spent £1000. Broadhurst in Southport looked better than ever, spruced up since old Mr. Broadhurst's demise, and Mr. Sankey, with a new young partner, had a lot for us. Continuing to Lancaster the same day, it was a must to stop at The Boar's Head pub in Barton. The McCormack shop in Lancaster was again good for us, and the town particularly attractive in the sun. And then back to Amy's for a well-earned cold drink with American quantities of ice, watching Mark, home from university, cut the grass. The weather was getting better and better, and warmer and warmer, and we rejoiced thinking ahead to the garden party. Next morning we took off with Amy to the picturesque, wee village of Cartmel, to see Norman Kerr Books, a wee shop under an arch, where we were, as Amy said, treated like children, were denied many books that they seemed to be hoarding. You always remember the "ones that get away:" there was a full set, eighteen titles, of the *Battles in Britain* series published by B. T. Batsford in the sixties. It was written by a group of fine naval and military historians, and always wanted by our people, but was also desirable to collectors of Batsford imprints; we were shooed away from it. We were allowed to see the books in the Priory Barn. The stock was excellent, and in spite of the restrictions, we were allowed to spend £900. We rewarded ourselves at the perfect rose-covered pub, where we sat in the sun and had beer and Cumberland sausage. Amy's photo of us there ran in the Fall catalogue, and many customers thirsted to know where it was.

We tore ourselves away from that charming spot and pushed on to Michael Moon in Whitehaven, which had been closed on our previous attempt. After all, it was not worth the extra mile, large but not very good, with too many ex-library books. That night, back in the Lake District, Amy had chosen a perfect country inn, the Pheasant, in Cockermouth. It was all dark wood, flowers, brass and copper, the right amount of chintz. In the lounge for coffee after dinner, we savored the long twilight; it was full light until ten.

We returned to our two good shops in Carlisle, then rented a car, parting from Amy at Sedburgh. When we had visited Mark's school there eight years before, we had not known of the magnificent R. F. G. Hollett shop. Mr. Hollett, who had started in business forty years before, was a delightful man and we enjoyed him. It was mutual, I believe, and we chatted about our travels thus far. "How did you get on with Mr. Halewood?" he asked, and we all laughed.

We headed for Kendal, near Sizergh Castle, where we were assigned, with others of the Maltese branch of the Strickland family, to the aptly named Heaves Hotel. We were greeted by the ineffable aroma of cabbage and bad furniture wax, and a maid who seemed weirdly spaced-out broke the news that there was no ice. We did learn that Roger Strickland and family were on the way, "and a lady from London," then beat a hasty retreat, thrice around the Kendal "speedway" traffic pattern, to find an indifferent Italian restaurant. We later found our Stricklands, appropriately, at the Strickland Arms pub, down the road from the hotel. Anne Strickland and her daughter were the Londoners. Anne was smart, sharp, and good-looking, reminding me of Charlotte Rampling, and we bonded immediately.

Before the festivities began, we again called on Brian Peet at Ewen Kerr in Kendal, in handsome new digs tucked away in a mews, with excellent stock. Once again, we managed to spend £1000.

The Sizergh weekend was blessed with extraordinary weather and a wonderful turnout. The Garden Party was out of Central Casting, and hats for the ladies were *de rigueur.* One had been pressed upon me by a friend before I left home; she and Felix both knew the drill and were insistent. Harris stood out as the American Indiscretion indeed in his summer khaki suit. He found cousins he had not seen since his teens, among them Margaret Kelly and her husband Peter who lived near Hay-on-Wye and were book-lovers. Richard Strickland arrived, with Dominic, Candace and Edward, all grown up and handsome and Dominic recently married. The next morning after a "family Mass" in the castle chapel, there were garbage cans full of Pimm's Cup. Richard pushed for a tour of the castle with a resident cousin, through the famous Jacobean paneled rooms, around by the formerly haunted staircase and up to the battlements. Harris hefted a long sword almost as tall as he. The ball featured really good, if a bit incongruous, Dixieland music in an ancient setting and, later, country dances in which we and the "Maltesers" were merry but inept. We danced until dawn, easy when dawn is about three a.m. On Sunday we came down to earth and went back to Amy, who had no ice shortage.

The three of us set out for Shrewsbury next day, to visit Candle Lane Books, an irresistible name, and another shop. At Candle Lane as well as other general stores, we usually found Churchill's *War Speeches*, in six volumes, very cheap in Britain, but very desired at home. We bought and sold them most often as odd volumes, but sometimes as sets. I got onto the first and second so-called "cheap" trade editions of Churchill's *The River War*, a celebrated book about the British reconquest of the Sudan in 1898–1899. The first edition, generously sized, with excellent maps and a fine gilt-navy cloth binding, was already well beyond the means of most of our interested readers. The slight, orange-golden "cheap" volume I came to recognize across the room. It was not much valued in England, but we could put a sizable markup on it. There were two copies at Candle Lane.

In the beautiful leather sets and antiquarian volumes we found in Britain, there was often an engraved bookplate, sometimes armorial; and often the little hand-written stickers on the front endpaper, which gave the shelf location in a great private library. So evocative. I particularly liked finding "prize copies," handsomely bound military classics awarded, as history prizes usually, in different "public" schools whose coats-of-arms were gilt-stamped on the front covers. A bookplate naming the student and the description of the prize was affixed inside. We found, at first, that these copies were not valued highly in England, in fact devalued because of the specificity of their ownership, and we could buy them very reasonably. I thought they were wonderful, each one with its particular history as a book, and I bought a lot of them in the eighties. But then they seemed to catch on, and became harder to find and afford.

At the other end of the spectrum, there were the unmistakable signs of Boots ownership. The large English pharmacy chain had, in olden times, a lending library. (In *Brief Encounter*, the Celia Johnson character goes to town to exchange books at Boots.) Boots ownership was denoted either by a little shield-shaped sticker in green and white on the plain, sturdy, cloth front cover, or by a sort of library binding with a little grommet at the top of the spine. Were they attached to the shelf before being rented? We bought them without prejudice because the books were often relatively scarce wartime and slightly postwar titles, when paper rationing was in effect. It amused us to list them as "Ex-Boots." They too had a story in themselves.

The weather continued sunny and ever warmer, a real heat wave, and we spent the night at the spectacular Feathers Hotel, a half-timbered Jacobean beauty in Ludlow. The paneled interiors were a marvel, the brass shiny, the food excellent. The town looked like a storybook and we wandered a while through the "black and white" streets in the gloaming.

We left promptly next morning for an appointment with a military specialist Amy had identified, George Harris in Bewdley. George was the picture of a military gent, big, bluff, ruddy, with fierce mustaches, and he and his wife Joyce were welcoming. Their house was full of books, upstairs, downstairs, and in, of course, the garden shed. George was sort of a collector run amuck. He did not see many customers, did the occasional show, and sent out some lists and quotes, which probably kept the inventory under control. George gave us sale prices on some uniform pictorials, to Joyce's relief, to clear some shelves. We put together a huge stack of books, which he opted to drive to our freight consolidator in Essex, with a little visit in London to please Joyce.

We went on about fifteen miles to Worcester, and there visited a shop where our subject was in the top of the old house, cramped, ill-lit, and expensive, and perishingly hot and stuffy. The Brits didn't know what to do with their heat wave, no one opened windows for a breath of air, and fans were unheard of. It was startling to see tan natives. Later, we strolled around the city and heard evensong at the Cathedral before continuing to an old coaching inn, the Falcon. The one-horse town of Bromyard was in the heart of the "black and white" villages, so-called for the quantity of old half-timbered houses.

We were positioned to assault Hay-on-Wye the next day, and our timing was good at Richard Booth's; they had a lot for us. I met Amy for lunch in the sun at a pub, but Harris worked through until mid-afternoon at Booth's. I went to the smaller shops and Harris was at the Cinema Bookshop until after six. Amy, left to her own devices all day, was understandably annoyed by the time we finally got on our way, through the beautiful Wye and Severn valleys south to Thornbury Castle. Between its splendor, and a very long day behind us, we decided to take it easier the next day and stay another night at Thornbury. The two of us made a run to Swindon, an unattractive town with a dumb store, and the pretty town of Marlborough where the Military Parade Bookshop was unaccountably closed. We found a fifteenth-century pub, good books and a corkscrew at an antiques shop, circled past Avebury and the White Horse again, and back to Amy at our fabulous castle, where she had spent the day sunning herself and watching the comings and goings at the helipad. At Thornbury in our stuffy turret room, the windows were closed and hard to open.

Our target was Bristol the next day, and before shopping we toured the S.S. *Great Britain,* fascinating to me after my last book project on transatlantic steamships. The *Great Britain,* launched in 1843, was the only survivor of the earliest ones, and had been rescued from the Falkland Islands, returned to her home port, Bristol, and was being restored. In Bristol we parted from Amy, spent a successful hour or so buying at William Georges, found a pub, and then entrained for London.

We had managed to get a reservation at our favorite Stafford Hotel in St. James Place; among its many virtues was an "American Bar" with ample ice—but no air-conditioning.

As usual, we went to the Sutcliffes our first day, and since it was Saturday we were invited for a family lunch. A happy time, what a civilized way to buy books, sipping a little wine, good conversation, sitting outside for lunch. Anne-Marie suggested Victor open the windows of the airless book room. They had long since been painted shut and Victor had to climb up on his desk with hammer and chisel.

On Sunday we had a beautiful day to visit the Leventhals for luncheon in the garden, and reveled in Lionel's book collections, his own publications naturally, and a remarkable assemblage of arms and armor books and other military history. The next few days were divided between Maggs and Peter de Lotz, a couple of times in each place. Of our former regulars, Henry Lloyd was in bad health, and Max Powling had died. We had a day in and near Guildford to see Traylen and Graham Palmer. In the meantime, there was a bonanza, thanks to Philip Kamil.

Philip Kamil, as a medal collector, had received a Christie's catalogue in New Jersey, and called us at the Stafford to alert us to an auction of British militaria and books. As we had seen dramatically in Cape Cod, books often got short shrift, not the proper attention from the auction house in a sale in which they were overshadowed by uniforms and weapons and medals, and the same happened at Christie's the week we were in London. Christie's had focused on the medals, and few of the books were on display, just the regimental histories; most were in too-large boxes we had to wrestle out from lower shelves to see and evaluate: no list, just a catalogue entry stating "two boxes military books." On auction day we were at Maggs in the morning and left Nicola the curator saying that we'd see her at the auction. She knew nothing about it. Christie's had not notified Maggs or any other book dealers, and Nicola was left flat-footed while we went off to Christie's. We had little competition, acquiring huge cartons of excellent if not rare British titles. One had to feel badly for the consignors, one of which was the estate of dealer Max Powling. We were not buying many British regimental histories by then. The prices had gone through the roof, artificially, like a bubble, and it had been impossible for us to buy them in England, but we were able to buy at this auction.

Mixed into the evenings were sightings of the Malta Stricklands, and Anne took us to the Royal Tournament at Earl's Court. The pageantry was wonderful as one would expect, but the most fascinating part to us was the contest involving exercises that mimicked the Naval Brigade's action in the relief of the siege of Ladysmith during the Boer War.

We flew home at the end of July, exhilarated by our successful trip and a time full of fun and interest, and carrying smoked salmon and Stilton, for immediate use. Michael Wray happened to call almost as soon as we got in, just arrived in New York himself. He came uptown bearing raspberries, and we had a feast and a debriefing, a memorable evening. When I trundled across Madison Avenue to our little video and film-developing shop to turn in our photos, "Fawlty Towers" was playing on their set—and thinking of the Heaves Hotel, I said, "I've just been there."

The two of us had a special date on Labor Day weekend: the day at the New York Public Library, each researching our Civil War interests, then dinner and a movie. A new level of togetherness.

Anticipating our enormous shipment from over forty-five English dealers, the

Ismael Medina and part of the British shipment.

fruits of our intensive three weeks and Jason's trip the previous month, John Catherwood was more than excited. Furtive calls from his desk (I could picture the hand cupping the receiver), "Is the boat in yet?"

At least two tons of books arrived at the curb. Arnold Brown volunteered to help that day, and Ish brought in a friend for a couple of hours. We loaded as much as we could into the back room of the basement; the boxes formed a solid block five feet high, like an iceberg, with a narrow path around them, from which we chipped away at the mass. There were plenty of boxes in the store itself, and I photographed Ish reclining on a stack four cartons high. John started coming up to the store a couple of times a week as the books were going onto the shelves; he was crestfallen when one caught his eye that had someone else's name on it. It seems I told him he could go down to the basement, where the unprocessed books were coming out of the boxes, and see what was there. John would come up from the bank at lunchtime to help unpack, so that he could set aside what appealed to him, descending to the basement wearing an extra white shirt to protect his banker's white button-down from the inevitable book dust. It was he who came upon the Gurkha picture lot, and staggered upstairs with several. I said, in astonishment, "We didn't buy those!" But we had, unknowing, in a lot of

John Catherwood in the basement.

Indian Army regimentals. A very personal collection, that British officer's photos of himself as a young officer of a Gurkha regiment, his subedars, his mementos and insignia, and a group photo with other officers, all nicely framed, graced the store wall for years.

John wasn't the only excited customer. M. E. B. wrote: *Your ship did come in! whew! A veritable jackpot. . . . . Thousand thanks for your ever faithful attention to my want list. . . . I really like reading about the intrepid Indian troops. At the moment I'm drowning in the recent wash of Navy books. Gurgle, gurgle.*

And a few days later, about a lost quote: *As my desk sometimes gets in arrears and resembles a toxic waste dump I was shocked to discover this error.*

The handsome young man in the mid-calf-length Armani camel-hair coat arrived with the silent fanfare provided by his entourage, clearly a bodyguard and a Secret Service agent. Who knew what threats might lurk in a military bookstore? He was primarily interested in the Ottomans, their conquests and their empire, and we learned that his close friend Timoor Daghestani had told him about us. Harris dealt with him that first time, and added him to the mailing list: nothing like the cachet of "H. R. H. Prince Talal Mohammed, Royal Palace, Amman, Jordan" on the print-out. (Not that the catalogues reached him.) On his later visits, the Secret Service was not involved, and the bodyguard's function, on one occasion, was confined to arguing with the credit card company. I did have trouble finding Talal's customer record in the computer when he was checking out—nothing under Talal or Mohammed—but knowing how Harris's mind worked, I looked under "Prince" and it came right up.

Linda Hughes-Willis had a scholarly interest in naval construction and was, she said, a naval expert. A small, bent, wizened woman, she talked knowledgeably to customers and staff. She was an advocate of concrete decks for aircraft carriers, this in the wake of a two recent disastrous fires, and went to naval conferences to promote them. She was homeless, but her checks were written on the J. P. Morgan bank, then like a very exclusive club. Arriving in several layers of clothing, with crammed shopping bags, she cruised the naval shelves, made her purchases, updated the staff on the latest conference, and had a little nap in our comfortable chair. She distinguished herself as being the only person who ever bounced a check on us and arrived to make it good even before we had heard from our bank.

We never knew the name of the African, fresh from Paris, and the glass of fashion. The look of the moment was a black T-shirt with a narrow white edge at the neck and a black chevron device embroidered on the chest, the same in golden thread on the breast pocket of his black blazer. Was it Comme des Garçons? Very chic. He spoke only French so Harris was summoned from the back, and they disappeared into the stacks together. Eventually they emerged with several large piles of counter-insurgency and espionage titles. Harris, in animated French, was addressing the customer as "Mon Père." With his utter obliviousness to fashion, he had taken the man for a priest! The disconcerted man paid cash and took the books with him.

Mon Père made one more visit and, as if to dispel Harris's impression of him, had the concierge at the Carlyle Hotel call ahead, and brought with him a nubile blond. She had a little, jet-lagged snooze in the wives' and girlfriends' chair, and destroyed her eyebrow pencil in our electric sharpener. Once more he cleared the shelves of his interest and departed.

This was all comical, and it was hard to take Mon Père too seriously. But maybe we should have. There was always a lot of activity in Africa, civil wars, coups, ethnic violence, a lot of job opportunities for the mercenary types who occasionally put in an appearance in the store. There were rather sinister, poker-faced men from an Ethiopian group, UTNA, who were buying counter-insurgency books around this time. Their address was a post office box in Washington, and they paid cash. At a later date, there was a Nigerian episode.

By contrast there was a good-looking young man in a well-tailored leather jacket with a dashing, white silk scarf around his neck, tossed over his shoulder. He was reading about soldiers-of-fortune and mercenaries, and seemed to be dressing for his fantasy, probably harmless.

Our neighborhood in its on-going gentrification had lost most of the services that had characterized it, due to mushrooming rents. Crabtree & Evelyn and especially Benetton were marching up Madison Avenue, and we no longer had a shoemaker or tailor. Most of the dry cleaners had turned into restaurants,

Carnegie Hill had sprouted many small, good restaurants in the eighties and nineties. We had done the rounds in our continuing tradition of a staff Christmas party, so we decided to go somewhere out of the neighborhood, having exhausted the more local possibilities. Harris and I had been a number of times to a place called Trastevere 84, on 84th Street near Lexington, not too far away. To accommodate Sheila's schedule, we made a late reservation: hard to get, in Christmas week. The group included the two of us, Jason, Sandra and Emily, and Sheila.

Sheila and I were in the vanguard, the first taxi, and the restaurant was a hive of activity, with a tumultuous mass jostling to get in. I pushed on, feeling responsible, and Sheila, following, said to me, "It says 'Now Kosher.'" I was just intent on getting our table; it would have been hard to go anywhere else: six people, already nine o'clock. The restaurant we had so enjoyed had become a Roman kosher restaurant, and we four Anglo-Saxon blondes felt especially out of place, and all of us unhappy about the food. As for the wine, a waiter left over from Trastevere's previous incarnation served us. Harris said, when he tasted the wine, "Well, I'll pay for it but I won't drink it." The waiter, who remembered him well, said, "Mr. Colt, you won't like any of the wine, it's all kosher, it's been boiled."

CHAPTER SEVENTEEN

"I apologize for the crude stationery but I am in Iraq . . ."

1990

Margaretta at Manassas Battlefield.

In the course of my project, the Military Bookman was a major asset. Jason, so involved with the Civil War and in charge of those incoming books, pointed out special arrivals, and I would take them upstairs for a good look. Some scarce books on Civil War medicine came along just when I needed them. I sequestered them for a few weeks in my parlor/work room before putting them on sale. At that very time, Diane Elliott's young son was assigned a science project in school. Junior Civil War historian Hank Elliott wanted to do a mockup of a medical officer's tent and instruments. His mother called and they came in and we made copies of some of the illustrations for him. Diane later phoned to say they were dyeing rags red in the kitchen sink, for bandages. The timing was lucky for Hank and me; we never had those books again. Hank's early focus on the Civil War led to a career in the National Park Service, at the Virginia battlefields.

For Jason, the Civil War had become more than a business interest; it was his avocation. He attended Civil War Round Table meetings and various seminars, and from them was acquainted with well-known historian Gary Gallagher. When Gary came to town, Jason asked him up to the store so that Gary and I could meet. Gary had vetted my chapter submitted to Broadfoot and was interested in my progress. Jason and I took Gary to lunch, at Piro's of course. He had just completed a massive compilation of the papers of Confederate Gen. E. P. Alexander, and told us he had managed to identify all but two of the multitude of people mentioned in the papers. I could tell that those two unknowns were bugging him. It had been my instinct to try to identify everyone named in the Barton papers, but this confirmed it, and I began to make weekly runs to the New York Public Library to work with the census records on microfilm. They held their own fascinations and frustrations. This was the time of the Gulf War, and business was slow as our customers followed the current conflict, so I felt I could take library days. Emily's presence and competence made me feel easier about taking time from the store.

Emily could be mischievous. No one could concentrate like Harris, and once Emily had some business that she considered important to convey to him. She talked on, but could tell he was engrossed in what he was doing to the exclusion of all else; so she lowered her voice to its most intimate tone, and said, "Oh, Harris, I've never been able to tell anyone about that before in my life, thank you for listening." He surfaced fast, "What? What?" and she just laughed.

The Gulf War engendered the all-time winner in the tacit "stationery received" contest. On a four-by-four inch piece of brown cardboard box stamped "Star Food Processing, San Antonio," Capt. P. F. Owen wrote: *Sir/Ma'am, I apologize for the crude stationary, but I am in Iraq and I am short of paper & envelopes.* He had several requests, including a catalogue and a Marine Corps book, which we were able to quote him.

There was a major auction of Travel and Military at Swann in March, over eighty lots for us to consider. Harris and I went down to look after doing the research; there was some very good military. And typically, some very military titles had strayed into the travel section: Drinkwater, *The Late Siege of Gibraltar,* and *Monro his Expedition with the Worthy Scots Regiment,* Davila on the French Civil Wars and others. Harris took Emily to the auction, as it was always good to have a second person when possible, and won some thirty lots. We bought many of the beautiful French pictorials familiar to us, two favorites by J. O. B., Fallou, Chelminski and another on the Polish army in the Napoleonic period; the *Livre d'Or,* the most-wanted book on the French Foreign Legion; several Frederick the Great titles and other Prussian books; Russian guards; MacMunn on *The Armies of India;* the remarkable Lienhart French uniform opus; and several large lots of less important but most saleable titles. I later took upstairs a group of eighteenth-century Prussian and Austrian uniform plates by Seele that hadn't sold, and continued to interest me for their limpid, clear colors and their many visual references to antique art.

Bill Muir bought a number of the fine pictorials over the months, on one occasion giving us a record day. Due to the new flexibility in the catalogue coding and the stepped-up schedule, we were able to list many of our acquisitions in the May issue. Sarah Gilmer bought *Monro his Expedition* as soon as it was listed—after I had found the "diligent and serious Souldier" passage that so resonated with us.

In April, Harris and I went to the Carnegie Hill Neighbors party: always a nice occasion, with music and dancing, in one of the old mansions, by then institutions, in the neighborhood. And as usual I had bought chances on the various contributions of local merchants, but we didn't stay for the drawing; it would have been a first to win anything. Very early the next morning, an annoyed and annoying voice called to say that we had won a prize, and it needed to be picked up immediately. I asked groggily what it was. "It's children's things, and it's not bulky except for the elephant." Hunh? We went as soon as we could, and collected some charming baby things and a very large, pale blue, stuffed elephant. In the store, I took them straight to Ish, "This is all for you." He was astonished. His little girl walked right into the pink corduroy dress and treasured the elephant, and the new baby had many accoutrements waiting when she arrived.

Harris went to Virginia with me that spring, partly because he was deeply involved in his research on Appomattox. We flew to Charlottesville and met a Nelson County historian with whom I had corresponded about an unnamed house in Randolph's story. She had identified it from his description, and led us to the imposing house, Pharsalia, set in a beautiful, secluded valley, a refuge from the Yankees. Then on to Appomattox, where Harris surveyed the battlefield and saw the White Flag.

The first year I was working on the book, I took a break one day in my transcribing and, almost as a whim, decided to pursue a Family Legend. Randolph Barton, who served in the Confederate Army from the First Battle of Manassas until the end, with intervals when wounded, described the final scenes at Appomattox. He had been detailed with two other officers to ride toward the Union lines to ask for a truce. They did so and immediately attracted Union attention, and fire. Realizing they needed something white, one rummaged in his saddlebag, finding a towel recently purchased in Richmond, and waving that, the three men arrived safely into the Union lines and virtually into the arms of General Custer. Barton claimed that Custer had appropriated the "flag," and that he had, in latter years, seen it displayed at the Smithsonian with the Custer memorabilia. I picked up the phone and called the Smithsonian and was quickly put through to a knowledgeable and helpful curator. Trying to dignify my query, I said I was attempting to verify a family legend about the white flag at Appomattox. "Oh," he said, "the towel?" Nonplussed, I said yes. "Well, when the museum was established at Little Big Horn, we sent the Custer relics out there." He supplied the number. Another call, to Little Big Horn: "Oh, you mean the towel? Well, we sent that back to Appomattox." I had paid my respects to the towel on my first visit there. Harris was more interested in the terrain.

Then we visited our Staunton cousins, and met a friend of theirs who was a military history reader, and recruited him as a customer. As we headed north and east seeing battlefields and cousins along the way, we identified other places in my history. At Fredericksburg, we met Robert Krick, whom we already knew, telephonically, as a good customer; he was Chief Historian at the National Park

Service in Virginia and author of numerous books on the Confederate Army. Bob had been the first person to whom Mike Mullins and Tom Broadfoot had shown Randolph Barton's memoir, and he had been somewhat dismissive of it in that form; he was most interested in what I was finding.

We wound up at the Taylors in Washington, and found we were going to a charity auction that night. Nancy showed me the catalogue and I waved it aside, saying, "I read too many auction catalogues." Nancy, always ready for an adventure, said, "Sometimes there're good travel deals." I seized it, read the first travel entry, "Dalmatian Dalliance," and exclaimed, "I've always heard that is gorgeous." The two of us, in front of our husbands, decided to bid for two weeks in a house on the island of Hvar, off the Dalmatian coast. She and I discussed when we could go and how much we could pay. The men paid us no mind and were unhinged when Nancy bid—and won. Keene, owl-eyed, and Harris, in shock, had major misgivings; they didn't know much about Dubrovnik, but they knew Yugoslavia was falling apart. Nevertheless, we planned to meet them in Dubrovnik in October, after some book-buying.

Before we had returned from Virginia, Emily had fielded a call from the owner of Pharsalia. When I called back, I was treated to a historical monologue by the lady, Perkins Flippin, descendant of the original family and heir to the Chapstick fortune. Pharsalia! We didn't know what the name referred to, and engrossed by Mrs. Flippin's stories I had not thought to ask her. Before I had even attempted to trace it, serendipitously, a book scout who came up with most unusual, and often unviable, items brought in an early-nineteenth-century French set on Caesar's wars and there was Pharsalia: Caesar's decisive battle against Pompey in 48 B.C. We did not buy the set, French being so hard to sell. We did take another French title on consignment, however, a big handsome set on the French Navy, heavily illustrated and with fine enamel insets in the covers. It eventually sold.

Lionel made his regular spring visit; he had been aware of my project for a while and took a lot of interest, always asking about my progress. One customer told me how to send for military records from the National Archives, a crapshoot as some were fascinating but many of the records had minimal information, and occasionally the wrong records were sent. A doctor researching Civil War medicine was coming in to the store regularly in those days. He had discovered a government archive of slides, tissue samples from Civil War soldiers, and I was amazed to hear about the esoteric find. I buttonholed him with variety of questions: consumption, confinement, phthisis, amputation, et al. Others who came to know what I was doing offered leads or tidbits of information.

Gavin Leckie was tall, fair, and British, and a new and serious Civil War customer. He and his wife found us by chance, roaming around Carnegie Hill after they had visited the Church of the Heavenly Rest at 90th and Fifth Avenue, where Gavin's parents had been married. They had recently moved to East 80th Street, and Gavin started walking up regularly, a Saturday stroll, often with wife and baby. Jason talked to him first, focused as both were on the Civil War books, then Jason told Gavin what I was doing. We found that he and I had something improbable in common. Each of us had a great-great-uncle who had been among the V.M.I. students called out to fight in 1864 against Union forces, which were moving south in the Valley and met the Confederates in battle at New Market. The cadets were known as the New Market Cadets, and those two boys surely knew each other.

Years before, I had lent Mike Rihn my precious copy of Randolph Barton's *Recollections*, and in his periodic floor-waxing and buying calls, Mike was excited to hear about what I was learning and my progress. The friend of the Staunton cousin had become a very good customer, mostly by phone with Harris; his cousin became my source for Staunton local history questions. In the course of my 7th Virginia Cavalry research, the name of Maj. John D. Richardson of Berryville came up, and I remembered that our poster consignor of yesteryear, John Richardson, a commonplace name, had been John D., III; the major was his grandfather.

Mike Mullins's book, *The Fremont Rifles,* had been published that spring, and he brought us a copy; we were happy for him, a labor of love realized. Sometime that summer, Mike came in with some copies for the store to sell, and to tell me that he had run into James I. Robertson, a well-known historian of the war in Virginia, and that Robertson was starting to edit a Civil War series for the University of Virginia Press. Mike had told Robertson about my project, and Robertson knew of the "six soldier brothers" of the Barton family, having spent time in Winchester years before. Mike put us in touch and we opened a correspondence, which led to my agreeing to submit my unfinished manuscript in a few months, a promising development. Indeed, it seemed perfect.

I still could not resist pictorial material for the store, and used some items to enliven the catalogue. From time to time at book auctions, I bought Civil War prints by Kurz & Allison, Ted Key cartoons from a cautionary series done for the U.S. Signal Corps, and cartoonist Robert Osborn's wartime training series on a Navy pilot, Dilbert, who was a real screw-up. I never paid much for them and priced them for the impulse buyer, and they were fun. A neighbor brought in on consignment some *Leslie's Weekly* engravings, some by Winslow Homer, from the Civil War. There were engraved maps long separated from their books, odd Nicholson plates, the occasional broadside or sheet music. Mike Wolfson found he had to have a French army conscription order from August 1914.

We had done so well with the Lester Hornby war art that I had high hopes for a large lot of vivid drawings from the South Pacific. The artist, George M. Harding, had been an Official Artist in the First World War, and despite his age, was determined to serve in the same capacity with the Marines in the Second. After two years in the Pacific he had sent home a footlocker of preliminary work, mostly sketches in pastels. Harding's finished paintings from that time were owned by the Marine Corps Historical Center, but they had returned the sketches to the artist. Harding's son contacted us and brought in the drawings and a finished painting of Marines in the jungle, on consignment. When we first advertised the art, the Marines received the catalogue, and fired a salvo: they claimed they owned all the Harding work, and that Mr. Harding Jr. could not sell it. (Mr. Harding Jr. had said the Marines hadn't wanted it and had returned it, so it was his to do with as he wished.) This was a little alarming but after all just huffing and puffing—no landing party arrived to recapture it. But, unfortunately, it meant the Marines wouldn't be buying.

Harding's work made me think of the brilliant colors of the movie, *South Pacific,* and had special interest, I thought, because there was so little of that war to be seen in color, and the collision between gorgeous settings and military subjects was dramatic. I worked hard trying to identify some of the places and people, and to pull out the most interesting pieces and organize the pictures in an appealing way; we illustrated it in every catalogue, and despite our somewhat muddy reproduction, it looked strong and interesting. I brought it to the attention of Rob Cowley, editor of *Military History Quarterly,* and he agreed that it was just right for the magazine. Rob was an old *American Heritage* acquaintance and an occasional customer, and was the author of an interesting book on the Western Front and other military titles. The *MHQ* article was excellent but brought in no business; the editors could not apparently say baldly that the work was "for sale" or even "available" at the Military Bookman. The magazine made a nice giveaway to buyers of the art, and we sold some copies of that issue. My old friend, Judy, whose then-husband had been in the South Pacific, bought several pieces reminiscent of his service, and of her attempts at learning to fly. Sheila bought one of an aircraft carrier, in memory of her father's service in the South Pacific. All together, we sold perhaps only two-dozen pieces. After several years I wrote of our mutual disappointment to Mr. Harding and together we gave up on it. He picked up the balance of the artwork and let us choose a nice naval watercolor sketch of the U.S.S. *Montpelier* for the store.

Philip Kamil had been in London in the spring, just at the right time to attend, as our representative, Lionel Leventhal's celebration marking his thirtieth anniversary in publishing. Philip later brought in friends visiting from England,

Diana Birch, editor of *Medal News,* and John Hayward, medal and militaria expert. Both had connections with Spink's and Christie's, and with the Orders and Medals Society, in London. Diana gave us a nice write-up in the latter's magazine, all to the good, and became a friend we saw in both London and New York.

A customer brought Harris a Sotheby's auction catalogue of antique militaria, quite spectacular, with lots of Napoleonic weaponry, the sale soon to be held in Monaco. Harris was excited and asked me what I liked, but there was so much that I couldn't take it all in. Harris, as usual, knew what he wanted. He singled out some French Napoleonic light cavalry sabers, handsome, and asked me which I liked best. I could play that game! He put in "low-ball" bids on several, hoping to get one, and in the meantime I ordered copies of the catalogue to sell in the store. Then we didn't think about it. Weeks later, Sotheby's called and asked for him. Well, I thought, it's not to tell him he got nothing. Harris's low bids had won him three stunning swords. Harris was elated, but he sheepishly had to borrow money from me to pay for them. They arrived in a substantial crate, which he and Ish, with great excitement, pried open in the front courtyard. So the dining room became militarized as well as the living room, with gleaming arcs of decorative brass and white metal.

We were approached by one of the veterans of the 95th Bomb Group about a complicated transaction. The 95th, part of the mighty Eighth Air Force, had been stationed in the midst of the gentle, tree-lined fields of Suffolk from 1942 to 1945. To commemorate their sojourn at Horham Airfield and their six hundred and thirty-two men lost over Germany, and for the fiftieth anniversary of their service, the vets had determined to raise funds to help restore the "Ring of Eight" bells in St. Mary's Church, said to be the oldest such Ring in the world. One of their fund-raisers was the auction of six copies of *Contrails*, their unit's history; but these were special as each had been signed by one hundred and fifty-seven vets, at their 1989 reunion. What a wonderful project: we were an easy touch for this, the Military Bookpeople all felt we should bid. We acquired one copy, which we listed in the August catalogue at a modest markup, and it sold quickly. We were pleased to be even a small part of this very appropriate endeavor. The next year, our contact in the 95th wrote to let us know that the bells had been reinstalled and had rung again for the first time in eighty years, and would be dedicated at a reunion of the 95th the next year.

Occasionally we acquired rarities like flight manuals from World War II, usually from veterans or their families. A notable package was saved by a man who had been a turret gunner with the 392nd Bomb Group, one of the first B-24 groups to arrive in England; the eight pieces included engine manuals and scarce electrical and radio handbooks. We sold it for $1500.00. A lesser group, a B-29 pilot's kit, five manuals and handbooks and some ephemera, went for $800.00. It was always easy to sell this material. Several times, we had little collections of Flying Tigers' signatures in a Fourteenth Air Force book, presumably collected at a reunion. We were starting to do more business in autographed books, especially generals' memoirs.

We had started seeing a lot of Philip Kamil after his wife had died the previous December, often for dinner at Buzby's, a neighborhood favorite, on Tuesday nights. It was like a club, where we discussed books, business, stamps (I listened), and occasionally Philip's Talmud class. Once when Harris and I went without Philip, the waiter said, "Where's the other one?"

Philip had resumed his regular jaunts to London but didn't know many people there, and it occurred to me that he might enjoy having Anne Strickland as a dinner companion. They naturally talked about his reasons for being there at that time, namely an auction of British medals at Christie's. Anne knew from medals: she was from a military family. She had a sad tale to tell; her late father had been Maj. Gen. Lionel H. Cox, and in a recent burglary at her mother's home, his medals had been taken. Of all things, Philip discovered that those medals were in the auction he was attending: one of three stolen lots in that auction, John Hayward later told him. Philip told Anne he would bid on them for her mother, but found himself bidding against the General's regiment, which was also bidding for her mother. It all came right in the end.

At the end of the summer, Harris and I went to visit Edith and Charlie Sheerin— and some more family papers—for a weekend at Saranac Lake. Harris went on from there for a rare and happy week of fishing in Canada with an old friend, and I returned to New York and spent that week with a self-imposed deadline, preparing twelve chapters to send to the University of Virginia Press two days before we went to Europe.

We had visited Ute and Peter Grauer near Stuttgart several times, and once or twice Ute had taken us in to town to the big old bookstore, Müller und Gräff. We had found books that sold, as German, such a military tongue, was the second language among our customers. We never had trouble selling German books in the store. We had conceived a German buying trip, on a smaller scale but along the lines of our English trips, but had been unable to do it in 1987. We would be very much more selective than in England; not only did we not want quantity, but choosing was challenging in a language unfamiliar to us. We each could fight our way through a title page; *kampf, krieg, schlacht* and *sieg* were key words, we knew. Harris returned to the idea that we try Germany, to fit in before meeting the Taylors in Dubrovnik, then still Yugoslavia, for our Dalmatian Dalliance.

Ute and Harris waiting for the würst.

Our "agent in place," Ute, was an indispensable part of our idea: planner, translator, guide. She had been encouraging us to come, and quickly began making inquiries and having catalogues sent to us from antiquarian bookstores all over West Germany. We decided to dip our toe in the bookish waters of southern Germany. Ute made herself available in late September, and she plotted our course, setting up appointments and reservations. We armed ourselves with traveler's checks in deutschmarks. Traveling with Ute, which I and we had done many times, always had its own zest and interest: discriminating to her fingertips, she and Peter were well-versed in history and enriched our visits with their local history and folklore. A discerning traveler, Ute always made sure we saw not only the significant sights but the everyday things she cherished, ate food and drank wine that were regional and seasonal specialties, and heard music, preferably in an ancient Kloster; and always there was an excursion to the Schwarzwald. Maybe she even arranged the weather; it was a perfect, sunny week.

It was a most interesting time to be in Germany. The Wall had come down a year before, and the longed-for Reunification was imminent. After the first euphoria, the Grauers and many others were a bit apprehensive, along the lines of "answered prayers." The East Germans were far behind the West Germans, their economy was primitive, they did not have the same work ethic, were perhaps uncouth and devious or criminal having lived under Communism for so long, did not know how to live in a democracy—all this was bruited about and speculated upon.

After a convivial weekend with Ute and Peter, we were ready to confront the challenge of German buying, not the least of which was the frequent necessity of selecting from catalogue slips before seeing the books. We started at Müller und Gräff, put together a good-sized lot, and presented our deutschmark checks—which were immediately refused. This was a shock; we had been so proud of having thought this out, after our British currency fiascos. The checks were acceptable elsewhere. We went on to nearby Tübingen that afternoon; the old university town was always a favorite visit. This time, of the several bookshops we went into, one that appeared to be a mixed bag was the most fruitful. It was a combination of antiques-cum-thrift shop, with books off on the side, but we found a number of good titles.

In most places the bookshops were in the old part of town, and we had assumed that there would be large general stores in sizable towns, like the one in Stuttgart. But the book scene in southern Germany appeared to be quite different, in our brief sampling: smaller shops, and very ephemeral.

We hit the road with some trepidation—those aggressive drivers roaring down the autobahn in their powerful BMWs and Mercedes—for the Bodensee, Lake Constance. We stopped at Meersburg, a castle-crowned, pretty, small town on the lake, then crossed on the ferry to charming Konstanz. In both places we puttered around in small shops; some of our targets had disappeared since the lists Ute had only recently obtained were compiled. A dozen books here, two dozen there. The weather was perfect, and we rested from our labors sitting in the sun drinking wine and eating würst, which was habit-forming.

We passed through Friedrichshafen, home of the Zeppelins, and went on toward Munich. Ute's big discovery, on the outskirts, was a military specialist, the Peter de Lotz of Germany, Gerhard Goldau. An older man, very reserved, almost unfriendly and perhaps secretive, he operated by appointment from his handsome house, beringed with geraniums. His inventory was very large and very impressive, with a multitude of German military titles we had never seen, in a big room with rank upon rank of steel shelving. It was, as Harris said, a "brain drain": the language, the selection, the currency conversion, and then the decision. We were there several hours, often the three of us with our heads together, Ute helping us understand what we were seeing. We bought a good bit, most memorably some World War I official histories, a variety of Wehrmacht publications and generals' memoirs, and two full sets of the semi-official *Schlachten des Weltkrieg* series as well as some (too many, as it turned out) odd volumes on the more famous battles of the World War. I had to buy the magnificent Teuber-Ottenfeld set of plates on the mid-nineteenth century Austro-Hungarian armies. At the end, we did not linger for pleasantries. It felt as if we were being moved out as a group of older men was arriving. Maybe it was Goldau's poker group, but in my fevered imagination they were conspiratorial Wehrmacht veterans.

We went in to Munich by train because it was Oktoberfest, the town was full and the traffic impossible. We were "booked out," having spent about $5000 in difficult buying that morning, and not up to any more bookshops, so Harris and Ute indulged me in some Bavarian shopping and the Baroque Assam church, before the mutual pleasure of a traditional brewery restaurant.

Next day, we followed the Isar River down to Landshut, a charming pastel town, lovely on a sunny day. It was mushroom season, and the *apothek* shops displayed warning posters of the poisonous ones in their windows; garlands of hops celebrated the harvest.

Our destination was Regensburg. That interesting Roman-founded town on the Danube had a couple of small antiquarian bookshops. Ute's priority was a small café by the ancient bridge; its sign read *Historische Würstkuche,* and it had served the same local sausage to the bridge-builders in the twelfth century.

The shops on Ute's list either were gone or had nothing for us, but we found a shop not listed that had a good military selection. In a few places we had asked for Third Reich material, for our serious propaganda collectors, and it was always in a hidden place, what the young dealer in Regensburg called the poison cabinet. Well after all, we didn't flaunt our Nazi material either, but it was there for the scholar.

At our hotel that evening, we availed ourselves of the special mushroom menu, listing many varieties and preparations, and the local wine. The next morning before leaving town, we visited the ancient abbey church that had been transformed in the eighteenth century by the Assam brothers into a celestial fantasy. We couldn't leave town without seeing the Roman ruins; around and around we searched, finding the major ones to be the foundations of our hotel.

Our last stop was Nürnberg, about an hour's drive, but we spent almost another hour breaching the walls and looking for our hotel in the labyrinth of one-ways and pedestrian streets. In desperation, we used one of Ute's best tricks: hiring a taxi to lead us. There was a magnificent antiquarian bookstore, with nothing for us; and elsewhere the booking proved fruitless. So next day we visited Albrecht Dürer's house and looked in at St. Sebald's church just in time for choir practice. Ute needed to do her grocery shopping in the medieval Hauptmarkt. She and I left Harris perched by the fountain in the square with his *Herald Tribune,* happily reading the football scores (the Giants were doing well that fall). We made our way through bevies of winter pansies, the first I had seen. Ute decided on a heavily mushroomy menu, and discussed recipes in detail with the market women. We were back with Harris, in position to see the famous pageant of moving figures as the Frauenkirche clock struck noon. We climbed up to the castle and had our usual wine and würst in the sun under a grape arbor on the walls before heading back home to the Grauers'.

When Ute presented us, next day, with a delectable mushroom dish and regaled Peter with the specials we had partaken of, he had dire words about mushrooms being most susceptible to the Chernobyl pollution, then very recent.

There was not a bookshop to be seen on the Dalmatian coast; well, we weren't looking. It was a beautiful time, that last season of peace.

Ute had found us a shipping consolidator in Stuttgart, so we had made those arrangements before leaving—we thought. The shipping consolidation was not only very expensive but incomplete. German efficiency had completely broken down. It took us a while, after the first books arrived in December, to make the shipper understand about the missing books. Perhaps worst of all, we had to bother Ute to pursue the shipper. The shipping problems and expense would have made us consider another such venture very skeptically, but the books unfortunately sold slowly too. Our German foray was a worthy experiment, interesting and fun, but not an unmixed success.

When we came home, everyone was talking about Ken Burns' Civil War series, which had aired while we were away. It accounted for another cresting, long wave of the never-ending Civil War interest and undoubtedly helped me find an agent to sell my book not much later.

Emily agreed with me about Jason's wardrobe, although we never discussed it. One morning she came in and told Jason she had dreamed about him, and that he was wearing a black turtleneck shirt: Emily's devious plot to upgrade his look. Then she and I got him one for Christmas. He was delighted, and started buying them himself, monogrammed, no less; I don't think he ever caught on. That Christmas, we added Philip to our list of regulars at the store party, and went right around the corner to Piro's, a safe Italian bet.

CHAPTER EIGHTEEN

"I don't want my beloved books to end up as garbage."

1991 — 1992

The Colts in the store.

Unbelievably I was called again for jury duty, and again for Grand Jury, at that. Another inescapable three-week commitment. Around this time, we had another kind of government hassle. The recent zip-code change had been bad enough: it affected all the stationery, catalogues, and other things you don't even think of.

Then we heard from the New York State Sales Tax authority. We were more than alarmed by the very word "audit," as anyone is. We felt persecuted; the auditors probably felt the same when they descended to our cave-like basement and confronted fat files of mostly handwritten letters: our customers' orders. Much of our business was out-of-state and thus not subject to New York sales tax, so we thought the low amount we were collecting might have raised some red flag. The only way for them to check was to read the correspondence files. An unenviable task, but sort of funny in retrospect. It was hard enough to decipher all that handwriting, but for them to figure out the transactions? Impossible. The auditors put in two or three days, for show I think, then retreated. They weren't heard from again. We later learned that they were going to all the other small businesses in the neighborhood, whose records were doubtless easier to read, so we hadn't been singled out.

We had a real treat in the midst of all this. Bill Hurlbutt, our Chicago Napoleonic customer, had won a sales competition for whatever it was he sold, the prize being a weekend in New York including dinner for four at Tavern on the Green. He and his wife invited us to join them, and it was a delightful evening. The Tavern was a vulgar extravaganza, and I thought a few times of *Ghostbusters,* Mark Cummings's favorite movie, with a hilarious scene shot outside the Tavern.

The University of Virginia Press's acquisitions editor was coming to town for the Modern Languages Association convention in January, and asked me to meet him at the Hilton for coffee. All their correspondence had made it clear that they wanted to publish my book-to-be, but their reactions were not what I had hoped. I knew the manuscript was too long, too much, but I needed the impartial eye of an editor to give me guidelines. Instead, in letters and in person, the editor dwelled on footnote form and how to handle the different kinds of text; it was as if he hadn't read it, just looked. There was no enthusiasm, no real interest in the material. The more I thought about it the more dissatisfied I became.

My friend, author and historian Jeffrey Simpson, had seen some printouts when I was first working to put chapters together, and had said, with only a little perusal, "Margaretta, this could be an important book." I was grousing to him about the dispiriting meeting with the Virginia editor, finding myself especially aggravated by his suggestion to differentiate my text with green pencil lines; I had already set it off from the letters by using italics, but the editor wanted that removed.

Jeffrey, hearing my frustration, especially with the green pencil, said, "Oh, Margaretta, this is ridiculous. Let me call my agent for you." Within days, Julian Bach had called and asked to see the manuscript. I ran another massive printout and sent it off. Julian must have read or vetted it over a weekend—such a fast response. He asked me to come in. I was completely unprepared for the star quality of Julian's large offices: framed dust jackets of the likes of Theodore White, John Fowles, Clifford Irving, Solzhenytzin, *The Preppie Handbook,* V. S. Pritchett, and Noel Barber hung on the walls. No sooner had we sat down in Julian's office than he said, "This book should be published." I was overcome.

It took me a while to prepare an updated version of the manuscript, an editorial statement, a picture selection, and so on, but then *Defend the Valley* was launched into the unknown by Julian. It began to make the rounds of publishers, each of whom kept it for a very long time before refusing it.

In the meantime, an implausible search paid off. I had deduced, from an 1863 letter and, separately, a newspaper clipping that Edith had sent, that a significant document, a home-made political cartoon, might be in the family of Robert

Barton's descendants, so I wrote to them about it. No, no, no from different ones, and then Yes from Dudley Lalley, my first friend in that family, with profuse apologies for not telling me about it before. It was a framed cartoon, hanging in her hall. Not surprisingly, she had not thought of it; it had almost become part of the wallpaper.

I was still researching and writing, not done yet. There was another brief week in Winchester in May. Always new leads, and hours at the Archives, and new conjunctions of cousins and connections. And as usual, I put in

Emily Katt in the garden.

an hour or so choosing a box or two of good titles at Rainbow's End, the local bookshop. One of our customers, Bill Smith, regularly went back and forth from Washington to central Pennsylvania, passing through Winchester and also making a pass at Rainbow's End. Sometimes he found nothing and was told the Military Bookman had just been there.

Emily had her own following. There was a spice merchant, in a family business; accordingly he was interested in twelfth-century China and the Silk Road, but he also bought expensive illustrated books. Emily helped a female colleague of a well-known newscaster find a present for him, the first New York edition of *The Red Battle Fighter,* by the Red Baron, German World War I ace Manfred von Richthofen. There was a man who habitually took white gloves from his briefcase before examining the naval books, his focus; it was unclear if he were phobic about dirt or dust, or whether he might have allergies. And a big, older man with bushy white hair came in with a succession of young girlfriends, each of whom wanted to buy for him—he must have been doing something right. Emily referred to one of her telephone customers as "Birdman;" his cockatoo was often audible in the background and occasionally Birdman would say, "Pete is in disgrace."

We all enjoyed John Ong, then chairman and CEO of B. F. Goodrich. He came to town regularly for Wagner at the opera and the Military Bookman, and told Emily he was building a new library with cherry wood shelving. We loved hearing that, and did our best to help him fill it. Once Emily found him eagerly waiting on the sidewalk before our ten-thirty opening. Mr. Ong collected mostly pre-1900, lots of classic, often leather-bound, nineteenth-century sets, and some antiquarian books. Mr. Ong was still a customer when he was the U.S. ambassador to Norway.

Our urbane and elegant travel agent, whom we had hitherto known only by phone, came in to see the store and buy a couple of books on India, his favorite destination. Our stationery printer, near Second Avenue, was a Korean War vet, and he wanted a few books on his war.

Sandra was going to the New York Antiquarian Book Fair, the stellar one at the Seventh Regiment Armory, which we rarely had time for. Emily went with her, deputized to buy judiciously; she came back with a fine early edition of Caesar and a three-volume prize binding.

With César, Harris and Ish went to Queens to buy the books of a commercial illustrator, up in years, who had worked on many military books and was a proud member of the Company of Military Historians. *I don't want my beloved books to end up as garbage.* Instead, some nine hundred volumes went into César's van. The artist's books were full of his working drawings, small ink sketches on the many subjects, tucked into the books.

In another parting, Mary Elizabeth Braun had determined to give away her collection. Her health was failing and she wanted to make provisions for her books. In anticipation of donating them to a library, she had bought our scarce and fairly unsalable Polish official history of World War II. She wrote with pleasure and in detail about the Colonel sending four Marines to pack and ship the books.

Thanks, thanks for all your loving care and service. This collection will benefit others for years to come when it becomes part of the U.S. Military History Institute at Carlisle Barracks, Pa.

Once again the hobby that grew and grew and grew has had its rewards. Little did I imagine the pleasure that your books have given me. Stories that would shame fiction in comparison were mine to enjoy—white-knuckle stories! The friendships that have developed through love of history and WWII experiences have enriched my life and are enduring. And finally, the decision to let go of the beloved books was the right one. I want you to share in the credit though. . . . thanks to the Military Bookman the books came in an endless stream (and still coming!).

M. E. B. continued to buy books from us and regale us with her reactions until a few months before she died.

As well as our "usual suspects," including Joel about once a month and the Lichtenbergs a couple of times a year, there was a new scout: Richard Lorand arrived talking a mile a minute, each visit with about thirty well-used shopping bags (which he wanted back) full of decent, general stock. He had found out about us from Murder Ink, a West Side mystery specialist that Jason patronized. Richard, dark and inquisitive-looking, worked as a night doorman, which left him the days for book scouting in Philadelphia and environs. Military had always been his favorite subject, so it was a natural match.

There were always collections. We combined seeing one in New Jersey with yet another visit to Sy Getchburg, and sent Ish and César to New Jersey for all of it. We bought another collection up the Hudson in Garrison.

Jason kept abreast of many of the book offers and auction catalogues that came along; he could do it sitting down. He picked up on a San Francisco auction with many listings of interest to us. It seemed a good idea for someone to go so we sent Jason. It was a productive trip, as he also visited the Bay Area shops and probably strutted his stuff. All of this, Jason's longevity and the store's egalitarian atmosphere, with Harris always referring to the staff as colleagues, may have misled Jason and added to his own delusions of grandeur. There were times Jason seemed to think he was the boss. Ish brushed him off when Jason tried to boss him around, and Emily told him off, memorably. He occasionally got on Harris's case. Harris acted as if he didn't notice, and maybe he didn't—until Jason went too far about something—and Harris went "whoa!" in a way that Jason finally recognized.

John Catherwood had been to California too, and saw a set of a scarce, five-volume classic, Arthur Marder's *From the Dreadnought to Scapa Flow*, about the Royal Navy from 1904-1919. It was very cheaply priced, less than $100.00, in a shop in San Francisco. When John came in next, he told us about it, and Jason reached for the phone. We all enjoyed that, our customers acting as scouts. Philip Kamil went to a lot of book shows, and would occasionally report on something we might want. He often ran in to Joel, who always looked furtive, and startled to be seen.

There continued to be improbable book sources. Someone called from Urban Solutions, which was sort of a recycling business taking donations of anything and everything, and had a warehouse in the South Bronx. They had been given some military books; Harris's questions were answered in a way that made it sound worth the trip, so off the two of us went by cab on a Monday. The books were really quite good, some unusual titles in decent condition. The guys put us and the books in their van and drove us back to the store.

The American Booksellers Association convention, and therefore Lionel's Military Book Show, rotated around to New York that spring. Lionel's inspired idea was to hold his show at the U.S.S. *Intrepid*. The famous World War II aircraft carrier had become the nucleus of a museum on the Hudson River. We were again invited to participate, and found it irresistible. We sent invitations to our local customers, and many came, including Oscar Schreyer, whom we still saw regularly, and John Catherwood. The temperature was in the nineties, an extremely hot day for May, and we were encased in metal, thinking of how much hotter it must have been on that aircraft carrier in the South Pacific.

Sheila's famous picnic, a movable feast, was actually on July 4th that year, and it was a sight to see Emily, like a little cat, secluding herself in a corner to concentrate on the fried chicken. There was another memorable picnic with Sheila, in Vermont. Brendan had moved there in pursuit of his new career, ghost-writing for Olivia Goldsmith on *The First Wives' Club* and later books. He was giving himself a birthday party and Sheila brought the good New York steaks, and Harris grilled them, and we saw the Aurora Borealis.

Dave was still in from time to time of a Saturday to work on Oliver; we would give him our accumulated problem-or-unfinished list, he would get through most of it, and say in parting, "We're almost there!" Sometimes we asked for a refinement of an existing function, and Jason could have qualified as an efficiency expert, so devoted was he to saving movement, preferring one-key commands.

On one occasion, Oliver reached into its memory and pulled up an old mailing list, printing out customers who had been dropped, and not those who had been added since the last round. Rather a disaster, because we barely had enough extra copies to supply those who had recently subscribed, and none to send as samples in the interval until the next catalogue. And in defiance of my logical deleting of inactive customers, one who had been dropped came back with a bang and placed a $2000 order from the issue he wasn't supposed to get. He was a doctor who had just retired and finally had time to read. It rocked me, throwing all my reasoning into a cocked hat. But maybe it was the exception that proved the rule; he was not heard from again. We could only hope I had not dumped other "live ones."

There was ongoing construction in the neighborhood, and there were numerous sightings of displaced rats on the street. Ugh. I saw one inside on the basement steps and told Harris; he pooh-poohed it, but it certainly wasn't a mouse. We got the exterminator who lavishly salted the basement with poison. It was before Dave had added in the duplicate-count computer function, and two of us still went down to the basement to count before the catalogue went out. As usual, Jason was the one sitting and the other dupe-counter was going down the shelves. When they took a break, the rat came out and died under Jason's chair.

We did now have the capacity to make special interest lists, and Emily was computer-interested and computer-savvy, so we chose a few narrow topics: Women in War, Poster Books, and Animals in War. She set it up in a page-makeup program, ran the special customer lists and, when Harris and I were in Wyoming and Idaho in an otherwise slow summer period, mailed them off to those who had indicated an interest. When we returned, Emily and Jason had a lot to tell us. They were excited about the sales from the lists, saying it was as busy as a mini-catalogue.

And a group of California plastic surgeons, in town for a convention, had spent $4000 among them—a really good day. One was African-American and interested in Buffalo Soldiers, the famous black 10th Cavalry Regiment, and we certainly expected more business from him, but none of them was ever heard from again. Robin Williams, having appeared in a Vietnam movie, had come in for some Nam books. Also in our absence, Jason threw out a customer whom he knew to be a "chop shop" guy, one who would have gutted a book to extract the beautiful plates. Everyone was so wound up with all the news that we all went out to dinner at a little café around the corner; it was a long and merry evening, so merry that Emily was under the impression the next day that we had been at Piro's.

We were with the Taylors on the Connecticut shore for Hurricane Bob and the attempted Russian coup. The storm came in from the Sound and seemed to go around the house and we kept watching Moscow on TV—both hypnotic. Trees were down on the roads, the trains were a mess, the phones were out, and we couldn't get home until Tuesday, when everyone was wondering where we were.

It had been the store's fifteenth birthday that summer, and we illustrated the first page of the Summer catalogue with staff photos, and with a photo of our favorite passage by Colonel Monro on the Reading Soldier; Sarah Gilmer had it copied for us from the book she had bought the year before. Harris and I had been given special Military Bookman watches by a friend: a bright red face, with our logo, very good-looking. We decided to have them made for our best customers and the staff, and they were a great success.

The birthday called for a celebration, and we had thought of one with a twist. *Song of Singapore* was an Off-Broadway show, a clever musical spoof set at the beginning of World War II, when the Japanese are coursing down the Malay Peninsula. In a dive in Singapore, the band and everyone else is panicking and the "low-down cheap saloon singer," who is amnesiac, comes to her senses and realizes she is Amelia Earhart. The show was downtown in a Polish social hall on Irving Place, an interesting venue, rather like the cafe of the story. We found the idea of a World War II musical funny, and appropriate. We, Jason, Emily and Sandra, Sheila, Ish and his wife, Dave and his wife, and Philip convened for a festive supper at home, Harris cooking in the fireplace as was his wont, then went on to the show.

Jason surprised us with a marketing presentation. He had given a lot of thought to new strategies to increase sales, and made a good case for credit cards and also a push for doing book fairs.

Before we took credit cards, we took in a lot of cash. We were always loath to leave much in the Polish cash box or in the store, so took it upstairs to various repositories until the next bank deposit. We kept thinking of new hiding places, especially when the amounts were large, and sometimes it was as if Harris and I were hiding it from each other. Once I had a large amount of cash upstairs under a planter in the bedroom, and had temporarily forgotten it. Joe Garabrant was doing some repair in that room and needed to move the planter. Coming back to the store in mock outrage, he said, "Margaretta, are you trying to tempt me?"

Judy and her then-husband, a staid engineer, were visiting for a few days, and he had come back from Egypt short of cash. Sitting at breakfast, he asked me if we could arrange for him to cash a check at our bank. I stood up, walked over to Harris's red leather chair in the corner, pulled up the cushion. The seat was paved with folding green. I said, "How much do you want?"

We started looking into credit cards, but Harris and I were deeply skeptical about the fairs. They entailed expense and a lot of work and considerable confusion in the store with books off the shelves for at least a week, and seemed unlikely to be worth it because we were so specialized. We had always figured the enthusiasts would find us and it was easier and more effective to spend money on ads. But we acknowledged we could be wrong, and Jason really wanted to try it. He laid out a schedule for the winter and the next year.

Mike Mullins reappeared in season, and on his visits to the store I regaled him with my research finds and my publishing hopes, and he loved hearing about my progress. He and I sat on the front stoop on a brilliant fall day, before another Virginia trip, and I told him how I had tracked down an important document, Dudley Lalley's cartoon; he was almost as excited as I was. Cousin Dudley had it, and had offered to send it.

Mike and I, knowing the perils of shipping, yelled in unison: "Don't send it!" That was the last time we saw Mike; he had a heart attack playing basketball that fall. He was only in his late forties, and among the many things he missed seeing was my book, in which he had played a pivotal role.

We were going to Virginia to celebrate my father's eightieth birthday; Harris and I were taking him and my mother back to his roots. We would show them the beautiful Shenandoah Valley, the landscape of his namesake-grandfather Randolph Barton's life and war. At the last minute, I put together relevant passages from my manuscript to read in the car.

It was a perfect October week, and we drove from Wilmington to Virginia, pausing at Harper's Ferry and then south, Harris or I reading about Sherman's advance on Winchester in 1864, on the route we were traversing. We stopped at Springdale and then found the place where Randolph was captured after the 1862 Battle of Kernstown, and read his account of it. Going south, stopping at the New Market battlefield and a special house in Staunton, and to Lexington and V.M.I., over the Blue Ridge past Pharsalia, all associated with Randolph's war, to Charlottesville and Middleburg and Marshall. On our way back, near Frederick,

Maryland, we found the farm from which, during the Battle of Monocacy, Randolph Barton had "borrowed" a horse, "Old Davy," which was, regrettably, killed under him. It was a happy, once-in-a-lifetime experience for all of us, and the story took on a reality for my father that my periodic presentation of chapter printouts had not.

In late October there was an auction at Tepper Auction Galleries, which operated in the same building as Swann, where the commercial spaces were lofts. It was unusual for Tepper to have book auctions; it may have been Philip who told us about it, as he was on every conceivable auction mailing list. Tepper listed a lot of Americana books, and a set of Fortescue's big, British Army history. I went alone, and fell into my auction technique, primarily attributable to anxiety, of raising my hand and keeping it up. It was a complete contrast to Harris's style: he waited to see how the bidding was going and got in toward the end. Whatever, either worked. I bought a lot, including the Fortescue, and later in the store, the curator of the Morristown National Historical Park, who had been at the auction, told Harris, "We all figured it wasn't worth bidding when Margaretta raised her hand." Not a strategy, just nerves.

Harris liked to send me out to visit widows who were selling their husbands' books, thinking they would be more comfortable dealing with a woman. Who knew what image "The Military Bookman" might suggest: an unshaven lout in fatigues? Accordingly, I went to see Hope Hope and her books on Park Avenue. Norman Hope had amassed a large and excellent collection of uniform-plate books, which he used to research his watercolor studies of uniform figures. Mrs. Hope's lawyer was there with her, to reassure both of them, I guess. After about fifteen minutes of chitchat he excused himself, convinced that I did not pose a threat. She and I had a good time together and we wished we could figure out what to do with the watercolors, which were very good. She was a lovely lady, so interested. She came to see us and the store after we had bought the books, and left feeling that they were in good hands.

Emily and Sandra had decided to move to Atlanta. Sandra's publishing job had ceased to exist in a company buyout, and she was ready to go back south, to Atlanta, where she had ties. Emily gave us plenty of notice and we went into mourning—and interviewing. Entirely too many interviews, all through the month of October: Jason ran the scheduling and wasn't selective enough. One woman came in, sat down, asked about the salary, stood up and left. We paid what we could but, as with most jobs in most parts of the book business, there was a financial sacrifice in doing what you enjoyed.

Over the years we had tried to refine the selection process, developing a list of interview questions, and then trying two interviews, but we came to the conclusion that you cannot tell until you work with someone. Some people had problems that were soon evident; others were not apparent until there was a cumulative effect, such as files in disarray. The Corner Bookstore had it right, we just never discussed it with them: they gave people a three-month trial before making them permanent.

This time we laboriously narrowed the applicants down to two: Mike Flint, with a publishing background and military interest, and Linda, who had had her own shop on the West Side. Jason was quite taken with Linda, and pushed for hiring her for her experience. We all liked Mike, and after our second interview, I wasn't so sure about Linda, but we figured that since Jason would work with her closely in our absences, we would defer to his preference.

We were due to go to Barbados for Clai Marshall's wedding and a vacation, and persuaded Emily to stay for those two weeks, even though Linda was starting. We had a farewell party for Emily before we left, and then she and Sandra house-sat for us. Sandra killed time playing Solitaire and Minesweeper on Harris's computer in the basement.

On our return, Jason didn't give us a day to come down to earth and do the laundry and read our own mail. He was on the phone Monday morning, when the store was closed, telling us Linda was a terrible mistake. His vociferous reaction seemed like overkill to me, and I became determined to bend over backward to give Linda a chance to settle in. After a week, I called Emily to see what she had thought of Linda. Her response was raucous but sympathetic laughter.

A plain, small, vigorous woman, Linda bustled around the store with total confidence. She didn't seem to think she had anything to learn, in a store dependent on computers and in a new subject, both foreign to her. She wanted to bring her dog to work—theoretically a nice idea, but the dog was as hyper as she was so we vetoed that. She could not get along with Oliver, which she regarded as an alien being with a mind of its own. That was crucial, if nothing else had been. She was arrogant, nosy, abrasive, and tried to tell us her bookshop methods were better, although obviously she had gone out of business. One idea: she thought we should mail the catalogue ourselves: 2000 catalogues to sort in zip-code order, bag in post office bags and schlep to our difficult post office? I don't think so.

Linda was the only one who was happy; we were all miserable and Ish was having migraine headaches. I tried to talk to her, to no avail. Harris told her she talked too much, so, in a snit, she stopped talking altogether. The customers disliked her too: Philip said, "Where did you get *her?*" Arnold Brown, who knew her from her West Side shop, freaked out when he saw her. Our Christmas party was "secret" that year—we waited until she left for the day and reconvened upstairs with Sheila and Philip and visiting Anne Strickland. Jason grumbled, "She's so nosy, she always asks what I'm having for lunch." I responded, "I can't stand the way she stirs her yogurt." When things descend to this level, you know it's hopeless.

Why in the world did it take us three months to let her go? When we did, she unloaded on me, and I gritted my teeth and kept telling myself, "I will *not* say I would lose the rest of the staff if I kept her."

It so happened that Mike Flint had paid a friendly call to look at Civil War books just before we fired Linda. Jason chatted with him, and I luckily was upstairs, so Jason phoned me and I was able to talk privately with Mike: would he still want to work for us? Linda's end was in a matter of days, and Mike disentangled himself and was with us a couple of weeks later.

We moved ahead with Jason's plan and got credit cards. For a long time we had had misgivings about the cost to us, and were squeamish about other people's credit card debt, especially some of the "addicts" we dealt with. I found it disturbing to see a buyer roll out a long folder of credit cards and have us run them one after another until he found one that wasn't maxed out.

As Jason said, it was a good thing we waited for credit cards until Linda was gone. With her antipathy to any technology, she would have really messed it up. She had been known to lean a book on the Oliver keyboard and then exclaim, "Look what it's doing," as Oliver unreeled unintelligible masses of letters.

As it was, we were a little gun-shy of the new gizmo, and it was thanks to a new customer and user that we successfully ran our first credit-card transaction. All of us clustered around the little machine as Ted Cook, an academic and author, showed us how to charge his purchase.

Jason's book-show plans included New York, New Jersey, and Baltimore. He worked very hard on the selection of books for the shows, and I figured out ways to make the booth attractive, such as cheap red tablecloths and a sign with the logo. Naturally we took stacks of catalogues. Bill Hurlbutt, who did a little dealing, had talked Harris into taking on consignment a couple of magnificent but off-the-mark antiquarian books, one by Sollysell, *The Compleat Horseman*, from 1717. The New York show, as were most, was fruitless, except for a man who perused our catalogue there, spotted the horse book, was sent uptown to see it, and bought it. The New Jersey show was unproductive; the predictable, cheap Osprey *Men-at-Arms* uniform books were selling, that was about all. The Baltimore show was most remarkable as Harris and Jason's rendezvous to collect Dudley Lalley's document.

Bill Waters, friend and globetrotter, had gone to Antarctica that winter, briefly stopping at the Falkland Islands. He returned bearing a most military souvenir for the store: a bright red, enameled metal sign from their war **DANGER MINES**, complete with skull and crossbones. It was installed under the rare-book cabinet by the coffee pot, and it was unclear whether the warning applied to the rare books or the coffee.

Lionel Leventhal was still coming to New York twice a year, marketing his Greenhill Books, which, among other military titles, did limited-edition reprints of scarce and noteworthy Napoleonic memoirs, both British and French. We decided to stock some of his reprints, and when we told him, the sight of his transformation from jet-lagged into an energized selling mode was comical.

Lionel wound in a continuing course through our business life, knew what I was up to and took great interest, checking my progress on each visit. That winter, he asked as always, "What news of the book?" The manuscript was then going the rounds, and I said, "I'm collecting rejections," adding that it was then at Orion Books. "Oh," said Lionel, "I'm calling on them tomorrow, I will just have a word with Steve and Peter." Lionel suggested to Steve that he visit the store as he lived nearby, and he came in to check it—and me—out. Perhaps the editors paid more attention with Lionel's "word." In any event, Orion did publish *Defend the Valley*.

Mike Flint started at the Military Bookman the day I went to midtown, through the usual St. Patrick's Day crowds, traffic and nasty grey weather, for my first meeting at Orion. Orion was part of Random House and it was déjà vu to be back in those offices because I had put in a freelance summer in 1973 working in another division there. And it just felt right: the editors said things like, "Where did you find all this great material?" They displayed the lively interest and so lacking in my University of Virginia Press contacts. Other than the necessity of chopping the manuscript, I had no reservations. I returned with an agreement, and my colleagues were dazzled and excited, as I was. Mike went home and told his girlfriend, who was at Dell Publishing, and she alerted them to the project. Dell subsequently bought the paperback rights.

I had about a year to do a massive edit and rewrite of *Defend the Valley*. Even then, sympathetic and hands-on editors were scarce, but I had been given one in Peter Ginna. The manuscript had to be cut substantially—painful to contemplate—but Peter's guidelines and suggestions and our discussions gave me the direction and impetus. The book was to be dramatically different from the manuscript.

This period in the store, when Jason, Mike, and Ish were with us, was one of the most congenial. Jason's guff didn't ruffle Mike and he was content to be the junior member. He was low-key, with a gentle sense of humor, interested, a good worker, and fitted in well. He was one of the most "normal" people who had worked for us, so it was interesting to learn that his girlfriend wrote science fiction and their roommate was a very large iguana. Mike drew cartoons in his spare time, occasionally selling them, and presenting us with hilarious Christmas cards. In season, there was a lot of football talk in the store: Harris was a dyed-in-the-wool

Giants fan, and Jason had become one in those years as he was growing closer to his father. Ish for some reason rooted for the Denver Broncos, and Mike for Dallas, as he was from Texas. Mike sat on the sidelines as Harris and Jason competed to remember ancient Giants' lineups, and it may be that he, tiring of endless talk of the Giants' superiority, started a football pool that the guys all enjoyed. The Cowboys were the bane of the Giants' existence in those days, and went to the Superbowl both years Mike was with us.

Our favorite part-timer, Robin Elenko, by then a lawyer, was marrying another lawyer. She invited us and Jason to the wedding, up the Hudson in an attractive place in Dobbs Ferry, overlooking the river. Jason had been taking driving lessons and offered to rent a car and take the three of us. He drove with great zest and impatience, a little unnerving. The wedding, on a sunny day in early spring, was lovely; Stuart, one of our first customers, was a proud and happy father and Robin a beautiful bride. Robin was astonished to see Harris dancing; she thought of him as humorous but mostly serious and intellectual—it was a new dimension for her. A wonderful time, aside from the alarming experience of driving home with Jason.

Harris and I combined one of my book trips to Winchester with a melancholy drive into the Appalachians to Davis, West Virginia, to rake through the Civil War and other books of Edith Sheerin's brother, Bob Barton, who had been so interested in and enthusiastic about my book project. Bob had died some months before and Edith asked us to go look at the books and buy what we could use. It may have been the biggest concentration of books in the Canaan Valley, surely in Davis, but they were in a jumble and many not in good shape. That time the station wagon, borrowed from my parents, was full, and for me the books we took were full of sentiment, many having belonged to their Civil War grandfather, Robert Barton, with some of the war texts annotated in his hand. There was also some classical history, including Charles Rollin's *The Ancient History of the Egyptians, Babylonians, Assyrians,* an 1831 London printing in eight volumes. I recognized the set in a special context: one of Robert's brothers, David, had mentioned in his brief 1858 diary that he was reading Rollin's *History*. Since these were books from that family, it was appealing, and pretty safe, to assume that these were David's books, moved from family house to family house, and then to the shelves of the Military Bookman. We saw the rugged terrain of the ill-conceived 1862 winter campaign of Bath, now Berkeley Springs, and Romney.

We "took the waters" at Berkeley Springs; it was a pretty little town, with an old bookshop where a "signed" U. S. Grant was displayed in the window. We tactfully informed them that there were no signed Grants, he having died before his memoirs were published. We passed near the headwaters of the Potomac, came down out of the choppy hills to the rolling farmlands of western Maryland, and shipped the books from Frederick.

There was plenty of book repair work in that lot, some requiring Lloyd Gayle's expertise, but many ministered to by Ish. With the turnover in our "shipping department," no one had ever been there long enough to train in book restoration until Ish came back, or had the aptitude, feeling and interest that he developed. Harris had learned a number of book repair tricks from Herb and developed some of his own, but Ish took those and ran with them. He really had a talent, and restored many books with taste and inventiveness. He stashed away spare parts of useless old books he thought might come in handy, in some secret place in the basement; Harris called him "the Squirrel." When he found a leather jacket discarded on the street, he brought it in, adding it to his cache.

Edith had provided me with many documents and related papers, and was always alert to new clues or artifacts. She sent a box of Civil War memorabilia that had surfaced in clearing out her brother Bob's house: a saddlebag and gauntlet, the leather dry and brittle; her grandfather Robert's Confederate Veterans uniform jacket; and the remains of a leather box that looked as if it had been run over. The jacket was, weirdly, a perfect fit on our nephew Ran, who so resembled Robert. As I handled the beat-up box, I realized that it was or, rather, had been a finely made toilet and writing kit, and a small card noted that it was used by one of the Barton brothers in the war. It was of black calf with a green silk lining, with silver-topped crystal bottles and boxes, and a bone-handled pen. I mulled over how to restore this once rather luxurious object, so full of associations, and thought to call Kauffman's, the famous saddlery shop in the East 20s, to see if they could repair it. I must have spoken to the proprietor; he did not brush off the odd query but gave it thought, then said, "What you need is someone like a bookbinder." I felt like a dolt. There I was, with a great resource ten feet away. I got off the phone and turned to Ish, who had heard my end of the conversation. "I've been thinkin' about that little box," he said. Ish talked to Talas, the bookbinding supplier, and obtained some special leather-reconditioning goo for the box, glove and saddlebag. He did all that sensitivity, imagination and skill could do, rebuilding the box structure with wood found somewhere, and reconditioning the leather, to make it handsome again.

While I was away briefly in Wilmington, Harris had an adventure. A young female researcher came in and asked for anything about the *Normandie*. Misunderstanding, Harris was pleased to lead her to the shelves on D-Day and the Normandy invasions. She quickly clarified that she wanted information on the burning of the magnificent French steamship in 1942, when it was interned in New York harbor and being converted into a troopship. Harris exclaimed,

"Oh I remember seeing her burning!" The sweet young thing was thrilled to have discovered an eyewitness; in short order, Harris was scooped up and transported to the shore of the Hudson River in New Jersey, with Manhattan in the background, to be interviewed for "Investigative Reports," Bill Kurtis's conspiracy-oriented TV series. The premise was the involvement of gangster Lucky Luciano and the Mob in the fire that gutted the great liner—pretty far-fetched, but it didn't matter. Harris was the star as far as we and our acquaintance were concerned. He vividly described going down Park Avenue, a six-year-old in a school bus, and seeing huge black clouds of smoke—and next day being taken by his father to see the stricken ship in her berth at the French Line, rolled over on her side. The program aired in 1993 and scores of friends, acquaintances and customers saw it, by design or by surprise, in re-runs which went on for a couple of years, and we would get excited and amazed calls. "Cookie" Wilson, in Florida, had left the bathroom door open: "I had the TV on, taping 'Investigative Reports,' and I heard that voice, I know that voice!" Harris really was good, a friend thought he should join the Screen Actors' Guild and make himself available.

Joel Block saw the show and was bent out of shape: "I saw it burning, why didn't they ask me?"

CHAPTER NINETEEN

"I'm going to sit down with these and a big glass of bourbon."

1992 – 1993

Peter Plimpton.

Ron Van Sickle was a Civil War specialist, a big bear and a bit of a wheeler-dealer; he seemed to move here and there and change business partners as often. His interest turned to the British Army, and he bought a lot from us and then went shopping in England. Maybe the pound was weak, but we heard tales of his buying prime, unusual copies of the classic British accounts and regimental histories, at high retail prices, flourishing wads of dollars, and, one hoped, not in the bright orange jumpsuit, vivid in my memory, that he later wore to 93rd Street. Maybe he was buying for himself, but in any event, before too long he wanted to sell his accumulation to us. Harris said it was the equivalent of a trip to England, and indeed we did not go buying in 1992. Ron's was such a large collection that we had to use the very top shelf in the British Army section, and even then there were several shelves of regimental histories in the basement. Regimentals had become so expensive in England, overpriced, Harris thought, that we had not been buying them since the mid-eighties, and our people were starved for them.

Mild-mannered, bearded Richard Link was a new customer for British Army books, who had seemingly discovered us just in time for Van Sickle's books to tempt him. I took him down to the depths to see the regimentals, where a few collectors were jostling each other. A certain amount of competitive bragging was going on, and Philip Kamil established his rank and seniority with the "new kid" in a most territorial manner. Richard was undeterred. He returned many times, often with his nice wife, until they moved to south Jersey.

Van Sickle's was a dazzling lot, almost all fine copies, with many unusual titles. Much of the best material never made it into a catalogue, because the local fanatics picked it off. Philip put aside so much he had to pay in installments. One particular temptation was an exceptional set of Sir John Fortescue's massive history of the British Army, handsomely bound, with a Latin inscription by the author:

Ecclesiastes 44:1, *Laudemus viros gloriosos . . .*—Let us now praise famous men . . . It was quite a sight to see Philip confronting that long row of leather under the rare book cabinet, perhaps raising his eyebrows but otherwise not changing expression. But we could feel his pulse rate go up.

That was a special set and had a life of its own; maybe it had belonged to the author, or a particular friend. For me, part of the appeal, the mystique of any old object, beyond its intrinsic merits and aesthetic attractions, was to think of where it might have been during its lifetime. And many of them have longer lives than we do. There was a two-volume set by Francis Vinton Greene on the Russo-Turkish War, rather scarce. The New York edition was bound in either bright blue or green cloth. The first volume was text, the second maps, and to some degree each could stand alone. Early on, we had the green text volume alone and supplied it to Brian Pieper in Canada. That volume had the added interest for us of a tiny sticker from a Madras bookstore at the hinge on the front endpaper, probably a sign of its first stop, and on the back endpaper the distinctive penciled code of Peter de Lotz (though we had not bought it from him). I later told Peter that the copy had passed through our hands and he said, "Oh, I remember that book, I bought it in Amsterdam." The wanderings of a book, and the memory of a book dealer. At a later date we were able to supply the map volume, in blue, to Brian. Still later, the mismatched set came back to us when Brian changed periods, and went on to another home.

It was a matter of some perturbation to us when our customers decided to go into our business themselves, even in a small or part-time segment of it. Over the years there were a number. We may have made it look easy and fun, but this was not exactly a compliment we wanted. A customer in Richmond got fed up with teaching and its low standards, and decided to try dealing in Marine Corps books and militaria, his own interest. Several Napoleonic collectors started producing their own lists. A young guy in Pennsylvania who frequently visited the store, and bought, set up as The War Room.

The most annoying was a customer in Texas who decided to create his own version of the Military Bookman there. He even aped our distinctive and unique logo, producing an ugly version. On top of this he wrote pushy, demanding letters, all questions about how we did business, as if he were entitled to be instructed on how to compete with us. He particularly wanted to know about how we bought books in England. These were certainly trade secrets that we were not about to share, but he was very persistent.

At first I didn't answer. He had the nerve to complain. I wrote what Harris would call an "airy-fairy" indeed very "feminine" letter, as vague and space-cadet as I could make it. He still didn't get the message, and sent a hectoring letter. Harris took him off the mailing list.

Peter Blum, who had originally seen us as some kind of threat but eventually had come to think of us as allies, talked to us about winding down the Soldier Shop. He had not been well for some time, and the Soldier Shop also was fading. Peter eventually called us in to buy from their inventory. He had stocked huge quantities of the very special uniform books (many European) published in the sixties, seventies and eighties—too huge, obviously—and was willing to accept very reasonable prices for them. But when we got around to discussing his mailing list, he was not reasonable. Mailing lists were crucial to our businesses, and we would have liked to rent his at any point during those years. By the time we were given this opportunity, the Soldier Shop had not mailed to its list in something like seven years, so it was far from current; Peter still wanted an unrealistic, even outrageous, price for it. We were there with Jeffrey Kleinbardt who was looking at the militaria, and even if we had split the cost with him, the price didn't make sense, especially for an untended list. With reluctance, we gave up on it, and I cannot imagine Peter had anyone else to sell it to.

Peter Plimpton had grown up playing with soldiers, at first flats and then Britains lead-soldier sets, visiting F.A.O. Schwarz and pining for the antique soldiers, and in his teens getting up the nerve to go to the Soldier Shop, where the staff could be gruff and snobbish. He was their main customer, or the most memorable one, who gravitated to the Military Bookman when the Soldier Shop was on its last legs. Tall, blond, spare, with thick glasses, always sporting a bow tie and bright suspenders with his banker's perfect suits, Peter was affable, gregarious, and an enthusiastic collector and scholar of uniform studies. He had started with prints, and continued, but from us he learned about the beautiful, old, plate books, which were a revelation to him. His timing was such that he started coming in shortly after we acquired the splendid Norman Hope uniform books. After a number of purchases, he chose Hauthal, *Geschichten der Sachsischen Armee*, and Harris, being Harris, said, "I can't sell Saxons: Germans, British, Russians any day, but not the Saxons." Peter's all-time favorite, acquired from us, was Dero-Becker and Martinet's exquisite *Galerie Militaire*. Ish was not the only one who breathed a sigh of relief when it sold, remembering that Jason had, typically, overpaid for it at the San Francisco auction.

Peter had been led by the uniforms to the history, and had a fine and growing appreciation of the literature, and a scholarly approach. He was one of those who welcomed Harris's, and my, guidance in their collecting. Harris knew how to "nudge" Peter one way or another, and said, when Peter made an important decision to buy Fallou, *La Garde Imperiale,* "This is your first copy of this book, you'll want a better one down the line." Indeed Peter later bought one of the numbered copies that had plates in two states—but not from us. Peter had a sense of custodianship which he claimed he picked up from me; I often remarked, in selling a precious book I particularly liked, "It's going to a good home." Peter lavished care and maintenance on his books, and sometimes consulted Ish on restoration. Ish had occasion to chastise him once for getting the leather lubricant onto the cloth part of the binding. We sent Peter to Herb Weitz for some spectacular bindings.

Doug Bandow started coming in about the same time. A nice-looking young man with a beard, he was an analyst and writer for the Cato Institute, a right-wing think-tank. His interests were broad, and he also collected the beautiful uniform pictorials, primarily the German ones. When he came to New York, he and John Catherwood would get together, having met when we referred Doug to John's wife's gallery for military prints. At a Virginia book fair, Doug saw a set of the Franco-Prussian War official history that he knew John would want, and John bought them and brought them to us to rebind. Doug was in New York regularly on business, and usually managed to fit in a store visit.

New to Carnegie Hill in the late eighties, Leighton Longhi lived around the corner on Fifth Avenue, and found us that naturally, walking his little dog or perhaps on his way to the Corner Bookstore or Patrick Murphy's Market. A very tall, very elegant dealer in Japanese art, he came to us for First and Second World War aviation, and always to talk to Harris.

A Swiss, Ralph Reinertsen, regularly visited New York on business, and had found our ad in a new magazine, *Military History.* He was an extremely good customer and an extremely nice one, who bought both in the store and from the catalogue. On one occasion, he called urgently to order from the catalogue and there were breaks in the conversation; he was on a train in the Alps and he was passing through tunnels.

A couple visiting obviously from "south of the border" spoke no English, and Ish was called up. He talked to them for several minutes, then said, "I can't help you, they're from Brazil."

Two new customers came on strong in the nineties, and while both bought from the catalogues, they ordered a lot by phone in long talks with Harris. Ed Somers, who lived near Washington, got to New York with some regularity and seemed to travel a lot, probably with some government-connected job. Ed's wife thought he was overdoing the books, and after I queried him about his lack of response to recent quotes, he told me with some embarrassment that he was "under pressure." It didn't slow him down much. Dave Schroer was a major when he signed up for catalogues. He was in the Army, in Special Forces, and read just about everything we could provide on post–1945 warfare, and elite units including the Marines.

Dave's career was stalled, he told Harris, before the Gulf War moved him along, and during the ten years he bought from us he rose to Colonel. He and Harris talked a lot, and Harris would emerge from his little retreat in the back closet with a big smile on his face, waving a large order to be printed up.

Two scions of real-estate families came and went for years, probably not encountering each other. One was "old money," very distinguished-looking, very reserved, and mostly interested in espionage; he "shimmered in," in the Wodehousian manner, not interacting except with Harris. He was startled when I addressed him by name. The other was an exuberant presence, wanting service and recognition; he taught military history and trumpeted that he was one of our best customers—if true we would not have lasted so long.

Not long after Al Qaeda's first attack on the World Trade Center, a woman came in to inquire for bomb manuals. She looked harmless enough, and it turned out that she was an architect working on the design of an American embassy in a country where there was a perceived need for a bombproof building.

More times than I could count, customers to whom I had just written out a postcard offering a new arrival from their wants list would call within minutes, a psychic communication that certainly saved on stamps. Mike Flint always got a visible frisson when this happened. David Feinberg, a long-time regular, called in some wants from time to time, but usually was a browser. When we had the South Pacific war art by George Harding, a relevant book came in. Harding was briefly on the U.S.S. *Montpelier*, a ship whose service was documented in seaman James Fahey's journal, published as *Pacific War Diary*. It was against regulations to keep a diary, so the book was singular and by no means common. Remarkably, a copy came in when I wanted it, and I snagged it to see if there might be any mention of Harding—and there was. The book was by my side when David called about it. He knew it was scarce, and voiced his request as pie-in-the-sky; I could feel the shock waves when I said, "It's right here on my desk." And Mike, of course, shivered.

A young woman who lived on 96th Street came in to see if we would be interested in a book that had come from Hitler's library. It was the German edition of an 1895 pictorial on Napoleon by Armand Dayot, and had not only Hitler's bookplate but that of an NSDAP (Nazi Party) office. With it was a 1945 letter from an American officer at SHAEF headquarters in Berlin, describing how he had acquired it. He had sent that and another book to her mother from Berlin. We always had mixed, if not queasy, feelings about Nazi items, but this was so unusual that we bought it, obtaining a letter from the mother about the provenance. She mentioned she also wanted to sell a stamp collection. We told Philip Kamil; one of his many interests was buying and selling lots of stamps, so he went to see it, and told us the woman and her mother were living in an almost bare apartment.

They had an accumulation of stamps, rather than a collection, but more Hitler bookplates. Philip bought it all.

Linda Hughes-Willis, our homeless naval expert, was still coming in, but there were some long intervals between visits; Emily had always suspected she was "away." At some point, Ms. Hughes-Willis asked us to keep for her the books she had bought, claiming that they would be stolen from her at the shelter. Probably true, but this quickly became untenable as we didn't have the space. It fell to Mike Flint to tell her, gently, that she must take her books away when she bought them. She left in a huff, and we never saw her again.

Mike was, and I guess we all were, taken by the repeated letters "sending friendly greetings," from a young couple in a tiny town in the Czech Republic. They were farmers, but in their spare time they took care of the public library in Myslejovice, Moravia. He was asking for book contributions, so eventually we rounded up an easy mix of Time-Life books and other pictorials and sent it off. An interesting little sign of the end of the Soviet period.

Actor Peter McNicol came in regularly to look for books on the Northwest Frontier and the Mountain Gunners, in India, the subject of many movies from *Gunga Din* on. After he moved to Hollywood, he still ordered from time to time. Michael J. Fox occasionally browsed the Civil War shelves.

A German resident in Manhattan, Agostino von Hassell, was collecting material on "elegant military food", an oxymoron, surely, and its influence on civilian food. Not particularly appetizing. We often had requests for Army or Navy cookbooks— *Take 10 dozen eggs . . .*—from people learning about cooking in quantity.

Known to us as an ardent Civil War reader and reenactor, Jay Monahan was better known as Katie Couric's husband. Jay read more widely than many reenactors, who generally confined themselves to the battles in which their units had participated, but he naturally wanted the Civil War manuals, especially for the cavalry. After he moved to New York, he came in frequently, and several times his friends called for a present for him, Katie's office having suggested us.

Mr. Maclaurin's courteous, British-inflected voice was instantly recognizable. His manners were old-fashioned, even courtly, and he wanted naval history. He lived in Connecticut but never made it in to the store, nevertheless was a very good customer. I always wondered how customers pictured the store, even after we included photos in the catalogue; frequently they seemed to have the impression we had a large staff and a big space.

A spry little Yank in a bowler hat, with a merry and flirtatious eye, was a veteran of both the First and Second World Wars. His son had heard about us, and he came hoping to find the history of his World War I unit's service. He had been a forward observer with an artillery unit in France—his nerves must have been steel.

All work halted in the store as he treated us to a few memories: of coming down to New York with a few friends from Yale to join up in 1917, and the hazardous duty of directing artillery fire from a church steeple in the middle of a battlefield, and of courting his future wife in our neighborhood. When not only his World War I but his World War II history was placed in his hands, he lit up, saying, "I'm going to go home and sit down with these and a big glass of bourbon."

Who should walk in, studiously casual, one day in March, but Mark Cummings. No warning, no expectation. He had moved to Brooklyn to seek his fortune in his mother's country. For the first six months or more, while waiting for a better offer, he did a lot of part-time work at the Military Bookman. We had not really needed a part-timer since Oliver came along, but the timing could not have been more fortuitous for us. I was in the countdown to my May manuscript deadline, and before long, each of my parents had serious health problems and I needed and wanted to be in Wilmington frequently. Mark was used to the store and its workings, having been with us so many times and always pitching in; it was also nice for Harris to have his company sometimes in my absences, which were many that summer. Mark also took on a project for Philip Kamil, cataloguing his library. Philip would collect Mark and take him out to his "book cave" in Fort Lee to work, and then return him. It took a long time; Mark made lists of the collection and then entered them in Oliver, with a special code for Philip. This enlarged our database, because Philip had a great many titles we had not seen. The lists were printed out in the store, and rechecked. Then Philip had a master list for the library, and a short-form printout to take on his travels.

Mark was in New York for a few years, and in his off-hours he sometimes wistfully trolled delis and specialty food shops searching for marmite. That dubious British concoction is something you have to grow up with; when he finally found it, he insisted we all sample it. No enthusiasm.

Dave had written me a little program that converted footnotes to endnotes, one of the last requirements in preparing my manuscript. By the end of May, I was ready for the necessity and anxiety of cutting a disk to send to Orion. Phil Haultcoeur, who usually came up from midtown at lunchtime, happened upon Harris and me at the end of the day when the disk-cutting time had come. Dave had told us what to do and how to do it, but we were nervous, so Phil oversaw the process and verified it. My editor, Peter Ginna, later told me that *Defend the Valley* was the first book ever that Orion had taken from a disk. I was my own typesetter, for better or for worse, and Orion saved a lot of money.

In late August, I went to Winchester, where I saw my cronies, did a little advance promotion, and met former National Park Service historian and sometime customer Joe Whitehorne. After meeting Harris in northern Virginia for a wedding, we added on some days with Judy and her then-husband to visit the battlefields of Antietam and Gettysburg, new to all of us, and looked for positions of "our" troops, the 2nd Virginia Regiment. In Gettysburg we visited the bookstore where John then worked. The Civil War naturally dominated the shelves and commanded top dollar, not a place to consider buying anything.

Despite my parents' continuing difficulties, things seemed to be stabilized with them, and Harris and I planned a buying trip for late September. Shortly before we went, I received a very unpleasant diagnosis of my own, and then sprained my ankle walking in Central Park. I went off to England with a sprained ankle on one leg, a recent biopsy on the other, and a cane. We were flying in to Manchester, but not to meet Amy. She had moved to the south coast, to Bexhill near Hastings. We took to the rainy road, getting mixed up in Leeds. When I got out of the car in York, I was struck with some strange malady which made me so weak I could barely get up the long flight of steps to our room with the Minster view at the Judge's Lodging. Harris took to the streets and the bookshops of York without me, but came back later and we, I haltingly, went to Taikoo Books together. Mostly I watched him spend a lot of money on great merchandise. I stayed in bed the next day until an afternoon appointment when I experienced the National Health Service. The nice young doctor at the clinic said that there was a virus going around in York, and I replied, sarcastically, that it must have been waiting for me just when I got out of the car. Nothing to be done, just wait it out, he said. I felt a little reassured and a little better, enough to go to a few shops, and vespers at the Minster, and better the next day.

Confused again in Leeds, but differently, we found our way to Halifax, in West Yorkshire, an ancient center of the wool trade. The book dealer was in the colonnade of the eighteenth-century Piece Hall, a large, handsome building which surrounded a big, open space where individual crofters had come to sell their piece goods, lengths of wool cloth. In a tightly packed shop with a most pleasant proprietor, we found a lot of good, reasonable books in all our subjects, three knee-high stacks. After lunch with the dealer in a funny little place in the colonnade, we went on to Southport. Though grey, it was a picturesque drive through the Pennines, little towns, sheep, steep hills, more sheep, stone fences. Harris was really pushing to get to Broadhurst Books before closing, and did. Mr. Sankey welcomed us, regretted not seeing Amy, stayed open late, and we accumulated a few more stacks. While the men were settling accounts, I sat with a little lady who was waiting for a ride home with Mr. Sankey. She looked just like a Toby Jug, ruddy round face, funny little black felt hat and no neck. I tried to converse with her, but she got a far look and intoned, "The nights are closing in." Indeed they were, and we were ready to settle in at our hotel but Harris took one look and pronounced it a dump. If Harris said it was, I surely wouldn't have liked it, so we circled around the town and found a classic Victorian hotel on the broad, leafy boulevard, a pretty place in the old style.

After a difficult drive with lots of traffic, we came to Bewdley and George and Joyce Harris in the late morning. It was fun to continue our acquaintance with our dealers; this year George was irate, face red and eyebrows beetling, about American dealers, the Culpins, who had stiffed him (and us), and we commiserated. And we had one or two bad stories about a couple of British dealers, and an Australian, who had never made good on transactions with us.

Between lots of buying and chat and teatime, we had a late start and another difficult, darkening, rainy drive on what must have been a spectacular route through the Malvern Hills to Ledbury, a charming market town. A kind young man led us to Hope End House; it was a hidden place in a valley lovely even in the rain, and inside, an interesting mix of modern and antiques, with good food, the first we had had that week. The sun came out in the morning for us to wander in the pretty grounds before we left for Hay-on-Wye.

By this time, Hay was very well known, indicated by the big parking lot outside the town. There were regular bus runs from London, making it a destination even for day-trippers (although they must have spent most of the time on the road). Our customers who visited Hay would come back deflated, saying, "It's all fished out." Well, it wasn't for us, because we were going for a wide range of subjects and repetitive titles, and collectors, by the time they were shopping in Hay, already had so much they were very selective. Many of them never seemed to realize that the more they had, the harder it was to add to it.

We headed first for the Cinema Bookshop and spent about three hours including coffee and a chat with the military curator. He drove us to Richard Booth's shop, where the military had been moved to a dingy, ill-lit, unheated annex. After two hours on that cement floor I couldn't feel my toes, and we were both glad to go on to the surprisingly good Swan Hotel to thaw out with a drink and dinner. We went to three small shops, then Booth again, all in the morning. Margaret Kelly, a cousin of Harris's whom we had met at the Sizergh Castle gala, lived about an hour away and came to meet us for lunch, a happy reunion though dimmed by the recent death of her husband Peter. We left Hay after our visit with Margaret, and it was over two hours to Broadway, in the Cotswolds. The late sun glowed on the golden village as it rose up the hill. We were just too late to get to the bookshop, but settled in happily at Dormy House, which was superb in every way; our cozy, cottage-like room under the eaves was a contrast to the grander public rooms.

The next day was Sunday, so it was no surprise that the bookshop was not open, but there was a book fair on the green, and the pleasure of sunshine, and we managed to spend a few hundred pounds by noon. It was about a four-hour drive with light Sunday traffic to Norfolk, and we stopped to see magnificent Peterborough Cathedral. The arresting Thorney Abbey, an ancient establishment, took us by surprise; we had never heard of it. It had suffered from marauders from the Vikings to Henry VIII, but in its restored condition it rose like a cliff by the highway, compelling our attention.

We looked forward to our return to gracious Congham Hall, near King's Lynn, and were in time for tea on the lawn. It was our base again to visit Tony Martin, farther north. Next day at Tony's, we chose eighty-five books, and Tony kindly shipped our gleanings from the book fair too. South to Cambridge, formerly a good book town, but it was disappointing this time, with some shops having converted to remainder books, or gone. Only Galloway & Porter was still really good. We spent the night nearby with cousin Jilly ex-Strickland and her husband Ron Maynard, who greeted us with a warm welcome and a dinner party. They lived in the sixteenth-century "Saxon House" in the tiny village of Ickleton. The house was fascinating, inside all half-timber and carved wood and different levels and vintages, and altogether charming, if hazardous, with many ups-and-downs and low (for me) doorways. We tried Cambridge again next morning, somewhat disgruntled, then braced ourselves for the confusing and difficult drive to London. I was driving and Harris navigating, and trying in vain to escape the inexorable pull of the intimidating Hyde Park Corner roundabout. We fetched up at our hotel on Half Moon Street in Mayfair about seven, too tired to care that it was cramped and shabby.

The next morning was the usual appointment-making, laundry-sorting, accounting and banking. We cabbed to Charing Cross Road and found almost nothing until we came upon Francis Edwards. The name had been resuscitated in Charing Cross Road and then around the corner in Great Newport Street, and once again it was known for its military and naval stock. We had found it "untouchable," the prices that is, when we had stopped in a few years before. But this time the prices were doable to the point that we spent well over £2000. Maybe it was because Glenn Mitchell, known to us by reputation, had taken over the military desk. Glenn was a knowledgeable, canny guy, and fun to deal with. After this visit, he started buying from us and continued to do so while at Francis Edwards. We went on to Maggs, and although the curator Nicola was not there, we were okayed for the basement, and then were locked in there until 5:30. We met Anne Strickland for dinner at Simpson's, both a treat; our English friends often humored us in going to a traditional British place rather than the latest trattoria.

Next morning back to Maggs, where we did a few deals with Nicola. We had some loose time and walked across Berkeley Square for some shopping of our own in Bond Street and environs (more shoes for Harris), before going on to Victor Sutcliffe. I was still a bit shaky so we were taking cabs instead of the Underground. We worked, visited, drank wine and waited for Anne-Marie, then went out to a French bistro.

Next day, we met a new specialist who had been sending his lists to us. Steve Tilston had taken a golden parachute from IBM and was doing what he wanted to from his home in Blackheath, south of the Thames. A good-looking, delightful man, he carried the IBM culture with him: he graciously picked us up at our hotel, gave us a little tour of the Heath, with great views and a little grisly history, and took us to lunch. Afterward as we drove down the littered street to his house, he said, "Oh, the foxes have been in the garbage again!" Harris immediately started making skeptical remarks, but the foxes indeed lived on the railway embankment behind Steve's house. Yanks might think them more picturesque than the scavengers in New York, but they were a regular, general nuisance, as they were in Hyde Park. In Steve's densely packed bookroom, we enjoyed spending close to £2000 on mostly twentieth-century warfare. A successful day, and Steve took us back to Mayfair, dropping us at the Burlington Arcade. Amy had come up to town from Bexhill to see us for a couple of days, and we joined her and Anne Strickland and Anne's daughters and went en masse to a snazzy Indian restaurant. Harris, surrounded by women, enjoyed the company more than the food.

Amy met us in the morning and we decided to pay our respects at the National Army Museum, in Chelsea. It had wonderful exhibits: paintings, uniforms, regimental plate, medals, et al., but it was disappointing to find that the Napoleonic wing was closed. Harris was resigned, but Amy charmed one of the guards and he turned on the lights and took us in. Afterward we started walking back, finding a great pub along the way. Somewhere in the crowded King's Road, I found later to my dismay, my priceless little notebook listing all our dealers and dealings was pinched from the open crevice of my handbag. Bummer. No value to anyone else, but precious to me. We came to Chelsea Rare Books and benign Mr. Bernard, and as before put together a box or two.

Then it was Sunday, and we met Anne Strickland for a very special date. Anne's half-brother was Maj. Gen. Christopher Tyler and he was the Governor of the Tower of London. We had been with Anne several times on this visit, and it had occurred to me that her connection might enable us to jump the lengthy lines and visit the Tower without that hassle. This got translated into Sunday dinner *en famille* in the Governor's residence in the Queen's House within the Tower. The Tudor house had a broad view of the Thames, thanks to later, larger Georgian windows, and was brightly, refreshingly decorated. The governor and his lady were attractive and delightful, and he later walked us out through the grounds.

Sunday should have been our own day, but we were interested in and felt compelled to check out something new to us. In the nineties, the Provincial Booksellers Association's monthly fairs had changed the business considerably, and we went for the first time to the Fair at the Russell Hotel: a hive of activity. The Fair was a movable feast, in different venues around the country, and an opportunity for small part-time or private dealers to make themselves known to new customers and to each other. We made the most of two hours at the Book Fair, buying from eight dealers—£12 here, £40 there, £170 there—and rediscovering Pat Quorn. Pat had moved shop and we hadn't found him when we were planning our last trip, but there he was and it was fun to see him again for books and chat. Pat had seen Lionel Leventhal and Peter de Lotz together the previous day and was reeling from "so much cleverness all in one place."

We spent the better part of the next day with Peter de Lotz, racking up our usual big bill, never immunized, despite all our buying, to his fine stock. Peter was already flogging a book he was publishing the next year, a fine and finely produced bibliography of the Boer War by dealer-collector Ron Hackett. This was a non-starter with us; there was little interest in the States in that literature aside from the most well-known titles. But we ordered a copy for our reference library and a couple more to sell; they moved glacially. After being over-caffeinated at Peter's, we were offered Bloody Marys by Tom Donovan, more good books, and eventually a ride back to our hotel. It was a horrible rainy night, but we went to meet Diana Birch, of *Medal News,* and her husband at the ancient and marvelous Rule's, near Covent Garden; they were a treat and so was dinner. Diana was a vegetarian but she indulged us: Rule's was famous for game, one page of the menu for "feathered" and one listing "furred." Next day, no book-buying: luncheon and book talk with Lionel, and paperwork for the shipper and a little shopping. We realized we were really tired and more than ready for a vacation.

We went on to France, I accidentally but symbolically leaving my cane on the plane. In the Loire Valley, we were to rendezvous with Keene and Nancy Taylor for a few days at an obscure château. When we arrived, there was a running footman with a light to lead us in along the raked, gravel drive, a room with the bath in a turret, and drinks by the fire with a lady who was more like a hostess than a hotelier. At a nearby restaurant with charm and divine food, I said to Harris, over an *amuse-bouche* of puréed artichoke, "We're not in Kansas anymore."

The Taylors came along after breakfast as we lazed in the stunning dining room in front of the fire, and we began a round of châteaux. It was gray and rainy and all the rivers were in flood. We tried to picnic and twice ate in the car, wondering how many rental cars were turned in with baguette crumbs on the dashboard. Eventually we headed for Paris, and thought it would be smart to turn in the car at Orly airport rather than contend with the confusion and traffic of the city. This was another kind of difficulty: we did not recognize the French word for car rental, *livraison*, (heaven forbid they offer a translation) and roamed all over the airport, finding ourselves almost on a runway and having a close encounter with a tank-like apparatus which shot water, for use in controlling riots and demonstrations. We had four chilly, dreary days in Paris, fortified by lots of onion soup, with the usual great mix of book buying, our own shopping, and Ste. Chapelle, the Marais, and the Musée de Cluny. Ute had planned to meet us for a day or two, but called that morning to say that Air France was suddenly on strike—so disappointing. It was one of those periods of random strikes in France, and we had seen a demonstration on the Boulevard St. Germain, sort of amusing but a bit alarming too, as the strikers were throwing firecrackers and the police were ready to crack down, one of their arsenal being the kind of water-tank we had seen at Orly. On the morning we were to fly home, there were strikers at our air terminal, and all flights were delayed unpredictably by the Air France strike. While we waited we were entertained by the outrageous talking robot we had seen years before in the Luxembourg gardens. Clouds of tear gas were rising over a nearby terminal, and we were given a terrible lunch: a sign that something was wrong in Paris!

At the store, everything had been fine in our absence, but soon was not. Jason was unhappy with his life. His father, to whom he was close, had died not long before. His long-term relationship had dumped him. His mother died days after we returned from France. Jason must have been mulling it over for a while, but abruptly decided on a complete change of scene, following his Civil War interest to Virginia. He had inherited some money so he indulged his fantasies, guess what, not changing his occupation or specialty and taking us as his model in many respects, he leased a handsome old house in Leesburg and planned to live over the store.

Jason sprang this on us within a week of our return from France, giving us two-weeks notice. While we understood his desire to act on his decision, two weeks was hardly enough for us to replace someone who had been an important part of our business. Furthermore, he knew I was scheduled for surgery and would be out for some weeks, and that Harris would be preoccupied with that. Jason was self-indulgent, as always. Somehow he was prevailed upon to stay until Thanksgiving and to do some preliminary interviewing for his replacement.

Jason left with our good wishes but with our wondering how he would fare. He intended to imitate what we were doing, by himself, a staff of one lazy person. He was going into a town that already had a couple of Civil War specialists. He was no businessman and loved playing the big shot: the house lease was expensive, and he ordered handsome, custom, walnut shelving and a lot of other frills. He cruised through New England in a fancy leased car, buying top-dollar inventory from specialists, and going to Britain to buy even before he opened. Really grandiose. He had learned a lot from us, but he had not taken in our frugality, or our work ethic. He confessed to me later that he hadn't realized how much Harris did!

The British books arrived December first, and we had to go slowly with them. I was not up to speed, Mike still had a lot to learn and our new employee was barely trained in the basics. Anne, one of two young women Jason had singled out for us to interview, was winsome, charming, cute, bright, but over-confident and over-familiar. She was a lawyer, but wanted a change from lawyering, so she was having a fling with bookselling.

Our accountant Melvin Kushel, who always begrudged paying authorities, inadvertently set in motion a painful, prolonged and expensive episode. He tried to get us a lower rate on our Workers' Compensation Insurance because in almost twenty years we had filed no claims for the Military Bookman, the hazards being mostly paper cuts, or dropping a book on one's foot, or back strain. The insurance company came down on us hard, sent some kind of examiner, and decided through some convoluted reasoning that we were a "wholesale" business because we shipped packages, and should be paying a higher rate, not lower. It still boggles my mind that anyone could define our business as wholesale, it couldn't have been more retail: one book at a time. We objected, utilizing Anne's legal training in an unanticipated way. She found an appropriate lawyer and did some of the work. No dice. We had legal fees and still the higher rate. It was cold comfort then to realize that we could opt not to include the proprietors in the coverage and at least deprive the insurers of that revenue.

Our store Christmas party was a particular delight that year because Amy and Mark were with us, Amy having come to spend Christmas with Mark. We had a merry time: Ish, Anne, Mike and his girlfriend, Sheila and Philip and the Cummings duo. I gave all the guys Christmas socks and Mike immediately put his on.

Mike Flint at Christmas.

CHAPTER TWENTY

"Did you write that review yourself?"

1994 – 1995

It seemed to set the theme for the year when Susan Murphy and her husband invited us to the Confederate Society Ball. Ulrich had been a Wall Street colleague of Harris's and was a sometime customer. Although German, he had a Civil War family connection through a Prussian officer, Heros von Borcke, who had gone into the Confederacy on a blockade runner, and served as an officer on Gen. J. E. B. Stuart's staff; this qualified Ulrich for membership in the Society.

During the winter I was involved with various parts of my book production. Even when I was in the hospital, Peter Ginna, my editor, asked me to place the photos in the text, which I was delighted to do—so much better than a picture section. Then, in relays: okaying the page proofs, checking and correcting the maps, checking the index, always in a rush. Peter thought a photo of the family papers and letters on the back of the dust jacket would express the nature of the raw materials of the book, and I turned to a photographer who had done copy work for our catalogues and later of the original documents that illustrated the book. Harris and I assembled the papers and photos and went up to his studio in Washington Heights where, as he said, he "made magic." A darkly handsome and evocative still life: we ordered a poster-sized blowup to hang behind the store desk, which looked much better than its reproduction on the title page spread.

Lionel had said, "Now you have to start thinking about promoting the book"— just when I thought I could relax—and launched my "speaking career" by telling Sidney Kramer Books in Washington about *Defend the Valley*. They called in February to invite me to speak in their Civil War series at the Arlington Public Library in the spring. I knew I had to say yes, but felt as if I were being thrown in from the deep end. I had never done any public speaking, but Harris helped me think out the talk, coached and rehearsed me indefatigably—he could have given the talk himself—and Susan, who taught public speaking professionally, gave me an invaluable afternoon of pointers while Lenny Golay and Harris and some stuffed animals approximated an audience. I gave it a not-very-good run-through with Sheila on our May garden-center expedition to Connecticut. After many rehearsals for many talks, Harris was mouthing the words with me— very disconcerting and very funny.

I had not imagined that an author was so involved in promotion. In March, Peter asked me what Civil War historians might be approached for the blurbs on the dust jacket, so I thought of Steve Sears, Bob Krick, and Gary Gallagher, all known to me. Edith Sheerin suggested Archer Jones, with whom she had some Richmond connection, and I threw in Frank Vandiver, whose biography of Stonewall Jackson was a standard. And I asked Jeffrey Simpson, who knew historian David McCullough, if he would call McCullough on my behalf. Already well known for his prize-winning books, McCullough had become the voice of American history with his narrations in the Ken Burns Civil War series, and others. David called and asked me to send him the proofs; my nephew Ran, impressed, asked, "Does he sound That Way on the phone?" Yes.

The historians' comments started coming in, so good that they crowded the documents photo off the dust jacket. The high point was David McCullough's letter: Peter Ginna faxed it to the Corner Bookstore and someone ran it over, and it was more than exciting. We all celebrated briefly, but I was so thrilled I couldn't come down to earth, good for nothing in the store. I went next door to show the letter to Felix, and he opened a bottle of champagne (which he did not drink) and we sat together at his kitchen table until the end of the day. I drank the whole bottle myself, so high already that I didn't feel it.

In the meantime, I was arranging a family weekend—a gathering of the clan, all my "book cousins"—around the book-launch festivities in Winchester in late May, and a book-signing party at the Military Bookman just a few days later. I was also involved with Rebecca Ebert, the archivist, and others in the planning of a special exhibit of the family papers and artifacts at the Historical Society in Winchester in conjunction with the book launch.

Lionel's appearances were always timely: in the spring, he visited Orion on his usual rounds, and then came uptown to us for dinner, bearing the designer's mockup of *Defend the Valley's* dust jacket and sharing the excitement of the countdown to publication.

In early May, a woman called from near Winchester, to talk about her father's tank books. I asked his name, and it was Pete Parham, who had collected books on tanks and armored vehicles. After about ten years and a lot of armor books, he had dropped out of our roster of Saturday regulars in 1989. Pete had, his daughter said, sort of disappeared about five years before, and now she had decided to sell his books that she had been storing. We were going to Winchester two weeks later for my book launch, and I had a wild thought that we could combine these ventures, but thank goodness suppressed it and asked her to ship them. Even more strangely, local tank-book aficionado, Arnold Brown, came in, a little spooked, saying he had had a vivid dream in which we had been offered a tank-book collection, and even more spooked when I told him we had.

In mid-May, Peter Ginna called and said The Book had arrived and he was sending it by messenger. By complete and perfect coincidence, Rebecca and her husband were in New York for the first time, and were visiting the store and going to dinner with us. We four and the staff hung around and hung around and the messenger finally came. Harris had champagne and roses at the ready, and then we celebrated some more with Rebecca.

Five days later, Harris and I went to Arlington for my first talk and signing, which I had been able to coordinate with the Winchester weekend. Washington

Margaretta signing, at the store's book launch.

customers and friends including the Taylors came, there was a good crowd, and the talk went well, in fact I enjoyed it. Edith Sheerin was there too, as a prelude to the weekend, and drove out to the Valley with us; we paused at Middleburg to look for one more house in the story, and to see if my book was in the local bookstore yet. It was, but Dick Francis's horsey mysteries ruled the shop window in hunt country; Edith inserted *Defend the Valley*, there for Randy and Peggy and Ran to see later that day on their way to the Valley.

My first duties on arrival in Winchester were the delivery of precious family papers, photos and artifacts for the *Defend the Valley* exhibit at Stonewall Jackson's Headquarters, part of the Historical Society—and a photo op there for the local paper, to accompany an interview I had given.

The festivities included the publisher's launch party at historic and beautiful Belle Grove Plantation. Sheila had come from New York, Dudley Lalley and some of her family and other cousins from Baltimore; still more, some previously unmet, from Virginia and beyond gathered, as did other friends. I had organized a tour for Saturday to show them places where *Defend the Valley* had happened. Cousin Frances Jones gave the quintessential tea party, with all the Virginia amenities, in my honor. It was perfect.

For the family dinner in a private room at the old Wayside Inn, my frequent entrenched position on Winchester visits, I had made a long printout of the genealogy connecting the family in the book with those present. We had copies of the book for sale, and some curious denizens of the bar wanted to buy it too. The next day the Historical Society's exhibit opened, with a book-signing at the

Stonewall Jackson Headquarters. There was such a good turnout that they ran out of books, and Rebecca sped down to Belle Grove to pick up more copies.

The next week, there was a book-signing party, our own launch, at the Military Bookman: many customers, book scouts, my editor, my agent, and friends on a rainy, humid evening. Diane Elliott and her husband brought me a *Defend the Valley* in chocolate, and Brendan was there from Vermont and taking the photos. It was a great party and a long one, as was evidenced by Mike Flint's logging of the sales, which with every entry became less legible.

Ten days later, Randy and Peggy, and my parents, who had not been able to go to Winchester, gave me a book party in Wilmington. I had also been invited to speak at the retirement community where my parents lived, so I stayed over for that and Harris returned to New York. That evening he called with an advance copy of the *New York Times* review. Peter Ginna had known the *Times* was featuring Civil War books the next Sunday, and one could only hope, even for an "In Brief" review. Harris said, "Get everyone on the phone." It was long and overwhelmingly enthusiastic. We were in tears. When it ran in the paper June 12th, there were many calls, including Clai Marshall, then in Texas, "Did you write that review yourself?" It was that good.

A couple of weeks later, at the Corner Bookstore, I gave my *Defend the Valley* talk. In July, jury duty, yet again, turned into book promotion after the voir dire moved some of my fellow jurors to quiz me, at a Chinatown lunch, about the Military Bookman and *Defend the Valley,* and to accompany me uptown to see the store and buy the book. More good reviews came in over the summer and fall. Harris took me by the hand over to Herb Weitz and ordered a handsome binding for my copy of the book, complete with an inlaid Confederate flag on the spine.

At the same time, the store was unusually busy. Fort Leavenworth, Kansas, was perhaps best known as a federal prison facility, but it was more important as the Army's Command and General Staff College. The Combined Arms Research Library had never been much of a customer, but they had built a new library, and suddenly had a large allocation for books to fill the shelves. They were buying a wide range of subjects, including antiquarian books, and Harris was only too happy to help Mr. Brown spend tens of thousands of dollars by the end of their fiscal period, which gave us a record year. Nevertheless, Leavenworth took an unconscionable amount of time to pay in spite of having a credit card, and then never paid the interest that had accumulated in six months.

Sales of *Defend the Valley,* which otherwise might have shown up as a nice bump in our revenues, hundreds of copies, paled in comparison. (It was the only time we ever bought boxes for shipping, which were otherwise gleaned from the Corner Bookstore or the nearby liquor store.)

It was quite a blow, that busy summer, when Mike and Anne left within a month of each other. Mike and the iguana were following his girlfriend's lead to move to New Hampshire. Mike had some shortcomings as a manager and disliked the responsibility, but was otherwise about ideal for the store. He was easy and fun to work with, and we really hated to see him go.

Two weeks later, Anne resigned, saying she wanted to go back to lawyering, and I wouldn't have minded her leaving if Mike hadn't gone at almost the same time. She was no great loss to us and probably no great gain to the legal profession. She was chronically late, always an issue as business started off with a bang at ten-thirty. I was a little tired of her glib and flippant manner, and especially tired of the way that by Thursday, her time on the store phone planning her weekend tended to exceed her business time. There were a lot of hung-over Saturdays. We did not part on good terms. When I cleaned out her spectacularly messy side of the partner's desk, the drawers were full of the Chinese mustard and sweet-and-sour sauce packets from her take-out lunches; all the paperwork was on top, including neglected parts of the ongoing Workers' Comp struggle.

The prospect of training two new people at once was gruesome. Almost as gruesome was the thought of the tedious and time-consuming interview process. But Harris had another idea.

For many years at Sky Books, Joe and Dan had presided, under the gimlet eye of the irascible and eccentric owner, Bill Dean. We had numerous referrals from Sky over the years, and Joe and Dan protectively sorted out which customers to send on (not the nut cases), and spoke of us in army code: as in, "Where did you get that book?" "Hotel Charlie," meaning Harris Colt.

We were aware that Sky was soon to close, and so when Mike was leaving, Harris approached both Joe and Dan to see if either of them would be interested in working with us. Goodness knows they had the background, even though they were each odd, rather sour, armchair generals.

Joe passed but Dan said he was interested, and came to work for us in August. A droll, chubby little gnome with thinning hair and a small mustache, he had cogent and entertaining things to say about the books and customers. He was so knowledgeable about the books and the subject that we thought he would be an asset. Dan was very taken with Oliver, the computer; he lit up looking at it, and marveled at its usefulness and information.

Julia had been "first runner-up" in Jason's selection process the year before, and we had liked her. We called her back to re-interview, and hired her. Julia was petite, very pretty in a gamine way, earnest and sweet. She had lived and worked in France; she was an artist and had done some drawings for the *New Yorker*, she told Ish. She was particularly scrupulous in shelf-checking and book-condition descriptions for the catalogue.

She and Anne may both have been among those with a bookstore fantasy; it always surprised me how common that was. People who loved books imagined that working in a bookstore equated with sitting around reading a lot, perhaps with a little dusting, and some interesting conversations, whereas it was a surprising amount of work, at least the way we did it. Catalogues and mail order generated so much paper work.

We were committed to going to Virginia in October, for a clutch of *Defend the Valley* happenings that I had fitted together. It was just for a week, but leaving those two novices in the store was worrisome. In beautiful October weather, we went first to Jason's new establishment in Leesburg, finally open, for a reading and signing. The next day, to Upperville, where Keene Taylor's cousin, who was a *Defend the Valley* fan, had invited me to speak for the benefit of the tiny old Upperville Library and its bookmobile. Keene and Nancy were there, and there was a great turnout for the talk in the Parish Hall of the church, a very responsive crowd. We sold a lot of books. Afterward, there was a dinner party in nearby Marshall given by a fourth cousin, and we learned there that the Disney project threatening the battlefield at Manassas had been cancelled, so it was an extra celebration.

I had been able to align those two speaking dates with the Cedar Creek Battlefield reenactment, where I had also been invited to speak as part of a symposium. It was held in a tent in the midst of the reenactors' encampments, on the battlefield surrounding Belle Grove plantation. I reached the place in my talk when I described my search for the white truce flag at Appomattox and recounted Randolph Barton's part in riding out to enemy lines and attracting Yankee fire, and at that moment, a musket was fired outside the tent. I threw up my hands and white papers as a truce flag and we all laughed.

These events were interwoven with very different, and pleasurable, research for an article commissioned by *Travel & Leisure* magazine, describing a Civil War weekend in northern Virginia—restaurants and inns and driving the battlefields, not archives—so we had an expense account to go with it. What fun.

Other talks, good reviews, and several radio interviews sprinkled the fall. One of the interviews was with a sometime-customer who had a late-night talk show, usually adversarial in tone, on WBAI. Another was by telephone from Winchester: an interviewer who supplied all the answers within his questions, leaving me little to say. In a third, more conversational, I was a last-minute substitute and the interviewer, Casper Citron, had scarcely been briefed, so I could actually explain what I had done.

There was also a lot of "fan mail," some wonderful letters: something I never expected, and very gratifying. I had never thought to write to an author about a book I loved, but this story provoked strong reactions. Several dozen new, and good, customers found us through my book. A New Jersey customer who was doing a lot of local history research in Jersey libraries always checked their catalogues for the book and took delight in telling me which ones had bought it. A local Civil War customer, who had talked to me many times about *Defend the Valley*, asked if there were any way he could read the complete letters of Frank Jones, excerpts of which had figured prominently in my early chapters. "I like Frank more than most of the people I know," he said. I made a special printout for him, and one for myself.

After a very full year, we managed to grab ten days in Barbados in February. We weren't happy and confident about leaving the store but we needed the break. We were beginning to get back to normal after the year in which *Defend the Valley* took priority.

By this time, Richard Lorand came in from "Philly" with a carful of books four or five times a year, parked on 93rd Street and unloaded; while we processed his finds he went off to check out his favorite New York sources. Richard had learned about us on one of his regular visits to Murder Ink, the mystery bookshop on the West Side, where Jason was a customer. Like most good finders, Richard never forgot when and how he came up with a winner: he regarded Gen. Liman von Sander's memoir of commanding Turkish troops in World War I as his best score for us.

Vic Kubelius was an enigma, probably a C.I.A. one. He lived in Washington but traveled extensively and, it seemed, rather luxuriously. Whatever he did, he had an almost uncanny instinct or nose for finding excellent and unusual books, and some very unusual sources, perhaps estate sales. He was so intense in pushing his product that I did not enjoy dealing with him, but he always had quality and his arrival was always full of interest. We never knew how he started coming in or where he came from, and then after some ten years, he just stopped coming. A mystery: did he decide to live abroad perhaps back in his native Baltic country? Did he go underground? Did he lose his interest, or his sources?

Faithful scout Joel Block usually orchestrated his presentations and, for dramatic value, rarely tipped his hand before appearing with his finds, but on one occasion the treasure was just too big to carry in on spec. Could we use the *Third Army After Action Report*, he asked. Any time, I replied.

This immensely detailed, huge compendium of Patton's operations in France and Germany in 1944 – 1945 weighed thirty pounds. "Take a cab," I said. Joel labored in with what could pass for an armored vehicle, and described its tiny imperfections with his usual painstaking attention to detail. I happily wrote him a large check, probably plus a dollar for the "want," meantime deciding to offer the set to all three customers whose wants were listed, "first come, first served."

I printed up the offers to be mailed, then turned my attention to the not-inconsiderable problem of where to shelve the behemoth. An impersonal, bland businessman, whom I had seen buying many times but did not know, came up and handed his selections to Dan. Dan asked his name to process the sale, and I grabbed one of the letters, "Mr. Devereux, we have one of your wants here on the desk." He did not change expression but came over, his eyes devouring the books. Coloring slightly, he said mostly to himself, "It's my fiftieth birthday, I think I'll give these to myself." Telepathy, psychic forces, mere coincidence—but a big one. When all was settled and the happy collector had departed, I called Joel, "Guess what?" Joel, alarmed and ever paranoid, "What's the matter with the books?"

Lionel and Greenhill Press were in the midst of reprinting some classic works by nineteenth-century American historian Theodore A. Dodge. Dodge wrote many fine military studies, but foremost among them was a monumental series called *Great Captains*, produced from the 1880s on. Alexander, Caesar, Hannibal, Napoleon and Gustavus Adolphus. A projected multi-volume set on Frederick the Great was in the works at the time of Dodge's death in 1906. We were pleased to see Lionel's reprints come along, and carried them, because although many of our customers preferred the original editions, those were scarce. We had bought a number of the originals that winter and they were on the shelves when our only South African customer, Achilles Kallos, came in. He had visited the store several times, but usually bought by mail, a difficult process for all. He already owned the Dodge titles we had for sale. Kallos then went on to London.

We subsequently had a comical letter from Lionel:

Mr. Achilles Kallos visited us at the London Book Fair last week, seemed very knowledgeable and your name came into the conversation. We had a wide-ranging discussion and part of it related to sought-after books. I mentioned that a book that some people were searching for was FREDERICK THE GREAT by Theodore Ayrault Dodge, but that it was never published.

He said that although he did not have it, it had been published and you had shown him a copy of it.

Is this correct?

Mr. Kallos said that the copy you had was in two volumes, and in quite poor condition, but was very definite that the book did exist!

Can you confirm this please?

Lionel enclosed a cartoon of a bookstore window with a sign saying something like "Books You Wish Existed."

Dan and Julia had been easy solutions but not good ones. Dan seemed gleefully appreciative of the magic of Oliver's performance; he looked at it fondly, like a new toy, but that didn't mean he used it properly. He never got it through his head that all transactions, incoming and outgoing, had to go through Oliver. Even in a short time this wrought havoc with the inventory and customer records—analogous to but worse than John's misfiling, years before. At Sky Books, Dan had not been in a mail-order business, and was not used to all the paperwork. There was a lot of shortfall, we later discovered, such as unfiled claims or tracers on lost packages.

Julia was conscientious but clueless and could not cope with the unpredictable, which we had plenty of. She did not have the skills to deal with customers' questions or to dodge them to cover up her lack of knowledge. Most memorably: "What do you have on the Black Watch?" That famous Scottish regiment was outside Julia's ken; she got that deer-in-the-headlights look and blurted out, "I never heard of it." I asked her later if she had heard, at least, of Black Watch plaid. No.

After about six months of these two inept people, we were beside ourselves. While Harris and I always had a lot to talk about, usually having had very different days although rarely more than thirty feet apart, at this period our talk was all about those two. One night upstairs after a day of cleaning up after them, Harris said to me, over a drink, "If we had known how hard it would be to get good help, we might not have done this."

I had ongoing *Defend the Valley* commitments which made it impossible to deal with a big staff change quickly: a speaking date at the Civil War Round Table in Wilmington, engineered by my brother, in April, others for a Winchester historical group and two in New York in May, and in between a trip farther south. An unknown cousin who taught at Emory and Henry College in the southwestern tip of Virginia invited me to speak there. I realized that I had to fly via Atlanta, so thought of a weekend with Sandra and Emily, and Harris was enthusiastic. We had stayed in touch with them, and there was continuing communication after Sandra became an acquisitions librarian at Emory University. They were pleased, and Sandra, ever the consummate networker, went into action to arrange for me to speak to the Friends of the Emory University Library. The talk at Emory was distinguished, for me, by the number of intelligent questions that followed. It was a great weekend, seeing some other old friends and doing some booking at Yesteryear and elsewhere. Harris went home from Atlanta and I continued to the Virginia hinterlands.

A more important and lengthier commitment lay in Wilmington. Harris and I had both had been urging my mother to have hip surgery, which she obviously needed. She wouldn't have it unless I stayed with my father, then an invalid. Her recovery was difficult and a good bit longer than expected, and Harris was at his wit's end in the store with two incompetents, one industrious but needing oversight and the other lazy and full of error. I kept saying to Harris, "Hang on, I'll come back as soon as I can and then we'll go to Colorado to see your grandchildren and do some booking, and then we will deal with them." Denver was said to be a good book town and we could see the Front Range of the Rockies.

Philip Kamil, with whom we also had traffic in mysteries, lending them back and forth, had given us *Booked To Die,* John Dunning's first mystery. Dunning was a book dealer in Denver, and his yarn involved the murder of a book scout who had discovered a valuable collection of modern first editions rigged to look like a mediocre lot. The three of us loved it, but we didn't tell Joel about it. Dunning had sent in a catalogue request, and we were glad to put him on the mailing list and probably sent a fan letter. When we were going to Denver, I felt I could ask him for some booking tips.

John's response was immediate and gracious. Not only some leads, but he and his wife invited us out to dinner. I hadn't wanted to be pushy about *Defend the Valley* and had intended to send it as a thank-you when we got home, but John had bought a copy that he wanted me to sign. He had just finished writing another book himself, and was still preoccupied with it, but we all had a good time. As well as leads to various Denver shops, John put us on to a dealer in Littleton with a strong history and military specialty. We walked into Aberdeen Books, a large bright shop, and there was the young proprietor, putting glassine dust jacket covers on each book as it came in. A lot of good stock, a pleasant man, an excellent little Mexican coffee shop down the road—it was a great day.

Dan was in charge while we were in Colorado. Dan opened the mail, so we had told him that in our absence we would be advertising in the *Village Voice* to replace Julia, and that he should put the responses in my desk drawer so that she wouldn't know. While we were in Denver, someone in Boulder, thirty miles away, called the store about a military collection for sale. Never before or after were we offered books in Colorado. But this piece of serendipity did not pay off. We could easily have visited but didn't have the option: Dan said he "didn't want to bother us," adding one more reason to those which caused us to terminate him a few weeks later. That and the fact that he failed to tell us Julia had seen the "help wanted" ad— well, she must have been looking—and was terribly upset, were two major errors of judgment. Dan just let us walk into the store, unknowing, and face Julia's distress.

I tried to let Julia down gently, but she left in tears. Her firing was followed a day later by that of our cleaning lady, who was overdue to be canned and had provoked both of us by her actions in our absence.

Dan was the last to go in this ten-day bloodbath. There was never a good venue or way to do the deed, but Harris took Dan out in the backyard for a brief conversation. Dan cleared out, and a little later, Harris mischievously asked Ish to go to the backyard with him, Ish in mock terror saying, "No, no, no," only to be given a raise. Sometime before, Harris had made Ish a badge saying "M. V. P."—Most Valuable Player—as indeed he was and continued to be.

We had received forty resumés, and conducted eight interviews and, for once, made short work of it. When we had been interviewing to fill Emily's spot in 1991, one of the people who applied was the still-weedy, bleached-blond clerk we remembered from our first buying visits at the Fourth Avenue Bookshop in 1976. We had not hired Peter then but, to his credit, he tried again and this time we hired him. Donald Phillips called in some embarrassment and distress; he couldn't make his appointment because his bicycle had been stolen from in front of his building in Brooklyn. We saw him the next day after work, went upstairs to confer, checked references and hired him.

Donald and Peter started the following week, at the end of August: once again the unhappy prospect of training two at a time.

Peter had worked in a great many bookshops and even an antiques store in the intervening years, and his experience in general did not get in his way in working for us, perhaps because it had been so varied. He ran his own search service on the side, and occasionally came across titles for the store.

Peter was a gentle soul, rather depressed but with a mordant sense of humor, and had a certain Edward Gorey-ish air. (Indeed he sent an inimitable Gorey Christmas card one year.) This was particularly in evidence when he approached my desk to deliver the occasional *Times* obituary he had found entertaining or bizarre. He took interest in my limited gardening efforts in the backyard and the pots out front, contributing some plants he thought I would enjoy: caladium, very showy, and before long stolen.

Donald had worked for peanuts at the Strand for five years, and had quit in disgust that summer, pushed over the edge by the lack of air conditioning in a broiling heat wave. Donald was lean and fit. With black hair slicked down, heavy-rimmed round black glasses, and usually wearing a shirt with a skinny black tie, he had an old-fashioned look; in the winter when he added fingerless gloves, his look became Dickensian. He rode his bike from Brooklyn to the Military Bookman in all weather except snow, and indeed everywhere, later participating in the "Critical Mass" demonstrations. He had a lot to say when he opened up which, after a fairly voluble interview, was not often enough. When he did, he was very observant and interesting, and drily funny when he allowed himself to be. He was conscientious, intellectually involved with the subject, and had a real feel for books. Donald did some writing, and visited many bookshops on his own time. His computer skills were good, but unfortunately he was almost congenitally unable to ask questions.

We were well enough known that other dealers routinely offered us unusual items or lots they came across. One such was a most fascinating World War II naval collection, or rather assortment, from the papers of Lt. Cdr. Harris A. James. James had been an intelligence officer in the Mediterranean, and there were "Confidential" documents from naval task forces and Eighth Fleet intelligence: titles such as *Survey of Assault Beaches,* a mimeograph with original photoprints of action and immediate after-action; *Panoramic Beach Sketches* in Northwest African waters (including an appendix "Determination of Underwater Gradients from Aerial Photographs"); *Invasion of Southern France, Report of Naval Commander Western Task Force,* also confidential and one of two hundred and seventy-five copies. Great raw material: it gave an immediate sense of planning and execution, and an inkling of James's participation. Interleaved with these serious documents were a piece of satirical sheet music, "Le Rommelon," from 1943 Casablanca and delightful items such as a menu from the Naval Detachment's Christmas dinner in Naples in 1944, a less formal "get-together at Lt Necce's shack," and a lengthy St. Patrick's Day mock-Irish missive about a *bit of a party . . . straight across the bay from Vesuvius, just two doors beyond a neat pile of rocks upon the sidewalk . . . Pensione Corona.*

We were offered other pamphlet and paper items, and scouts, especially Joel, loved to find obscure titles for us. The pamphlets looked small and inconsequential, but a clutch of early nineteenth-century U.S. Navy publications was evocative of early American naval history. One of several relating to the Seminole War was a dry little 1832 report on Live Oak in the Carolinas and Florida; Harris's comment line was, *One reason for the Seminole War.* (Live oak was used for wooden ships.) One from 1849 reported Punishments, and how many were administered by a cat-o'-nine-tails. Letters from the Secretaries of War and Navy on "Ardent Spirits" proposed a monetary allowance instead of the rum ration. There was a nineteen-page "Letter to the Chairman . . ." of 1813 relating Commodore Perry's victory on Lake Erie. Decatur and the Barbary pirates. The Comptroller of the Treasury regarding "Unsettled Balances of Officers who have not Rendered Their Accts.," seven pages of text and eighty-four pages of charts. Prize Cases in New York, 1864. Gen. Zachary Taylor and Cdr. Jefferson Davis's report on the occupation of Monterey published in 1848. These all went out at a brisk pace for $75.00 to $125.00 apiece.

CHAPTER TWENTY-ONE

"I can't help you, they're from Brazil."

1995 – 1998

Ish at the packing table, with his binding work.

We detected the networking of Sandra Still when we heard from the library of Oglethorpe University, a small liberal arts college in Atlanta. They became active buyers and, really surprising and refreshing, as I noted in their record, fast payers. Peter suggested another institutional customer, the little-known David Library of the American Revolution, in Pennsylvania.

Peter was very informed about and cognizant of the book world, and made us aware of Metropolitan Book Auction on West 18th Street, where, on two occasions, we bought very well.

As it happened, our first auction at Metropolitan offered a lot of Americana, just right for the David Library. That sale was the more exotic: de-accessioned fine old sets and some antiquarian titles from the New-York Historical Society. These items—it would be hard to call them books, they were almost all disbound—were mostly from the library of an Old New York name, J. Watts De Peyster, who had been among other things a historian. It was ironic and sad but not uncommon that a collector entrusted his books to a library in the faith that they would be valued, and was mistaken. These books had been stored in the damp basement of the Society, quite appalling, and the covers had fallen off. The texts were relatively unmarred. Needless to say, we bought them very cheaply, in large lots, at the auction, and we had plenty of work for Ish and Lloyd the binder. Some really good and scarce material: Fumée, *History of the Troubles in Hungary . . . the Pitifull Losse and Ruine . . .*, 1600, and Maimbourg, *History of the Holy War . . .*, 1686, on the Third Crusade, a very rare book. There were important seventeenth-century manuals, and the 1599 Guicciardini on the wars of the Italian Renaissance. There was unusual and interesting Americana, particularly local history, such as small and obscure battles of the Revolution; one was a little booklet published for the Centennial of Evacuation Day in New

York, when the British left in 1783, with a memoir by a participant. *The Siege and Reduction of Fort Pulaski* of 1862 had belonged to a Lt. Loomis in Beaufort, South Carolina, and Harris colorfully described the covers as *stained by damp Southern air and burned perhaps by a candle.*

Harris had regular conversations with one or two colonels at the Army's Military Research Institute at Carlisle Barracks, home of the Army War College, and they did occasionally buy. He had learned that their library could supply us with photocopies of, for instance, a missing map that had made a book defective and unsalable, so we could make the information complete, without any intent to deceive. When we received the copies from the Institute, they would be inserted at the right places in the texts before giving the books to Lloyd for a rebind. On these occasions, Ish drew on his secret stash of spare parts, taking the dead-white copies from Carlisle and recopying them on to old paper that toned in harmoniously with the old texts, and then the copy of the copy would complete the book.

Ish retrieved his street find, the leather jacket, from the basement, and the good parts of that derelict jacket were utilized for a respine on this one, and new corners on that. Pieces of the jacket were used for a new spine and corners on a good edition of Sir Edward Creasy's mid-Victorian classic, *Fifteen Decisive Battles of the World*. It's odd to think of that jacket going in all directions on a variety of books. Ish occasionally consulted Lloyd, but his binding techniques, increasingly sophisticated, were mostly self-taught; he had some of the usual tools, and someone brought in a book press found on the street. Ish made ingenious use of items such as a rolling pin and a cheese shredder. For regular cloth bindings, we could print out spine labels on the computer. But in one noteworthy case, the ravaged, British-red, board cover, distinctively imprinted in a handwriting style, *Nicknames & Traditions in the Army,* was xeroxed onto the right red paper to recreate the cover.

That fall, I had some more speaking dates, and Harris went with me to Virginia again, to a book symposium in Staunton. We stayed with cousins Cal and Susan Thomas, then went on to Winchester for some book-related happenings. My *Defend the Valley* commitments continued into 1996, though naturally tailing off. My friend Judy, then living in Kansas City, had set in motion my being invited to speak at the Civil War Round Table there. There was a good turnout, overshadowed by a very tall, bearded gentleman, magnificently attired in the uniform of the U.S. Army of about 1850; the shako brought his height probably to seven feet. He was a sometime-customer from the Fort Scott Kansas Historic Site. I stayed on an extra day to visit Independence, where Judy and I made the bookshop rounds and saw the Truman house.

On vacation in Martinique, the only books we looked at were paperback mysteries, although Harris also took his dog-eared paperback of John Keegan's *A History of Warfare*, which he read again and again. A rainy day in a Florida visit was more bookshop browsing than buying, but I found a scarce Virginia Civil War book for myself, undervalued in Florida. We went to Washington for another auction with the Taylors, and then to Second Story Books. We had a special reason to go to Boston in June: Ran's wedding. But we added on a day for the bookshops.

We heard again from a former customer, Marshall Silver, who had amassed a large and comprehensive World War I aviation collection and then had moved to Vietnam, leaving the books in storage in Chicago. He still hadn't focused on the problems of selling it, inherent in his list. I wrote: *We do remember the prolonged, tantalizing and unsuccessful attempts to arrive at a meeting of the minds [eight years ago]. The list was in our pending file for years, and there was considerable difficulty due to what appear to be double listings or items that we would catalogue differently.* Despite all our previous dealings he seemed too scattered to act on our offer of a down payment before shipping the lot, and the books may have continued to reside in storage.

Around this time, David Feinberg came in and headed for the shelves, but soon circled back to me and sat down across the desk. He said he was thinking about selling his library; his wife wanted the space and he agreed, having kids and not so much time for the books. I always was a little sorry about such acquisitions, and said so, but added that certainly we would buy them. "I don't need a list, you have such good taste in books." This was the first personal conversation we had ever had, David being rather reserved, I telling him about my publishing background and learning that he was a senior editor at ABC News. He brought in his books, but still came in from time to time, so we didn't lose him.

I went down one morning and joined Donald who was going through some big boxes. Donald was his taciturn self, but I thought the whites of his eyes showed a little more than usual. The boxes were being hefted in by . . . someone in a dress. We both recognized the seller, but just kept our heads down going through the books. He was from north Jersey, and had been a customer since 1978, always rather withdrawn and impersonal. There was no etiquette for this; one couldn't know if this person wanted to be recognized or wanted to be perceived as someone entirely different. We worked as quickly as we could, and when the seller was out getting more boxes I said to Donald, "Just ask, when we're done, 'how shall I make out the check?'" I was sort of hoping Harris wouldn't come out of the back; he could be tactless. I briefed him that evening. The person was coming back with more books the next day. Donald and I were in shock, haunted, thinking of the enormity of his situation.

Harris and Ute at the right pub, London.

Donald and I were the ones who didn't know how to behave. Harris, the next day, was perfect, just his friendly interested self; and the customer-in-transition, more open than we had ever known him to be, told Harris that the books would help pay for his sex-change operations.

That October, we went to Europe for ourselves, not for books. We were flying British Airways to London, and were early at JFK for once. The BA clerk checking us in lifted the phone and intoned discreetly, "The Colts are here." What did that portend? We had been subjected to special scrutiny years before, after Lockerbie, because of the Maltese stamps in our passports. We thought there must be some mistake when we were "invited" to the First Class Lounge but we didn't want to correct it, and then were dumbfounded when we were ceremoniously ushered into the plane's First Class section. What a treat. Somewhere over the dark Atlantic, it dawned on us: Ute's fine German hand, upgrading us. It was easy to get used to; during the night, Harris said, "I belong in first class." I wrote that out in my trip diary and had him sign it.

We had ten days in England to visit Amy in her new home in Bexhill, near the White Cliffs and all the Battle of Britain names and 1066; then to London to see the various Stricklands, Lionel, Diana Birch, and Ute who came over from Stuttgart for a day. We took one book-ish afternoon, visiting Glenn Mitchell in his new posting at Maggs. When we showed up, Glenn exclaimed, "I just ordered from you!" Glenn had done his best to civilize the grotty basement, with even a rug on the floor, and to get the books priced and organized, and started producing fine catalogues. A new broom. We went on to Tuscany to meet the Taylors for ten days, and then to Malta again.

That fall there was another auction "for us" at Metropolitan, and we sent the experienced Peter to bid after we had looked. There was a lot of unusual material in

German: the official Bavarian history, ten volumes covering 1604 – 1914, *nothing ignored in peace or war* was Harris's catalogue comment; a World War I history of a Hussar regiment; battle and divisional histories and generals' accounts; and again, the massive Austro-Hungarian official history of World War I. All had been de-accessioned from the West Point library. In addition, there were always-wanted good World War II titles such as the *American Forces in Action* series, and some unit histories. Sort of surprising that West Point would get rid of all these; conceivably they were duplicates. Peter brought home thirty-eight lots.

About that time, one of our scouts, Dick Snyder, came in with a handful of early books about the Revolution. They bore the stamp and signature of Gen. C. A. Waite, and Harris's research showed that Waite had been a brigadier general in the Mexican War, brevetted twice for gallantry. Strangely, Dick had found them near West Point.

Peter, who was sort of sickly, came down with shingles. It was not a disabling attack, but, quite probably from him, Ish got chicken pox, a related disease. Ish was miserable for a while, and never forgave Peter, directing baleful glances at the back of his head from the packing table. It occurred to Ish much later that there was another suspect: Mr. Abdelsamad, a Sudanese customer and Japanese sword collector who usually went to chat with Ish at the packing table.

A couple visiting obviously from "south of the border" spoke no English, and Ish was called up. He talked to them for several minutes, then said, "I can't help you, they're from Brazil." About the same time, an Argentine man visited the store and became a good customer, and a fifteen-year-old Argentine boy began ordering by mail. They each managed to buy a lot, which was never easy at that distance.

Inigo de la Huerta was dynamic, attractive and friendly, an international person with an apartment in Manhattan, an office in Staten Island, a house in Southampton, a ranch in Spain and probably more. He piled up a stack whenever he came in; he was particularly interested in Spanish subjects like their Civil War, in which his titled father had fought with the Nationalists, and in the Foreign Legions, French and Spanish. Inigo had served in the latter. He bought uniform books too, and anything in his interest; he did not mind buying duplicates, which were simply sent to another of his houses. Whenever we saw Inigo, it was not only delightful, it was a good day for sales. He was usually in transit to Southampton, and accompanied by one or two or a pack of Jack Russell terriers. One August day it was too hot to leave the dogs in the car and Inigo asked if he could put them in the backyard, about eight of them. That breed is hyperactive and nimble, and they were all over the place, jumping up on the garden wall to look in the back window for their person. It was a cute and funny sight. Suddenly a tremendous crash: they had overturned the big window box. What a mess! Inigo rushed to the back door, the over-excited dogs ran into the store, and two of the dogs ran out onto the street, Harris and Inigo in hot pursuit. It was so hilarious that I didn't even mind about the window box, which Inigo offered to replace; it was late in the season.

Our customers and contacts continued to be assets, providing leads and help of various kinds. Thanks to Philip Kamil we learned that a British medal dealer had come by a cache of a scarce and much-wanted Second Anglo-Afghan War title. *My God, Maiwand!*, by Col. Leigh Maxwell chronicled a British disaster in Afghanistan in 1880. It was a recent book but unaccountably elusive, and there was little coverage of that war. We immediately ordered twenty or thirty copies and they went out at a brisk pace, within the year certainly.

A man called from Wyoming and beat around the bush for a few minutes. Harris asked probing questions and determined that this fellow had an army surplus vehicle in need of servicing; he obviously needed a technical manual, a TM. Harris patiently extracted the information that he was a park ranger at the National Elk Refuge near Jackson Hole, where they used the vehicle to take feed to the elk. For some reason, he could not tell Harris exactly what the "elk feeder" was, not the model or designation; Harris thought it sounded like a half-track. He was intrigued—we had seen the Refuge on our Western trip—and got in touch with Jim Controvich to try to figure it out. Speculative xerox images passed back and forth. Harris often consulted Jim on similar esoteric questions.

The elk feeder was one of the "wilder" questions . . . At first I couldn't figure out why [Harris] would ask me but after questions and answers back and forth, he filled in one of the more important missing "facts" about the "elk feeder," it was a surplus army truck. I seem to recall it was a member of the M520 family, a heavy cargo truck that could carry eight tons. I imagine it could carry lots of elk feed just about anywhere you might want to go. Well, I didn't have a manual for one even though I have more than my share of unusual titles. But I informed him that the National Technical Information Service (NTIS) could provide copies of any army manual. He forwarded the NTIS info to the Forest Service guys and they were happy that he came through for them and the elks lived happily ever after.

Harris often went out of his way when a query appealed to him. We received a letter in Japanese, and he had it translated by new regular, Ted Cook, a professor of Japanese history. The correspondent was a veteran of the little-known Aleutian campaign of 1942, and was writing his memoirs. Harris knew just the book for him, Brian Garfield's rather scarce *The Thousand Mile War*, which we did not have at the time. Harris called Phil Haultcoeur at Random House which had just issued it in paperback, and Phil offered to send the paperback to the vet, and included a tongue-in-cheek note from Phil, "Compliments of Harris Colt." It was Harris, rather than Phil, who received the thank-you letter.

Peter drew a big customer in Santa Fé, Tom Meaders. He had been, years before, a minor buyer and then had dropped out. But he returned in strength and spent about $5000 in 1996. Then it got sticky. We wanted to supply his wants, but Meaders only wanted to place large orders. He had no patience with one-at-a-time wants, and the $3.00 shipping charge was intolerable to him. We were willing to make accommodations for good customers but it was hard to effect these exceptions because it just got confusing. In any event, Meaders was something of a flash-in-the-pan: a burst of activity, then dropping off before long to nothing.

A Floridian named Dane Delcontivo was a very active customer in the early nineties. He did spend a lot of money, but it was always a cliffhanger as to when we would get paid, whether the check would clear, and when we should ship. At the same time, Delcontivo's collecting was very ambitious and his wants list all top-of-the-line. The difficulties of our dealings exhausted the space in his customer record screen. He seemed like a dubious character and at one point was doing all his buying through his business account. Then he left the country for some years, came back and bought some, lost his job and offered us his books. I expected, with his grandiose wants and big buys, to have some good titles coming in, but it was most disappointing, with a lot of shabby books that we couldn't use. Maybe it was the low end of his collection.

We got some bad news from our printer, KNA Press. In sleepy little Kennett Square, their building, two blocks from the main street, was falling victim to eminent domain because the town wanted the property for a parking building. KNA couldn't fight it, and Dick Taylor was nearing retirement age, so he packed it in. We followed KNA designer Debra Gallek to a printer in Philadelphia, who was more expensive. After about a year, we went to the cheap and sometimes slipshod and slow Eagle Press, a sideline of the well-known *Berkshire Eagle* newspaper in Massachusetts.

We took ten days in the spring, when the catalogue was at the printer, for a break in the South: Savannah, Beaufort, and Charleston. Interspersed with old houses and lovely gardens, we visited the Marine Corps museum at Parris Island, and took the boat out to Fort Sumter in Charleston Harbor. Booking was irresistible, and we went to Atlantic Books and found enough to go back the next day, there encountering a long-time customer from Washington, to our mutual surprise.

On our return, we regretfully let Peter go. He was a kind and sentimental man, and interesting in his quirky way. Even when he was hung over, which was often, he was early for work. We liked him and appreciated his knowledge, but he was fogged in a lot of the time, and he simply could not adjust to Oliver and its demands—another old dog who couldn't learn computer-age tricks.

The job applicants we saw had some computer skills, which we belatedly had recognized should be a requirement. We interviewed for a couple of weeks, and narrowed it down to two men, each of whom had a ponytail. Harris had had a problem with this on a previous hiring round and we had told him that under no circumstances could he ask someone to cut his ponytail! Ed Nebel had a red one, very curly. He was a sweet guy, light-hearted, outgoing, very interested in history, and had been writing audio books on the subject. Paul Kaplan had a big, black beard and a big, curly, black ponytail. And he was big, well over six feet, and had been working as a security guard and office temp, but had a history education and an academic bent. Donald was in on these discussions too, and he thought it would be good to choose someone different from himself, to give some balance and levity, Donald being so serious. We hired Ed, and he was off to a good start, but after a month he developed some sort of health problem that led to a month's absence and then his graceful resignation. We got back to Paul, who was still available and was able to start in August. Paul proved to be great for the long term, interested and flexible. He had a good sense of humor, and his eyes virtually disappeared when he laughed. He always carried a large military-green backpack, though I almost never saw him take anything out or put anything into it.

Ish overheard Donald briefing Paul on certain aspects of working for the Colts. Harris and I from time to time publicly and volubly disagreed on procedures or other minor decisions in the store, and Paul was naturally perplexed when we contradicted each other on his instructions. Donald, trying to clarify, told him, "If Margaretta tells you to burn the store, burn the store!"

Donald also told Paul about the time, with Terry Dotson's five- or six-carton order stacked up against the wall to be shipped, a customer approached me with half-a-dozen books and started badgering me for a volume discount. I told him no, but he persisted, and finally I said, "See those boxes over there against the wall? That's all one guy—*he* gets a discount."

A few months after Paul arrived, late in the day, a phone call came in from England, from someone who wanted virtually all the books on small unit actions and counter-insurgency we had in stock, about seventy titles. Harris and Paul were all over the store rounding them up, and then discussed shipment. The customer wanted them shipped to Nigeria in the fastest way possible, by Fed Ex. They settled on three-day delivery, and the shipment cost more than the books, but money was no object. When there was a coup that failed in December, Paul was bug-eyed at the implications.

Paul took a call from a rather sporadic Connecticut customer, usually a few books every so often. Paul was perplexed to be answering questions about dust jackets. Not that we didn't have callers who were fussy about d/js and their condition, but the man was asking about, for instance, what shade of red it was. He could feel Paul getting annoyed and confessed that his decorator had mandated certain dust jacket colors to go with the new look. We couldn't do much with that.

Paul and Harris engaged in conversation with a man who asked what they had thought of *Saving Private Ryan*, just out. Most of their comments were positive but Paul unwittingly put his foot in his mouth, saying that some of the characters were flat, the standard war-movie stereotypes. Turned out the guy was the screenwriter.

There were some antiquarian books for us at a Sotheby's auction that summer. One was the first English edition of the earliest European book on Genghis Khan, *The History of Genghiscan . . . First Emperor of the Moguls and Tatars . . .* published in London in 1722, "from the French of Monsieur Pétis de la Croix, of Louis XIV's court." It had a fine, old, paneled-calf binding. To me, it had Mike Wolfson's name all over it, and I was excited to call and tell him about it. He came right in, of course, but did not exactly jump at the beautiful book. I felt deflated. Mike later wrote:

Your style wasn't so much to talk me (or others) into something as to afford me the opportunity to talk myself into something, a little bit of appreciative admiration of the virtues of the book, and more. I think that my problem was that it was more of a collectible than a source book. De la Croix wasn't a historian and prepared his history by translating and reading the works of Asian historians and memoirists. Ultimately you or I convinced me of the desirability of owning the book and I've never been anything less than pleased.

Mike's deliberations couldn't have taken too long—the book was sold nine days after the auction.

In September, we flew into Madrid, where one evening we met Timoor Daghistani, and his wife for dinner. Timoor had gone from his Washington posting to become Jordan's ambassador to Spain. In due course, he went on to be Ambassador to the Court of St. James: more and more responsibility, and less and less time for books. We worked our way south from Madrid, through miles and miles of olive trees, for our rendezvous with Ute and Peter Grauer in Andalusia.

That summer, I had started buying by mail, box by box, cheap uniform books listed and sent by Betty Risley in upstate New York, all the Osprey uniform series, for a start. Betty was the widow of Clyde Risley, one of the founders of Imrie-Risley Miniatures, a line of fine, pewter model soldiers. The Ospreys, I felt sure, were the tip of the iceberg.

By the end of the year, Betty had sent a series of lists, and a number of boxes, laborious for her. I sensed that she was comfortable with our dealings, and suggested that we just go and pick up all the rest. Betty lived north of Albany, so it was a good excuse for us to visit the ever-hospitable Edith and Charlie Sheerin in Albany.

Meeting Betty the next day was a pleasure, we all felt we had encountered kindred spirits, only partly because she had been involved in her husband's business. Her grandson was with her to help us pack and load, and the rented van was filled up to the roof, so full I think I had books under my feet. I barely managed to slide in a large *New York Times* World War I pictorial from Edith. We headed south running ahead of the threat of snow, a few flakes starting around Poughkeepsie. Eventually, we sent a Military Bookman T-shirt for Betty's grandson along with the final check.

The van must have contained every uniform plate book published in the last half of the twentieth century, and some uniform-plate series. Peter Plimpton was soon on hand, champing at the bit, and bought the plates by the French artist Lucien Rousselot. Peter brought in a French sword and consulted Harris; yes, Peter had swords too, and there was one he found hard to identify. Harris took Peter upstairs and found a similar model hanging on the living-room wall, which proved to have the same *chasseur á cheval* blade.

Peter was becoming a friend, and we occasionally had lunch together, once with Philip Kamil in order to show Peter Philip's two Ackerman treasures, the Wellington Funeral and another smaller-scale foldout, *Line of March of a Bengal Regiment of Infantry in Scinde.* The latter I found completely captivating: the troops with all their camp followers and colorful impedimenta, and replete with camels, elephants, and sheep. Philip had found the Indian title elsewhere and we never had it, but I noted in the computer record, "the next one will be a severe conflict of interest for MBC." I did occasionally take a particularly appealing book upstairs for a while: *Jezebel the Jeep,* a cartoonish book set in occupied Japan, *Curry and Rice for Forty Plates,* a portrait of a British hill station in India, and the Chinese artist Th. Yung's bird's-eye views of Napoleonic battles, among others, had a sojourn in the living room before going on sale. I absconded with a worn but delightful book by Fritz Kredel, of German war songs: deft, sophisticated, colorful and faintly comical depictions of Napoleonic German soldiers patterned the pages and framed the calligraphic lyrics. It was published in 1933 on cusp of a grimmer era, when German soldiers had to be taken very seriously. The staff were welcome to borrow books as long as that was noted in the Oliver record; sometimes when a book was ordered, we would have to say to a usually amused or at least tolerant caller, "Oh, Paul has it at home, we can't ship until tomorrow."

A few years before, we had had another Ackerman title, views of Moscow, bound with a title on Russian costume by Edward Orme, both dating from the first decade of the nineteenth century. Each was a slim volume of about a dozen delicately hand-colored, large plates, in a fine calf binding. It had the added interest of the bookplate of a man who had been Britain's ambassador to Catherine the Great.

It was expensive and although we expected it to be a problematic sell despite the Napoleonic period, I believe it sold quickly in the store. It had to be seen.

It was in 1998 that we geared up for five catalogues a year. It made a rush, too rushed to shelf-check and proofread well, but we wanted to get more offerings out there. The entries seemed to me littered with typos when I saw the finished product, but our subject presentation was getting better, with a new focus on small segments, a different way to present the inventory. We had the coding to do it.

In the Summer issue, we had announced our website and email address. We had realized the year before that we should "stake our claim" on the internet, so we had found a freelance person to get the domain name and set up the very simple web site, passive at first. Before long, Paul volunteered to work on this new project; amazingly enough, the word "internet" had not even been mentioned when we interviewed him. Getting it all started was a simpler exercise then, and Paul had done some programming, and got technical pointers from Dave, and editorial ones from us. Paul became completely involved in the development of our internet presence and business, finding the service provider who helped with a number of details, such as the secure page for credit card payments. Listing the books on our website would have been just too much work, so we opted for selected listings on the two out-of-print sites, ABE and Bibliofind; their fees were much cheaper then, before they were gobbled up by Amazon. And at first they did well for us.

We went to Colorado again, in a wintry week, for a family occasion and some book-buying. To Denver first, for another large buy at Aberdeen Books in Littleton, and then a big barn of a general store we had not visited before, Ichabod Books. Most of what we bought in Colorado was familiar, but there were always new and unusual items coming in, interesting for us and adding spice to the catalogue.

Joel's most significant finds, in his eyes, were several different sets of German Wehrmacht maps published shortly before World War II, which had been developed to prepare for their invasions of France and Russia. We had seen the tip of this iceberg a few years earlier, with four British map sets we sold for $2000; they were part of the set for Operation Sea Lion, the projected German invasion of England, compiled from British sources ranging from the Ordnance Survey maps to postcards, as well as espionage. The maps of France were a blueprint for blitzkrieg, *detailed intelligence work designed for rapid movement and precise positioning of units*, Harris wrote. Superbly executed, they showed everything from electrical grids, canals, roads and rail, industrial sites, to telephone exchanges, population density, and city plans. Joel brought them in in several batches over a period of months, and Harris and he had a great time collating them and putting the sets together. Harris talked to his sources at Carlisle Barracks and from them acquired a lot of bibliographic information on the German army's maps, which in his scholarly and obsessive way he added to the Oliver records, in case Joel came up with more. The Russland set, covering both European and Asiatic Russia, was the most complete and the most valuable. It comprised eight text volumes, ten photo albums, seventy large maps, and more. Harris noted: *We have been unable to locate a collection or set in the main military repositories.* It was listed in the Summer catalogue for $7500. Harris sold it to Kenneth Rendell, the well-known dealer in historical autographs and documents. Ken was putting together a World War II collection, which he turned into a most unusual museum near Boston.

Poster dealer George Dembo, whom we hadn't seen for years, brought in a curious item that had surfaced in his wife's family. It was a brief typescript memoir, in English and enhanced by sepia photos, by a Russian cavalry officer in the Russo-Japanese War. He had been in command of the Circassian Free Riders, a scouting party. It sounded pretty exotic to me, and we agreed to give it a try, on consignment. I found it fascinating, but then I had a penchant for unpublished documents. I ran it by Rob Cowley, as a possible article for MHQ, but it didn't work for him.

It didn't sell. It remained an enigma to me that our customers were so reluctant to buy an unpublished manuscript or art in its original form. To me, the unique was appealing, the original that the artist or writer had created. But most of our people seemed to want only published books, as if that supplied some validation they needed. Similarly, it was easier to sell "war art" in a book than originals.

Glenn Mitchell was a very active buyer for Maggs, and we were buying more from them too, long distance, because of Glenn's catalogues. He was turned loose in the States that spring, and spent time and money with us, his visit punctuated by the not-unusual call from Harris to me, still two floors up, to drop a can of coffee out the window into the backyard, the store supply having been exhausted. Harris was working on selling Glenn some of the British regimentals remaining from Van Sickle's lot; prices for regimentals were still very high in Britain, so Glenn could buy well from us. Glenn couldn't get over Harris still using a slide rule for currency conversions. On the other hand, Glenn's light-powered calculator was not working too well on the ground floor. There was a lot of negotiating and they were having a good time. Glenn bought handsomely and was rewarded with a Military Bookman T-shirt. In time he acquired a few more of them, resisting offers to buy one off his body in a London pub.

Glenn also visited Philip Kamil and his remarkable library of India before the 1857 Mutiny; Glenn was blown away by the quality and extent of it. Philip did not confine himself to that one subject, but wanted anything extraordinary that appealed to him. Glenn particularly remarked the run of the fine British periodical, *Navy & Army Illustrated,* in sixteen volumes from 1895 to 1904, purchased from us. "But there are only supposed to be fifteen!"

We regularly took an off-season weekend at the Jersey shore, and in May it was bracketed with afternoons at Christie's. A customer had told us about the auction: a huge Napoleonic collection, that of one donor, was being de-accessioned by the Western Reserve Historical Society. It had seasoned for years in their boardroom and was being sold because it was definitely not their subject, Ohio. The breadth of the collection was fascinating: furniture, paintings, uniforms, militaria, even wallpaper, and some important books, and many leather sets. A familiar story, the books were again secondary and badly described. Harris and I went to the viewing and developed our ideas, and then left for a peaceful weekend, planning to return to the city on the morning of the auction in plenty of time. Traffic was horrendous and we had to go straight to Christie's, where the aging post-debs weren't coping too well with admitting the bidders, even those like us who had preregistered.

At the sale, we were repeatedly frustrated by a private bidder who kept his hand up and took the lion's share of the books. We came home figuring to pick up our purchases when the dust settled at Christie's in a day or two; instead we got a rude call from a passive-aggressive clerk threatening to send the books to a warehouse in Long Island City if they were not collected forthwith. The next afternoon, I sent Paul off for the books, and it was a mess. Far from being put together and packed to go, the beautiful leather books were slowly assembled and then dumped into not-sturdy-enough shopping bags by the same nasty clerk, who acted as if it were all an imposition. Later, when Paul struggled in with multiple bags, we were surprised to see how much we had bought.

After our 5:30 closing, Harris and I started working on the books together, doing the descriptions and pricing, with a drink—it was our idea of fun to process such unusual material together. And there was quite a surprise. The nasty clerk had carelessly given us Sloane's *Life of Napoleon Bonaparte,* a magnificent, extra-illustrated, four-volume set in red morocco that had been won by the big bidder. Christie's would never have been able to track it down, but after a long Memorial Day weekend of talking playfully about how handsome the books would look upstairs on our own shelves, I called them. The same clerk was awfully casual about a $5000 item; his attitude was such that I fully expected him to ask us to take it back to them. Instead an out-of-breath, good-looking, young intern arrived to collect it. He got very prissy and proper when I asked him who the big bidder was. We got no thanks for our honesty, and they must have lost the set again when it got back to Christie's, because five months later the head honcho in the book department called to see if we knew anything about it. I told him in no uncertain terms what had occurred and he said, "Thank you so much, what can we do for you?" Never fast on my feet, I did not say, "A dozen roses or a couple of bottles of champagne might be in order," or "Who was that masked man?" Instead, I told him that we had had to find out about this auction from a customer, and asked that he send their book auction catalogues, which, no surprise, never happened.

We tied another New Hampshire school reunion with the Taylors to a book fair in Concord, where we met some dealers known to us by reputation or by some mail or phone dealings, and found some books. Books kept coming, with two local collections the next month.

Paul and Ish were to pick up the library of a Saturday regular who had lived in Danbury. He had quite recently died, and the widow, or rather their daughter, was wasting no time. There was a problem with renting the van: Paul didn't have a credit card and they wouldn't take mine because I wasn't driving. To my chagrin, I found myself going off in the van to Connecticut with Paul and Ish and Paul's pack, rather than having a busy Saturday in the store. Saturdays were fun, social days with many regulars, lots of selling, shopping bags of books going out, and often new customers. The Danbury lot was useful, but certainly did not hold the interest of the next one.

A collection often speaks suggestively about the person who assembled it. Bob Schepps, late of the Soldier Shop, came in to introduce a widow whose husband had been dead for some years. Mrs. Connor was ready to part with his books and brought in a list but I couldn't do much with it; the material was so unusual. I explained to her that the books would have to be examined and evaluated in the store. She understood, and I took Donald, Paul and Ish and a down payment downtown to collect the books. I recognized Frank Connor's picture in their Greenwich Village apartment. Frank was a pleasant, reticent man with warm brown eyes, curly, eventually graying, reddish hair and an open face, who had come in periodically for years, even in the old store. He never engaged, it was as if he didn't want to bother anyone; he would quietly browse the shelves, and usually leave empty-handed. When I saw his books I knew why we had so little for him: he had painstakingly assembled an esoteric collection of Central Asian history, of nomad warriors long gone or assimilated. It conjured up obscure peoples springing from the earth like the mythical dragon's teeth. Frank's interest had apparently been generated by their elegant weaponry.

We went to Mrs. Connor's on a summer day interrupted by a summer downpour, which had fortunately ceased by the time we left with the books in two taxis. The Central Park transverses were swamped by the storm, and our macho cabbie insisted on driving through deep water despite my protests—"I can make it!" The water reached the trunk, and the bottoms of the boxes were damp when we quickly unpacked them. Most of the books we had not seen before and knew we would not again. A relatively small holding but choice, and an education to catalogue: *Turkish Archery and the Composite Bow*; *The Long Sword and Scabbard*

Slide in Central Asia; The Magyars in the Ninth Century; A History of the Georgian Peoples; The World Conqueror; The Tibetan Empire in the Early Middle Ages. Connor's was a fine and refined collection, and it merited a special catalogue listing, implemented by the creation a new code: Central Asia. When the books went on the shelves the first person we called was Mike Wolfson, and he added a few Mongols to his already large library.

During two gorgeous weeks in southwestern France, we learned from local tourist information that we were near the site of the Battle of Castillon, the final battle of the Hundred Years' War. So we diverged from our wandering and wine-tasting to look for it. A hand-made and very imprecise sign pointing down a country road was the only clue. We drove into the suggestively named Château de la Bataille vineyard to inquire, Harris confronting the formidable dogs and speaking French to them and the proprietor. The hospitable vintner, hands grape-stained, took us into his barn-like *cave* for a tasting and we bought some wine for our picnic. He shrugged off the battle, saying that the French, with their long history, don't bother much with markers. This was the most military we got, aside from Carcassonne, the somewhat fanciful but enormously impressive and evocative Viollet-le-Duc restoration. In our few days in Paris, we bought no books: Petitot was out of business, and Clavreuil too expensive.

Our trip had been a respite for me. My dear father, after five difficult years as an invalid, had died several weeks before we went to France. He had taken great interest in our endeavors and such pride in my book, and had always marveled at our, to him, improbable success.

CHAPTER TWENTY-TWO

"It speaks to me."

Philip Kamil's temptation.

The phenomenon of the collecting urge was on display for us on a daily basis, fascinating to behold, and ever mysterious.

Many years ago, I read an article in the *New York Times* about kids' collections. Their reasons for choosing what to collect seemed to be random, as I know by now that many adult collectors' are. One little boy collected yogurt tops, not for any special reason, he said, *but now I find them helpful in many areas. When my mother yells at me, I go to my room and count them. I find it relieves a lot of tension.*

As redoubtable and omnivorous a collector as Electra Havemeyer Webb, whose Americana treasures at the Shelburne Museum encompassed everything from a steamboat and a lighthouse down to circus models and jugs, mused: *I do not believe I have ever heard any reason why certain people collect.*

Whatever the nature of the impulse, it seems to be inborn. David Magee, a well-known San Francisco book dealer, described in his delightful memoir, *Infinite Riches,* his childhood collecting in London. He wanted but couldn't afford books, and he discovered in church porches penny pamphlets of religious tracts, numbered. He bicycled all over North London to parish churches, striving to complete the sets, which lay in neat stacks on his shelves. Nothing he would ever think of reading: Transubstantiation, say, or the Nature of the Trinity.

Collectors are inscrutable, even to themselves. It is sometimes unpredictable to them and to close observers (like merchants or spouses) what will appeal to them. Collectors arrived with a palpable sense of expectation, ears pricking up, sniffing and on the hunt. It was always fun for us to dangle special—major or minor— titles in front of them or, alternatively, to leave the books on the shelves to be discovered. Emily observed the emotional side of being "intellectually hooked"— "intimate and aphrodisiac . . . the heart leaps up and the hand shoots out." I certainly experienced the charge, the visceral excitement and thrill of the chase, on the threshold of an old bookstore new to us. It was the treasure hunt, each time. Gavin Leckie wrote, *A visit to the store for me was just like a visit to my grandparents' attic . . . full of surprises and a place where one could just lose oneself.* Simon Barker-Benfield remembered *rounding the corner and finding the Scots Guards.*

Harris grew up with a father and grandfather who were book collectors; maybe it was genetic, or catching. Most little boys go through a soldier phase, and Harris was one of those who had not left it behind. As he grew into adolescence he wanted to maintain the French fluency of his childhood, and began to read Napoleonic history. By his mid-teens he knew what he wanted, and sought out the classic French Napoleonic titles, mostly those with uniform illustrations. Each summer in those years, he was shipped off to Europe to some family connection, and each time he managed to save enough from a meager allowance to buy a Napoleonic cavalry saber. In a Seine-side bookstall, he found a broadside of the famous 29e Bulletin, called by Napoleon the "Bulletin Terrible," the grim account of the retreat from Moscow: "the Emperor's health has never been better."

Harris collected and read World War II books for years until he put those books into our starting inventory, and from then on he limited his book acquisitions to titles about Malta in the war, and the occasional fine Napoleonic pictorial, usually a present from me. He had an ever-changing library in the store to draw upon for his reading, but rechanneled his collecting urges into Maltese stamps.

Mike Rihn remembered devouring his aunt's American Heritage Civil War book, which he read before he was ten. His was a dormant interest until the Military Bookman called for floor-waxing, and then, he didn't know why, he zeroed in on the Confederates; it may have had to do with endeavoring to understand the conflicting loyalties of the West Pointers who chose the Southern side. He didn't have Civil War books before he found us, then bought very little elsewhere.

Gerald Forrette came to us from Ray McGuire's list, and he was already amassing unit histories. He may have been interested in World War II before he fixed on these books, but when a client had shown him his own unit history, the

Mike Rihn's temptation.

504th Parachute Infantry Regiment, a/k/a "Those Devils in Baggy Pants," (part of the 82nd Airborne), Gerry was hooked. He was a tough, irascible labor lawyer who seemed older than he was, cynical and jaundiced perhaps. His legal practice brought him from Minnesota to New York occasionally, and into the store. He usually complained to Harris about the prices, and it rolled off Harris; it was obviously part of Gerry's hectoring lawyer persona and it was done with humor. They both knew he had to have it!

John Catherwood started with model planes, and remembered his first book purchase, an encyclopedia of airplanes; he had kept his books in boxes at the foot of his bed. Always alive to history, but military history, he was already a collector in graduate school. John talked about the "work" of collecting: reading bibliographies, dealers' catalogues, his own record keeping, on index cards (from whom, how much) and studying other sources. Serious work, not a hobby!

John bought mostly First World War from us. He said the technology fascinated him: he would talk at length about war with the new dimensions of railroads, submarines, airplanes, motorized vehicles, artillery, which was not understood by the command. John couldn't get enough of it. He gradually collected all the British Official Histories, for the maps—"you can't read that stuff," he said—as well as the other classics of that conflict. But he also wanted accounts of nineteenth-century wars, including the official histories, particularly for the maps.

Bill Smith said that budget was his only limitation. His collecting was well defined in his own terms. World War II had dominated his childhood: war bond drives, blackouts, air raid sirens, war movies and newsreels. He was focused on the American participation, and particularly wanted the unit histories and *American Forces in Action* series for their after-action interviews; he compared accounts and statistics, and maintained that the official history versions often overstated casualties in "the fog of war." I saw him standing for long periods at the shelves, reading, comparing the information, always looking for an unusual item that would fill a gap, before buying. As it did for many, the immensity of the conflict held the fascination: the geography, the combined services and the scale of the effort in the U.S., and the fact that all Americans were involved, focused and together, and on the Right Side. For Bill, the home front stories were integral: rationing, civil defense, industry. But in some categories, Bill collected just to collect: the slippery slope of the technical and field manuals, numbered. "When you start, you have to complete the set." When he lived in Maine, he found a full set, over a dozen, of the FM-1 series of manuals covering the Army Air Corps. Expensive, but he had to have it.

The "baseball card syndrome" was perhaps best exemplified by a Navy vet who wanted every edition and every printing of the Navy *Blue Jacket Manual.* The small book of regulations, distributed to every new sailor, was first published in 1902 and there were twenty-three editions in our records, and who knows how many printings—and needless to say, very repetitive. Not to say dull.

Heaven help the collector if what they want is numbered. The marketing of series is diabolical. Publishers know that anything with numbers magnetizes and addicts people: to wit, the many aircraft or warship series, the Osprey uniform series, Ballantine's various World War II series, army yearbooks or naval and aviation annuals. The Ballantine series was so successful that the publishers just kept churning them out to feed the appetite, and at one point not even Ian Ballantine had a complete list of the titles.

Gavin Leckie ascribed the collecting of numbered things as a way to create order out of chaos. Perhaps it is comforting to define a limit even if it turns out to be a large universe. There were those who seemed to fixate on things that came in sets. A man who lived nearby on East 86th Street wanted only the Osprey uniform series, in a neurotic way; you could tell he needed the strictures of the numbered set. He also wanted *Tradition Magazine*, a short-lived but excellent British uniforms periodical. When a full run, seventy-six issues, came in, we let him know. It was a desirable set, but I felt he hesitated because if he bought the set he would not have the pleasurable compulsion of an ongoing quest.

It can be deflating to complete a search and not have any wants left. As sophisticated and scholarly a collector as Peter Plimpton said, "The finding might be more rewarding than the having."

If collectors fasten on one thing they like, they want more of it: aside from his Mongols, Mike Wolfson wanted all titles by Charles W. C. Oman, so we were always pleased to turn up one we hadn't seen before for him. Some readers want everything they can find on a narrow subject. But what at first sounds like a narrow subject, such as Philip Kamil's focus on the British Army in India before 1857, can turn into hundreds or even thousands of books. In its worst form, collecting knows no limits, like the Kiralfy obsession.

Philip gave a lot of thought over the years to what people collect and why they collect it. He didn't know. "It speaks to you," he said of his various interests and treasures. And no matter how much they have, collectors never forget and continue to bemoan the ones that got away. Twenty years later, Philip was still lamenting that he hadn't bought Shadbolt's *Afghan Campaigns of 1878-1880* from us when he had the chance in 1994. He hesitated because although it was beautiful, it was not strictly in his purview, and while he deliberated, it escaped him.

In the bookstore-as-*Cheers*, the recognition of fellow addicts made for a camaraderie as well as occasional rivalry among them. When Philip encountered a former British officer in "his" section, they started talking and ended up going for drinks at the Carlyle after the store closed. Philip also chatted with Alex, a young man who came in from time to time with his little girl. Alex had little money, but he had some old letters from India he wanted to research, and Philip lent him some books. At the same time there could be a sense of rivalry and competition even at long distance and between strangers. From Jan van Weerden in the Netherlands: *I'm glad two of the items ordered were still available after the ravaging visit of your Detroit customer [Gerald Forrette]. . . . I hope to receive them soon and also wish you a pretty Easter Parade.*

How people are led to their subjects can be immediate and straightforward. A Puerto Rican customer was captivated by the Spanish fortifications in San Juan, and some denizens of the East Coast focused on the mid-nineteenth-century forts and coastal artillery that had protected its river mouths and harbors. Local history was enthralling to many. The Civil War was the primary focus in the South, the Indian wars in the West, and Texans would buy anything about Texas.

Jordi Jové of Barcelona wanted, most of all, books on the War of the Spanish Succession, still a sore subject for many in Catalonia, which as a result had lost much of its autonomy within the Spanish kingdom.

In my experience, it was only Poles, and many of them, who asked for their national history: *anything, really, on the history of Poland.* Maybe it was so compelling because Poland had been run over and suffered fragmentation time and time again.

Uniform collectors were drawn by the glamour, the intricate and meaningful detail, the tradition, the magnificence of the eighteenth- and nineteenth-century array. Mary Elizabeth Braun was hooked on British uniforms and had bought the outstanding Ackermann panorama. *I have a marvelous collection of miniature British soldiers in their best uniforms, authentic in every detail . . . I guess I'm just mad about uniforms, I admit it.*

Romantics were drawn to World War I aviation and to the Spanish Civil War and perhaps the Confederate "Lost Cause." The scale, ferocity and extreme conditions of the Russo-German war, and the sheer magnitude, the geographic sweep, the numbers involved, drew many serious readers. Others fixed on the larger-than-

life grandiose figures such as Patton or
Custer or Napoleon, megalomaniacs who
channeled their craziness into sophisticated
destruction, sometimes new levels of total
war. I was drawn to reading about Patton,
but I think the movie and George C.
Scott had a lot to do with it. Some readers
became fascinated by the nature of heroism,
wanting to plumb the mystery of the act in
the intense moment—a peak emotional
experience and its ephemeral nature.

Then there were the "hardware"
collectors. The womb-like shelter and small
space, and the sense of invincibility, of tanks

John Catherwood.

and subs were appealing to some. (It would be repellent to others, claustrophobic
and scary.) You don't need to be Freud to get it.

On the other hand, jeeps had the appeal of sturdiness, the compact power and
sheer practicality. They were sort of cute.

The fine line between passion and obsession was probably crossed many
times in the stacks of the Military Bookman. We saw symptoms of hoarding—
compulsion—addiction. John Catherwood had a lot to say about the "pathology
of collecting": needing a goal, such as completing a set, and the challenge, like
a mission. Seeing John's books, visitors would ask, "How many books do you
have?" John would answer, "Not enough," which understandably made Margot
crazy. Margot caught John one day when he was measuring a spot for more shelves
and, John said, "did an intervention." John thought he had 1000 to 1500 books
(I think more) before he winnowed it down to the Pacific War and early Japanese
operations, and World War I tactics and command. But he observed, ruefully, that
collectors, if they get one category under control, just move on to another; the
urge is still there. He should have had an implicit warning in his visit to Henry
Sirotin, who was Kiralfy-weird about his books. John said the apartment was lined
with full shelves, two books deep, and with a maze-like, chest-high spiral of books
in the dining room—which were off limits. "If you knock them over they'll be out
of order!" Henry remonstrated. What order?

Phil Haultcoeur's collecting had no spatial or wifely limits—until he found that
the perhaps 7000 books were too much for the floors of his house and decided
to divest himself of a few thousand. Jim Controvich, who had been a collector
since boyhood (starting with baseball cards), began reading military history in
college and had gradually decided to concentrate on the American Army and

then focused on unit histories. He confessed that he didn't read most of them. It was the hunt he enjoyed, and presumably the record-keeping which resulted in a number of bibliographies on the American Army. His collection was no threat to the flooring; Jim kept his thousands of books in his basement.

Peter Plimpton's strategy was to "exhaust a passion, sell out and move on." He made rules for his own collecting, setting himself space limitations and refining his parameters "to keep his sanity." He spoke of collecting Richard Cannon's nineteenth-century British regimental series as "like a drug," and the high of finding Goddard and Booth's magnificent set, *The Military Costume of Europe,* on our shelves. He remembered where he got what with amazing accuracy, and the circumstances that in some cases made it all the more enjoyable.

We loved helping customers pursue their interests, nourish their intellectual curiosity and build their collections, and Harris was especially gifted not only at remembering what they had, but knowing and telling them what they would want. And what they should prefer: "you don't want this one, you want that one."

We were sometimes asked about books as investments, a concept we never encouraged. It was not only unpredictable, but it was not why we were in the book business. There were books that were pricey enough that a collector might want reassurance, or might want to justify it to himself, or someone else. I believe Harris told John Catherwood, teetering on the brink of a Fortescue purchase, that it would be a good investment. But that was the only time I know of. I usually said, "Well, they're not making any more of them." Most of our collectors understood that the real return on investment was their own pleasure and satisfaction.

CHAPTER TWENTY-THREE

"E loves 'is books."

1999 – 2000

We never knew or knew of the small shop, London Pride, in Bogota, so we asked Philip Kamil, who lived in north Jersey, if he did. Philip did not, but was curious enough to go spy it out though it was closed, pressing his nose to the glass, even taking polaroids of the outside, while we waited for the appointed day. The owner was dying and his daughter was not waiting, was selling with unbecoming urgency, and in a way, it turned out, calculated to offend everyone, most especially her father.

We thought, as did other dealers, that we were getting first crack at it. I minded the store while Harris took all our guys off to Jersey. The sale turned into a bit of a free-for-all, lots of grabbing at the Osprey series especially. Philip was there too. A safecracker was brought in to open a six-by-six foot vault in the basement that was expected to contain medals and other important militaria. The safe, after all, had nothing of significance, just some odd items of erotica. Philip zeroed in on an unnoticed treasure in the disconnected walk-in refrigerator, a first edition of Darwin's *Descent of Man,* which he bought cheaply and handily resold to great advantage at auction. There were no treasures for us; it was quantity not quality. Our crew returned with fifty boxes of decent but not exciting merchandise, and lunchtime regular Phil Haultcoeur walked in on their arrival, and pitched in to help unload.

Jury duty, yet again. This time, the waiting around was enlivened for me by George Lowry of Swann Galleries, in the same pool of prospective jurors there for the selection process. We chatted away the time, and he asked why they hadn't seen us recently at Swann. The answer was simple: not much in our subject had been on offer. Later that year, Swann had a lot for us.

We got a call from the library of the Council on Foreign Relations, on Park Avenue, which published Harris's favorite periodical, *Foreign Affairs.* The books for sale being largely in poor condition, I didn't buy anything.

But across the avenue, there was a holding at the august Union Club. The humorless librarian summoned us as if it were an emergency. It was a hot week in early June, and the store was busy, but I reluctantly obliged. She met me in the grand marble lobby, but rushed me off behind the scenes; I never saw the handsome library. As she and I rose in the freight elevator, I tried to lighten her up with the story of a lot sent us from the Union Club years before, a run of mid-nineteenth-century U.S. Navy *Registers of Officers* that also did not fit into their library. The naval books had been delivered to us in Bordeaux wine crates—what class! As I was reaching this punch line, we walked into the storeroom and there was the current lot—all stacked up in wine crates.

The librarian was not interested in my making a considered offer; everything was urgent. I threw out a number and she accepted it. Then it was urgent, for her, that the books be removed ASAP. I said we could do it by the end of the week: panic, the library closed early on summer Fridays. I told her I would send Donald and Paul: panic, "You're not coming? How will I know them?" "They'll have a check."

I found this collection especially interesting because it was the very personal accumulation of the donating member and I learned about him from his books. Clarence Van Schaik Mitchell was of an old New York family, and had attended all the right schools. He had served in France in World War I, as a Captain in the 302nd Machine Gun Brigade of the Twenty-sixth Infantry Division. Afterward he was a Wall Street lawyer, commuting to Summit, New Jersey, and going frequently to Boston on the Merchants' Limited. He read on the train and he read on ships to Europe. His bookplate was in most of the volumes, and he had neatly annotated in pencil when and where he read each book, with a few marginal comments when it related to his experience. There were novels too, and although we had previously carried only a few notable World War I novels by the likes of Robert Graves and Siegfried Sassoon, Arnold Zweig and Erich-Maria Remarque, we decided to broaden our coverage on this occasion because Mr. Mitchell had thought they were of value. The priceless Joel supplied a catalogue from William Reese of New Haven, a leading dealer, to help us evaluate the literature.

That spring Sheila and I decided to share a share in the local "community supported agriculture" which the farm delivered weekly to the nearby Church of the Heavenly Rest. It was sort of a medieval scene, like a European market huddled against a church, and we enjoyed going over to collect our share, always full of surprises. There were often veggies we had never seen, and might not have chosen if we had. I said to a dubious Harris of some, "We'll try it once, but we don't have to do it again." After one try, we passed on the kale and the collard greens and the soybeans; but they found a willing taker in Donald, a most-of-the-time vegetarian. Off he would go to Brooklyn on his bike, its basket sprouting a bouquet of greens.

Donald set the tone in the store in latter years; he was so serious and so withdrawn that Paul, at first anyway, was subdued. It was not the merry mode of yesteryear, or even very chatty. Both Paul and Donald were often transfixed by computer screens, to the detriment of customer interaction and even welcome. Paul had much to do with the internet inquiries and listings, and just the deletions of junk took a lot of time before filters came along. When Paul was on vacation, I took a turn and was amazed at what a huge proportion of our emails were Viagra and Russian virgins and Nigerian scams rather than book inquiries.

Donald did have certain customers he related to, one a retired naval officer. Captain McLaren captured everyone's attention with his low-key but animated description of his recent cruise on a nuclear sub in the Arctic.

Paul Newman, a part-time neighbor on Fifth Avenue, made a brief appearance, just inside the door, asking for airplane pictures. Despite reflective sunglasses, he could not hide, his elegant persona was impossible to disguise. He was too late for aircraft prints, we had given up on those long since.

James Gandolfini, a/k/a Tony Soprano, loomed large in the doorway one evening. We were not familiar with the program, but one didn't need to be: he made quite an impression. Paul said he sounded just like Tony. He was looking for books that related to his next role, as commandant of a military prison, taking a "method" approach. He bought several, including a Liddell Hart title.

The paperback of *Defend the Valley,* published by Oxford University Press, finally made its appearance and went on sale in the store. It was pleasing to think that the book would be more accessible and affordable, for instance at the National Park Service bookstores at the Virginia battlefields. A year later, in Fredericksburg for a speaking date, I tracked down Hank Elliott, the little boy with the Civil War school project, now a National Park Service ranger at the battlefield Visitors' Center. He was in the bookshop, and told me that he always put my book out front, and recommended it. Beyond its inclusion in a one-page ad of all its new publications, Oxford did nothing to promote it, but we sold a good number.

The two-inch picture of *Defend the Valley* in the ad prompted me to ask Ish to use it for a miniature book of the paperback. Years before, Peggy Barton had made us some little military books—including the red catalogue—to decorate our Christmas wreath, and we recycled them each year. Ish's paperback joined a miniature leather one he had already made of my book. From time to time, for select occasions and recipients, he created one ingeniously from odd bits of leather and marbled paper, sometimes with a little gilt on the spine. A visit from "our Amy" may have occasioned the first. Ish made a little beauty for my mother, with a flower illustration. Sheila's was the most elaborate: a boxed "folio" in gilt leather with a leather slipcase, designed to go with her particular "logo."

One for me was fashioned from an aged, cracked piece of 1747 leather, with ribbed spine and a tiny red label, and wittily marked "as is," as we frequently did with books in debatable condition. The Twenty-fifth Birthday edition was oblong, three-quarter leather with a red label, and gilt inlay of our logo on the cover, jazzy endpapers, and four gilt plates of toy soldiers copied from the store bathroom's wallpaper. I suggested that Ish develop his own sideline in the little books; miniature books were collectable. But he only wanted to make them for people he cared about.

The Millennium was approaching, along with fears of how many computer systems of every description would be messed up by the new and alien 2000. Once again we called on Dave, who came in and made some adjustments that made the milestone a non-event for Oliver. (For good measure, Paul unplugged the machines for the turn of the New Year.) Dave brought in a new program for booksellers; we scrutinized it and it couldn't compare with Oliver. We talked again to Dave about a title-search program for Oliver, one piece of unfinished business and more necessary by then as we were getting a different kind of customer on the internet, people who didn't know from authors. Dave was too busy to take it on, but said he would be on the lookout for a programmer who could help.

We had early on thought of doing the catalogue layouts in-house, and Dave had brought in a PageMaker program. I had experimented with it to produce a booklet for my father about his 1991 Virginia birthday trip, as a learning experience without deadline pressure. It was a terrible struggle: the illustrations kept slipping and the caption placement was a horror. At one point, we imported Ran, a computer whiz, to help, but he found the same problems I had. Oddly enough, my document was almost exactly the length of our catalogue, so it was theoretically a good test. When I resorted to calling PageMaker's 900 number and describing my problems, the consultant said, ominously, "If I were you I would finish that off and get out of that document as fast as I could."

Paul knew that page layout programs had improved, and soon started to design the catalogues in-house. Arnold Brown, who loved technology in all its manifestations, was constantly promoting our acquisition of various systems and equipment, most totally unnecessary for us. He worked at Columbia University, which apparently was always upgrading and discarding not-too-used equipment, and he provided us with a scanner, for the catalogue illustrations, and a fax as ours was over the hill.

We seemed to have entered a "Russian Period." We joined the Taylors on a Russian river cruise that summer. Our Christmas party was to be at a short-lived Russian restaurant not far away. And in due course, Dave crashed through, and sent us a programmer. It was by then almost impossible to find anyone who knew DOS programming; but Yuriy Shkolnikov hailed from backward Ukraine, and DOS was still used there. Yuriy, small and swarthy, accomplished the title search itself rather easily, but when it came to inserting it into the Oliver system, he and Paul struggled. Many too many evenings they huddled over Oliver, then would sit back and say to me, "Check it out." The new part always threw all the old records out of sync, and we tired of too many Yuriy hours being spent; we settled for a title search outside the main program, as we should have much sooner.

Internet sales were in many ways a different ballgame. Email revealed new quirks; customers had addresses like "Thucydides" or "Homeric." There were some big hits from the internet, undeniably, but they could be accompanied by selling problems we hadn't had before. One buyer, for whom we were grateful, wanted a big-ticket French atlas, by Napoleonic Marshal Gouvion St. Cyr, which had been a bad buy in Paris years before. The atlas was made to accompany the Marshal's memoirs, but it was better geography than battle plans. We were delighted to have a buyer, especially one who didn't balk at the price. But when he received the book, he made a big fuss about a previous owner's bookplate, considering that to be "ex-library." That was not our definition of ex-library, but it was his. He kept the book.

Peter Plimpton had discovered internet book shopping and was very actively buying, sometimes in lots; he brought in items he didn't want for credit or against his choices. Sometimes, they weren't very good for us, and on one occasion, Peter took back some that had failed to sell. I thought Harris allowed Peter too much on some of these items, because Peter was a good customer and a friend. I didn't like it, but was powerless in this case. Peter's buying was our first intimation of the scope and competition inherent in the internet.

In December, a Swann auction was full of good things for us: many of the classic nineteenth-century French uniform pictorials, also British in plenty, and the Americans as covered by Ogden and Walton. On a few of these we were bidding for Peter Plimpton. There was also a complete set—well, we labored mightily to ascertain that it was complete—of the German official history of the Franco-Prussian War, in five text volumes and three map cases. It was most unusual to find it whole, the maps being loose in cases; the set went very cheaply because it was in wretched condition, the map cases flattened. But we knew Ish could fix it. We turned it over to his sensitive and resourceful attentions, and he cleaned it and rebuilt the map boxes. Harris and he worked together to collate it, and as we had thought it was all there, with even a few extra maps. The text volumes were on the shelf near Ish's work table and he was putting together the map cases when Ralph Reinertsen arrived from Switzerland, and had to have it. We had put a teaser in the Winter Extra 2000 catalogue but the set was gone before the first calls.

From several sources, an unusual small group of Scottish titles had come together, so we ran a special Scotland section in the catalogue, just a couple of pages. It had escaped us that Gavin Leckie, a Scot, might be interested; we thought of him as mostly a Civil War reader. Gavin was too casual about reading the catalogue and missed out on *Scotland Forever,* a nice old pictorial on the glory of the Scottish regiments. One of the lot was a most unusual antiquarian book about William Wallace, the Scottish patriot, which came to us complete but in pieces. Ish ministered to it, salvaging and resurrecting the old leather boards, re-spining it (perhaps with remnants of the jacket), and piecing together and lining the title page. He did a fine job. Probably due to the recent and highly fictitious Mel Gibson movie *Braveheart*, the handsomely restored book sold before it hit the shelf.

That issue had an interesting Nineteenth Century array: the many small wars, German and Italian unification, the Balkans, French colonial actions in Africa, a couple of odd Latin American pieces, such as an artsy book *El Motín de los Artilleros*, about a mutiny in Punta Arenas, Chile in 1877. It made for an unusual grouping, but we could never sell Latin America, and there wasn't much interest in the French colonial period unless it starred the Foreign Legion. There were also a number of scarce and contemporaneous titles on the Hungarian Revolution of 1848. Sometimes books seemed to have a magnetic force to attract like titles; these had come in from several sources, as if drawn to each other. We had never seen them before and they went out fast.

Harris's stepmother occasionally sent us packages of family items, and we never knew what to expect. Over a period of years, she had sent us some rare books, remnants of a magnificent collection of *fête* books she had gradually been donating to the Folger Library in Washington. *Fête* books were commissioned to record exceptional occasions, usually royal: coronations, weddings, victories. We had stowed them in the basement and had half-forgotten they were there, but on a day off, we were rummaging around in the back room looking for something else, and realized what we had. We called in Ursus Books, a leading New York rare-book dealer, who bought with alacrity; but we decided to try one from the Napoleonic period in the catalogue. This *fête* book had been published for the city of Strasbourg in 1806, to commemorate its celebration of the Emperor's victorious return from Germany after the battles of Ulm and Austerlitz. It was a large folio in diced red calf, with gilt spine and a large, gilt, imperial eagle and N on the cover. The engraved plates showed the triumphal arches and other elaborate constructions made for the occasion. The book had the cachet of a well-documented relic of the Imperial Library at the Empress Joséphine's Malmaison—all quite splendid. It was a little out of our line, but after all Napoleon sold, and it did, quickly.

Sheila and I finally decided to cash in Harris's bet with me, and went off to Oaxaca, Mexico, in March. A few weeks later in a weird April blizzard, Harris broached the subject of an English buying trip, the next month. He thought it was time to enrich and deepen and spice up the inventory, fine by me, I was always ready to go, and we scrambled to plan. As we did so, I realized that we had never been in England in the spring. We had fallen into the September pattern in the eighties

British bookshops. Clockwise from top left: Cecil Court, London; Beeleigh Abbey; St. Paul's Street Books, Stamford; Ashley Book Shop, Bournemouth; Margaretta and Mr. Sankey, Broadhurst Books, Southport; Harris and Amy take a break; Addyman Books, Hay-on-Wye.

because of the seasonal lull in the catalogue schedule in those days. But this time the gardens would be at their peak, and I made Harris understand that a couple of famous gardens must be on the agenda. We did a number of things differently that year; for one thing, by then phone rates were cheap and time was short, so we called for dealer appointments. We contacted our usual sources and "suspects" and found to our dismay that our shipper had gone out of business—quite suddenly, Lionel told us, with ships at sea. True to form, Lionel had an alternative at his fingertips and was good enough to give us the name.

We left May 11th for almost three weeks. London was hot and sunny, and I congratulated myself for getting prescription sunglasses. As soon as we headed west out of town, I didn't need them.

On our first day in London, we went on to Maggs, which had only become better under the aegis of Glenn Mitchell. The military department had been upgraded to the newly renovated stable behind the house, a handsome setting. Glenn's office and that of his secretary were in the stalls. We took our time, chose judiciously and only picked about fifteen books. We had taken one minor, leftover *fête* book to London and tried to sell it to Maggs. No deal, but we went on to Sotheran's where they gave us £50 in cash.

We had sticker shock with all our London specialists and I don't think it was the exchange rate, prices just seemed to be much higher. In Tooting Bec with the Sutcliffes, we bought sparingly, only eight books, for an embarrassingly low total of £190. So there was time to visit Anne-Marie at her new post as Head of an ancient and impressive school. After wine in their garden and idly deadheading the fuchsia, on to an Indian restaurant. We found little the next day in the Charing Cross environs, and plenty of high prices at Francis Edwards; nevertheless we managed to spend over £1000 there. We recovered at an ancient and wonderful pub near Covent Garden, which was by then like a combination theme park and mall, with mimes thrown in. Of the Bloomsbury shops, one was not worth the struggle: new, old, and remainders in a muddle. At Waterstone's we found a lot, but there was a prolonged hassle about our check, barely worth the effort. We had a happy dinner date with the Leventhals at a French restaurant on the Thames, sitting outside despite a dull evening, and Lionel drove us the long way back past the lighted monuments, like the tourists we didn't have time to be. We had decided to start in London because the Book Fair was on that weekend, at two hotels. We separated at the fair, and Harris made some sizable hits, while I picked up odds and ends and made some contacts to visit in Bath and Nottingham. We had dinner with Anne Strickland and daughter on the roof of the Oxo building, sunny, hot and leisurely, with a great view of St. Paul's and the river.

Next day, we hit the road west, not without the usual difficulty with car rental; this time they upgraded us to a car, the only one available with automatic shift, which was so large as to be unsuitable for country lanes. Harris was not happy. We were going to see Lt. Col. R. J. Wyatt, finally, at Lionel's urging. Bob was the sometime editor of the Military History Society's journal, the author of a couple of books on military collecting, and also a darling. He lived in Wokingham, in a charming cottage, where he sat us down for coffee and "bikkies" (cookies) and book talk, and clearly enjoyed showing us his own treasures, British Army as expected and very fine. All the rooms were shelved and stacked with books, but somehow it was not creepy like some other oversized collections we had seen; there was life in its constant use. Bob was in the midst of building a new library, and his own books were mixed up with those for sale. Instead of a nice, neat garden shed, he had two garages, one an almost falling-down barn, for his overflow. I found myself dressed to meet a colonel, on a hot, sunny afternoon, clambering over and digging through random stacks of dusty periodicals, mountains of pamphlets and other unsorted, unshelved material in the barn. It was as if Bob had gathered these things to save them from destruction. The rummaging was worth it: there was a great supply of wartime publications, such as those by the British Information Office on different branches and theatres, in multiple, good propaganda pieces. There were many small interesting pamphlets, home front material such as air-raid warden manuals and little recipe booklets for stretching rations; *The Detection and Identification of War Gases; The Post Office Went to War; Hitler Invaded Sark* (published in Guernsey). *Red Sky over Manchester,* published by the local paper. *History under Fire* documented air raid damage in London. Published in 1941, it was a collaboration between the eminent art historian John Pope-Hennessy and the even more well-known photographer Cecil Beaton. Beaton did a lot of war work for the Ministry of Information. So unusual: I found such material very evocative. We did well, and enjoyed working with Bob.

Bob told us not to bother with the shop we had thought to try in Reading, so we headed for Marlborough, cross-country on tiny roads lined with cow parsley (Queen Anne's Lace, to Yanks), buttercups, fruit trees and horse chestnuts, all blooming luxuriantly. We found a few things at a small shop in Marlborough and looked in at the Military Parade, which had good stock but too dear for us. We pressed on to Bath and got spectacularly lost beating around in residential areas for almost an hour to find our golden, Gothic Revival hotel on a tranquil hillside. We had a drink beneath a wall of blooming wisteria with a sweeping garden view accented by magnificent ancient trees, and felt the grime and grit of Bob's garage falling away. We took time to walk in the gardens in the morning, then went off to find the India dealer I had met at the book fair, winding around the hills above the town. After the mandatory coffee and book chat, we went, of course, to the garden shed, where by the light of an oil lamp we found some good stuff, at a twenty percent discount for "combat pay." The dealer sent us on to Margaret's Buildings in Brook Street, a pedestrian street near the Royal Crescent and Circus, for three small shops where we spent a total of £700. The first was especially charming, presided over by a rubicund gent who was clearly amused to see us dig in to the military in his rabbit warren of a basement; it was another treasure hunt, and we found a lot. Going to three shops gave me time to consider a wonderful handbag I had veered off to see in Brook Street; on the way back to the car, I told Harris I wanted it. "But you have a lot of handbags!" "Not one with pears on it."

The lady in the last shop had told us that William George's shop in Bristol now had only new books, so we decided to skip Bristol, have a quick tea, and head straight for Wales, to cousin Margaret Kelly's, in Welsh Newton. Across the spectacular bridge over the Severn River, we followed the Wye River, with a pause at ruined and poetic Tintern Abbey, and up the valley, past signs "! Badgers 2 miles." The country felt more remote, the roads ever more narrow, cow parsley slapping against the sides of the oversized car Harris so disliked, as we came to Margaret Kelly's green valley. Margaret lived in The Lower Cwm, a barn converted by her late husband Peter, quite eccentric and interesting and comfortable. We had a warm, family welcome and a wonderful evening, as if we had known each other much longer and better. It was more than interesting to learn that Margaret had worked at Bletchley Park, England's decryption center during the war, decoding German High Command messages on one of the Colossus machines. She and the other women who had worked there had been so schooled to downplay or deny their work that she usually said, "Oh, I just changed the tapes."

In the morning, we tore ourselves away from Margaret's view and garden, full of yellow poppies and pink honeysuckle. We had a picturesque, twisty and somewhat hair-raising drive to Hay-on-Wye, and visited Richard Booth's first, working hard in dankness and poor light. We tried a few small shops, then went on to Cinema Books; it was real work but easier, and we spent twice as much money as at Booth's. A few more shops, some deceptive but worth the looking, ten books here, twenty there, thirty in another, and considerably more at Addyman, where we were given a welcome cup of tea. We were "knackered," Harris especially so as he was fighting a bad cold. Done for the day, we had a short but pretty drive to a most unusual inn, Penrhos Court. Our destination was a fairy tale, an ancient, half-timbered farm complex with wisteria and clematis climbing over it, and the smell of wood smoke. Some of the buildings, we were told, were almost seven hundred years old; at the core was a large, tall hall that originally had a fire hole in the center, no chimney. What an atmosphere, enhanced by the chatty proprietor who loved being near

Hay and was intrigued by our business travels. We could hear the sheep from our window in the morning but we did not linger; we ran back to Hay to pay bills and hit a few more small shops.

By midday we were on our way to Bewdley, for a date with George and Joyce Harris. George was out looking for us when we came along a little late, and they insisted on giving us lunch. Did we want salad? I said I would love salad, and was treated to the spectacle of George going out to the garden, returning looking fierce, presenting like a trophy a whole head of perfect lettuce, roots and all, pulled from the vegetable patch for my delectation. George was still booking despite arthritis, and his stock was great. Fondly Joyce said, " 'E loves 'is books." He came to me while I was browsing and asked so sweetly about my book, and I had brought a copy of *Defend the Valley* with them in mind; they were so pleased. A good time and a lot of spending.

It was my turn to drive, to Stow-on-the-Wold, in the golden Cotswolds, through sun and showers and pretty country. We had never shopped in the Cotswolds before, and all the little towns with quaint names had bookshops, it seemed. We spent two nights in a charming inn; The Grapevine really had an ancient grapevine in an ancient greenhouse which had become the dining room.

In Evesham, we found a lot of good buys at Bookworms (even a couple of cheap copies of the cheap edition of *The River War*), and as we left, a customer pursued us and gave us some tips. Pershore had two shops, Coach House Books where we put together three boxes, and droll Ian Pugh for thirty-two books. We never found the Stow shop open, and there was a no-show dealer with whom we had made a firm date by email from New York. It hardly mattered. How could we resist Moreton-in-the-Marsh or Bourton-on-the-Water, whether they had bookshops or not? They did. All of these were an easy distance from Stow. The weather continued changeable but the spring countryside was gorgeous, rain or shine.

The next morning started well, but had clouded over when we reached the ravishing Hidcote Manor garden. After two hours wandering, it was time to check out the shop, near the Market Hall on Sheep Street in Chipping Camden. Draycott Books was tiny, charming and interesting, and we left £320 behind.

From there I drove and Harris navigated our way, with Edward Strickland's scrupulous instructions, to the Nottingham vicinity, to visit Edward and Elisabeth in their new dear little house. They had been married for only a few months, and we were their first guests. A happy time. A great pub for dinner, a taste of haggis, and the next day we all went to a completely contrasting famous garden, that of Chatsworth House. We saw Nottingham Castle, and Sherwood Forest, what was left of it, was blanketed in bluebells.

We left early on Monday, Edward leading us to the Bulwell section, and luckily the dealer, met at the Book Fair, was early too. A productive visit, over fifty books. It wasn't far to Stamford, a pretty town where there seemed to be a great many bookshops, several closed, but we found Undercover Books open. After lunch, the most charming shop, St. Paul's Street Books, in a house half-timbered inside and out, was open. It was small but good for us. We had an appointment near Peterborough with an aviation specialist with his own books and his inventory in his house. Brian Cocks was a nice, shy man with an impressive collection of his own, and we bought some excellent titles. We went on to Ickleton, to Jilly and Ron Maynard's again, and it was getting gloomier and rainier and we were running out of gas. Once in tiny Ickleton, we went round and round not recognizing the Maynards' house—we passed it several times—as it had not only been painted green, but renamed. Once there, it was a delightful reunion.

We set off early the next rainy morning and shopped without much result in Cambridge; we would have done better to go back to Stamford. Cambridge had been "malled," and we found only one decent shop, Albion, down near the bridge, where we put together a small lot of thirty books. At the Mitre pub we had a pint and a sandwich before the train to London. We had decided not to drive to London, to ditch the car in Cambridge, but the train was a different set of problems, including a forty-five minute delay due to a lorry hitting a bridge. At King's Cross Station, the crush was like the Tokyo subway and Harris, encumbered by our suitcase, barely made it off the train in the stampede of frenzied commuters getting on. But things got better quickly; Philip Kamil was in town and he and Anne Strickland collected us for dinner.

Next day, we went off to Peter de Lotz, always the last and best. But Peter was talking about retiring soon, and floated the idea of our buying a lot of his inventory. We bought very carefully, only about two stacks. The books were not as tempting; Peter had never before had ex-library books on his shelves. We only spent £715 and our usual tab was in the thousands. Tom Donovan had moved to Brighton and was producing reprints, so that was not our coda after Peter. We still bought from Graham Palmer, and he from us, but mostly by email. Graham was already becoming disenchanted with the internet: the impersonality, the ignorance, the unsatisfactory nature of the dealings.

Amy had come to town to meet us for a day or so, and Anne picked up the three of us in heavy rain to rendezvous with Philip; it was a surprise for Amy to see Philip and a great dinner party. The next day was to be special: Amy and I had tickets for the Chelsea Flower Show, a famous event, and Harris was going to a big stamp show, hoping to connect with a Malta stamp authority with whom he had been corresponding. The Queen had had heavy rain at the Flower Show opening;

but we had the most perfect day, so invigorating, so intoxicating and brilliant that Amy and I walked around and around for hours. Harris returned crestfallen; his specialist was unwell and they did not meet, and the rest of the show didn't make up for that.

Next day we had a date with Steve Tilston: coffee and chat and a lot of buying and a Italian lunch, more chat, and more buying. An enjoyable but full day, then the pleasure of meeting Mark Cummings, perennial student, at Rule's for dinner. We had a real weekend, Bank Holiday, for the British Museum and visits to the young Strickland cousins and their families. With everything closed on Monday, we went to the Changing of the Guard and had a long lunch with Anne; we completed the usual paperwork for the shipper and customs, like homework.

We were home at the end of May, and I had a college reunion near Boston the next weekend, which I did not impose on Harris. Somehow his reunions were much more fun than mine. Afterward, Harris met me in Boston, for a little more book buying and a visit to the U.S.S. *Constitution*.

The English books did not arrive until July 11th. Richard Booth's was the culprit this time; they had delayed the shipment because they had ignored our instruction sheet and couldn't be bothered to put their name and return address on the packages, so the shipper couldn't identify their packages and know the shipment was complete. And they had mangled several items in their careless packing, including a rare pamphlet on the Indian Air Force. Our subsequent complaint was brushed off.

Despite the fact that ninety cartons arrived at 93rd Street, we had the disturbing sense that this trip was not so successful. We had just not found the top of the line material of yesteryear. Peter was selling ex-library books, and much other material was not only very expensive but not so tempting. Perhaps more meaningful, the only antiquarian book of note, Bentivoglio's 1652 *History of the Wars of Flanders*, which we had bought from Francis Edwards, was found to be defective when we collated it; we returned it.

CHAPTER TWENTY-FOUR

"Now we can meet each other in cybernetic space."

2001 – 2002

Donald Phillips.   *Paul Kaplan.*

Scott, of Feldman's Housewares, paid us a call to tell us that his aunt wanted to sell her late husband's books. Ish and I went off to Flushing, Queens in a van. When we met Mrs. Levine, it was clear she resented everything about the books and her husband's collecting. She was right; from what Scott said, he had left her in an unenviable situation financially. And he certainly had bought a lot of books. Most of them were decent stock for us, but only one set was unusual. We both packed, and Ish trucked it all down to the van—it seemed to take forever, the freight elevator being out of order—leaving me to chat up the sour widow.

This accumulation included a beautiful set of Churchill's *The World Crisis*, the first London edition in a custom, navy morocco binding, which I took on consignment because Mrs. Levine wanted more than I wanted to pay for it. It certainly dressed up the ever-popular Winston Churchill section, but did not sell in the next catalogue.

Anxious Mrs. Levine called shortly before the agreed-upon six months had elapsed, to see what was happening. I asked her to let us keep the Churchill a little longer; I just had a feeling. About a week later, and nine days short of six months, we sold it to a hitherto-unseen young woman who wanted a birthday present for her father, a doctor in Connecticut. A wonderful present indeed, and gift-wrapped in our special, rare-book patterned paper.

Most women at least tolerated or admired or even enjoyed their husbands' arcane interest, if it didn't encroach too much on their time, space, or budget. One called from the West Side, and she and her son brought in a unique small lot. Her late husband had been an intelligence officer in Europe during World War II, and had picked up the flotsam and jetsam, pamphlets and ephemera, that he came across in deserted Nazi offices, as well as some more substantive material. This included some uncommon and fascinating propaganda material: an NSDAP (Nazi Party) booklet celebrating the Führer's visit to a newly conquered Poland; another NSDAP title on storming England's gateway, another on the Westwall as Europe's impregnable barricade; the Nazi liberation of Alsace; *Krieg im Westen,* von Wedel's album of stereopticon photos; a pictorial of Spring in the Balkans with the Wehrmacht, 1941, not a carefree sight. There were pamphlets in French recruiting French workers for the Reich, showing photos of well-fed Ukrainian and Slovak laborers: *Travailler pour l'Europe; Le Vrai Visage d'Allemagne; Travailler en Allemagne.* Also intriguing was a small pamphlet on the ordinances regarding confiscation of black-market currency and penalties for speculation. These were items whose survival was so unlikely that they might be unique. *Go find another,* as Harris said from time to time in catalogue descriptions. The woman had kept the material carefully and nicely filed, so the condition was fine. I was genuinely enthusiastic about it, it was so interesting and unusual although its monetary value was not significant. She took pleasure in knowing that her husband's accumulation had found an appreciative buyer.

It was possible to overdo the enthusiasm. Early on, Harris was impressed and excited by one veteran's books, and said so, to the point that the man decided they were important enough to keep for his children.

Since the beginning of our acquaintance, Rita Wolfson had aided and abetted Mike's collecting. When someone arrived in the store offering a handsome Chinese painting of Mongols, Harris, thinking of Mike, took it on consignment. Rita wrote,

Harris called me one spring day out of the blue and asked if I wanted something really unusual for Mike's next birthday. I said of course . . . and he said that normally he didn't like to deal in paintings but because of the Mongol subject matter he immediately thought of Mike and took the painting and called me. I said I would be in the next day, took one look and fell in love with it myself. Harris wrapped it up in brown paper and it stayed hidden in the back of my closet for five months, until Mike's birthday on September 1. Mike wanted to hang it in his office . . .

The Company of Military Historians had decided to disband what they called their reference library, which was made up of members' donations. This well-known organization was devoted to the study of American military history, particularly its units and uniforms. They called us, and it certainly sounded good; they didn't tell us Brattle Books, from Boston, had been there first. Donald and Ish went off in a van on a long trek to Massachusetts. It was a load of books, to be sure, but ultimately disappointing. Some of the big, important sets were incomplete or shabby, and in other cases, such as Nicholson's *Wars of the French Revolution* set, the donors had extracted the fine uniform or map plates from the rare books before giving them to the Company. It was a very mixed lot, all the signs of contributions rather than focus. We didn't pay for the junk, and indeed Donald and Ish had left some behind. Ish resuscitated others, most notably a set of the memoirs of the Duc de Sully, French soldier and minister during the sixteenth-century religious wars. Ish rebound the five volumes, newly handsome in caramel-colored calf, with marbled paper boards. There was a clutch of books on Rogers' Rangers, the French and Indian War militia unit: John Cuneo's biography, and a two-volume, privately-printed set we had never seen before, and a volume on Col. Robert Rogers' trial for treason. It was certainly unusual to have those all at once. There was also British Richard Oswald's 1781 *Memorandum on the Folly of Invading Virginia*, the title drily amusing to me; Oswald negotiated the Peace of Paris the next year, ending the Revolutionary War.

The lot also included U.S. Navy Official Histories of both the Quasi-War and the War with the Barbary Pirates. The former was a drug on the market because the Quasi-War, a sideshow of the French Revolutionary Wars, was little known; the latter was not often seen and relatively desirable, but lacked the last volume. The *Naval Documents of the American Revolution* set was also incomplete. The naval *War of the Rebellion* set did sell readily. The enormous *War of the Rebellion, Official Records* was complete but shabby, but we priced it to sell, and it did, quickly. There were other large Civil War sets such as the *Southern Historical Society Papers*, and Gavin Leckie saw his chance and found the space. An original set of *Medical and Surgical History of the Civil War*, in six volumes, was very scarce, but that didn't mean it flew off the shelf. There were masses of the annual Army Registers, and New York and Massachusetts publications relating to their militias, and Harris created a Militia subject in the next catalogue. There were many unit histories on the Spanish-American War, and Navy Registers. Not too scintillating, but saleable.

Iraq was in the news; the International Atomic Energy Agency was sending in inspection teams to look for Weapons of Mass Destruction. One of their weapons inspectors came in to the store, fresh from Iraq, and told us there were no WMDs.

And Enron was in the news. A Fifth Avenue couple who worked at Alliance Capital and were both customers, often walked up to the store on Saturdays. When Enron went into freefall and Alliance Capital was impacted, they asked to be taken off the mailing list.

Our London dealers and friends, the Sutcliffes, had a standing invitation to stay with us, and they took us up on it in April. It was fun to show them the store, and to have them in and out and enjoying New York. Lionel was in from London too, for his spring visit, and to introduce his son who was joining him at Greenhill Books: the old guard, with intimations of change.

Joel Block still came in on a regular basis, as often as we would let him. His situation was somewhat altered. He had always accumulated more than he had sold, and I knew he had a storeroom or storage locker somewhere. The enormity of his situation became apparent when a leak developed in his apartment, and the landlord couldn't get at it because of the book accumulation and went ballistic. Joel's family (who did not live with him) forbade him to buy any more until he had worked off his inventory—he had more books than money—and then he found a number of great titles for us under his bed. Poor Joel, for whom The Hunt was his calling and addiction. I didn't like to think about his apartment.

Emily and Sandra remembered that July 5th would be the bookstore's twenty-fifth anniversary, and invited themselves to our celebration. They arrived with their red Military Bookman T-shirts and wore them all weekend. We hadn't been planning much, but put together a party July 5th in the store, decorated for July 4th, for some good local customers and associates and anyone else who happened along: some of the long-time regulars, John Catherwood, Mike Wolfson, Peter Plimpton, Gavin Leckie, Philip Kamil of course, and some newer regulars, including John Mercurio, Frank Delia and Stan Heisler. Stan read ancient history, and since the Ancient section was in the front of the store, I had seen a lot of him. He was very gregarious and I knew he would come. Mr. Mercurio was an older man who trekked in from Staten Island quite frequently. He was taciturn or shy, and I was surprised to see him come to a party—still serious but evidently enjoying himself. The Corner Bookpeople and Joel, always up for a party, were in attendance. We hung out and had drinks in the store and the backyard, and gave out the T-shirts remaining in our stock, with one reserved for our nice mailman. It was a restrained but happy time. There was a suspicion that Emily had instigated their visit as much for Sheila's Fourth of July fried chicken as for the store party.

Once again, we ran a "scrapbook" in the Summer catalogue, showing the current staff and some from the past; Mike Rihn with Harris, both beaming about a Civil War book; Philip Kamil confronting Fortescue; Arnold Brown looking serious, or puzzled; a happy Peter Plimpton with a new acquisition. A number of new customers loved the photos. A Brazilian, Rogerio de Oliveiro Souza, wrote, *It is very good to see our booksellers, like human being and not only like an e-mail face. By the way I am sending a picture of mine. Now we can 'meet' each other in the cybernetic space.* A few customers were confused because I chose to put a photo of the store on the cover of the catalogue, with the dates, not the usual logo, although inside it was the stated eighty-fifth issue. Many customers sent their congratulations on this anniversary, and Jacques Lacasse wrote exuberantly, *In October of 1976 I bought my very first book from your establishment—Lachouque's* The Anatomy of Glory, *and I am still the proud owner of that book!*

We must have bought at auction the scarce and off-beat 1796 book of French uniform regulations, *Reglement concernant les Uniformes des Generaux et officiers* Harris's comment read, *This detailed piece could only have been of interest to tailors, not the general public!* It was certainly very rare, and fascinating in an arcane way. Harris thought Peter Plimpton should buy it. Peter certainly was the most ambitious and sophisticated uniform-book collector on our roster, and this book was too rarified and probably too expensive for anyone else. All through 2002, Harris worked on it; Peter bought, in an elaborate trade, bringing in books he had lived with long enough, or had bought in a lot.

Sandra, in her capacity as acquisitions librarian at Emory University, vetted book gifts to the library. The library had annual book sales of thousands of donated titles that they could not use, and soon after Sandra and Emily had visited, Sandra invited us to come down to Atlanta for a first crack at Emory's sale, which that year was dominated by the spectral presence of a Russian professor who had left Emory his books. Excellent and unusual titles, especially on Russian and Central European history, at $2.00 apiece: we were on the next plane. We must have found about two hundred books, and later Sandra sent more. We had the weekend to see our various friends and hit four Atlanta bookstores, including Yesteryear, a fine shop we had visited previously. And we had a great Russian Empire category for the Winter catalogue.

We were sound asleep when Harris's local son, Alex, called on the crystal-clear morning of September 11th. A plane had crashed into the World Trade Center. Even in the fogginess of waking it seemed an improbable accident on such a day. We went straight to the TV like the rest of the world and didn't leave it except to make coffee. The second plane crashed into the second tower. In the Bronx, Paul had left home early to vote in the mayoral primary elections and came on to 29 East 93rd and upstairs to us. Ish was walking to work from the West Side through the northern, hilly part of Central Park, saw what was happening and turned around and went home. Donald called from Brooklyn—he had seen everything from his apartment.

There the three of us sat, two still in bathrobes, glued to the tube, hideously hypnotized. News came of the Pentagon strike—and the crash in a Pennsylvania field. Friends were calling for reassurance and to be in touch. My mother too—it was a bad time to be alone. Jeffrey called; he lived in Greenwich Village, and had come out of his breakfast place to Seventh Avenue in time to see the second tower struck. Jeffrey said, "Who could it be? I can't imagine the Palestinians being well-organized enough for this." I heard myself saying, "Osama Bin Laden." About two o'clock, I said, "I'm getting a shower and going up to Mt. Sinai Hospital to give blood."

We three went. The fighter jets were flying low, crisscrossing the skies over Manhattan, and that was thrilling, reassuring, and frightening. Streams of people in business dress and in shock were walking resolutely uptown on Madison Avenue. At 99th Street, the line was out the door at Mt. Sinai, and blood wasn't, after all, needed. Paul headed home to the Bronx, having heard that the uptown subways were running.

No one knew what to do with themselves. The Corner Bookstore was as busy as it had ever been; people wanted to do something normal, semi-social, with the comfort of the familiar. I went down to the store; I couldn't cope with any more TV, nor could I face customers. Not even turning on most of the lights, I did something mundane and relatively mindless, pruning the mailing list. Nevertheless some people came in so I turned on the lights. My hairdresser called to see if I was going to keep a haircut appointment. No. The phone became impossible; from all over the world people were trying to check on friends and loved ones, and customers were trying to reach us to see if we were all right.

Alex had been working in Forest Hills, Queens. He hitched a ride to the 59th Street Bridge, and walked over to Manhattan. He wasn't allowed to go home to the East Village: it was below 14th Street and off limits. So he made his way to us, and spent the evening frantically calling his friends to check on their well being and to see who could take care of his dog. Later, we three straggled up to Hanratty's.

Everyone in the city was running a list in their heads, to think of anyone they knew who might have been downtown. We didn't know until much later that Mike Wolfson's offices were in the World Trade Center. He had not yet gone downtown that morning, having stayed up into the night to finish an overdue library book. As he was about to get a late start, Rita, in front of the TV, said, "You're not going to work today." Mike hadn't gotten around to taking the Mongol painting to the office, so it too was spared.

And we hadn't known that Dave Liebman was then working in the Deutsche Bank building next to the Towers, which was heavily damaged when they fell. We heard months later from him about his harrowing and dangerous escape.

We had agreed that the store would open the next day, and we were all there. In the next weeks, we heard from many customers and business friends. Paul talked to . . . *a customer way down south, whose accent you could cut with a knife. He apologized for not calling to buy anything and said he just wanted to see if we were all OK, and I told him yes, and how much we appreciated so many of our customers calling and writing. He paused then, and said that he had always thought of NYC pretty much the way most people in his neck of the woods did . . . then said that he'd been watching everything on the news, and hearing about how New Yorkers were acting, and ended with 'Ya know, y'all gotta helluva city there.*

Foreign customers were particularly eloquent and moving. One who managed to get through on September 12th was calling from Israel—a rough-voiced, recent customer and ordinarily a tough one, rather cantankerous, spoke in great empathy.

From Mme. Clavreuil, our Paris bookshop: *It is with great chagrin and grief that we have followed the tragic events . . .*

From George and Joyce Harris, in England: *All Britain shares your grief . . .*

From Dr. Albert Merzweiler, in Germany: *Our sympathy is with all the victims of this detestable crime but also with you for the hours of anxiety and uncertainty and with the poor city as well.*

From Giambattista Raimondi, in Italy: *In these exacting moments I would like to express my solidarity to you and to all American people. . . . May God accord success to the struggle led by your Country against the barbarians.*

We had planned to go with friends to Turkey and Greece that fall, but none of us were up for it. It was not the time to do something fun and happy, and many people were nervous about flying. We were able to postpone the trip, but I said to Harris after ten days or so, "I want to go somewhere," and he agreed. We set off for New England in October, meeting those friends in Vermont for a couple of days, and seeing Brendan in New Hampshire. Otherwise, unstructured wandering as far as Mount Desert Island in Maine, through beautiful fall weather, with apples and picnics and American flags everywhere. People came up to us because of the New York plates on our car, to express their feelings and sympathies. Fall color, no books; we searched out one battlefield, the only Vermont battlefield of the Revolution, in tiny Hubbardton. Our escape smoothed us out; it was restorative.

In the first catalogue of 2002, we ran a new subject, "Heroes and Heroism." We had been giving a lot of thought to the mysterious and various nature of heroism (by this writing a word that has become all-too-common currency). We mustered an interesting array of heroic figures, decorated and undecorated—*Deeds of Valor,* as one title had it—from warrior monarchs like Charlemagne and Boudica, through Victoria Cross and Congressional Medal of Honor winners, air aces, the British troops at Rorke's Drift. Their lives and reputations were forever defined by a surge of adrenalin or fear or both, combined with training or a sense of duty, that prompted exceptional acts: was it reflex, impulse, or choice? There were more sustained efforts, such as those of Joan of Arc and the enigmatic Lawrence of Arabia, caught up or trapped in their own mystique. Heroes' later lives were sometimes burdened by others' expectations of them, some exploiting the deed, riding their reputations into movie stardom or the Senate—others, like Sgt. Alvin York, feeling it something of a curse to have been a "hero," never allowed to be unnoticed or average again.

By December, things were closer to normal. Amy was not afraid to fly, and came for a New York week. Around the same time, I happened on a Lufthansa deal, and we decided to have a February week in Germany with Ute and Peter Grauer.

We had had an intermittent friendship with Bill Smith, which had resumed telephonically with Harris when Bill started buying from us in the mid-eighties. Bill, a hands-on buyer, moved around a lot and browsed and bought wherever he was. My old friend Judy had known Bill only a little, as a friend of her late husband, and wanted to talk to him about old times, and Bill's memories of her children's father. How do you find a moving target named Bill Smith? Ask the Military Bookman. We put them in touch, and did they talk! A few months later, Bill stopped in to see us on his way from Maine to Missouri and points west, to visit friends. He said he was planning to see Judy and visit his old friend's grave, but Harris, ever intuitive, picked up on something to which I was oblivious. A few days later, we went off to Germany. By the time we got back, Judy and Bill were talking marriage. Another Military Bookman romance!

There was to be another Bethesda auction, and we sent Donald and Paul off together. They had worked closely with Harris on developing bids from our records, and bought very successfully, winning many British and Commonwealth official histories in fine condition. But when the books came to be priced, Paul started checking internet listings, and then it did not seem so successful. Lower prices, often much lower, were to be found on the net. A few weeks later, an unprecedented number of "wanted" books, a long row of important titles, had to be taken off the quote shelf, unsold.

The daughter of a Wehrmacht officer, living in South Carolina, called Atlantic Books in Charleston about his books, most in German. Atlantic was good enough to refer her to us. Her shipment included a number of cigarette-card albums, so popular in Germany between the wars, and one of them was new to us.

Manner in Dritten Reich was one of the scarcer albums, perhaps because in the midst of the 1934 production of this Nazi propaganda piece, the Night of the Long Knives, the purge of the SA (Sturmabteilung) branch of the Nazi party, occurred. The album was altered during production to eliminate the SA leaders, and sixteen biographies were dropped. But a number of the cards themselves had already been distributed. The Wehrmacht officer, probably a teenager at the time, had collected the cards, and added eight of the missing leaders including the most notorious, Ernst Röhm, on blank pages in the back of his album, with terse handwritten notes on their fate: *erschossen*—executed. A fascinating document, which ended up in a propaganda collection at Emory University.

On the proverbial dark and stormy night, pouring rain, the store was very quiet, and Harris was in the basement playing Minesweeper. An older man, impeccably dressed, materialized at the door. Not a raindrop blemished his beautifully tailored blue suit. He told Paul and me that he wanted some special naval books for a friend who would never treat himself to something expensive. Paul worked with him, and they settled on a fine selection, including a venerable U.S. Navy submarine manual and another official publication, *The Magic Background of Pearl Harbor*, eight volumes of the intercepted Japanese diplomatic communications. The mystery man ran up quite a tab and when the credit card and shipping info were revealed, we learned that it was Michael Ovitz, the big-league Hollywood agent, buying for Tom Clancy, best-selling author of *The Hunt for Red October* and other naval titles. Ovitz vanished into the night under the shelter of a large umbrella held by an unseen hand, all the way to the limo.

CHAPTER TWENTY-FIVE

"What if I came one day and they weren't here."

The store was too quiet. When Emily and Sandra had called with great excitement about the store's twenty-fifth birthday party, I muttered, "It might be more like a wake." The signs were all there to be noticed, and we did, around the edges of what else was happening.

Harris's numbers showed that sales were undeniably falling, and one hardly needed a sales analysis to know there was not enough action. A day's transactions didn't fill enough space in the sales ledger. Equally compelling to me was my more modest but very straightforward index: the number of catalogue subscriptions had gone into a steep decline in the late nineties. In 1995 we had about seven hundred catalogue requests, with over half of those subscribing; in 2001, there were only ninety-nine new subscriptions. We had taken such good care of our long-timers that they were replete or at least not buying at the same pace. Some of the new subscribers were enthusiastic buyers; others undoubtedly used the catalogues for information and comparison shopping. With the vast array offered on the internet, a rare or scarce book was not so scarce any more. Our premium on, for instance, Australian official histories looked bad to an internet shopper who was willing to wait for months for a book that could be had for a much cheaper price from Australia, where it was relatively common.

We were selling a lot of books on the internet, but I observed that most of those sales were like one-night-stands rather than long-term relationships. We did attract some new subscribers from the net, but most of those buyers were never heard from again. Yes, they were from all over the world, and that was fun and interesting, but ultimately it was a so-what.

Paul ran the internet listings and they were accessible only on his computer. I asked to see our listings on ABE or Bibliofind. Straight across the store from my desk were the Aviation shelves, and I focused on the Battle of Britain section, checking on a good book we didn't have all the time, *The Narrow Margin,* by Derek Dempster and Derek Wood. Not a common book. On the site there were about twenty-five copies listed, by price; ours was almost the most expensive, at $27.50. Uh-oh.

No more mimeographed lists came from Alma Anderson, whom we later learned had leapt directly into the internet selling age. No more little book offers on index cards from a myriad of finders. Yard sale pickers were playing at bookselling on the net, had no idea of what they had, no knowledge, no perspective, but perhaps more important, no costs to cover, no overhead. It was amateur hour. Some internet sellers were semi-literate. One so-called dealer, querying our book description, asked, "What is 8vo?" This may be the most basic book term, octavo, which describes the size of a usual book.

Aside from all this, the internet was so impersonal that it just wasn't fun. There was no conversation, no interchange.

Donald and Paul wanted to try eBay, and since we were not busy, they had a fling with it, listing some gun books and lesser aviation items we wanted to unload. By the time we factored in the effort and fees involved, it was a worthless endeavor.

We had thought, with the advent of the book superstores around 1990, that the out-of-print business would not be affected, and at first this was so for us. Later, every so often, one of us had occasion to breeze through our local Barnes & Noble on Lexington Avenue. The size of the military history section was impressive. The sheer quantity might satisfy many readers and not send them questing for the older, seminal books. The multitude of new publications were authored by a new generation of good military historians, but also a bunch of second-string guys, hacks—or as John Catherwood would say, scathingly, journalists—who were churning out rehashes of respectable histories long since written, offering no new approach, research or insights. Desktop publishing enabled the production of many worthy books with small readerships, but also the appearance of numerous amateurish, ill-digested, badly-produced titles, some on ever-more-obscure and finely-parsed topics. All these were competing for the book dollar.

Reprints were the first nail in our coffin, another kind of competition. At first these were mostly unit histories, but later some of the classic texts, even official British histories, and the Marine Corps World War II titles, were reprinted. Despite the inferior quality of many of these productions, the maps especially, they eventually eroded our market.

We had stopped paying ourselves. I had gathered the staff for our standard five-minute meeting and told them there would be no raises for that year; I could tell they were expecting worse. We had told our scouts we had to start paying them a lower percentage; interestingly enough, none of them stopped coming, and I thought, cynically and belatedly, that we could always have paid them less. Harris had always said he wanted to be fair to sellers; I was overdue in rejoining that we needed to be fair to us.

It had been my mantra that the *New York Times* was the first place we advertised and would be the last. Without conscious forethought, I heard myself saying to Regina, our long-time *New York Times* classified ad rep, who regularly phoned to confirm its continuance, "I can't believe I'm saying this, but I think I'll cancel the ad." Regina was shocked and I was too, but I must have been mulling it over for a while. "It's gotten so expensive and it just doesn't draw enough anymore." We didn't need to cancel our perennial ad in the *Antiquarian Bookman's Weekly;* they had quietly stopped publishing in 1999, more evidence of the internet's effect. I reevaluated our other advertising: I had already dropped some of the small magazines. The many Yellow Pages ads, so successful for years, were expensive and no longer producing as much, but I continued them.

Through 2002, Harris lost himself in the books and kept on keeping on, emerging regularly to present the declining sales numbers to me with distressed eyes, as if I could fix it, pull some rabbit out of a hat as I sometimes had. All I could think of was a mailing to the list of the *Journal of Military History*. We sent it out in August. There was some response, several of them very enthusiastic and immediately buying a lot. But it was too little, too late.

We were going away in the fall to Turkey and Greece, the trip we had postponed, and as people do, we deluded ourselves that business might pick up while we were gone. After all, Gen. Tommy Franks was quoting Sun Tzu, and the new war in Afghanistan might generate interest in Britain's fruitless nineteenth-century Afghan wars. On our return after three weeks, there was nothing to encourage us. A couple of days later, Paul was plumping for a new printer, then not so cheap, for Donald; I told him we would think about it. Upstairs after work I said, "Paul's talking about a new printer and I don't even want to order more stationery!" Harris came out of his denial and we had some thoroughgoing discussions of how and when to close the Military Bookman. It was wrenching, all so painful. And ironic that we finally had a good and stable staff in place, and very good inventory, and were positioned to do a lot of business—but in the old way.

We talked about it for a few days and then told Ish and Donald and Paul. On some level they had been expecting it. They knew the Military Bookman had never been a "hobby." It had to be a viable business. We discussed the final catalogue and how to set it up, and Paul suggested the discount schedule, which he had thought about more clearly than we had. After the first of the year, Paul and Donald each went on half-time, as they chose to plan the days between the two of them; Ish continued full-time.

Soon we told our scouts that we would be winding down, so they would not keep buying for us, asking them to keep it confidential. Our timing for the closing sale was dictated by Harris's and my physical woes. In November, Harris was afflicted with a agonizing and prolonged attack of sciatica, precipitated by too many hours at the computer, where he had immersed himself in a new bibliographic project for post-bookstore. He really suffered, tried to tough it out and waited too long to get help. It was horrible. I had known I needed a new hip—I had fretted all through our wonderful trip about whether I would be able to walk up the Acropolis to the Parthenon—and was able to schedule it for January. When we came out from under these problems, in mid-February, we began to implement our plans. Since neither Donald nor Paul immediately found another position, they were available through the closing days.

The doleful discount signs went up in February, and we had sent letters in January to our best customers, telling them that there would be a final sale.

Mike Wolfson: *I received your note today. I can't tell you how shocked, saddened I am. The Military Bookman—and you and your staff—are part of what make Carnegie Hill and New York City special. The Military Bookman won't be replaced by the internet and we'll all be poorer for it. . . . I will be in Saturday afternoon, to commiserate and to say bad things about progress. . . . . I was there at the beginning, but I don't like being there at the end.*

Tom Burdett: *I was not a very good customer, but I am surely one of the oldest and your red catalogues (and those two yellow ones long years ago) were always a source of pleasure and hopeful anticipation . . . The Internet is fine for searching for titles on a want list, but it is no substitute . . . in finding titles one never knew existed. And it certainly is no substitute for the excitement of receiving a new catalogue in the mail. I will miss The Military Bookman as an earlier generation of collectors regretted the passing of old Fourth Avenue.*

James Hiatt: *I 'discovered' The Military Bookman in 1980, on a trip to New York; since then you have added enormously to my pleasure, and (I hope) knowledge regarding my life-long interest. . . . I don't know what I appreciate most: the books, your tremendous range and depth of knowledge in your specialty, the dry humor with which the catalogues are laced, or your unfailing courtesy and help. I guess the answer is: all of the above. I know that when those red catalogues arrive, whatever else might be going on that evening, whatever work I might have carried home from the office, would have to wait.*

Kazuhiko Yoshida: *The other day I received a very sad piece of news that you are closing for ever. I will miss you as long as I live.*

Giambattista Raimondi: *On behalf—I think—of many other readers, I wish to thank you for all that: I think it has been a job, but also a work of love.*

The store was never short on interesting or humorous episodes, even in the final months. In March we received an internet order from ARCENT Qatar, the U.S. Third Army's position in the Persian Gulf, for a 1957 study, by C. R. S. Harris, *Allied Military Administration in Italy.* Well, better late than never. That told us all we needed to know about the lack of foresight and preparedness for the consequences of the Iraq War: someone thinking to inquire two days after the invasion was launched.

Leighton Longhi was there one evening when the Last Sale was starting, and a small curly-haired woman in dark glasses arrived. She stopped just inside the door. "Do you have 'War for Dummies'?" Paul walked her through the store: "When I'm watching the news they're talking about regiments and battalions and all that and I want to know what they're talking about. Do you think we should go into Iraq?" She was a little dynamo and led Paul a merry chase around the store, talking non-stop. He helped her select four or five bags of books, which he and Ish later delivered to 94th and Fifth Avenue. She left me with her credit card to process the order while she did an errand. Harris, curious by now, was moved to come out from his lair in the back closet, "Who was that?" Bette Midler, I replied. Harris, usually oblivious to contemporary "culture," knew who she was, because Brendan had written her character in *The First Wives' Club* with Bette in mind. "How do you know??" As if I were in a credit card ad, I held up her Visa.

Our final catalogue would list everything in the store, and both to cut costs and make a mourning statement, we published it on newsprint—no red cover. It was a larger format, about eight by ten, and eighty pages. The preface read:

The Military Bookman, founded in 1976, is coming to the end of a long and happy existence. We will miss the books and our relationships with you, our knowledgeable customers. Recently, our sales have been eroded considerably by the plethora of new book titles and reprints, and also from internet listings, where erratic and continually falling prices are affecting all specialists.

We sent it to Eagle Press in February and it was done and sent to us in a timely way, but unbelievably, the printer had left out page one. Eagle then took three weeks to redo it, apparently feeling no compunction for their screw-up. Then they heedlessly put on wrong mailing permit information, taken from an old layout, which despite the pleadings of the mailer, the post office would not accept. Paul came up with the solution of a sticker, which the mailer affixed to about 2000 catalogues. And this took more time and money. It was excruciating. It was finally in the mail April 16th.

Then the mails were awful, the catalogue not arriving in places like Delaware and Carnegie Hill until early June, so this prolonged the already wrenching process —and made me mindful of a few things I wouldn't miss, like printers and the post office. We had figured on closing July 4th, completing our twenty-seventh year.

The first-class catalogue mailing had been sent from the store in early April, so that made for a lot of activity, and customer lamentations. Their distress was in some cases eloquent, in others muted as they were too upset to articulate.

I took an order from one man who said he was "heartbroken" and was almost too choked up to talk. I came close to joining in. He said he had marked all the books he wanted, knowing it was his last chance, and it added up to over $5000, which he certainly could not afford. He tentatively asked about the discount and if it were flexible. I told him I would get back to him, got off the phone, calculated what it was and later Harris and I talked about the discount, and offered him a larger one.

In spite of the laggardly catalogue, May was really busy, kicked off on the first by Doug Bandow spending over $4000 on books he had been flirting with. Tom Burdett at UTEP, ever a good customer, put in a large last order. The Naval War College placed a sizable order. The Marines got their act together and sent a big order in June. Our old guard was coming in time and time again, realizing it was the last chance of being there, and constantly rethinking what to latch onto while they could. Philip Kamil was in often, just to watch the action. Mike Wolfson came in several times, Phil Haultcoeur and Mr. Mercurio almost weekly. John Catherwood was there several times in May, as was Gavin Leckie. John Hartnett showed up for the first time in years. Many of our mail-order regulars were placing multiple orders, clearly mining their subjects time and time again.

The Pig, galvanized by discounts, was in all the time, scooping up a variety of subjects and insisting on an ongoing discount. One of the obnoxious naval historians was in at the kill, or I could tell that's what he thought. Without even a show of condolence, he gloated about getting a good discount on an expensive set he had been eyeing.

A local regular, who had always seemed unhappy and almost furtive, always frowning, never connecting, said without eye contact when he arrived, "I'm sorry about this; I always felt comfortable here." He probably couldn't say that in most of his world.

We posted a catalogue-red GOING OUT OF BUSINESS SALE sign in the store window, and later one on the railing of the stoop, an eye-catcher from Madison Avenue. Before long, I thought we might as well put a stack of the large number of extra catalogues on the stoop, and that brought in many people, curious passers-by, neighbors who had always meant to have a look, a few crass and unsympathetic "waddaya gonna to do with the space" types. At times it felt like a feeding frenzy and someone said to me, "This is so successful maybe you shouldn't go out of business." It gave me pause, as I thought about what it would take to put Humpty Dumpty back together again.

There were many small sales and two $1000 sales from the stoop catalogues. One was a set of Charles W. C. Oman's *History of the Peninsular War,* the listing found by a passer-by, an Australian woman whose father had long coveted it; it was to be the only complete set of that Napoleonic classic in southern Australia, she told us. In the continuing principle of "there's a person for every book," *Der Danske Underofficer,* by Kroier and Hinge, a nineteenth-century uniform survey that was a languishing leftover from the Hope collection of 1991, found its person. A young woman of Danish extraction bought it for her father.

We stayed open late for Museum Mile in early June, which we never had thought worth the effort, and someone wandered in and spent $600.00.

The way the catalogues on the stoop brought people in was an eye-opener. I, marveling, said to Ish, "Maybe we should always have done this!" Ish, ever a class act, said, "No, no, no!"

With many pangs, we were selling most of the wonderful images that we had collected to decorate the store. Gavin bought two of the "Books Wanted" poster series and I was happy about where they were going. Bill Waters, who loved penguins, went for the wintry Coal Administration poster. A customer in Scotland bought the British officer's Gurkha photo collection, sight unseen. A local doctor, new to us, had to have a marvelous, large, Japanese print of the 1184 Battle of the Uji River, with ribbons of cavalrymen fighting through the water. The Pig bought the big, beautiful, French print, alas. The large Liberty Loan poster we had "restored" ourselves in 1976 had long since been superseded behind the desk and consigned to the basement. As the walls emptied, I thought "Why not?" Ish hauled the fierce Liberty goddess image upstairs, dusted it off and I put $150.00 on it, and it went. Someone asked about the old, ragged, plane model Lloyd had brought in years before, and I pulled it down from its perch over the Aviation section, and said "fifty bucks," and off it flew. Ish said, "Watch out, everything's for sale!"

Lionel, with his son, paid a last call on us on Memorial Day weekend on his spring business trip. A week later, John made a sentimental journey, driving in from Gettysburg for lunch and to hang out in the store once again. Jordi Jové, our faithful Barcelona customer, was in town for his annual visit in June, found a couple of books and took photos of the store, and us.

In the midst of the hubbub, a not-unfamiliar man hovered near my desk. He reintroduced himself as Barry Singer of Chartwell Books, a Churchill specialist in midtown, and said he would be interested in buying the inventory. I answered, "As you see, we're in the midst of the sale." He said that when the sale had run its course, he would like to talk.

I was trying to sell or give away equipment we wouldn't need, and called Arnold Brown about the fax machine he had provided. As usual he had a list of "beneficiaries." He left a message that the Korean man who ran his local pizzeria (Arnold doubtless a frequent customer) could use it and would pick it up. The man called, and shortly before he came, called again to ask, "Can I bring you some pizza?" I declined, saying we were going out to dinner, whereupon he said, "What about something to drink?" He arrived, admired the space, asked why we were going out of business, and what was I going to do now? I said, "Write a book." He said, "You don't look like the type." So I showed him *Defend the Valley*. In parting, he said whenever we were up around 115th and Broadway we could come in for pizza.

In due course, having tried to give away the book press, we put it out on the sidewalk; it was a handsome object in itself, and I hoped it would be adopted. Within two hours, a couple of workmen came down the street and one was very excited to see it. Was it there because it could be taken? Yes, he knew it was heavy, he had a car. But what if someone came and took it first? (Now really, what were the odds.) Not to worry, put it in the courtyard. Anything will be adopted in New York, just as there is a person for every book.

It was time to talk to Barry Singer. He came up to the store and we had a very good discussion. We ran the numbers on the inventory in Oliver to establish a value, and Barry wanted the mailing list too, and a link from the Military Bookman to his web site. His offer was more than fair and we shook hands on it. It was a most civilized transaction at a painful time. People were still coming in while we started to box up the inventory.

Alex with his dog came to help pack and enlivened the depressing process with his rough humor. He and Ish went foraging for boxes in the worst kind of steamy, New York summer weather, coming back dripping. I was managing, directing traffic, labeling the boxes packed by subject, trying to get the wretched process over with. Harris was too depressed to participate fully, taking refuge in his bibliographic project for spells of time. Ish objected but Alex understood.

My brother checked in with a sorrowful letter and an aviation book order, and Sheila bought one more copy of *Defend the Valley*. One of the last sales was to Ed McHugh, a regular who came in from north Jersey and was not on the mailing list. He hadn't been in for a while, and as he rounded the corner onto 93rd Street, he said to himself, "What if I came one day and they weren't here."

We planned to keep Ish on even beyond the store closing, and Paul continued part-time for some wrap-up things, computer records and to teach Harris about the internet. Ish had many melancholy tasks to perform, including the physically and emotionally difficult chore of taking down the shelves, which he said was saddest thing he ever had to do.

On August 13th, Barry sent his people with a van to pick up the books. It was a scorching, humid day in a heat-wave week, and a hard time. We were in the store the following day, a pretty mournful place, literally echoing with the absence of the books. There was still a lot to do—paperwork, small piles of books in the few subjects Barry didn't want—but it all felt pointless. As a denouement, the lights went out in the late afternoon. When we went out to the street, the traffic lights were out too. It was a citywide blackout, due to extreme heat, and I immediately went to Patrick Murphy's for a bag of ice. When the store got as hot as the outdoors, Harris and I went up to the still somewhat cooler parlor. We spent the evening with a young neighbor who, not wanting to be alone, came over with her dog, and we drank by candlelight until the ice gave out. It was too hot to think of eating. The electricity did not come back until late the next day.

We were in business for a generation. We had inherited veteran collectors from whom we could learn, and many were with us for the duration. We saw and helped young people discover their interests and shared their excitement in learning. We enjoyed the ripple effect when we heard from our customers' sons or friends or fathers, or more improbable connections. Some older clients had wound down their collecting, if not their reading, and sold us all or parts of their libraries, and the books recycled through our hands to find new homes. At the end, at least two regulars told Harris they'd have to change their wills.

In 1976, we could not have imagined the long and happy relationships the Military Bookman brought to us, the endlessly fascinating and rich variety of people and books and the places we found them, the wealth of subjects we would discover . . . and the good times we would have.

People came looking for the store for years.

The French couple stood forlorn and unbelieving, disconsolately gazing at 29 East 93rd Street as Ish came down the block. Still its self-appointed caretaker, he asked them courteously if he could help. They were looking for The Military Bookman and he had to tell them that it was gone.

They might have been the young couple who had visited about fifteen years before. It was their first time in the United States and they were embarking on an ambitious American tour. They had only one day in New York, so they each chose one sight to see: hers was the Statue of Liberty, and his was The Military Bookman.

Acknowledgments

Recent conversations and correspondence with the following not only confirmed but clarified certain memories. Many thanks to: James Bloom, Christopher Busa, John Catherwood, James Controvich, Jean Crocker, Amy Cummings, Robin Elenko, Michael Flint, Philip Haultcoeur, Philip Kamil, Paul Kaplan, Emily Katt, Sheila Keegan, Lionel Leventhal, Richard Lorand, Claiborne Marshall, Ismael Medina, Peter Plimpton, Michael Rihn, William B. Smith, Victor Sutcliffe, Michael and Rita Wolfson.

Thanks also to Deborah Harkins, Mary Ann Joulwan, and Jeffrey Simpson.

Page 18. Larry McMurtry, *Books: a Memoir.* New York, Simon & Schuster, 2008, p. 161. Page 290. David Owens, quoted by Georgia Dullea, *New York Times,* May 11, 1979. Electra Havemeyer Webb quoted by Edward Rothstein, *New York Times,* May 20, 2011, from Lauren B. Hughes, *To Collect in Earnest: the Life and Work of Electra Havemeyer Webb*, Shelburne Museum, 1997.

Cover photograph by Anthony Edgeworth, 1981.
From left: Jesse, Michael, Oliver, Margaretta, Harris, Mel; Sheila on the stoop.

Illustration page 11. Col. Robert Monro, *Monro, his expedition with the Worthy Scots' Regiment . . .* London, 1637. Courtesy Sarah Gilmer Payne.

Book design by Debra Gallek, DG Design.

Made in the USA
Charleston, SC
13 August 2015